Rethinking Social Movements after '68

Protest, Culture & Society

General editors:
Kathrin Fahlenbrach, Institute for Media and Communication, University of Hamburg
Martin Klimke, New York University Abu Dhabi
Joachim Scharloth, Waseda University

Protest movements have been recognized as significant contributors to processes of political participation and transformations of culture and value systems, as well as to the development of both a national and transnational civil society. This series brings together the various innovative approaches to phenomena of social change, protest, and dissent that have emerged in recent years, from an interdisciplinary perspective. It contextualizes social protest and cultures of dissent in larger political processes and sociocultural transformations by examining the influence of historical trajectories and the response of various segments of social, and political and legal institutions on a national and international level. In doing so, the series offers a more comprehensive and multidimensional view of historical and cultural change in the twentieth and twenty-first centuries.

Recent volumes:

Volume 31
Rethinking Social Movements after '68: Selves and Solidarities in West Germany and Beyond
Belinda Davis, Friederike Brühöfener, and Stephen Milder

Volume 30
The Walls of Santiago: Social Revolution and Politial Aesthetics in Contemporary Chile
Terri Gordon-Zolov and Eric Zolov

Volume 29
The Aesthetics of Rule and Resistance: Analyzing Political Street Art in Latin America
Lisa Bogerts

Volume 28
Political Graffiti in Critical Times: The Aesthetics of Street Politics
Edited by Ricardo Campos, Andrea Pavoni, and Yiannis Zaimakis

Volume 27
Protest, Youth and Precariousness: The Unfinished Fight against Austerity in Portugal
Edited by Renato Miguel Carmo and José Alberto Vasconcelos Simões

Volume 26
Party Responses to Social Movements: Challenges and Opportunities
Daniela R. Piccio

Volume 25
The Politics of Authenticity: Countercultures and Radical Movements across the Iron Curtain, 1968–1989
Edited by Joachim C. Häberlen, Mark Keck-Szajbel, and Kate Mahoney

Volume 24
Taking on Technocracy: Nuclear Power in Germany, 1945 to the Present
Dolores L. Augustine

Volume 23
The Virago Story: Assessing the Impact of a Feminist Publishing Phenomenon
Catherine Riley

Volume 22
The Women's Liberation Movement: Impacts and Outcomes
Edited by Kristina Schulz

Volume 21
Hairy Hippies and Bloody Butchers: The Greenpeace Anti-Whaling Campaign in Norway
Juliane Riese

For a full volume listing, please see the series page on our website:
http://berghahnbooks.com/series/protest-culture-and-society

Rethinking Social Movements after '68

Selves and Solidarities in West Germany and Beyond

Edited by

Belinda Davis, Friederike Brühöfener, and Stephen Milder

berghahn
NEW YORK · OXFORD
www.berghahnbooks.com

First published in 2022 by
Berghahn Books
www.berghahnbooks.com

© 2022, 2026 Belinda Davis, Friederike Brühöfener, and Stephen Milder
First paperback edition published in 2026

All rights reserved. Except for the quotation of short passages
for the purposes of criticism and review, no part of this book
may be reproduced in any form or by any means, electronic or
mechanical, including photocopying, recording, or any information
storage and retrieval system now known or to be invented,
without written permission of the publisher.

Library of Congress Cataloging-in-Publication Data

Names: Davis, Belinda J. (Belinda Joy), 1959- editor. | Bruhofener, Friederike, editor. | Milder, Stephen, editor.
Title: Rethinking social movements after '68 : selves and solidarities in West Germany and beyond / edited by Belinda Davis, Friederike Brühöfener, and Stephen Milder.
Other titles: Rethinking social movements after 1968
Description: New York : Berghahn Books, 2022. | Series: Protest, culture & society | Includes bibliographical references and index.
Identifiers: LCCN 2022016088 (print) | LCCN 2022016089 (ebook) | ISBN 9781800735651 (hardback) | ISBN 9781800735668 (ebook)
Subjects: LCSH: Social movements--Germany (West) | Social movements—Europe—History—20th century. | Identity (Psychology)--Germany (West) | Identity (Psychology)—Europe—History—20th century.
Classification: LCC HN460.S62 R47 2022 (print) | LCC HN460.S62 (ebook) DDC 303.48/40943—dc23/eng/20220413
LC record available at https://lccn.loc.gov/2022016088
LC ebook record available at https://lccn.loc.gov/2022016089

British Library Cataloguing in Publication Data

A catalogue record for this book is available from the British Library

EU GPSR Authorized Representative

LOGOS EUROPE, 9 rue Nicolas Poussin, 17000, LA ROCHELLE, France
Email: Contact@logoseurope.eu

ISBN 978-1-80073-565-1 hardback
ISBN 978-1-83695-654-9 paperback
ISBN 978-1-80758-493-1 epub
ISBN 978-1-80073-566-8 web pdf

https://doi.org/10.3167/9781800735651

Contents

Acknowledgments — vii

List of Abbreviations — viii

Introduction. Social Movements after '68: Histories, Selves, Solidarities — 1
   Stephen Milder, Belinda Davis, and Friederike Brühöfener

Part I. Working with—and against—the Past

CHAPTER 1. Leaving the Borderlands ... but for Where? 1968 and the New Registers of Political Feeling — 23
   Geoff Eley

CHAPTER 2. Conceptions of Democracy and West German New Social Movement Activism — 46
   Michael L. Hughes

CHAPTER 3. New Social Movements and the New Role of the Intellectual: From the "'68ers'" Critique (of the Intellectual) to (the Typus of) the "Specific Intellectual" — 67
   Ingrid Gilcher-Holtey

CHAPTER 4. Fighting with Feelings: Experiences of Protest and Emotional Practices in the Autonomous West German Women's Movement during the 1970s and 1980s — 88
   Bernhard Gotto

Part II. "Start Where You Are"

CHAPTER 5. "Break Down the Violence in a Place Where It Is Vulnerable": The Urban '68 and Its Aftermath—Expert Critique, "Tenant Campaigns," and Squatter Movements — 111
   Freia Anders

CHAPTER 6. Running Over Trees in Germany: Social Movements and the US Army, 1975–85 — 133
   Adam R. Seipp

Chapter 7. Radical Change Close to Home: Transforming the Self
and Relations in West German Alternative Politics 153
Belinda Davis

Chapter 8. Changing the World for the Better: Women Activists'
Redefinitions of Identities, Relationships, and Society 173
Friederike Brühöfener

Chapter 9. From Self-Organization to Self-Management:
Paradigms of Social Movements in West Germany from '68
to the Early 1980s 193
David Templin

Part III. "Learn to Live in Solidarity"

Chapter 10. The Gay Movement in 1970s West Germany:
Liberation in Its Multidimensional Context 217
Craig Griffiths

Chapter 11. Radical Protest or Shadow Diplomacy?
The Decolonization of Zimbabwe and West German Maoism,
1960–80 238
David Spreen

Chapter 12. Supporting a Revolution: West German Nicaragua
Solidarity and Its Transnational Connections with the
Nicaraguan Sandinistas 259
Christian Helm

Chapter 13. East German Environmental Activism and
the West: Connections, Common Ground, and Difference
across the Iron Curtain 283
Julia E. Ault

Chapter 14. Activists Divided? Continental Imaginations
in West Germany's 1968 and Beyond 303
Anna von der Goltz

Conclusion. Democracy in the Streets, Social Change
in the Countryside: Grassroots Struggles, Solidarity Work,
and Political Power after '68 324
Stephen Milder

Index 338

Acknowledgments

Generous support for work on this volume was provided by the Center for European Studies and the Dean's Office of the School of Arts and Sciences at Rutgers, as well as Rutgers Global; the German Academic Exchange Program (DAAD); the German Embassy of the United States "Campus Weeks"; the University of Groningen's Institute for the Study of Culture and its Sustainable Society Institute; and the German Research Foundation (project no. 423371999). At Rutgers, Christina Pasley, Martine Adams, and Dustin Stalnaker all supported this project. Eimear Shine took time from her studies at the University of Groningen to proofread much of the initial manuscript. The editors are very grateful to Chris Chappell, Sulaiman Ahmad, Keara Hagerty, and Ryan Masteller at Berghahn Books, with whom it has been a pleasure to work, as well as to the press's outside readers. Finally, the editors would like to thank the volume's contributors, who responded remarkably promptly and with unflagging good cheer to many rounds of comments and queries. This volume speaks to grassroots politics "after '68." It remains "after '68," and we hope this collection offers inspiration to producing change going forward.

Abbreviations

AfD—Alternative for Germany / Alternative für Deutschland
AGW—Working Group Westend / Arbeitsgruppe Westend
AHA—General Homosexual Committee / Allgemeine Homosexuelle Arbeitsgemeinschaft
AI—Amnesty International
APO—Extraparliamentary Opposition / Ausserparlamentarische Opposition
AstA—General Students Committee / Allgemeiner Studierendenausschuss
BBC—British Broadcasting Corporation
BBU—Federal Association of Citizens' Initiatives for Environmental Protection / Bundesverband Bürgerinitiativen Umweltschutz
BDP—Federal Scout Association / Bund Deutscher Pfadfinder
BVerfG—Federal Constitutional Court / Bundesverfassungsgericht
BURN—Citizens' Action for Environmental Protection Rhine-Neckar / Bürgeraktion Umweltschutz Rhein-Neckar
CAWT—Cooperation and Working Together
CDU—Christian Democratic Union / Christliche Demokratische Union
CFDT—French Democratic Confederation of Labor / Confédération française démocratique du travail
CR—Consciousness Raising
CSD—Christopher Street Day
CSU—Christian Social Union / Christliche Soziale Union
DFU—German Peace Union / Deutsche Friedens-Union
DGB—German Trade Union Confederation / Deutsche Gewerkschaftsbund
DIY—Do-it-yourself
DKP—German Communist Party / Deutsche Kommunistische Partei
DM—German Mark / Deutsche Mark
EDS—European Democratic Students
ETH—Swiss Federal Institute of Technology / Eidgenössische Technische Hochschule
FDJ—Free German Youth / Freie Deutsche Jugend

FDP—Free Democratic Party / Freie Demokratische Partei
FLN—National Liberation Front / Front de Libération Nationale
FM—Field Manual
FRG—Federal Republic of Germany
FSLN—Sandinista National Liberation Front / Frente Sandinista de Liberación Nacional
FU—Free University of Berlin / Freie Universität Berlin
GA—Joint Committee / Gemeinsamer Ausschuss
GDR—German Democratic Republic
GIP—Information on Prisons Group / Groupe d'information sur les prisons
GIM—International Marxist Group / Gruppe Internationale Marxisten
GG—Basic Law / Grundgesetz
GSG—Union Students' Group / Gewerkschaftliche Studentengruppe
GSR—Society for Sexual Reform / Gesellschaft für Sexualreform
HAW—Homosexual Action West Berlin / Homosexuelle Aktion Westberlin
IBN—Information Office Nicaragua / Informationsbüro Nicaragua
ICCS—International Union of Christian Democrat and Conservative Students
IM—Unofficial Informant / Inoffizielle Mitarbeiter
ISC—International Student Conference
KB—Communist League / Kommunistischer Bund
KBW—Communist League of West Germany / Kommunistischer Bund Westdeutschlands
KHG—Communist University Group / Kommunistische Hochschulgruppe
KJV—Communist Youth Federation / Kommunistischer Jugendverband
KPD—German Communist Party / Kommunistische Partei Deutschlands
KPD-AO—Communist Party of Germany (Organizational Structure) / Kommunistische Partei Deutschlands (Aufbauorganisation)
KPD-ML—Communist Party of Germany (Marxists-Leninists) / Kommunistische Partei Deutschlands (Marxisten-Leninisten)
LAZ—Lesbian Action Center / Lesbisches Aktionszentrum
LGB—Lesbian, Gay, Bisexual
LGBT—Lesbian, Gay, Bisexual, Transsexual
ML—Marxist-Leninist
MV—Markish Quarter / Märkisches Viertel

MVZ—*Markish Quarter News / Märksiches Viertel Zeitung*
NATO—North Atlantic Treaty Organization
NRW—North Rhine-Westphalia / Nordrhein Westfalen
NSM—New Social Movement
OPEC—Organization of Petroleum Exporting Countries
PCI—Italian Communist Party / Partito Comunista Italiano
RAF—Red Army Faction / Rote Armee Fraktion
RCDS—Association of Christian Democratic Students / Ring Christlich-Demokratischer Studenten
REFORGER—Return of Forces to Germany
RWTH—Rhenish-Westphalian Technical University / Rheinsch-Westfälische Technische Hochschule
SB—Socialist Office / Sozialistisches Büro
SC—*Socialist Correspondence-Info / Sozialistische Correspondez-Info*
SDS—Socialist German Student League / Sozialistische Deutsche Studentenbund
SED—Socialist Unity Party of Germany / Sozialistische Einheitspartei Deutschlands
SEW—Socialist Unity Party of West Berlin / Sozialistische Einheitspartei Westberlins
SFB—Radio Free Berlin / Sender Freies Berlin
SHB—Social Democratic University Union / Sozialdemokratischer Hochschulbund
SJD—Socialist Youth of Germany / Sozialistische Jugend Deutschlands
SPD—Social Democratic Party of Germany / Sozialdemokratische Partei Deutschlands
TU—Technical University / Technische Universität
UJZ—Independent Youth Center / Unabhängiges Jugendzentrum
UN—United Nations
USA—United States of America
USAEUR—United States Army Europe
USSR—Union of Soviet Socialist Republics
WES—West European Socialists / Westeuropäische Sozialisten
WCC—World Council of Churches
WG—Living Community / Wohngemeinschaft
ZANLA—Zimbabwe African National Liberation Army
ZANU—Zimbabwe African National Union
ZAPU—Zimbabwe African People's Union

Introduction

Social Movements after '68: Histories, Selves, Solidarities

Stephen Milder, Belinda Davis, and Friederike Brühöfener

On 14 October 1979, from a stage in Bonn's Hofgarten, Walter Mossmann called for "Resistance at every level!"[1] Three seconds later, his words, amplified by "two four-meter-high towers of loudspeakers with a power of 12,000 watts," echoed off the buildings across the park.[2] In the meantime, they had been heard by the 150,000 opponents of nuclear energy assembled in front of him. Mossmann's reverberating call to action was only the latest evidence that the midsized university town and "provisional" capital of the Federal Republic of Germany (FRG, or, West Germany) had been overwhelmed by antinuclear activists. Sixteen chartered trains had arrived from across the country, holding up traffic at Bonn's small train station, which was filled with "thousands of singing and clapping activists."[3] At the city's outskirts, police tried in vain to halt a column of tractors driven more than 300 kilometers by members of the Rural Youth Association of Westfallen-Lippe.[4] Some 400 *Spontis* from Frankfurt, Marburg, and Gießen had arrived already the previous evening—by riverboat. To the frustration of some participants, members of the East German–oriented German Communist Party (DKP) took part in the protest vociferously, using a loudspeaker car to drown out chants "against reactors in East and West."[5]

The diverse, cacophonous mass of protesters had come from all across society, from all over the FRG, and beyond. While the majority of the demonstrators were young people in their twenties, significant numbers of older people took part, including "far more women than men."[6] Future chancellor Gerhard Schröder, then already thirty-five, positioned himself at the head of a contingent of the mainstream Young Social Democrats, as featured prominently in new coverage after the fact.[7] From the stage, Herb Pletchford, "an Indian from the USA," described "resistance against uranium mining on Indian land," while Kathy McCaughin of Harrisburg, Pennsylvania, spoke about the near-meltdown at the Three Mile Island nuclear power plant.[8] In the crowd, activists from France waved signs against "the mammoth atomic reactor in Cattenom." Austrians, Swiss, Dutch, and British opponents of nuclear energy had also "come in droves."[9]

The demonstration in Bonn epitomized the diversity and the growing prominence of social movement activism in West Germany in the 1970s and 1980s. The motley crew of participants, some affiliated with national organizations or political parties, some members of local "citizens' initiatives," others attending on their own, was typical of many of the era's social movements.[10] So too were connections to activists from abroad. Some connections—like McCaughin's reminder that the world had been watching what happened at Harrisburg—made the Bonn demonstration seem part of a global movement. Others, such as the anti-Cattenom signs that dotted the crowd, suggested transnational links among particular struggles. Given such diversity, not only of participants but also of networks, conflicts among participating groups, like those incited by the DKP's attempt to exempt socialist reactors from the demonstration's focus, were common to many of the era's mobilizations. The conflicts notwithstanding, the Bonn demonstration then, brought together people with a wide variety of motivations from all across society, in the name of a common cause. It exemplified the way that activists who came from very different personal and local contexts stood in solidarity with one another, at once empowering themselves and collectively building the social movements of the 1970s and 1980s. Drawing on transformations in thought and practice begun already in the 1960s, these "new social movements" comprised activism emerging not out of rigid structures and tight hierarchies but rather from the loosest networks—as likely based across group houses and squatted buildings as in individual organizations identified via common ideology or even issue.

Understanding social movements in the decades after the perceived zenith of the student movement in the late 1960s—a period that we refer to throughout this collection as the years after '68—requires looking beyond any individual protest action, however. The Bonn demonstration's format—a handful speakers addressing a mass audience from the stage—made it highly legible to the press. Yet, focusing too closely on such mass demonstrations might draw a reader's attention away from the bottom-up organizing that had brought such a diverse crowd to the West German capital. Like most other mass demonstrations and street protests, the Bonn demonstration concluded at the end of a single day. It "crumbled apart around 4pm" as the tens of thousands of demonstrators "hastened back to their buses and chartered trains." But for the demonstrators, the Bonn protest was "only a single step in the long-term struggle against the atomic state."[11] Mossmann's impassioned call for "resistance at every level" was based precisely on his experience of the power of grassroots organizing and the limited potential to effect meaningful change through established political channels. Hence, understanding the social movements of the years after '68 requires studying activism that took place where people lived, that built on alternative conceptions of power, and that was often framed in a transnational context. Examining contemporary grassroots politics requires us thus to analyze the tangible transformations that activists had already spurred on in their own lives, at the local level, and across borders. To better understand social movements after '68 and to reassess their significance, this volume presents a range of case studies, showing how the movements were organized, what concerns and ideas motivated their protagonists to act, and how they related to one another—and to society as a whole. This broad body of empirical research reveals how social movements after '68 brought together diverse demographics, often across geopolitical boundaries, and empowered individuals to act, both in their own interest and in solidarity with others.[12]

While this volume is closely focused on the movements of the 1970s and 1980s, and studies those movements' characteristics and commonalities, our research does not support the idea that they were wholly new or unprecedented. We do not describe the period we study as the years *after '68*, therefore, in order to suggest a clean break between "old" and "new" social movements.[13] We do so, instead, because of the long shadow that '68 casts on the movements of the 1970s and 1980s and that shadow's ongoing influence over the way the broad public and even many scholars have perceived them. The activism of the late 1960s—and responses to it—wrought real social and political changes that influenced later movements. But "'68's" near-immediate "mythologization" was perhaps even more important for the perception of the movements that came afterward.[14] The perceived apogee of postwar protest was not the only influence on social movements in the years after '68; indeed, for many contemporaries, '68 specifically represented also a nadir of their activism, in terms of official and other attacks against them and the attendant despair and disunity. The activism of the late 1960s—and that beginning already years before—constituted a powerful but also highly diverse set of influences on what followed. At the same time, other elements were also critically influential. The shift from the galloping growth of the postwar "economic miracle" to the challenges of the later "crisis decades" shifted the context of protest just as it reframed the way that social movements were understood. In elucidating this historical context, this volume addresses not only the movements' characteristics and internal histories but also the ways in which they have been perceived. It is only by approaching the movements in their historical context, we argue, that we can understand their meaning for West German politics, society, and democracy. The remainder of this introduction outlines our approach to social movements after '68. It first situates the movements of the 1970s and 1980s by considering their historical context and what this has meant for the way we tend to understand them. Drawing on the research presented in this anthology, three further sections, corresponding with the three sections comprising the volume as a whole, articulate our understanding of the movements themselves. We begin with activists' own multidimensional relationships with the past, showing how they built on historical achievements even as they sought to address the problems of the past. Next, we take up the often personal and localized starting points of activism after '68, looking at the ways in which activists connected themselves, and their own experiences—via local issues and personal concerns—with other people, other places, and larger causes. Finally, we turn to the networks within which social movements developed. By following protest across ideological, societal, and geographical boundaries, we examine the meaning and the salience of solidarities for the era's social movements.

After '68: Explaining an Era—and Its Social Movements—by What Came Before

As the title of this volume indicates, the social movements of the 1970s and 1980s have been defined primarily in terms of that that came just before them. The broad West German New Left is widely regarded to have "disintegrated into a multiplicity of splinter groups" immediately after '68.[15] Accordingly, some activists perceived the 1970s as a comparatively "leaden time."[16] Scholars' interpretations of the era have often drawn in turn on a similar sort of comparison with the immediate past, though recent work now challenges that perspective, often looking explicitly to a longer period of postwar activism (1962–78; even 1963–89) that coheres as a single whole.[17] Work in this volume suggests still longer relevant trajectories, from at least the "generative and enabling" moment represented by 1945—while at once challenging assumptions that inhere in such characterizations as "the red decade" of 1967–77.[18]

Broader shifts in context are also essential to understanding the transformation of popular politics. The collapse of the Bretton Woods monetary system in 1971, as well as the 1973 and 1979 oil shocks, were important markers of what Eric Hobsbawm termed the "crisis decades."[19] That appellation jarringly juxtaposed the 1970s and 1980s with the sparkling image of the preceding "golden years." In West German historiography, as a result, the period has come to be known as the time "after the boom."[20] Yet, as with the "red decade," it is important to simultaneously appreciate scholars' characterization of that context and critically review attendant understandings, as they relate to popular politics and otherwise.

Defining the "long 1970s," as some scholars have cast it, primarily by what preceded it has deep consequences.[21] It can seem to turn the unprecedented economic growth of the 1950s and early 1960s—and the social and political conditions that accompanied it—into some kind of norm. Emphasis on the economic growth of the miracle years also precipitates depictions of "'68ers" as callow youth knowing only prosperous, easy lives.[22] Accordingly, master narratives of systemic crisis and precipitous decline foist a set of presumptions onto our understanding of social movements in the years after '68. The narrative of breakdown has been extended to the movements themselves, which are also seen as little more than the remnants of a former sepia-toned Left, which splintered as the economy stagnated.[23] From this vantage point, debates over the uses of history can appear as a longing for a bygone era, intimating that new movements that fostered change in individual lives and particular communities were only isolated fragments, characterized dismissively by a lack of leadership.[24]

Recently, historians have begun to revise their perspective on the era, linking the "long 1970s" with the future instead of the past. Konrad Jarausch, for example, has interpreted the 1970s as a "pre-history of the problems of the present," while Niall Ferguson has described the 1970s as the decade "in which the seeds of future crises were sown."[25] While this has permitted fresh insights, it can likewise cast the era's activism, along with the issues that occasioned it, in highly inauspicious terms. The issues that have been portrayed as problems and crises of the present range from globalization and migration to environmental destruction and climate change, and thus have myriad links with the social movements of the 1970s and 1980s; it can seem that the earlier activism failed entirely—if not actually contributing somehow to the problems.

Debates on the perceived "crisis of democracy," which have been widespread in recent years, epitomize the extent to which teleological perspectives on the 1970s affect our understanding of the era's social movements. Since the contemporary crisis of democracy is perceived as a problem with roots that go back to the seventies, the era's movements have been implicated in it.[26] Particular initiatives and individual "single-issue movements" have been recast as threats to traditional parties; transnational solidarities have been said to ignore and thus challenge liberal conceptions of citizenship. Seeking change from the self outward has been portrayed as a neglect of real politics. Most alarmingly, efforts to work around and beyond national parliaments have become threats to parliamentary democracy as such.[27] The social movements of the 1970s and 1980s, in short, have become handmaidens of democracy's ongoing deconsolidation.

Our research into the era's social movements draws on a different interpretation of the 1970s and 1980s. We avoid narratives based in the idea of a complete break between "miracle years" and "crisis decades," which obscure the movements' deep roots. At the same time, we refrain from seeing the seventies and eighties as part of an ongoing present, which neglects the distinct contexts of these two eras and suggests the sudden emergence of path-dependent processes that remain on track in spite of the copious, widely diagnosed crises of the past fifteen years.[28] By transcending the binary of rupture and continuity, we also open up space to rethink the results of contemporary activism in its highly diverse forms.

West German activists' own perspectives on the 1970s and 1980s clearly moved beyond these binaries. They experienced the years after '68 as a time of both promise and frustration. The period can be bracketed by the "student uprising" and the climax of the monumental peace movement of the mid-1980s. It also saw the emergence of a new political formation in the Greens (Die Grünen) that sought to transcend the divide between a conventional political party and a grassroots movement. Its beginning coincided with the new country's first change from a Christian Democratic–led government to one led by Social Democrats, a government that came into office on Willy Brandt's pledge to "dare more democracy." And yet, few of the era's movements could claim obvious and immediate victories in terms of the issues that animated them. Grassroots protests did not stop the proliferation of nuclear energy production just as mass demonstrations did not halt the deployment of NATO's new Euromissiles. The Brandt government did usher in changes in democratic praxis, but it did not precipitate a radically different, more participatory form of parliamentary democracy in West Germany; instead, it began a decade precisely of SPD-led assaults on popular political expression in the name of "militant democracy."[29] The emergence of the Greens was not just a boon for movement activists, but could also be viewed as a diminution of the potential of the social movements that party leaders claimed to speak for, since party leadership attuned itself increasingly to parliamentary politics rather than broad protest campaigns.[30] Yet, none of this warrants imagining the period as a time of failure for popular politics, nor does it suggest that we should see the era as one of absolute success as far as popular political engagement was concerned: to choose either would be precisely to take the period out of time.

Because we understand the 1970s and 1980s as neither a period of terrible disintegration nor a time when only crises were sown, we approach social movements after '68 in a way that opens the door to a different conception of the contemporary history of democracy. We look to the ways that the era's movements struggled to build on a past that contained achievements as well as missteps, at the ways they enabled a broad cross-section of the population to engage itself in political debates, at the ways they positioned personal and localized actions as the foundation of deep societal transformations, and at the ways that they encouraged—and even depended on—unexpected cooperation between unlikely partners, domestically and also internationally. As a result, we see the years after '68 as a moment when parliamentary democracy opened up to a more participatory democratic politics.

While the fullness of activists' participatory vision was realized only in glimpses here and there, the ideas that underpinned it have nonetheless left a lasting imprint on the ways that democracy was practiced in later decades. Specifically, they have created widespread expectations that parliamentary democracy must privilege public inclusion over elite leadership and transparency over backroom decision-making. These expectations, of course, do not ensure that parliamentary democracy will always be more inclusive. They do, nonetheless, serve as an important precedent and thus as a premise for demanding a more inclusive democracy, one that moreover includes attention to sites of expression beyond party politics and to sites of action and influence at every level of society. Indeed it is more than this: contemporary grassroots activists themselves rethought timelines of change. They saw each successive political experiment as a chance to learn and grow; each "failure" was instructive for the next efforts. They challenged the very notion of any end of history, realization of any utopia, and replaced the view with the need to doggedly keep at it. This may be one of contemporary activists' most signal lessons—and one of the very sources of challenge to notions of rupture versus continuity.

Movements and Histories: Working with—and against—the Past

The chapters in this volume look critically at social movement activists' own engagement with the past, particularly with histories of activism and democratic practice. In line with our understanding of the period's complicated position in longer historical trajectories, our research shows that activists looked with a mixture of pride and derision at past advances toward greater social equality and enhanced democratic participation, and even the histories of their own movements. By seeing the past as both a supporting basis for their actions and a reminder that so much remained to be done, activists declined to see the movements of the 1970s and 1980s as the falling action after the climax of postwar protest, or as evidence that democracy itself had passed its zenith and entered into a phase of deconsolidation.[31] So too did many of these activists refuse to see their demands for participatory democracy as a rebuff of the parliamentary democracy that West Germans had carefully constructed in the wake of World War II. Elucidating this multidimensional perspective on the past is essential for understanding not only activists' motivations and goals but also their place within Germany's postwar history and the longer continuum of social movement activism.

Perhaps the most salient example of activists' multidimensional perspective on the history of democratic advances is their relationship to what Geoff Eley calls the "post-1945 settlement," a phrase he uses to describe the social and political compromise that emerged from the rubble of World War II. That settlement, he argues, "sutured democracy and social justice firmly together inside a discourse of social recognition and public goods." The postwar era's economic boom and its stable—if staid—practice of parliamentary democracy, amid which youthful insurgents of the late sixties and early seventies came of age, made their mobilization possible.[32] Activists' attitudes toward the Basic Law, the 1949 provisional constitution that underpinned West Germany's new democratic order, exemplified this relationship. Protagonists of social movements made good use of the Basic Law's provisions: they availed themselves of democratic participation via "elections and votes" and also depended on its guarantees of freedom of expression and of assembly in order to protest. This was so despite efforts in the Bundestag to chip away at these guarantees from at least the late 1960s, as well as official efforts to restrict them on the ground.[33] As Michael Hughes shows, however, the same activists sought to transcend the very parliamentary democracy that the Basic Law prescribed, working to realize their own varieties of the direct democracy and council democracy that their predecessors had advocated from World War I.

It was precisely the combination of embracing the post-1945 settlement even as they sought to transcend it, Hughes and Eley argue, that shaped activists' primary contributions to democracy. Hughes finds that activists' aspirations for more, deeper participation motivated their challenges to the Basic Law and "ultimately established new norms for political citizenship." Even though they came nowhere close to installing a council democracy in the FRG, in other words, social movement activists succeeded in making parliamentary democracy as it existed in the FRG a far more participatory enterprise and, all the more, in legitimating a wide range of popular political forms. They also spurred the politicization and reimagining of human relations broadly, at every level, such as between women and men, and also between adults and children. Indeed, it was not so much critiques of the post-1945 liberal democratic order per se but rather the activists' "largeness of aspiration, big ideas, and cultural militancies" that effected the greatest change in the long run, Eley finds.

The ways activists understood the history of activism, and even their own movements' pasts, were also multidimensional. Feminists' assessment of where the women's movement was headed, their ideas about "the possibility of changing the society, and . . . of what it meant to be a 'true' feminist" were highly dependent on their experiences within the movement, Bernhard Gotto shows. While women who had been engaged in the movement since the 1960s tended to feel that the movement was declining and becoming depoliticized by the late 1970s and early 1980s, women who joined the movement in the 1970s believed broader possibilities for meaningful action were just now opening up.

Activists' changing understanding of intellectuals' contribution to social movements revealed a similarly conflicted, multivalent view of past movements, as Ingrid Gilcher-Holtey shows. On the one hand, activists distanced themselves from earlier movements by rejecting the idea of a "universal intellectual," who could intervene in a social struggle from the outside, as a purveyor of abstract, universal values and thus reshape public opinion. The emergence of the "specific intellectual," who was expected to deploy actions as well as words in support of movements, on the other hand, revealed an emphasis on multiple viewpoints rather than metanarratives. Reflections on the past, then, promoted a more pluralistic approach to the problems of the present.

The research presented in this volume reveals that the past resonated with activists in the years after '68; but it also shows that their relationships to the post-1945 settlement and even to the histories of their own movements were complicated and multivalent. Rather than thinking in black-and-white terms about contemporary history or about their predecessors, or desiring to cut themselves off from the past completely, activists after '68 celebrated, critiqued, and sought to build on past accomplishments. Such a perspective on the past shaped the movements they organized, making them more open to divergent viewpoints and causing them to seek common ground amid a variety of viewpoints. Understanding activists' will to work with—but also against—the past is key to reintegrating those movements into longer histories—from master narratives on economic progress and the consolidation of democracy to microhistories of individual movements—as led by the example of contemporary activists themselves. Those longer histories extend toward the present as well, challenging the explanatory importance of individual historical "flash points" and reminding us that change occurs unevenly and contingently but always connected to the past, just as to imagined futures.

"Start Where You Are"

Social movements in the years after '68 were organized by diverse casts of protagonists, who hailed from all across society. The deep engagement of "ordinary citizens" and "local people" fostered broad conceptions of societal problems and multifaceted approaches to them.[34] The same diversity supported the development of grassroots leadership and self-organization. Such diversity drew on local engagement, epitomizing Green party cofounder Petra Kelly's adjuration to "start where you are." Kelly linked grassroots work with big-picture changes, proposing that getting started at the local level would bring about greater transformation. Far from amounting to a withdrawal from politics writ large, beginning with personal matters and issues close to home fostered new sorts of political engagement and led to the development of new political coalitions, effectively allowing activists to transcend the shortcomings of "high politics" (*große Politik*).[35] The brand of popular politics that this approach generated expanded political participation to new populations at the same time as it provided a basis for connection with the needs of others, in the same town and also across the world.

Debates over living space and living arrangements provide evidence of the importance of the self and of one's own experiences as a basis for far-reaching political engagement during the 1970s and 1980s. As Freia Anders shows, discussions of what Henri Lefebvre termed the "right to the city" had their basis in individuals' own life situations and ability to access housing and other urban resources.[36] From this perspective, the practice of squatting in vacant buildings is hardly the work of a radical fringe but rather one tool in a broader toolkit that also included tenant organizing campaigns, rent strikes, expert critiques, and the presentation of alternative visions for urban life. In rural regions too, debates over the use of space were linked with much broader issues. Adam Seipp shows how, in the region around the Fulda Gap, where NATO expected the Warsaw Pact countries to strike in a potential third world war, inhabitants' efforts to protect their hometowns from the ill effects of US Army tank maneuvers linked concerns about the destruction of the local environment with the fears about preparations for world war and even questions about German sovereignty.

Changes in personal relationships were building blocks for shifts with effects throughout society. Within individual dwellings, as Belinda Davis shows, activists undertook experiments that fundamentally questioned the nuclear family and also the primacy of the couple's relationship. Inhabitants of living communities (*Wohngemeinschaften*, WGs) refuted essentialisms concerning "what women do," and "who men are." This intense work helped redefine the political itself, transforming activists' thinking concerning how and where change takes place and fostering new understandings of the timeline of change (transcending "revolution" versus "reform," and the success versus failure of individual political experiments). The "moral utopianism" voiced by West German women after '68 also drew on the idea that changing the self and interpersonal relationships would be the basis for any transformation of society as a whole. By working against the attribution of emotions on the basis of gender while repudiating the exclusion of emotions from political debates, Friederike Brühöfener shows, West German women sought likewise to create change starting from their own lives and experiences. In the long term, their work aided the development, in the FRG, of what Thomas Kühne has described as a "culture of peace."

David Templin's study of the changing meanings of the terms "self-organization" and "self-management" offers further examples of ways in which the restructuring of spaces for work and recreation proved transformative in the years after '68.[37] Apprentices' "self-organized" meeting spaces enabled them to express concerns that had been overlooked or downplayed by union leadership, while self-organization within activist groups became a means of demonstrating that a new society was possible, and living in it now. By the 1980s, efforts to create "self-managed" youth centers focused on the active engagement of participants in the centers' programming: sustaining independence had become an end in and of itself. As these different projects suggest, self-managed spaces were part of a collective effort directed toward the emancipation and empowerment of people who were often left out of preexisting decision-making structures.

By starting where they were, and by focusing on interpersonal relationships, activists confronted the extent to which the fundamental circumstances of their lives were shaped by both political decisions and social norms. By beginning from this most basic and personal level, their engagement showed them how changing personal circumstances could underpin deep societal transformations. In making changes to their own lives, they made themselves, their needs, and their experiences into the bases of an alternative society in the present. Indeed, asserting one's own right to decent living conditions was easily linked to the parallel rights of others. Both as models and on account of the way they transformed their protagonists, new sorts of personal relationships and self-managed groups and spaces often served as building blocks for the broader transformation of society, meaning that the self was almost always viewed in relation to others, and as a starting point for activists' work that transcended the shortcomings of "high politics."

"Learn to Live in Solidarity"

In the years after '68, the idea of a shared, overarching struggle enabled a wide range of activists, focused on various particular issues, to feel that they were part of something far larger than themselves. Even if many increasingly approached their work from the basis of their own experiences and their own self-interest, they refused to see themselves as isolated individuals. Instead, they saw themselves and their own concerns as part of a broader emancipatory struggle, as they "learn[ed] to live in solidarity."[38] Such an outlook enabled activists to build common cause with people who had very different experiences, different concerns, and different approaches to politics. Not only did such networking link various sets of concerns together, it also frequently extended across borders and spanned oceans. As efforts to build connections and channels of communication across the Iron Curtain made particularly clear, however, even earnest strivings for solidarity did not always succeed in creating equal exchanges among their participants. But such efforts did blur the boundaries between groups and struggles that are often understood primarily in terms of their seeming difference from one another.[39] In short, the emphasis that activists placed on building solidarities deeply affected the way they saw their projects, the way they related to society, and thus the social change that they worked toward.

Protagonists of movements ostensibly devoted to a single issue conceived of their own struggles in relationship to other ongoing political projects, making particular interests the basis for broad solidarities. As Craig Griffiths shows, 1970s gay activists conceived of their movement only within the context of a wider struggle against capitalism. Realizing their own oppression as both homosexuals and workers, and seeking to build reciprocal solidarity with other oppressed groups, gay activists saw their politics not as a single-issue campaign limited to others with the same experiences but rather as part of a broad movement for social emancipation. Coming together around a particular cause or issue was the basis for engagement in broad movements with transformative goals. Indeed, coalition building and networking far outweighed the sectarianism, infighting, and self-isolation by which the era's grassroots politics have often been characterized.

Networking particular campaigns and building common cause in the name of a larger, shared struggle extended social movement activism far beyond the borders of the FRG in the long 1970s. The Maoist Communist League of West Germany (Kommunistische Bund Westdeutschlands—KBW) was well-known for its domestic networking, which consisted largely of "infiltrating" other activist organizations, from antinuclear citizens' initiatives to working groups focused on the abolition of the FRG's abortion ban. But, as David Spreen shows, the KBW also networked with anticolonial groups in Southern Africa, like the Zimbabwe African National Union (ZANU), and this networking benefitted the KBW. In providing the ZANU with funds, armored vehicles, and other resources, KBW activists came to see themselves as part of a "global revolutionary movement." The West German solidarity campaign in support of the Nicaraguan Sandinista movement, though quite different in nature than the KBW's support for the ZANU, had similar effects on its German participants. As Christian Helm shows, the unitary movement that West Germans built in support of the Sandinistas helped activists conceptualize political and societal change outside established frameworks and beyond national containers, even shaping the development of a "people-to-people diplomacy" that circumvented the Foreign Office and linked West Germans directly with Nicaraguans.

Building solidarity across geopolitical borders was not always a reciprocal project, even if claims to solidarity had deep effects on those who made them, as well as on those they claimed as their new partners. As Julia Ault shows, West Germans who sought to aid environmental activists in East Germany conceived of environmentalism as a single phenomenon in East and West. Such a conception helped West German activists to push their work forward within the FRG, but it did not always draw on accurate conceptions of the conditions in the GDR or reflect a relationship based in equal exchange. Indeed, efforts to act in solidarity with East German dissidents were shaped by West Germans' different understandings of the dissidents' situation and their political demands. Thus, Anna von der Goltz shows, some self-described leftists in West Germany, whose solidarity had its basis in advocacy of revolutionary transformation on both sides of the Iron Curtain, had a harder time connecting with dissidents than did West German conservatives, who shared GDR dissidents' critiques of state socialist repression. Unequal exchanges across the Iron Curtain reveal the role of misunderstandings in the building of solidarities, but they also show that solidarity could nonetheless prove useful—and even meaningful—for activists on both sides.

Building—and imagining—solidarity among struggles and across borders enabled activists in the years after '68 to see themselves as part of a larger, transformative project. To some extent, at least, their vision was vindicated. In fact, the idea of living in solidarity underpinned their sense of themselves and their activist work: not only could many activists not understand themselves and their movements without such cooperation but they also depended on it to demonstrate the broader emancipatory potential of their action, regardless of its roots in particular circumstances. The idea of a common project, and strivings to realize it, helped activists to give meaning to their own work, to think through the links between their particular interests and their broader goal of multifaceted societal transformation, and thus to lay the foundation for an inclusive, popular politics that extended far beyond a limited, activist milieu, but also far beyond the formal structures of the FRG's parliamentary democracy. Solidarities, in other words, were essential to imagining—and acting upon—new conceptions of politics and participation.

Conclusion

By showing how the activists of the 1970s and 1980s started where they were, but nonetheless dedicated themselves to living in solidarity, this collection places the era's social movements into the center of important political and social debates in the years after '68. By analyzing the ways that activists interpreted the past, these essays position the era's movements within a longer historical trajectory. Indeed, this collection comes at what feels like another moment of possible deep political change, related not least to the rapid rise of the radical-nationalist party Alternative for Germany, mirroring political trends across Europe and the world, as well as to the concurrent rise of Black Lives Matter, in iterations across the globe, all in the midst of a pandemic that makes us more aware than ever of how we are all connected. The new prominence of radical nationalism cannot be cause for elitist retrenchment in the name of a notion that the masses and their political voice simply need to be better controlled from the top.[40] Indeed, notable responses across the United States and Europe (including non-prosecution of the removal of statues, official acknowledgment of the atrocities of imperialism, mainstream discussion of reparations for slavery, and the promise at least of entirely rethinking public security) offer a reminder of the changes bottom-up politics can engender, even if most often as a means from the top to protect the power of the status quo.

We remind ourselves that, here again, these new movements did not come out of nowhere: they are part of shorter and longer histories, of popular memory, and of trajectories that connect these flashpoints. Awareness of this history; related thinking on the nature of change, leadership, political organization, and politics itself; and efforts to work with these broader contexts inspired contemporary activists. It can remain a source of political inspiration today.

Stephen Milder is lecturer on modern history at the University of the German Armed Forces in Munich. He is the author of *Greening Democracy: The Anti-Nuclear Movement and Political Environmentalism in West Germany and Beyond, 1968–1983*.

Belinda Davis, professor of History at Rutgers University, is author or co-editor of five books, including *The Inner Life of Politics: Grassroots Activism in West Germany, 1962-1983* (Cambridge, 2026); and, ed. with M. Klimke, C. MacDougall, and W. Mausbach, *Changing the World, Changing Oneself: Political Protest and Transnational Identities in 1960s/70s, West Germany and the U.S.* (Berghahn, 2010, 2012). Her current book project is entitled "Apartheid Planet: An Environmental History of Europe and European Reach from 1500."

Friederike Brühöfener is Professor of History at San Jose State University, where she also serves as Assistant Vice Provost for Faculty Excellence and Teaching Innovation. She is the co-editor, together with Karen Hagemann and Donna Harsch, of *Gendering Post-1945 German History: Entanglements*, published by Berghahn Books in 2019.

Notes

1. Walter Mossmann, *realistisch sein: das unmögliche verlangen; Wahrheitsgetreue gefälschte Errinerungen* (Berlin: edition der Freitag, 2009), 248.
2. Micha, Holger, Frank, and Uli, "Pressionen und Impressionen," *die tageszeitung*, 16 October 1979.
3. Uli Beller, "Mit Sonderzug nach Hannover und Bonn," in Christoph Büchele, Irmgard Schneider, and Bernd Nössler, eds., *Der Widerstand geht weiter: Der Bürgerprotest gegen das Kernkraftwerk von 1976 bis zum Mannheimer Prozess* (Freiburg: Dreisam-Verlag, 1982): 136–38.
4. Micha, Holger, Frank, and Uli, "Pressionen und Impressionen."
5. M.S. and H.B., "Legt ihnen das Handwerk!" *die tageszeitung*, 15 October 1979.
6. Micha, Holger, Frank, and Uli, "Pressionen und Impressionen."
7. *Frankfurter Rundschau*, 26 October 1979.
8. Micha, Holger, Frank, and Uli, "Pressionen und Impressionen."
9. M.S. and H.B., "Legt ihnen das Handwerk!"

10. On the concept of "citizens' initiatives," see Peter Cornelius Mayer-Tasch, *Die Bürgerinitiativbewegung: Der aktive Bürger als rechts- und politikwissenschaftliches Problem* (Reinbek bei Hamburg: Rowohlt, 1976).
 11. Micha, Holger, Frank, and Uli, "Pressionen und Impressionen."
 12. This volume also offers a correction to literature, scholarly and otherwise, that continues to characterize grassroots politics on the left after '68 as collapsing entirely, outside of a tiny number of dogmatic and/or violent activists.
 13. On the distinction between "old" and "new" social movements, see Ulf Teichmann and Christian Wicke, "'Alte' und Neue soziale Bewegungen: Einleitende Anmerkungen," *Arbeit Bewegung Geschichte* 17, no. 3 (2018). Cf: Craig Calhoun, "'New Social Movements' of the Early Nineteenth Century," *Social Science History* 17, no. 3 (Fall 1993).
 14. See for example Gerd Langguth, *Mythos '68: Die Gewaltphilosophie von Rudi Dutschke—Ursachen und Folgen der Studentenbewegung* (Munich: Olzog, 2001); Wolfgang Kraushaar, *1968 als Mythos Chiffre und Zäsur* (Hamburg: Hamburger Edition, 2000).
 15. Andrei Markovits and Philip S. Gorski, *The German Left: Red Green and Beyond* (Oxford: Oxford University Press, 1993), 58. On the "fragmentation" of the student movement, see also Geoff Eley, *Forging Democracy: The History of the Left in Europe, 1850–2000* (Oxford: Oxford University Press, 2002), 418.
 16. On the idea of the 1970s as a "leaden" decade, see Christiane Peitz, "Die Bleikappe des Schweigens: Margarethe von Trotta über ihren Ensslin-Film, das Sympathisantentum und deutsche Kontinuitäten," *Der Tagesspiegel*, 28 April 2007.
 17. Cf. Timothy Scott Brown, *West Germany and the Global Sixties: The Anti-authoritarian Revolt, 1962–1978* (Cambridge: Cambridge University Press, 2015); Carla MacDougall, "Cold War Capital: Contested Urbanity in West Berlin 1963–1989" (PhD diss., Rutgers University, New Brunswick, NJ, 2011).
 18. See Geoff Eley, "Leaving the Borderlands . . . but for Where? 1968 and the New Registers of Political Feeling," in this volume; cf. Gerd Koenen, *Das rote Jahrzehnt: Unsere kleine deutsche Kulturrevolution 1967–1977* (Frankfurt a.M.: Kiepenheuer & Witsch, 2002); and Wolfgang Kraushaar, Karin Wieland, and Jan Philipp Reemtsma, *Rudi Dutschke Andreas Baader und die RAF* (Hamburg: Hamburger Edition 2005).
 19. Eric Hobsbawm, *Age of Extremes: A History of the World, 1914–1991* (New York: Vintage, 1994), 403–32.
 20. Anselm Doering-Manteuffel and Lutz Raphael, *Nach dem Boom: Perspektiven auf die Zeitgeschichte seit 1970* (Göttingen: Vandenhoeck & Ruprecht, 2008). Konrad Jarausch, ed., *Das Ende der Zuversicht? Die siebziger Jahre als Geschichte* (Göttingen: Vandenhoeck & Ruprecht, 2008).
 21. On the "long 1970s," see, e.g., Martin Deuerlein, *Das Zeitalter der Interdependenz: Globales Denken und internationale Politik in den langen 1970er Jahren* (Göttingen: Wallstein Verlag, 2020).
 22. On challenging the notion of activists as having grown up in material and other forms of comfort, Belinda Davis, *The Internal Life of Politics: Extraparliamentary Opposition in West Germany, 1962–1983* (Cambridge: Cambridge University Press, forthcoming).

23. See, for example, Tony Judt, *Postwar: A History of Europe since 1945* (New York: Penguin, 2005).
24. This is all aside from the substantial, ongoing literature that asserts the highly destructive character of "'68" itself. Cf. Götz Aly, *Unser Kampf: 1968 – ein irritierter Blick zurück* (Frankfurt/Main: Fischer, 2008); Kraushaar et al, *Rudi Dutschke Andreas Baader und die RAF*.
25. Konrad Jarausch, "Verkannter Strukturwandel: Die siebziger Jahre als Vorgeschichte der Probleme der Gegenwart," in Jarausch, *Das Ende der Zuversicht?*; Niall Ferguson, "Introduction: Crisis, What Crisis? The 1970s and the Shock of the Global," in Niall Ferguson, Charles S. Maier, Erez Manela, and Daniel J. Sargent, eds., *The Shock of the Global: The 1970s in Perspective* (Cambridge, MA: The Belknap Press of Harvard University Press), 18. Frank Bösch lists numerous historians, political scientists, and journalists who have interpreted the year 1979 as the beginning of the contemporary age, and the problems that accompany it. Bösch, *Zeitenwende 1979: Als die Welt von Heute Begann* (Munich: C. H. Beck, 2019), 14–15.
26. Colin Crouch's influential 2004 book *Post-Democracy* might be seen as the opening salvo of the latest chorus on the crisis of democracy. Crouch, *Post-Democracy* (Cambridge: Cambridge University Press, 2004). For overviews of recent literature on the "crisis of democracy," see Wolfgang Merkel, "Krise der Demokratie? Anmerkungen zu einem schwierigen Begriff," *Aus Politik und Zeitgeschichte* 66, nos. 40–42 (October 2016): 4–11; and Jan-Werner Müller, "Democracy's Midlife Crisis," *The Nation*, 22 April 2019, https://www.thenation.com/article/how-democracies-dies-how-democracy-ends-book-review/.
27. On deconsolidation broadly, e.g., Roberto Stefan Foa and Yascha Mounk, "The Danger of Deconsolidation: Democratic Disconnect," *Journal of Democracy* 27, no. 3 (2016): 5–17. On the idea that seeking change from the self outward amounts to a neglect of real politics, see, for example, Judt, *Postwar*; see also (though focused on the Unted States) Todd Gitlin, *The Twilight of Common Dreams* (New York: Metropolitan Books, 1995); On the threat to traditional parties, see, for example, Franz Walter, *Im Herbst der Volksparteien: Eine kleine Geschichte von Aufstieg und Rückgang politischer Massenintegration* (Bielefeld: Transcript, 2009); Wolfgang Merkel, "Ist die Krise der Demokratie eine Erfindung?" https://www.akademie-forum-masonicum.de/wolfgang-merkel-ist-die-krise-der-demokratie-eine-erfindung/; and Peter Mair, *Ruling the Void: The Hollowing of Western Democracy* (New York: Verso, 2013); On internationalism as a retreat from national politics, see, for example, Samuel Moyn, *The Last Utopia: Human Rights in History* (Cambridge, MA: Harvard University Press, 2010), 8.
28. On the 2010s as a decade of crises (and comparisons to the 1970s), see Andy Beckett, "The Age of Perpetual Crisis: How the 2010s Disrupted Everything but Resolved Nothing," *The Guardian*, 17 December 2019. See also, Craig Calhoun and Georgi Derluguian, eds., *The Deepening Crisis: Governance Challenges after Neoliberalism* (New York: New York University Press, 2011).
29. See Larry Frohman, "*Datenschutz*, the Defense of Law, and the Debate over Precautionary Surveillance: The Reform of Police Law and the Changing Parameters of State Action in West Germany," in *German Studies Review* 38, no. 2 (May 2015):

307–27; cf. Karrin Hanshew, *Terror and Democracy in West Germany* (Cambridge: Cambridge University Press, 2012).
30. On activists' apprehensions about the Greens' emergence, see Natalie Pohl, *Atomprotest am Oberrhein: Die Auseinandersetzung um den Bau von Atomkraftwerken in Baden und Elsass (1970–1985)* (Stuttgart: Franz Steiner Verlag, 2019), 272–78; and Stephen Milder, *Greening Democracy: The Anti-Nuclear Movement and Political Environmentalism in West Germany and Beyond, 1968-1983* (Cambridge: Cambridge University Press, 2017), 238–46.
31. On '68 as the climax of postwar protest, see, for example, Ingrid Gilcher-Holtey, "Introduction," in *A Revolution of Perception? Consequences and Echoes of 1968*, ed. Ingrid Gilcher-Holtey (New York: Berghahn Books, 2014). On the idea that democracy was on the downward slope by the 1970s and 1980s, see Crouch, *Post-Democracy*.
32. On staid, but stable democratic praxis in the postwar era, see Martin Conway, "The Rise and Fall of Western Europe's Democratic Age, 1945–1973," *Contemporary European History* 13, no. 1 (February 2004): 67–88; Claudia Gatzka, *Die Demokratie der Wähler: Stadtgesellschaft und politische Kommunikation in Italien und der Bundesrepublik, 1944–1979* (Düsseldorf: Droste Verlag, 2019).
33. Davis, "Jenseits von Terror und Rückzug: Die Suche nach politischem Spielraum und Strategien im Westdeutschland der siebziger Jahre," in Klaus Weinhauer and Jörg Requate, eds., *Terrorismus in der Bundesrepublik. Medien, Staat und Subkulturen in den 1970er Jahren* (Frankfurt a. M.: Campus, 2006), 165; also Eckart Conze, *Die Suche nach Sicherheit: Eine Geschichte der Bundesrepublik Deutschland von 1949 bis in die Gegenwart* (Berlin: Siedler, 2009); Jeremy Varon, *Bringing the War Home: The Weather Underground, the Red Army Faction, and Revolutionary Violence in the Sixties and Seventies* (Berkeley: University of California Press, 2004), 26–27.
34. On the concept of "local people," see John Dittmer, *Local People: The Struggle for Civil Rights in Mississippi* (Urbana: University of Illinois Pres, 1995). On the practice of wide populations including conservatives borrowing on strategies such as citizens' initiatives, see Martin Geyer, "Elisabeth Noelle-Neumann's 'Spiral of Silence,' the Silent Majority and the Conservative Moment of the 1970s," in *Inventing the Silent Majority in Western Europe and the United States*, ed. Anna von der Goltz and Britta Waldschmidt-Nelson (Cambridge: Cambridge University Press, 2017), 251–74; on populations across the political spectrum in new social movements, see Horst Pötzsch, *Die Deutsche Demokratie*, 5th ed. (Bonn: Springer, 2009), 54–55.
35. Petra Kelly, "Ohne Frauen ist kein Staat zu machen," in *Ist das alles? Frauen zwischen Erfolg und Sehnsucht*, ed. Norbert Copray (Munich: Kösel-Verlag, 1991). Reprinted as "Ist das alles? Frauen zwischen Erfolg und Sehnsucht," in Petra K. Kelly, *Lebe als müßtest du heute sterben* (Düsseldorf: Zebulon, 1997), 167.
36. Henri Lefebvre, *Le Droit à la ville* (Paris: Éditions Anthropos, 1968). See too MacDougall, "Cold War Capital."
37. Historians have begun to join other scholars in addressing these issues. Compare Sven Reichardt's exhaustive *Authentizität und Gemeinschaft: Linksalternatives Leben in den siebziger und frühen achtziger Jahren* (Berlin: Suhrkamp, 2014), 351–459; also Detlef Siegfried, *Time Is on My Side: Konsum und Politik in Der Westdeutschen Jugendkultur Der 60er Jahre* (Göttingen: Wallstein, 2006); Detlef Siegfried and Sven

Reichardt, *Das Alternative Milieu: Antibürgerlicher Lebensstil und linke Politik in Der Bundesrepublik Deutschland und Europa 1968–1983* (Göttingen: Wallstein, 2010); Detlef Siegfried and David Templin, *Lebensreform um 1900 und Alternativmilieu Um 1980: Kontinuitäten und Brüche in Milieus der gesellschaftlichen Selbstreflexion im frühen und späten 20. Jahrhundert* (Gottingen: Vandenhoeck & Ruprecht, 2019); and Timothy Scott Brown, *West Germany and the Global Sixties: The Antiauthoritarian Revolt, 1962–1978* (Cambridge: Cambridge University Press, 2013).

38. Cristina Perincioli, *Berlin wird feministisch: Das Beste was von der 68er Bewegung blieb* (Berlin: Querverlag, 2015), 29.
39. On the challenges but also the promise of such networking across borders, see Andrew Tompkins, "Grassroots Transnationalism(s): Franco-German Opposition to Nuclear Energy in the 1970s," *Contemporary European History* 25, no. 1 (February 2016): 117–42.
40. See, e.g., Steven Levitsky and Daniel Ziblatt, *How Democracies Die* (New York: Broadway Books, 2019); and Jason Brennan, *Against Democracy* (Princeton, NJ: Princeton University Press, 2016).

Select Bibliography

Brown, Timothy Scott. *West Germany and the Global Sixties: The Antiauthoritarian Revolt, 1962–1978*. Cambridge: Cambridge University Press, 2013.

Davis, Belinda. *The Internal Life of Politics: Extraparliamentary Opposition in West Germany, 1962–1983*. Cambridge: Cambridge University Press, forthcoming.

Eley, Geoff. *Forging Democracy: The History of the Left in Europe, 1850–2000*. Oxford: Oxford University Press, 2002.

Ferguson, Niall, Charles S. Maier, Erez Manela, and Daniel J. Sargent, eds. *The Shock of the Global: The 1970s in Perspective*. Cambridge, MA: The Belknap Press of Harvard University Press.

Glicher-Holtey, Ingrid, ed. *A Revolution of Perception? Consequences and Echoes of 1968*. New York: Berghahn Books, 2014.

Jarausch, Konrad, ed. *Das Ende der Zuversicht? Die siebziger Jahre als Geschichte*. Göttingen: Vandenhoeck & Ruprecht, 2008.

Koenen, Gerd. *Das rote Jahrzehnt: Unsere kleine deutsche Kulturrevolution 1967–1977*. Frankfurt a.M.: Kiepenheuer & Witsch, 2002.

Kraushaar, Wolfgang. *1968 als Mythos Chiffre und Zäsur*. Hamburg: Hamburger Edition, 2000.

Markovits, Andrei, and Philip S. Gorski. *The German Left: Red Green and Beyond*. Oxford: Oxford University Press, 1993.

Reichardt, Sven. *Authentizität und Gemeinschaft: Linksalternatives Leben in den siebziger und frühen achtziger Jahren*. Berlin: Suhrkamp, 2014.

Part I
Working with—and against—the Past

Chapter 1

Leaving the Borderlands . . . but for Where?

1968 and the New Registers of Political Feeling

Geoff Eley

Rewriting Politics

In *Landscape for a Good Woman*, Carolyn Steedman writes of "lives lived out on the borderlands . . . for which the central interpretive devices of the culture don't quite work."[1] Many elements in the full and messy diversity of a society's lived experience, she argues, drop outside the available historical narratives, certainly those most widely established or effectively embedded and understood. In such scripts, neither the range and directions of contemporary societal change nor the multiplicity of past trajectories are sufficiently acknowledged or captured. In *Landscape for a Good Woman*, Steedman offered a history radically at variance with the accounts we thought we knew. She told a story of gendered working-class lives that failed to fit—that escaped the available scripts of socialism, the postwar democracy of opportunity, and the vaunted solidarities of working-class culture—a story not easily folded into the best-known frameworks of social history and cultural studies. Steedman's arresting metaphor can also be read via the particular history of its writing. It suggests the disruption and dramatic enlargement of Europe's polities during the "long 1968."[2] Born in 1947, Steedman exactly figures that distinctive generational time.

The "borderlands" here were partly literal, meaning those historically distant, isolated, or disadvantaged regions of a country, "the provinces" in English parlance or *Provinz* in German, where postwar prosperity leveled differences unevenly upward and brought them more effectively into the nation: South Derbyshire, in my own case, for example, buried deep in the East Midlands at the very southern tip of the English North. But "borderlands" also suggests the journeying of class. Raymond Williams based his first novel *Border Country* (1960), written between 1946 and 1958, around the relationship of a London-transplanted academic son (an economic historian) and his ailing South Walian railwayman father, tracking them through the never-resolved back-and-forth between upwardly mobile metropolitan arrival and the confining place-based solidities of local working-class community. In the words of its back cover, the book charts the fractured continuities of these interrupted yet indissoluble relations across their "many invisible frontiers."[3] Analogous settings can easily be found: gender, obviously, but also sexuality; likewise race, colonialism, and so forth. In each case, "borderlands" denotes both a physical space and a cultural condition, not only a type of location or actually existing material habitation but also a mode of identity or [re]cognition.

The metaphor brings the bases of political change in the later twentieth century under a particular lens. My theme hinges on the contrasting structural possibilities of two overarching eras: the century linking the 1860s to the 1960s, and the present time running from the 1980s. I am interested in how those eras might be thought together, with the "long 1968" as the bridge. Many iconic images from 1968 itself disclose an interesting generational mix. Beside the youthfulness of the big demonstrations was the presence of an older contingent: not only Dany Cohn-Bendit but also Jean-Paul Sartre and Louis Aragon; not only the students but also the veteran Renault trade unionists; not only Hilary Wainwright and Tariq Ali but also Vanessa Redgrave and Ralph Miliband; not only Helke Sander and K. D. Wolff but also Ernst Bloch—and Herbert Marcuse.[4] While the '68 movements rose in angry contention with the political cultures forming after 1945, in other ways those postwar settlements remained generative and enabling. They secured above all an unprecedented enlargement of democratic citizenship in Western Europe, establishing for the first time full democracy of the franchise, with its countless entailments and sprawling ramifications. That applied both to class and to gender.[5]

In 1945 democracy and social justice were sutured firmly together inside a discourse of social recognition and public goods. The ensuing consensus was cemented by a persuasive script of social betterment, composed from a critique of the mass misery of the Depression and the egalitarian ethos of the victory over fascism. The radicalisms then emerging around 1968 displayed complex dialectical relations with those postwar values, angrily impatient with many of their aspects, yet entirely impossible without them. Thus, "1945" and "1968" were joined in an intensely contradictory symbiosis.

On the one hand, the postwar settlement secured genuinely far-reaching reforms. A new broadly founded societal consensus was inspired into being by popular wartime mobilizations and the accompanying hopes, decisively institutionalized through the post-Liberation alignments and negotiations. Sustained by a liberal public sphere, that consensus was shaped around the social contract of the welfare state and its corporative trade union presence. Cold War narrowings and reversals notwithstanding, those changes settled popular loyalties around ideals of social citizenship reaching well into the 1960s. In Britain, these embraced social security "from cradle to grave," the National Health Service, the Butler Education Act, progressive taxation, strong public-sector policies, corporative means of national economic management, and unprecedented trade union legitimacy. The resulting politics was sealed by a larger cultural script about national-popular unity and accomplishment, whose meanings percolated through the public culture of those postwar years. If the preceding social misery of the 1930s fueled demands for improvement and redress, while mass unemployment and poverty, punitive social policies, and ineffectual governance became almost universally decried, then wartime sacrifices fired an expansive vision of how the postwar world could be made, fusing patriotism to broadly diffused beliefs about democracy and the public good.

If chastened and policed by rigors of the Cold War, on the other hand, these popular gains—not just via the growth of juridical democracy, winning of rights, and new social entitlements but also by modestly attained material security and psychic well-being—profoundly enhanced people's confidence in a reliable future. This was initially a matter of survival, social renormalizing, and day-to-day needs: "Everybody eats. Food for all. At the time, that was the most urgent problem, rather than alienation, say, or man-machine relationships."[6] But by the late-1950s, higher living standards meant not only housing, nutrition, full employment, and the welfare state but also rising real wages and greater disposable incomes too, with novel access to new consumer goods. New acquisitions included vacuum cleaners and electric irons, washing machines and refrigerators, and TV sets and cars, not to speak of gramophones, long-playing records and 45s, transistor radios, and electric guitars.[7] While arising out of a very different immediate past—and under a conservative government—West German politics too relied on a new labor legitimacy in a corporatist model and the adoption of Britain's "New Consensus" in the form of basic social protections. British (and US) cultural influences likewise stood alongside the emerging "Economic Miracle" in that country.

For younger generations, these circumstances became combustible. While clear beneficiaries of the widening postwar chances (not least in the

1960s growth of higher education), younger people bridled against the conservative cast of postwar culture and its perceived cautions and complacencies. Clothes, long hair, sex, drugs, rock 'n' roll, and the many forms of stylistic militancy and experiment were only the sharp hedonist edge of a cultural politics that veered pointedly away from earlier received grounds. For David Fernbach, from a London Jewish family of modest means, forming his teenage rock band meant "a whole new way of being," reflecting the "basic aspiration to live our own life in a way that accorded with things that gave us pleasure."[8] From a bourgeois background in Milan, sixteen-year-old Laura Derossi saw cosmetics, chic dresses, and serious adult cinema in the same way, as the "first acts of rebellion." They enabled "a special type of friendship, a generational union, in place of the traditional family-based friendships like my mother's. We changed everything, inherited nothing."[9] Ingrid Schmidt-Harzbach recalled escaping home at night in small-town West Germany to meet other youth at music clubs.[10] Such defiance was bitterly upsetting for parents. Fernbach's parents "were keen for me to study hard and get a good professional job. Throughout my teens, there was this conflict between what they wanted for me and doing my own thing here and now."[11] So instead he became a socialist militant, gay activist, and translator of Marx. For earlier antifascist generations, who went through World War II as adults and now led Western Europe's Communist and social democratic parties, such departures were simply not legible:

> These people are not Socialists. They are not even respectable Marxists. They are a new brand of anarchists, very different from the endearing characters whom many of us know. . . . They are wreckers who . . . are concerned only to disrupt society. Their weapons are lies, misrepresentations, defamation, character assassination, intimidation and, more recently, physical violence.[12]

1968: A Longer Conjuncture

In harvesting the proceeds of the post-1945 settlement, sixty-eighters were simultaneously burying its hopes. Their emergence was not imaginable without the protective and enabling resources of the settlement's endowment. Improved housing and nutrition, medical services and public health, universal secondary education and places at university, social services and income support, full employment and the welfare state—these were the vital conditions of possibility. So too by the 1960s was the new openness of ideas in a radically liberalizing public sphere, with energizing experimentation all across the arts, an inventively oppositional aesthetic, and radical pedagogies of many diverse kinds.

Yet, it was precisely the settlement's main architecture that attracted much of the younger radicals' ire. They urged directly against representative democracy; participatory against parliamentary forms; rank-and-filism against union officials; self-management against workplace authority and alienation; tenants' movements and claimants' unions against social service bureaucracies; direct action against polite and ossified proceduralism. Extolling the virtues of theory inside an insurgent politics of knowledge, they brought schooling and the university under fundamental critique. Through the resulting contention, they opened essential spaces where new movements could elaborate the challenge—second-wave feminism, gay liberation, sexual dissidence, critiques of family and intimate relations, a new politics of everyday life.

Into the same space rushed an aggressively rightist politics of backlash. This had many forms. One was a storm of vehemently "anti-permissive," sexually conservative, and socially Christian morality campaigning, which during the 1970s effectively captured public debate. Exemplified in Britain by Mary Whitehouse and her National Viewers' and Listeners' Association formed in 1964–65, this varied across Western Europe, often within church-sponsored conservative mobilizations. Roiled by feminism, gay sexuality, and the cultural excesses of youth, such movements rose to defense of family, conventional morality, and decorums of public decency while raging noisily against sex education, access to contraception, and reproductive rights, no less than pornography and violence in the media and arts.[13] A second front assaulted progressive changes at all levels of education.[14] Policing and the politics of "law and order" became a third scene of fighting, visible for example in West Germany, as politicians both urged police to crack down harder on young protesters and goaded citizens to take on the job themselves.[15] Increasingly linked across each of these areas, "race" was also constructed as vital for this right-wing counterattack, first during the 1960s in Britain, then across Western Europe more generally. With Enoch Powell's infamous "Rivers of Blood" speech (20 April 1968), racialized grievances erupted into the very heart of the British '68 itself.[16]

The meanings of '68 are best grasped inside this larger conjuncture, as the post-1945 stabilities began messily coming apart. Usually tagged as "the student revolt," the popular insurgencies of those years (say, 1967–74) actually encompassed a far greater diversity of social militancy and social movements, shaped around the largest pan-European strike wave since 1917–20. The wider country-by-country turbulence ranged from the variegated direct actions and extraparliamentary challenges in France, Italy, and West Germany to the Prague Spring, the 1974 Portuguese Revolution, and the long crescendo of Anti-Francoist protests in Spain. Considered inside this longer narrative of political dissolution, the '68 rebellions emerge as disorderly symptoms of longer-run changes whose character and effects only clarified after the event. Whether as sociopolitical turbulence or many-sided cultural excess, new radicalisms were the chiefly unanticipated effects of sociocultural changes generated during the *trente glorieuses* or long postwar boom. Those changes had remade the landscapes where politics would have to occur.

Within this framing, the 1968 events themselves were only inchoately understood. According to their own lights, the movements were everywhere a failure. Student life in Western Europe shifted, to be sure: an intrusive paternalism *in loco parentis* was abolished, including gate hours, sexual regulations, and social rules. But overcrowding was not reduced; curricula were not transformed; universities were not democratized, let alone turned into "red bases," as some had dreamed. De Gaulle was never toppled in France. The May events triggered a national political crisis, but June elections left Gaullism apparently unscathed. Equally vigorous Italian and West German student revolts likewise foundered. The great Vietnam solidarity actions failed to shift national governments out of their cravenly US alignment. Francoism survived in Spain. Eastern European student movements in Poland and Yugoslavia were beaten back. In Czechoslovakia, reform Communism expired.

But those new radicalisms were more disorderly symptoms than consciously directed movements. They remained flashes from societal futures still in process of being made—class structures being recomposed; manufacturing and extractive industries entering long decline; labor movements losing their distinctive organizational cultures and community ground; service industries dominating labor markets; new technologies and labor processes transforming habits and rhythms of everyday life; novel discourses of alienation and self-management shaping an emergent cultural critique. Indeed, it was only through the dramas surrounding "1968" that social theorists, political actors, and ordinary citizens could begin to discern what that future was likely to contain.

Structural counterpoint to this narrative of political dissolution and societal change was the world economic downturn following the oil crisis of 1973–74, combined with fallout from the Indochina War and collapse of Bretton Woods in 1971. As the postwar boom neared its end, so did the promise of permanent growth and continuously rising prosperity, receding before the new norm of high inflation, rising unemployment, and low growth. This magnified the effects of underlying changes in the economy—reorganizing of labor markets, manufacturing decline and deindustrialization, reconfiguring of class, general capitalist restructuring. With economic stagnation, Europe's welfare states also entered disarray. They were too costly, too inefficient, too bureaucratic, too corrosive of individual morale, too open to abuse. Their machineries of public provision and language of public goods were denounced as corrupting. Demands for privatizing services grew ever louder. Along with the former Keynesian orthodoxies—deficit financing, demand management, strong public sectors, full employment—the common sense of politics was brought angrily into question. Fordist-era verities started to crumble, from the economics of mass production and the associated corporatist arrangements with trade unions to the prized securities of rising real wages and full employment. New priorities of post-Fordist transition started entering their claims.

If postwar reconstruction assembled the ground from which an effectively social democratic politics could unfold, involving much broader acceptance of societal responsibilities and public goods, then the 1970s took such ground brutally away. The postwar system of governance had seemed anchored in popular-democratic experience, as a concerted response to shared hardships of the pre-1939 depression and antifascist solidarities of wartime and liberation, supplying a deep reservoir of practical legitimacy. This normative cement crumbled amid the turbulence of 1967–74. It was then consciously demolished by the sustained political divisiveness of the next two decades.

Via capitalist restructuring in the last quarter of the twentieth century, politics became decisively reconfigured. In place of the long-lasting but unfinished coherence of the postwar settlement came a bifurcated political culture: on the one hand, the grassroots, direct-action citizenship of a variegated social-movement politics; on the other hand, the forms of governance suited for the newly globalized, deregulated labor markets and transnational financial circuits celebrated by an entirely ascendant neoliberalism. The resulting social logics permanently damaged the viability of the national-reformist politics previously animating the post-1945 settlements. As what we now call globalization deprived social democrats and other reformers of their ability to manage national capitalisms in the interests of working-class supporters, deindustrialization drastically reduced the old working class itself. Brutally reorganized labor markets transformed the character of available work, disrupted the accustomed meanings of class, dismantled the given institutional, spatial, and cultural bases of class formation, and redistributed social inequality in dramatically unfamiliar ways. How these twin phenomena—the fragmentary, localized dispersal of activist citizenship and the gutting of socially grounded national-political process—might be shaped into a politics with continuities comparable to those of the earlier socialist tradition remains an unresolved question of contemporary political history.

Interposed between 1968 and today is that other big watershed year of our times, 1989. The decisive political endings of 1989–91 occluded and placed beyond reach an entire space of future-oriented oppositional thought. For any practical progressivism or radical vision of politics, 1989 interrupted the feasible imagining of what the transformation of society might now be allowed to mean. In the words of Göran Therborn, it brought not so much the "end of history" as the end of the future "as a new place [available to] be visited." By this he meant "the end of the epoch [in which various] futures of progressive, emancipatory revolution or reform [might be imagined], the era of radical modernity opened up by the French Revolution."[17] He meant the end of the epoch in which the future per se could be confidently projected, the end of an optimism that envisaged how modernity itself could be completed. This discrediting of the attainable ideal of a possible future, in which *society as such* might be reimagined and remade, in which the unlimited capacities of science, technology, nature, and production could be mobilized for creating the good society—the discrediting of that ideal decisively recast the reach of the possible.

An accustomed political space was closed down, narrowing the possible terms through which political futures might be thought. Communism's collapse was already preceded by the slow dissolution of Western social democracy. That in turn accompanied the end of the postwar boom and the crisis of Keynesianism since the late 1960s. Capitalist restructuring was engineered via deindustrialization, dismantling of welfare states, shedding of labor corporatism, rolling deregulation of national economies, privatization, the pervasiveness of market values, and the entire machinery of post-Fordist transition. The Left's predicament followed from the *fait accompli*. The old ties binding the locally rooted subcultures of the Left so successfully into the nationally organized arenas of politics had all but disappeared. Indeed, by the 1990s the classic means by which democratic gains had mainly been realized during the twentieth century had definitely gone—namely, socialist parties as mass-based political formations simultaneously embedded in local residential communities and drawing around them variegated popular energies and wider social hopes.

The socialist political tradition as previously constituted belonged to a very particular period of European history between the late nineteenth century, when the various parties were founded country by country, and the 1960s, when they started coming apart. That tradition was shaped by definite social histories of industrialization and the associated urban concentrations of working population, residentially segregated inside particular frameworks of municipal government based around public employment and delivery of services. That singular alignment of urban economies, municipal social administration, and working-class residential communities, replicated region by region across Europe, was the necessary infrastructure for the rise of labor movements. Gradually during the twentieth century, with great political unevenness and frequent reversals, those movements gained popular legitimacy, access to government, and growing emplacement within the national economy. But now, after four decades of sustained deindustrializing, privatizing, and large-scale capitalist restructuring, with the attendant dismantling of earlier welfare states and local government systems, the social infrastructures and popular machineries of socialist political culture have receded into the past.

This is a momentous change. During a long century of democratic enlargement in Europe—from the big constitution-making conjuncture of the 1860s to the crisis of 1968—the socialist tradition came gradually to *hegemonize* the Left. But after the clarifying struggles of the 1970s, that ceased to be true, in a process ratified by Communism's 1989–91 collapse. This being so, how might ideas of willed or directed social transformation be reentered onto the practical political agenda? How might the utopian possibility of reorganizing human relations into a different kind of socially organized world be reengaged? What kinds of politics are producing the sounds for which hope might then be the echo? I think of utopia here as an impulse or kind of subjectivity, whose active presence is an essential ingredient for any reformism aspiring to popular resonance or staying power—as a kind of longing, a dreaming of what might be, a necessary imagining, a credo of possibility, a willingness to think beyond. More concretely, this is how the politics of the 1970s and 1980s might be approached: as the nascent, open, and disorderly realm of possibility released and enabled by the events of 1968 and their surrounding conjuncture. What were the political goods of 1968, and how might they be recuperated and made available?

Speaking across Generations

Before he died, Teddy Adorno was in fraught correspondence with his old Institute for Social Research friend, Herbert Marcuse, who had stayed in the United States after 1945, teaching from 1965 at the University of California, San Diego. In early 1969, battles between students and authorities in both California and West Germany had reached a sustained peak. On "Bloody Thursday," 15 May, Governor Ronald Reagan unleashed police into Berkeley's People's Park, killing one student and severely wounding 128; the National Guard occupied the city; other California campuses struck in solidarity. This drama waylaid Marcuse's letters with his friend, who watched similar events in Frankfurt. But there was a difference, for Adorno was himself in the eye of the storm. Attacks on the political quietism of Adorno's Institute came to a head on 31 January 1969, when students, including Hans-Jürgen Krahl, one of Adorno's own prized doctoral students, occupied an Institute room. Adorno called in the police, who arrested Krahl and 75 comrades. After much dithering, amid broadening confrontations, Adorno pressed charges against Krahl alone, for trial in July.

To Adorno's disquiet, Marcuse planned a trip to Frankfurt to meet with the students. The university was in utter turmoil. The blurb for the mass market edition of Marcuse's *One Dimensional Man* put him in a pantheon with "Mao Tse Tung, Che Guevara, and Ho Chi Minh." As Marcuse's notoriety gathered pace, Adorno's lectures triggered ever-worsening contentions. The two friends' letters teetered toward estrangement. With a heavy heart, Marcuse wrote that things had "decisively" changed:

> If I accept the Institute's invitation without also speaking to the students, I will identify myself with . . . a position I do not share politically. To put it brutally: if the alternative is the police or the left-wing students, then I am with the students. . . . Occupation of rooms . . . would not be a reason for me to call the police. . . . I still believe that our cause (which is not only ours) is better taken up by the rebellious students than by the police . . .

He continued in a vein of ethical frankness and resolution:

> You know me well enough to know that I reject the unmediated translation of theory into praxis just as emphatically as you do. But I do believe that there are situations, moments, in which theory is driven further along by praxis—situations and moments in which theory kept separate from praxis ceases to be true to itself. We cannot banish from the world the fact that these students are influenced by us (and certainly not least by you)—I am very glad of this and I am ready for patricide, however painful that can sometimes be. And the means they use to translate theory into action? We know (and they know) that the situation is not a revolutionary one, not even a pre-revolutionary one. But this situation is so terrible, so suffocating and demeaning, that . . . one can bear it no longer, one suffocates, and one needs some air. And this fresh air is not that of a "left fascism" (*contradictio in adjecto!*). It is the air that we (at least I) also some day want to breathe, and it is certainly not the air of the establishment. I discuss with the students, and I attack them if I

think they are being stupid and playing into the hands of the other side, but I would probably not call to my aid worse, more awful weapons against their bad ones. And I would despair about myself (us) if I (we) would appear to be on the side of a world that supports mass murder in Vietnam, or says nothing about it, and which makes a hell out of any realms that are outside of its own repressive power.

Adorno had been digging himself in. He drew the line tightly around the West German status quo, including its international alignment with the anti-Communist United States, while deriding the proceduralist obsessions of participatory democracy and invoking "the danger of the student movement flipping over into fascism." In response, Marcuse mounted a careful defense of the student movement's critical potential. He affirmed the need to defend "parliamentary-democratic institutions where they still work in favor of freedom rights." He had no patience for the ultra-left slogan of "destroy the university," which would be "a suicidal act." But refusing to support "*this* democracy" unconditionally did not mean sliding inevitably into "neofascism." Despite all its confusions and excesses, and its vulnerability to provocateurs, the student movement was now a vital source of critique, an impulse toward principled dissent, and a "catalyst" for change, one that enabled the "new, very unorthodox forms of opposition" then emerging. Here, critical theory's responsibility was to offer support: "It is precisely in a situation such as this that our task is to help the movement, theoretically, as well as defending it against repression and denunciation."[18]

Even as Marcuse wrote (in late July 1969), the witch hunt was at full throttle, now joined to his dismay by another close friend, Max Horkheimer, quoted by *Der Spiegel* as accusing him of simplifying and coarsening "Adorno's and my thought." Thus Marcuse's private professing of his ethico-political standpoint occurred in lurid counterpoint with this frenetic public theater. On 18 June Adorno canceled his lectures on the "Introduction to Dialectical Thought." In mid-July, Hans-Jürgen Krahl received a suspended sentence for violating a ban on entering the university and a fine for disturbing the peace. Against this backdrop, Adorno found Marcuse's defense of the students "monstrous" (*ungeheuerlich*). Relations headed for a rift. Then, on 6 August, Adorno died. Six months later, on 14 February 1970, twenty-seven-year-old Krahl was killed in a car crash.[19]

Out of this correspondence I want to draw three things. The *first* gets too easily effaced, especially in the mealy-mouthed, weasel-worded *mea culpas* of some anti-'68 critics. A key driver in the protest movements of the later 1960s was moral outrage at the escalating violence perpetrated by the West's elected governments, most especially in Vietnam but more widely in southern Africa, Latin America, the Middle East, and earlier in Algeria. There were many more localized spurs—in Northern Ireland, for example. Longer-standing opposition to nuclear armaments, identification with US civil rights, gathering awareness of the politics of race were likewise vital to that critique. Here is Anthony Barnett, who was a student in Leicester and Cambridge: "There was the bombing and the relentlessness of the bombing—the headlines of the bombing, and I put a map of Vietnam on my wall. I think people now probably don't understand that, but it was just terrible." And Nelly Finkielsztejn at Nanterre: "Napalm, bombings, mass graves, executions—the fury of military and economic might against a small population of a different race—that was the Vietnam War for me. It was intolerable. That's why we went out into the streets . . ." Or Fiorella Farinelli in Pisa: "We had a poster we'd made, a skull on a blue background, with a quotation from Tacitus: *They made a desert and called it peace.*"[20] West German activists hosted congresses against the Vietnam War in 1966 and 1968, drawing thousands of participants from across Western Europe and well beyond.

This was a defining feature of the modalities of public engagement essential to what became the New Social Movements—not as a discrete, stand-alone motivation but as an indissoluble ethico-philosophical element during the broadest moments of coalescence. That became especially clear for radical ecology, for peace activism, for major parts of feminism, and so forth. However schematically, the social science literatures of the 1980s and 1990s on *value change*, *culture shift*, and *postmaterialist values* sought seriously to address that altruist momentum, which ran from the counterculture and New Ageism to the alternative scenes and New Social Movements.[21]

Second, I want to highlight the compelling *eventfulness* of an experience like the 1969 Frankfurt sit-in and the wider mobilizations surrounding it—the exceptional intensity and perduring consequences of joining a direct action of that kind, whose energizing charge came not just from the local immediacy alone but also from everything else happening in the wider radicalized worlds of politics. This can never be exaggerated. The giddying sense of possibility released through such actions was fueled not just by events in other universities and colleges all across the world but in countless other contexts (socially, nationally, globally) where collective actions occurred. In their fusion of local and larger meanings, in the directness of the unity between immediate actions and wider understanding, and in the dramas of personal change, such times radically exceed their particular moment. Learning one's politics in the laboratory of practice is a rare privilege. The sheer intellectual and political excitement of being *inside* the event is extraordinary—the existential rush of participating in direct action, the exhilarating novelty of so much collective discussion, the unprecedented ease of spontaneous communication, the rapidity of the political learning process, and even, from time to time, the temporary high of success. Those intensities leave an indelible imprint. It is the aggregation of those experiences, their electrifying resonance with countless events elsewhere, and their promiscuous interarticulation that allow us to speak sensibly of a '68 generation.[22]

This Mannheimian view of generation as being shaped around shared life-defining events suggests a *third* meaning of the Marcuse-Adorno story, returning us to that contradictory symbiosis of "1968" with "1945." If sixty-eighters in the narrower sense were children of the higher education expansion of the 1960s, then the wider youth culture grew from conditions of full employment and expanding consumption from the late 1950s, which heightened in turn some sociocultural consequences of the postwar settlements. Those settlements normalized a particular passage into adulthood for 15- and 16-year-olds based on a freshly cohering set of reasonable life expectations: *either* immediate full-time industrial or white-collar employment, preferably linked to some kind of apprenticeship, *or* a deferred professional future linked to higher education.

This was an extraordinary historical departure. The social changes of the 1950s and 1960s normalized a dependable structure of supports and entitlements placing young people inside a practically realizable relation to the future, as a visible horizon, even a set of reachable destinations. The elements included: school reform; expanding higher and further education; construction of the nuclear family ideal; the elaborate machinery of social services in the welfare state; discretionary spending in the consumer economy; full, regular, and secure employment; and a labor market that from the later 1950s increasingly shunted unappealing jobs onto a specifically recruited low-waged, mobile, insecure, and unprotected Mediterranean and postcolonial reservoir of cheap and unregulated labor power. For a brief historical moment, young white people in Western Europe lived as though the future was predictable and assured. The political upheavals and longer-term trends arising from the 1960s and 1970s were inseparable from this condition of possibility.

Across Generations: Transmitting the Political Goods

As a result of capitalist restructuring, that particular normality has patently gone. Imagining a reliable future based on regularity of employment as part of an assured passage into adulthood was the transitory accomplishment of the postwar settlement and lasted barely two decades. How exactly it could be taken away is a key question for the following period and a vital ingredient in the social movement politics after '68. The activism of the 1970s and 1980s presumed a mass of young people marginal to mainstream society, whether socially by lack of jobs and reliable economic futures or culturally by modalities of existential disaffection: highly educated, yet displaced from career paths and partially employed, they were stylistically rebellious while subsisting inside distinctive collective arrangements and informal economies, often with bohemian or multicultural links, as in the Hafenstraße in Hamburg's St. Pauli and Kreuzberg in West Berlin.[23] This was a transitional society, one still relying on the long aftermath of the postwar prosperity, before the neoliberal onslaught of privatization had dismantled the only recently institutionalized machinery of income supplements, social services, unemployment benefits, retraining schemes, work creation, and public subsidies for the arts, museums, and local cultural initiatives. In the starkest of contrasts, the subsequent sociology of the contemporary metropolitan scene, already coalescing in the 1990s, confirmed in the 2000s, and made spectacular since 2008, reflects a fundamentally different set of labor markets and career prospects for the young. Whereas in the 1970s young people could postpone the future of a settled adulthood for a variety of consciously chosen reasons, the time of "youth" today is brutally elongated, disabled in relation to a future now indefinitely deferred.

By the 1980s a very different topography was coming to shape the possibilities for Left politics, comprising three distinct sociologies. One described the New Social Movement trajectories of campaigning groups, civic associations, and grassroots citizenship bridging out of the late 1960s; a second comprised the autonomisms that coalesced from the countercultures and alternative scenes during 1977–86; and the third crystallized through the partial reclaiming of existing Socialist and Communist Parties, often on a very specific city or urban neighborhood basis. This was a threefold concurrency: each sector had its own rhythm and temporality, but the boundaries were permeable, they frequently overlapped, and often coalesced—during elections, in local campaigning, above all in the peace movement of 1980–84.

At one end of the resulting spectrum was the organized activism of women's liberation and later feminisms, gay-lesbian politics, ecological and environmental groups, antinuclear and peace activism, antiracist organizing, Sicilian anti-Mafia campaigning, and so on, all of which intersected more readily with the given party-political and parliamentary sphere. At the other end were more amorphous alternative scenes, festival and music cultures, travelers, DIY politics, squatters, autonomists as such.[24] *Their* relationship to the party-based urban lefts of the early 1980s was usually hostile and fraught. But neither activist sector was legible for the mainstream Left. They often violently collided: the Italian autonomists of 1977–78 defined themselves through ebullient confrontations with the PCI in Bologna and Rome. That politics of refusal was at best an ambivalence against parliamentary politics, at worst a profaning of democratic values. Extraparliamentary activists had few affinities for older Left parties, which by then seemed exhausted—a Eurocommunism (Italy, France, Spain) that failed to break through; a sclerotic social democracy (West Germany, Low Countries, Britain) stuck in its accommodations to capitalism; and a technocratic socialism (France, Spain, Greece) shedding its relation to labor movements.

Since the 1980s, the clefts have grown ever deeper. Capitalist restructuring has destroyed the infrastructures making the earlier broadly based socialist cultures possible, reducing those parties to mere husks of their former selves, existing only for the intermittent purpose of contesting an election. In extraparliamentary arenas, meanwhile, an inventively vigorous social movement activism remains highly localized and mainly disconnected from any national party framework, outflanked in its turn by the militant equivalents of autonomism. So there are now three quite distinct Left formations with separate but overlapping existence. If in the first two-thirds of the twentieth century the city housed the stable working-class formation that sustained democracy's earliest successes, it is now a fundamentally changed space of sociality, employment, everyday practice, and political identification. Boundaries have been redrawn, redistributing the societal space where politics has to occur.

In the complex relationship between "1968" and "1945" a key issue has been generational transmission, i.e., how were the political goods from one time of change passed down to people in another; how were those goods transferred and redeployed? How can we bring together the ideals and exigencies of two starkly differing conjunctures—the "post-1945" and the "post-1968"? Where were the reciprocities between the popular-democratic postwar and the new political languages of the "post-1968"? How should we think about the *bridging* of generations in that sense? Where might we find the coherence of a new political formation joining them together?

Unfortunately, this was a site of generalized political failure. Using Eric Hobsbawm as a case, I argued elsewhere that this was a big political deficit; Edward Thompson would be another such example, as indeed would Teddy Adorno and Max Horkheimer.[25] Exceptions may certainly be found: Ernst Bloch and Wolfgang Abendroth; Raymond Williams and Ralph Miliband; Jean-Paul Sartre, Simone de Beauvoir, and André Gorz; Rossana Rossanda and Lucio Magri; and so forth. If we go down the generations somewhat, to the effects of 1956, we can find figures like Raphael Samuel and Stuart Hall. But in the main, earlier generations did not respond well to the youth insurgencies of the 1960s and 1970s, still less to those that came after. But this same question of generational transmission might be put to sixty-eighters themselves. How far, and in what ways, have the political goods of '68 been transmitted to the political cultures of the post-1989? How do we locate the spaces of experimentation that both sustain a relationship to the earlier radicalisms and open imaginations to the future? How does the space of experience enable or occlude the horizons of possible expectation?

One very familiar answer is a condescending narrative of disavowal. One version alleges the self-indulgent narcissism of middle-class privilege, where the rebelliousness of "sex, drugs, and rock 'n' roll" becomes sundered from the politics and turned into a demeaning tale of hedonist irresponsibility and excess. It becomes constructed as a kind of phase, something finite and ephemeral, something that was "not inhaled."[26] There is a larger version too, through which the cultural divisiveness of the intervening present is traced back to the excesses of an earlier cultural radicalism and its supposed destructiveness. In that way, "1968" becomes joined to "1989" in a seamless story of the dangerousness of any big thinking about social transformation. From the liberal sector of the culture wars of the 1990s and early 2000s there came many homilies of this kind. For translating political disappointments into strategic and epistemological warnings, pundits like Todd Gitlin or Richard Rorty were always on call.

But there are other ways of telling this story. Achievable gains and practical continuities came *precisely* from the largeness of aspiration, big ideas, and cultural militancies that Rorty wanted to banish. Born in 1950, Mary Kay Mullan was an eighteen-year-old student at Queen's University Belfast when she joined People's Democracy during the Northern Irish civil rights struggle. After a year's frenetic agitation ("marches, meetings, pickets, leafleting, sit-ins, traffic disruption, and all types of non-violent public direct action"), she marched from Belfast to Derry in December 1968, when the brutality of Ian Paisley's Unionist vigilantes at Burntollet Bridge radicalized civil rights into a thirty-year civil war. After traveling abroad in 1972–75, Mullan returned to Derry to teach, forming her feminism via a CR group and a course on "Women in Irish Society." She helped found Woman's Aid Refuge ("squatting, negotiating, publicizing, fundraising, learning about Social Security, housing laws, and laws affecting women's status, . . . organizing petitions, lobbying MPs and Ministers"). While organizing campaigns against rape, domestic violence, and sexual abuse, she came out as a lesbian. In 1978, she began Bookworm Community Bookshop, which flourished into a workers' cooperative. By 1988, activity had diversified: a women's health collective; a Rape and Incest Line; a Family Planning Association branch; a Women in Trade Unions group; Women's Aid; creche campaigns and playgroups; study groups; assertiveness classes; the monthly *Derry Women's Newssheet*; and a set of connections to Sinn Fein and Prisoners' Relatives Action Committees, from an independent feminist standpoint.[27]

Two decades on, Mullan was still active in Derry. More to the point, her various contexts were also alive and well, as the websites of Derry's civic activism could quickly confirm. Ten years after that she stayed active as ever, still in Derry. Building from her "background in community development and adult education," she trained in Gestalt Psychotherapy, with further qualification in community drama, working mainly as a Gestalt psychotherapist. According to her website, she "has a particular interest in promoting social, economic, and political change through facilitating learning as a shared group experience. For example, through her interest in equality and diversity she worked in CAWT (Cooperation and Working Together), a Cross-Border Social Inclusion Project facilitating health courses, researching LGB service issues, and presenting LGB Awareness Training to Health Professionals."[28]

Conclusion

My first and main point is very straightforward: 1968 was a truly generative moment. With the Adorno-Marcuse-Krahl melodrama in mind, I turn to another story. Like many such existentially dramatic "here and now" moments, mine occurred not in 1968 itself but two years later in February 1970, when the University of Oxford entered turmoil over the so-called "files" issue. On 11–12 February, students occupying the University of Warwick Registry had stumbled upon secret files containing political surveillance of students and faculty. Amid ensuing uproar, protests mushroomed across Britain, raising issues of transparency and surveillance, policing and freedom of information, university governance, the relationship between democracy and education, and capitalism's corruption of the university. Students in Oxford marched to a central administrative building, breached the gates, and occupied a wood-paneled room. The sit-in was sustained for a week, galvanizing an extraordinary collective discussion across the university as a whole. It ended in a march to join the first open meeting ever held in the University of Oxford on 2 March 1970, when some twelve hundred students passed a series of resolutions on the university's governance and the keeping of files.

Three elements stick in my mind, each reflecting a general theme: one bridging from the past; one showing the generation gap; one pointing forward.

- The first involved working-class Communist Party members attending Ruskin College on trade union scholarships, about ten to twenty

years older than the rest, who supplied much of the discipline and stamina needed to keep the occupation going overnight, especially by guarding the doors.
- My second memory is of Iris Murdoch visiting the occupation, climbing onto the table, and demanding to know, in inimitably patrician tones, what we thought we were doing. At first I thought this rather impressive. Later, it was the haughty entitlement and sheer incomprehension that stuck with me most.
- Third, the occupation coincided with the first National Women's Liberation Conference, meeting in Ruskin at the time. These were very early days—only very few women joined the occupation. The announcement that Liberated Women would march to the occupation in solidarity was another of those truly revelatory moments.

Between 1967 and the mid-1970s, with varying rhythms and intensities country by country, a generic militancy traveled across institutions to excite the political imagination. In some version or degree, change in the interior relations and practices of the university reached most of further and higher education, whether in particular departments or disciplines or more widely across an institution. This was the oxygen of student life. The *openness* of the possibility of radical change had become generalized across the student cohorts of the later 1960s and the small numbers of their teacher allies. Until we can grasp the rapidity and extent of this generalized generational shift, key lines of indebtedness, impact, and affiliation will not emerge.

Mary Kay Mullan's story can be replicated many, many times. Involved was a definite sociology of recruitment into the professional, technical, managerial, and administrative jobs that the higher education expansion always meant to accomplish, with the twist of an activist ethic and understanding of public service. (This was so even in West Germany, notwithstanding the corrosive effects of the 1972 "professional ban" [*Berufsverbot*], threatening the career prospects of those active with a wide range of oppositional political groupings.) Arguments about "value change" and "culture shift" crystallizing during the 1980s around New Social Movements rightly captured this logic. Participants in the demonstrations, marches, and sit-ins went on to work at all levels of education, social work, healthcare, law, civil service, media, and the rest of the professions, for which expanding public sector employment, information services, and business services were opening the way. What held these cohorts together was *not* the collective resources or organized sinews of any party-based subculture, despite many recruits to Western European Eurocommunisms or the resurrected urban Labour Party branches in Britain. Rather, this was what Raymond Williams called a "structure of feeling": a presumed continuity of common understanding, an imaginative architecture, a shared collective sensibility, with definite if shifting social and political coordinates. More than just attitudes and values, this was a common texture of assumptions about how to conduct an integrated personal life. "Structure of feeling" described the relationship of cultural forms to the practices and relations of everyday life. It described the fields of tension linking programmatic ideas and a generalized political outlook to the personal spheres of the quotidian.

So I *am* thinking Mannheimianly: "generation" coheres around the impact of a collectively encountered life event or concentration of events.[29] But "1968" also presumed definite enabling conditions—expanding educational opportunity, full employment, consumer affluence, and general prosperity—which came abruptly to an end in 1973–75. For a privileged generational cluster, born into the right moment of history, those conditions of possibility crucially informed the coming social movement politics, whether immediately in the 1970s and early 1980s or further down the century. These were forms of politics that unfolded in dialectical counterpoint with the earlier conditions of material life and their subsequent disappearance. In another single but not singular example: Angie Pegg (born 1950) was a young small-town Essex housewife who noticed *The Second Sex* in a bookshop, devoured it voraciously, and decided to go to university and study philosophy. The experience was similar for Frenchwoman Florence Hervé, married to a West German and living in Bonn. That choice presupposed the growth of higher education, student grants, and the opening of political space in the 1960s and 1970s.[30]

What big societal crises like the "long '68" leave behind may only cohere long after the noise has died away. The relation of lasting effects to willed desires will be dripping with ironies and disappointments. What people want will differ from what they actually get. As William Morris famously put this in *A Dream of John Ball*: "I . . . pondered how [people] fight and lose the battle, and the thing that they fought for comes about in spite of their defeat, and when it comes turns out not to be what they meant, and other [people] have to fight for what they meant under another name."[31] The chemistry of the immediate crisis really mattered: that combination of determined, daring, and often reckless direct action, largeness of vision, institutional vulnerability or readiness, and surrounding popular ferment, which together unlocked the space and gave power holders of the necessary courage and astuteness the fleeting chance to seize the time. Outcomes are unlikely to coincide with demands; they may amount to seemingly modest changes. But they only came to the agenda in the first place by the crisis and its disruptions, by all of the unmanageable, luxuriant, troublemaking excess.

Geoff Eley is Karl Pohrt Distinguished University Professor of Contemporary History at the University of Michigan, Ann Arbor. His most recent works include *Forging Democracy: The History of the Left in Europe, 1850–2000* (2002); *A Crooked Line: From Cultural History to the History of Society* (2005); (with Keith Nield) *The Future of Class in History: What's Left of the Social?* (2007); and *Nazism as Fascism: Violence, Ideology, and the Ground of Consent in Germany, 1930–1945* (2013). He is currently writing a general history of twentieth-century Europe.

Notes

1. Carolyn Steedman, *Landscape for a Good Woman: A Story of Two Lives* (London: Virago, 1986), 5.
2. By the "long 1968," I mean the surrounding conjuncture brought to a spectacular head during that emblematic year. Pertinent events spilled backward and forward into the mid-1960s and early 1970s, whether through impressively Pan-European industrial militancy, fallout from university-centered insurgencies, international antiwar protests and similar social movement activism, housing and welfare mobilizations, feminisms and sexual radicalism, stylistic and aesthetic challenges in cultural politics and the arts, or critiques of family, intimate relations, and the social settings of everyday life. In each of those spheres, across Europe as a whole, the turmoil ran from ca. 1965 to ca. 1976.
3. Raymond Williams, *Border Country* (London: Chatto & Windus, 1960).
4. See also the contribution by Ingrid Gilcher-Holtey in this volume.
5. I have made this argument in detail elsewhere: Geoff Eley, *Forging Democracy: The History of the Left in Europe, 1850–2000* (New York: Oxford, 2002), esp. 278–336; "What Produces Democracy? Revolutionary Crises, Popular Politics, and Democratic Gains in Twentieth-Century Europe," in *History and Revolution: Refuting Revisionism*, ed. Mike Haynes and Jim Wolfreys (London: Verso, 2007), 172–201; "When Europe Was New: Liberation and the Making of the Postwar Era," in *The Lasting War: Society and Identity in Britain, France, and Germany after 1945*, ed. Monica Riera and Gavin Schaffer (Houndmills: Palgrave Macmillan, 2008), 17–43. See also the contribution by Michael Hughes in this volume.
6. Alessandro Portelli, "Luigi's Socks and Rita's Makeup: Youth Culture, the Politics of Private Life, and the Culture of the Working Classes," in Alessandro Portelli, *The Battle of Valle Giulia: Oral History and the Art of Dialogue* (Madison: University of Wisconsin Press, 1997), 241.
7. Consumer capitalism reached Western Europe at the turn of the 1960s. In 1958–65, refrigerator ownership in Italy rose from 13 to 55 percent of households, washing machines from 3 to 23 percent, TVs from 12 to 49 percent. West Germany had the same pattern. Consumer spending rose in Britain by 45 percent during 1952–64, while consumer durables more than doubled their share of household budgets, driven in 1959–60 by the slashing of sales tax and novel forms of consumer credit. My mother did the washing in the 1950s with a tub and mangle, by the early

1960s with a machine. See John M. Foot, "Mass Cultures, Popular Cultures, and the Working Class in Milan, 1950–1970," *Social History* 24, no. 2 (1999): 134–57, and "The Family and the 'Economic Miracle': Social Transformation, Work, Leisure, and Development at Bovisa and Comasina (Milan), 1950–1970," *Contemporary European History* 4, no. 2 (1995): 315–38; David Forgacs, "Cultural Consumption, 1940s to 1990s," in *Italian Cultural Studies: An Introduction*, ed. David Forgacs and Robert Lumley (Oxford: Oxford University Press, 1996), 273–90; Michael Wildt, "Plurality of Taste: Food and Consumption in West Germany during the 1950s," *History Workshop Journal* 39 (Spring 1995): 23–41; James Obelkevich, "Consumption," in *Understanding Post-war British Society*, ed. James Obelkevich and Peter Catterall (London: Routledge, 1994), 141–54.

8. Ronald Fraser et al., eds., *1968: A Student Generation in Revolt* (New York: Pantheon, 1988), 76.
9. Ibid., 77.
10. Ingrid Schmidt-Harzbach, "Rock'n'Roll in Hanau," *Perlon-Zeit:* Wie die Frauen ihr Wirtschaftswunder erlebten, ed. Gisela Breitling (Berlin: Elefanten, 1985), 37–40.
11. Ibid., 78.
12. Edward Short (1912–2012), Labour Party Secretary for Education (1968–70), denounced student radicals as "academic thugs." See Paul Hoch and Vic Schoenbach, *LSE: The Natives Are Restless: A Report on Student Power in Action* (London: Sheed and Ward, 1969), 210.
13. See the now-classic treatments in Martin Durham, *Moral Crusades: Family and Morality in the Thatcher Years* (New York: New York University Press, 1991); Anna Marie Smith, *New Right Discourse on Race and Sexuality: Britain, 1968–1990* (Cambridge: Cambridge University Press, 1994); Stuart Hall, "Reformism and the Legislation of Consent," in *Permissiveness and Control: The Fate of the Sixties Legislation*, ed. National Deviancy Conference (London: Macmillan, 1980), 1–43. More recently, Lucy Robinson, *Gay Men and the Left in Post-war Britain: How the Personal Got Political* (Manchester: Manchester University Press, 2007); Lynne Segal, "Jam Today: Feminist Impacts and Transformations in the 1970s," in *Reassessing 1970s Britain*, ed. Lawrence Black, Hugh Pemberton, and Pat Thane (Manchester: Manchester University Press, 2013), 149–66; Lawrence Black, *Redefining Politics: Culture, Consumerism, and Participation, 1954–70* (Houndmills: Palgrave Macmillan, 2010).
14. See *The Attack on Higher Education: Marxist and Radical Penetration* (London: Institute for the Study of Conflict, 1977), the last of the Black Papers on British education (a play on official government White Papers), beginning with Brian Cox and A. E. Dyson, eds., *Fight for Education*, and Brian Cox, ed., *Crisis in Education* (London: The Critical Quarterly, 1969). For broader context, see CCCS Education Group, ed., *Unpopular Education: Schooling and Social Democracy since 1944* (London: Hutchinson, 1981); AnnMarie Wolpe and James Donald, eds., *Is There Anyone Here from Education?* (London: Pluto Press, 1983).
15. See especially Stuart Hall, Chas Critcher, Tony Jefferson, John Clarke, and Brian Roberts, *Policing the Crisis: Mugging, the State, and Law and Order* (London: Macmillan, 1978); compare, e.g., "Filbinger: Rückfall in faschistische Methoden," *Die Welt*, 17 April 1968.

16. See Stuart Hall, "A Torpedo Aimed at the Boiler-Room of Consensus," including the text of Powell's speech, *New Statesman*, 17 April 1998, 14–19.
17. Göran Therborn, "The End of the Future," *Marxism Today*, November 1991, 24.
18. See detailed documentation in *Frankfurter Schule und Studentenbewegung: Von der Flaschenpost zum Molotowcocktail 1946 bis 1995*, ed. Wolfgang Kraushaar, vol. 2: *Dokumente* (Hamburg: Rogner & Bernhard bei Zweitausendeins, 1998), 530–696. Specific quotations are from the following: Marcuse to Adorno, 5 April 1969, 601–2; Adorno to Marcuse, 19 June 1969, 653; Marcuse to Adorno, 21 June 1969, 653–55.
19. See Esther Leslie, "Introduction to Adorno/Marcuse Correspondence on the German Student Movement," *New Left Review* 233 (January–February 1999), 118–36. Also Hans-Jürgen Krahl, *Konstitution und Klassenkampf: Zur historischen Dialektik von bürgerlicher Emanzipation und proletarischen Revolution; Schriften, Reden und Entwurfe aus den Jahren 1966–1970* (Frankfurt a.M.: Verlag Neue Kritik, 1971).
20. Fraser et al., *1968*, 100.
21. Ronald Ingelhart, *The Silent Revolution: Changing Values and Political Styles among Western Publics* (Princeton, NJ: Princeton University Press, 1977), and *Culture Shift in Advanced Industrial Society* (Princeton, NJ: Princeton University Press, 1990); Alberto Melucci, *Nomads of the Present: Social Movements and Individual Needs in Contemporary Society* (Philadelphia: Temple University Press, 1989); Ulrich Beck, Scott Lash, and Anthony Giddens, eds., *Reflexive Modernization: Politics, Tradition, and Aesthetics in the Modern Social Order* (Cambridge: Polity Press, 1994); Manuel Castells, *The Information Age: Economy, Society, and Culture*, vol. 1: *The Rise of the Network Society* (Oxford: Blackwell, 1996); Charles Leadbetter, *Living on Thin Air: The New Economy* (London: Viking, 1999).
22. See, classically, Karl Mannheim, "Das Problem der Generationen," *Kölner Vierteljahreshefte für Soziologie* 7 (1928): 157–80, 309–50.
23. According to George Katsiaficas, *The Subversion of Politics: European Autonomous Social Movements and the Decolonization of Everyday Life* (Atlantic Highlands: Humanities Press, 1997), 87–88, 99–100, 128–31, Kreuzberg had an alternative scene of forty thousand, along with forty thousand Turks and fifty thousand "normals" in 1989.
24. The other contributions in this volume address this range of more and less organized forms of activism.
25. See Geoff Eley, "A 'Slight Angle to the Universe': Eric Hobsbawm, Politics, and History," in *History after Hobsbawm: Writing the Past for the Twenty-First Century*, ed. John H. Arnold, Matthew Hilton, and Jan Rüger (Oxford: Oxford University Press, 2017), 309–27.
26. Challenged during the 1992 presidential campaign over his drug use, Bill Clinton said: "I experimented with marijuana a time or two. And I didn't like it, and I didn't inhale." Anthony Jay, ed., *The Oxford Dictionary of Political Quotations*, 2nd ed. (Oxford: Oxford University Press, 2001), 90.
27. Mary Kay Mullan, "1968: Burntollet Bridge," in *'68, '78, '88: From Women's Liberation to Feminism*, ed. Amanda Sebestyen (Bridport: Prism Press, 1988), 15–24.
28. Mary Kay Mullan's webpage on the Gestalt Centre Belfast website, retrieved 3 November 2018 from https://gestaltbelfast.org/gcb-people/mary-kay-mullan/.

29. Compare Bernhard Gotto's contribution to this volume.
30. See Penny Forster and Imogen Sutton, eds., *Daughters of de Beauvoir* (London: Interlink Publishing, 1989).
31. William Morris, *A Dream of John Ball* (1887), quoted by Edward P. Thompson, *William Morris: Romantic to Revolutionary*, 2nd ed. (London: Merlin, 1977), 722.

Select Bibliography

Brown, Timothy Scott. *West Germany and the Global Sixties: The Antiauthoritarian Revolt, 1962–1978*. Cambridge: Cambridge University Press, 2013.
Davis, Belinda, et al., eds. *Changing the World, Changing Oneself*. New York: Berghahn Books, 2010.
Eley, Geoff. "A 'Slight Angle to the Universe': Eric Hobsbawm, Politics, and History." In *History after Hobsbawm: Writing the Past for the Twenty-First Century*, edited by John H. Arnold, Matthew Hilton, and Jan Rüger, 309–27. Oxford: Oxford University Press, 2017.
Fraser, Ronald, ed. *1968: A Student Generation in Revolt* (New York: Pantheon, 1988).
Häberlen, Joachim C. *The Emotional Politics of the Alternative Left: West Germany, 1968–1984*. Cambridge: Cambridge University Press, 2018.
Hughes, Celia. *Young Lives on the Left: Sixties Activism and the Liberation of the Self*. Manchester: Manchester University Press, 2015.
Sedlmaier, Alexander. *Consumption and Violence: Radical Protest in Cold-War West Germany*. Ann Arbor: University of Michigan Press, 2014.
Siegfried, Detlef, and Sven Reichardt, eds. *Das Alternative Milieu: Antibürgerlicher Lebensstil und linke Politik in Der Bundesrepublik Deutschland und Europa 1968–1983*. Göttingen: Wallstein, 2010.

Chapter 2

Conceptions of Democracy and West German New Social Movement Activism

Michael L. Hughes

The 1970s appearance of citizens' initiatives, new social movements (nsms), and widespread public protests was a new, but deeply rooted, development in political citizenship in Germany. Germans have always protested in various ways, but Germany's political cultures had generally repudiated citizen activism. Traditional elites had wanted citizen participation only as a source of information and support necessary for defending the realm and for political stability. Democratic elites accepted some popular voice, but they have almost universally sought to limit and channel that voice to ensure that the experts (themselves) would be in charge. Traditionally, German citizens seemed generally to accept such limitations, often dismissing public protest as disorderly and repugnant. Indeed, reacting to 1967/68 student demonstrations, some bystanders demanded the protesters be shot or gassed. Hence, the subsequent expansions of activism and protest and their eventual acceptance were notable developments. They reflected new conceptions of democracy, ones that challenged the model the *Grundgesetz* (GG) had established, that faced continued opposition among policymakers and citizens but that ultimately established new norms for political citizenship—not least, but not only, for nsm members. This chapter will demonstrate this transformation after '68, with reference to the longer history of popular political expression in modern Germany.

Nineteenth- and early twentieth-century German attitudes toward political participation were complex. Military and political elites had known since the Napoleonic Wars that some citizen engagement was indispensable, but they did not actually want citizens to have any decision-making role.

Even socialist leaders sought to keep the masses under their tutelage. Yet the "stab-in-the-back legend" after 1918, via which military leaders attempted to pin Germany's defeat in World War I on Social Democrats and other "reformers," only strengthened the perception that citizen engagement was crucial. Hence, Nazi leader Adolf Hitler later crafted key policy decisions to maintain popular support, while insisting that he alone knew the people's will and interests, so that his absolute rule was "true democracy." Nonetheless, German citizens often sought to influence policy through political protests. Catholics actively defended their church during the 1870s *Kulturkampf*. Socialists in the Second Empire (*Kaiserreich*), 1871–1918, used political funerals to promote their movement and demonstrations to seek universal male suffrage at all levels. Even proponents of authoritarian governance openly challenged the kaiser for insufficient assertiveness in the early twentieth century. And during World War I, women resorted to food riots (extraparliamentary democratic action).[1]

Popular political activism was ubiquitous in the Weimar Republic (1918–33), but Germans increasingly demanded a state that could exercise authority. A revolution driven by popular activism made the republic possible. A general strike saved it from the 1920 Kapp Putsch. Farmers engaged in tax strikes, boycotts, intimidation at foreclosures, and the occasional bombing to protest government policies and inaction. Millions of Germans attended innumerable political meetings. Except for the farmers, Weimar-era political protesters generally promoted not specific policies but a political party, movement, or individual. Protesters could be using democratic means to support democracy—but, crucially, protesters often used democratic means to undercut the democratic Weimar Republic so they could replace it, perhaps with a "democracy capable of exercising authority" but usually with some nondemocratic alternative.[2]

In 1949, West Germans drafted and implemented their constitution, the Basic Law (*Grundgesetz*, GG), in reaction to historical experience. Elements of parliamentary government in Germany went back to the early nineteenth century. Yet Germans had feared "parliamentary absolutism" in the Kaiserreich and indeed in the Weimar Republic. And they had seen the Weimar Republic collapse amid parliamentary dysfunction and violent political conflicts. They then suffered the persecutions and bloody failure of dictatorship. They now wanted strong but nondictatorial government.[3]

The GG established in the Federal Republic (FRG, or West Germany) a representative parliamentary democracy. With few apparent exceptions, post-1945 German elites (political, economic, and intellectual) blamed the "masses" for Hitler's coming to power, despite conservative elites' decisive 1933 role in maneuvering Hitler into the chancellorship. They feared "massification" and any substantive role for masses, whom they considered vulnerable to demagoguery. So they established a system in which parliament made the laws and also chose the executive. The president was not directly elected. And they allowed plebiscites only on changes in state borders. They thereby repudiated plebiscitary-democratic elements and ensured that representatives, shielded from direct citizen influence by multiyear terms, were the ones making decisions.[4]

Still fearing parliamentary absolutism, the GG drafters set constraints on parliament. One was federalism, but legal constraints were crucial. The GG forbade the limitation by any means, including constitutional amendment, of some key political rights. It established the FRG as a state of law (*Rechtsstaat*) to constrain governmental arbitrariness and to guarantee that democratically made decisions would be implemented. Moreover, the GG established the Federal Constitutional Court (BVerfG) as a check on governmental, including parliamentary, actions. These elements played key roles in creating political spaces for citizen activism.[5]

The GG granted political parties an implicitly privileged position that expanded to include certain large formal interest groups. It charged political parties to participate actively in "forming the political will," granting them a constitutional legitimacy they had never previously possessed. Hence, in the 1950s and 1960s, the parties, not individual citizens, successfully claimed a preeminent role in determining public policy—and indeed what issues would even be on the agenda. The parties expected to hear from members, but they looked primarily for support, not ideas on policy. Scholars often refer to 1950s/60s West Germany as a "parties democracy." As Ilona Klein noted, the GG had thereby provided not "rule of the people" but "rule for the people." The parties also acknowledged as key actors large formal interest groups such as business associations, trade unions, expellee organizations—i.e., interest groups that were simply too large to ignore and could provide significant support.[6]

Crucially, political elites (from the Christian Democratic CDU/CSU to the Social Democratic SPD) generally anathematized popular protests as "Nazi and Communist tactics" of "pressure from the streets." West Germans did occasionally take to the streets in the 1950s and early 1960s, and those who did faced suspicion and disdain. For example, August-Martin Euler (Free Democrats, FDP) could in 1950 assert that the parliament (Bundestag) must never submit to "pressure from the streets." German Civil Service Youth leaders in the mid-1960s argued that "in a democratic Rechtsstaat, political differences of opinion are not to be conducted in the streets." Often, citizens in the 1960s not only rejected student protests but condemned as "capitulation to the streets" any suggestion one should take demonstrators' concerns seriously. Contempt for the masses, memories of 1930s street battles, and elitism predominated. Indeed, when in 1969 Willy Brandt famously invited West Germans to "dare more democracy," he immediately specified that they would do so "not only through hearings in the Bundestag, but also through our constant contact with representative groups within the population and by offering transparency about government policies." He invited *not* public protests or nsms but more of the traditional West German focus on parties and formal organized interests.[7]

Notably, the BVerfG's 1958 Lüth decision strengthened considerably West Germans' right to freedom of expression. When Veit Harlan (director of the Nazis' viciously antisemitic *Jüd Süß*) released a new film in 1950, Social Democratic journalist Erich Lüth called for a boycott. Using a Civil Code tort provision, the film's distributor got a court to enjoin Lüth from promoting a boycott. Lüth appealed to the BVerfG on free expression grounds. The court ruled in his favor, affirming that the "free-democratic basic order" that the GG referenced made freedom of expression a central value that generally had to prevail over other legal and constitutional provisions. This decision significantly bolstered citizen rights to protest.[8]

The students who sparked 1967/68 protests did not invent protest in Germany. Across the decades, Germans from every segment of society had protested. Student protesters, from the country's future elite, did raise protesting's visibility and spurred development of protest techniques.[9]

Student activists had multiple reasons to doubt how democratic the FRG's parliamentary-representative system was. The 1966–69 Grand Coalition had reduced parliamentary opposition to a tiny, ineffectual minority of FDP delegates. And that coalition planned to amend the constitution to establish state-of-emergency provisions that aroused fears of a repeat of early 1930s erosions of democracy. Student activists also recognized the ways in which government, parties, and large interest groups were making policy behind closed doors, with no significant popular input, except—to a minor degree—at elections. And they were also convinced that the media, especially the powerful Springer publishing empire, were grossly misleading the public about the issues so that citizens could not make autonomous, democratic decisions.[10]

Given the power of media and government, student activists committed to strong, often deliberately provocative, protests as indispensable, efficacious, and democratically legitimate means to waken citizens from their apathy. The Grand Coalition reflected mid-1960s West Germany's broad, comfortable consensus. Student activists argued that rising real wages and consumerism had co-opted the citizenry, so that as a tiny minority with limited influence they struggled to make an impact. Initially they dressed conservatively, to reassure adults of their seriousness and maturity, but they soon embraced changes in dress, deportment, and culture that challenged prevailing norms. Already in the early 1960s, Dutch activists had deployed provocation to attract attention, and West German student activists increasingly concluded that they too must do so. Sit-ins, blockades, and happenings became increasingly common, as activists sought to secure the media's attention and confront the citizenry with alternative visions of the future. And a debate developed over whether force or violence (*Gewalt*) against things or even persons might be necessary to attract citizens' attention.[11]

The grassroots democracy that student activists were promoting provoked a sharp reaction from West Germans who feared that it threatened the reason and objectivity widely seen as crucial for legitimate political action.[12] The Nazis had rejected reason and objectivity and embraced will—with brutal, disastrous consequences. Postwar Germans instead embraced rational argumentation and rational discourse while denouncing emotion. West Germans in the 1960s could then dismiss a demonstration as "*ein Happening*," merely a frivolous expression of emotions. The increasing 1960s role of television, which focused on symbolism, emotion, and violence, only exacerbated such concerns. Germans hence generally seemed to believe that demonstrations were only legitimate to the extent that they furthered rational discourse on public issues. Moreover, student leaders were convinced that they could transform West German society through bottom-up political activism, through acts of will. Political philosopher Jürgen Habermas (in)famously denounced as "left fascism" the emotion and voluntarism of some student leaders. He quickly renounced that phrasing, but he and other left-liberal and social-democratic intellectuals—and common citizens—continued to reprove or even revile protest movements that strayed from reason and objectivity.[13]

Opponents of the new activism continued to denounce "pressure from the streets"—but activists argued that politics was about pressure. Interest groups, they pointed out, sought to influence policymaking all the time, with threats of economic and electoral consequences. As Johannes Agnoli argued, any letter from a major business group exercised far more pressure on policymakers than any student demonstration. And in a pluralist society, activists argued, pressure was just fine. This pluralist democracy repudiated Germans' traditional emphasis on a single national interest that the political system was to promote, instead of private interests. It had developed gradually across the 1950s and 1960s, as the de facto pluralist FRG flourished and as Germans increasingly seemed to accept that society in fact consisted of a multitude of groups entitled to promote their interests, and that multiple parties were preferable to one party. It opened the way for multifarious voices to seek to influence the political process, without facing the traditional delegitimization of being materialist egoists.[14]

Student activists often argued for a future direct democracy in Germany. Dubious about representative democracy, they sought an alternative to secure substantive citizen control of political decision-making. The council's democracy movement of the 1918 revolution offered a potential model. Some activists promoted the project. Moreover, various groups sought to organize themselves on a grassroots-democratic basis. These efforts could produce moments of intense engagement for individuals, though they are often seen as contributing to the inefficiency and hence inefficacy of such groups.[15]

Women's political roles changed, slowly but dramatically. Women had gained formal political rights in 1908 and 1919 but faced continuing de facto marginalization. The 1970s women's movement helped redefine the boundary between the private and the political.[16] Much energy went into nontraditional projects (e.g., women's shelters, nonauthoritarian education) and issues (e.g., abortion). Traditional male dominance in the formal political sphere continued in many ways (e.g., 70 percent of party members were male even in the 1980s). But, in surveys, openness to women's political participation more than doubled from 1965 to 1976. And especially in the nsms women undertook increasing, including leadership, roles. The Greens then initiated a process that brought more and more women into political leadership positions. By the 1980s, women's activism had increased substantially, and polling suggested that most Germans accepted in principle, if not yet in practice, that women were equal citizens.[17]

In 1970, reacting to the student demonstrations, the new SPD/FDP governing coalition promulgated legal changes that made protesting less risky. Previously, if even a few demonstrators acted violently, any demonstrators could be arrested, if they did not disperse *immediately* at police orders (whether they had been able to hear the orders or not); thousands of arrests resulted, usually of peaceful demonstrators or innocent bystanders. A 1970 amnesty law cleared most demonstration-related convictions, to integrate the overwhelmingly peaceful protesters into West German democracy. Crucially, a criminal code revision meant that mere presence at a demonstration that turned violent was no longer grounds for criminal proceedings, even if police ordered protesters to disperse. The CDU/CSU sought vehemently, for years, to reverse the latter amendment.[18]

The FRG's continuing commitment to "militant democracy," the notion that suppression of "antidemocratic" expression might be necessary to protect a parliamentary system, had negative but ultimately limited consequences for democratic citizenship. German governments had since the Weimar Republic banned organizations deemed antidemocratic. Renowned activist Rudi Dutschke's proposal for a "long march through the institutions" led to fears that Marxist radicals were working systematically from within the civil service to subvert the FRG—perhaps a Left "totalitarian" version of conservative jurists' and civil servants' subversion of the Weimar Republic. In 1972, Brandt sponsored a "Decree on Radicals," intended to provide a just consistency among federal and state governments in reviewing and barring from office current and future civil servants suspected of antidemocratic attitudes. Governments investigated many thousands of citizens and dismissed from or denied government jobs to hundreds or thousands (depending on the sources). This policy potentially threatened a protesting individual's career prospects, as implementation varied in unjustly arbitrary ways. Antiterrorist legislation and rhetoric contributed to the anxiety. An indeterminate number were intimidated. For example, in 1971, 85 percent in the FRG thought one could freely express oneself; in December 1976, only 73 percent agreed. Nonetheless, West German politics did become more participatory. So, the policies constituted a deeply problematic attack on people's rights and a de facto reaffirmation of traditional efforts to channel popular activity into the parties and large interest groups; yet it proved in practice less threatening to democratic expression than it seemed or might have become, especially had CDU/CSU proposals prevailed.[19]

The burgeoning citizens' initiatives from around 1970 repudiated the 1950s/60s model of democracy. The parties and formal interest groups had claimed not only a right but the ability to be sole representatives of citizen interests. By 1970, however, increasing numbers of Germans recognized that the parties and interest groups were incapable of representing the full range of citizen interests. Citizens' initiative members exercised their right to seek collectively to convince, or pressure, officials to meet citizen needs. For some activists from the start and increasingly by the mid-1970s, citizens' initiatives were seeking to change policy by appealing to the courts or by lobbying elected officials. Citizens' initiatives, concerning issues from the erection of stop signs to the building of nuclear power plants, could use personal representations to government officials or suits, but they also deployed various forms of public protest. The appearance of thousands of citizens' initiatives demonstrated that the parties and interest groups were not giving people the representation they desired. Indeed, Helga Grebing wrote, the GG's party-based political will formation turned out to *require* citizens' initiatives to address the full range of popular desires.[20]

While West Germans increasingly accepted citizens' initiatives as legitimate, the initiatives did face sharp criticism in the 1970s. Opponents asked just how representative they were. A group of individuals might demand a traffic light, but did they represent any significant share of their neighbors?

Many citizens (over half in some polls) passionately opposed nuclear reactors or nuclear missiles, but others (over half in some polls) welcomed one or both. Moreover, some commentators had been expressing concerns that too much popular participation was problematic because it raised expectations that the society might not be able to meet. Indeed, political mavens such as Gabriel Almond, Sidney Verba, and transplanted German Ralf Dahrendorf had in the 1960s urged more citizen engagement but warned against too much participation. The citizens' initiatives could in the 1970s seem to promote excessive participation, contributing to "ungovernability" because of system overload—a concern across the liberal democratic world in that period. Some commentators also opposed citizens' initiatives as a threat to the GG's parliamentary democracy, in which elected representatives were to discuss complex issues autonomously, rationally, and objectively, and reach reasoned compromises.[21]

Citizens' initiatives and nsms could lean toward grassroots democracy. Convinced that representative democracy could never accurately reflect majority opinion on the enormous range of issues a modern society faced, some Germans looked to more participatory alternatives. One suggestion was to move decisions to the lowest level possible, where citizens might secure more influence. Proposals for an imperative mandate, in which voters or party members instructed parliamentary delegates how to vote on each issue, were appealing to some. It was unclear, though, how that might happen in practice, and the GG Art. 38, affirming for parliamentary representatives the right to make decisions "freely," as representatives of the "entire people," seemed to make it unconstitutional. Various activists also proposed replacing the GG representative democracy with a council's democracy, where delegates could be recalled if they failed to follow popular will. The Greens experimented with various mechanisms, such as rotation of offices, to secure a grassroots democracy. Squatters and site occupiers, rejecting majority rule as a dictatorship over minorities, usually embraced a consensus decision-making process involving every participant in place of representatives and votes (though opponents noted that could involve browbeating holdouts into abandoning sincerely held opinions). Such direct-democratic options retain supporters but have failed to secure widespread acceptance.[22]

Citizens' initiatives and nsms developed amid changes in values and education that affected attitudes toward democracy and political citizenship. The rise of "postmaterialist values" significantly broadened the scope of political action. As individuals matured in more secure circumstances and procured more education, they became less concerned with immediate economic needs and more concerned with quality of life. They focused less on duty, order, and obedience and more on self-expression and self-development.

Politics and political citizenship hence embraced not only the struggle over economic resources but also a new range of issues, from local quality of life to women's status to global human rights. Some data suggest that people with postmaterialist values are more likely to participate politically, albeit the value shift probably affected more the range of issues and the tactics than the number of protestors. Increased education levels, by increasing knowledge and self-confidence, were probably more important for increased participation but do not themselves explain it.[23]

A new emphasis on emotion challenged the prevailing emphasis on reason and objectivity. Seeing rationalism as inherently cold and inadequate, some Germans urged joy, empathy, or imagination as the basis of political action. Emotion could seem authentic rather than, like reason, calculated. A "new subjectivity" meant that the individual and society should value individuals' feelings, perhaps above all. *Betroffenheit* (that an issue or value directly touched one) became central for more Germans. Some Germans characterized rationalism as capitalist or patriarchal oppression and inherently antidemocratic. Other demonstrators concluded that reason could not win over the masses but only emotion and symbolism, especially on television. The emphasis on emotion did decline, though not disappear, by the mid-1980s.[24]

Violence proved a fraught issue in the 1970s and early 1980s. Militant communist and anarchist groups sought a mass base in the 1970s; having given up on the working class, they hoped to find an alternative base in the nsms. Some West Germans continued to think that the state relied on indirect violence (unemployment, advertising, imposed social mores, state monopoly of force) to maintain its power, denying citizens true freedom. The Federal Republic was then a pseudo-democracy that needed to be overthrown. Moreover, police often saw any challenge to authority as an attack, against which they often responded with police brutality—gratuitous official violence that conservatives never questioned. Communist and anarchist groups then argued that "counterviolence," such as planned violence at antireactor demonstrations, was necessary: as legitimate self-defense, to reveal the existing order's brutality, to draw recruits, and to prepare the way for revolution leading to true democracy. And debate continued as to whether violence versus people or only versus things was acceptable.[25]

Yet despite continuing appeals to emotion and debates about violence, convincing policymakers through rational argumentation—and without violence—has remained the goal of political activity for most Germans who comment publicly—into the twenty-first century. Movements saw lively debates on tactics, as they grappled with the same problem that had led 1960s activists to embrace provocation—how to engage citizen attention to make one's case and influence public action. Movement activists often promoted "imaginative" protest tactics. Yet observers, even some sympathetic ones, repeatedly still dismissed any but cool and rational events as happenings, that is, those frivolous distractions that trivialized serious issues. Long after Nazism's irrationality and violence, such attitudes still had a hold. So when opponents attacked emotion and provocation in order to delegitimize issues by delegitimizing tactics, they could influence otherwise sympathetic fellow citizens who preferred rational, objective politics. Hence, groups usually focused on enlightening the masses and policymakers through well-reasoned debate. And observers and participants frequently asserted that throwing stones could not constitute rational argumentation, so that violence was unacceptable at demonstrations.[26]

Moreover, polling and other sources show that most Germans, especially in the nsms, embraced nonviolence as central to democratic citizenship—for ideological and pragmatic reasons. The logic of democracy was to provide for the peaceful resolution of social conflicts and the peaceful transfer of power, obviating any need for violence. Some Germans committed themselves to the sanctity of human lives and so opposed violence on principle. And some activists argued that means determine ends, that one could not get peaceful and democratic ends with violent means. Such activists often looked to the American civil rights movement, with its moral and pragmatic objections to violence. And participants could see that, in a democracy, violence would likely prove politically counterproductive. Correlation does not prove causation. However, when widely reported violence accompanied anti-nuclear-reactor demonstrations and squatting in 1977–81, polling showed a decline in popular support for demonstrations. Indeed, in a 1982 poll, 44 percent approved police "beating demonstrators" if a demonstration turned violent. Conversely, a post-1981 decline in violence accompanying anti-nuclear-reactor demonstrations and squatting, and a rise in determinedly peaceful anti-nuclear-missile demonstrations, was accompanied by growing support for demonstrations. According to polling, most Germans believed that violence would only be acceptable in extremis, particularly in the face of a new Nazism. And nsms, and apparently almost all demonstrators, embraced nonviolence.[27]

Pressure became by the 1980s a much more acceptable purpose of protest. Democracy *purely* as reasoned discourse would delegitimize any "pressure," and some commentators continued to reject "pressure from the streets" by self-selected minorities as undemocratic, especially in the GG's representative democracy. Yet protesters could see their activities as both sparking dialog *and* exercising pressure on policymakers. They certainly recognized the pressure other political actors exercised on parties and government. Some talked openly of raising the political costs to policymakers who did not promote the protesters' preferred policy. As West Germans came to accept pluralism, they generally also accepted that varying interests within the pluralist society had the right to and would seek to pressure parties and government. If so, citizens were just as entitled to do so as narrow interest groups.[28]

Compulsion has seemed more problematic in a democracy. Some issues (e.g., nuclear waste, nuclear weapons, access to housing) have seemed to some so crucial that the citizenry was entitled to resort to compulsion to overcome unresponsiveness by the political system, or at least to secure public debate. West Germans were likely to reject compulsion, however, seeing it as a minority seeking to impose its views on the majority. Moreover, the penal code (§240) criminalized coercion, at least if it was "reprehensible." The highest federal appeals court had interpreted §240 as meaning that a protest blockade that imposed compulsion counted as violence that could be reprehensible and hence criminal (though the appeals court and the BVerfG have traded dueling decisions on the details into the twenty-first century). The resort to civil disobedience in the 1970s and 1980s then led to sharp debates on coercion in a democracy.[29]

Civil disobedience seemed to its supporters a necessary tactic in the face of official failures. Government and parties, they complained, often ignored citizens, even when people protested, so that citizens were entitled to resort to civil disobedience. They often referred to GG Art. 2's right to bodily integrity to justify compulsion aimed at the government—as self-defense, e.g., against the dangers inherent in nuclear reactors. To legitimate such illegal actions, theorists argued that in a democracy one had to acknowledge majority rule and the constitutional order by being willing to accept arrest and legal punishment. And one had to be completely nonviolent.[30]

Supporters of civil disobedience grappled with some of these issues. Some wanted to use it to elicit dialog and rational discussion, but others wanted to compel policymakers to accept protesters' policy choices. Indeed, if the issues were vital enough (life and death), some claimed a right to veto policies that threatened life or health, even if the majority of the Bundestag and of citizens supported those policies. While a few German theorists were willing to go to jail, virtually no other German civil disobeyers were. Indeed, the latter denounced the arrest of citizens for civil disobedience as the "criminalization of dissent." Virtually all who promoted civil disobedience insisted on nonviolence, but small groups occasionally engaged in violence at protests. Civil disobedience continues to be a protest tactic into the twenty-first century in Germany, though less frequently, but these disagreements remain.[31]

Across the history of the FRG, many politicians, scholars, and citizens, though, rejected civil disobedience sharply. Some feared for the maintenance of order, of the Rechtsstaat, and of democracy, as civil disobedience promoted deliberate law-breaking. All too easily, opponents feared, people would conclude that they could break any law by claiming that their conscience made them do it. The Rechtsstaat was arguably indispensable to democracy, to ensure that democratically arrived-at laws and regulations were implemented; hence, conservative commentators argued, undercutting it was antidemocratic. Moreover, any dissatisfied minority—from far Left to far Right—might veto majority decisions with civil disobedience, especially as proponents usually denied that they should face any penalty for breaking the law.[32]

A 1968 GG amendment provided a "right of every German to resist anyone who undertakes to overthrow this [constitutional] order, when no other remedy is available," a provision some protesters expansively embraced. From the 1960s some activists rejected the FRG as delegitimized by inadequate denazification or by effective rule by capitalist elites; and into the 1980s and beyond the GG's failure to allow sufficient citizen input on crucial issues such as nuclear power and nuclear weapons continued to influence some Germans to question the system. For some, three decades of democratization following 1949 had not gone far enough to legitimate the GG and FRG. West Germans also had come to respect "resistance" because of the high valuation, retrospectively, of those who had resisted Hitler; they felt that Germans had a special responsibility to resist immoral policies. They concluded that the GG Art. 20 (4) "right to resistance" granted constitutional sanction for using illegal means to secure one's goals.[33]

Most observers sharply attacked this line of argument. The GG provision explicitly applied only when the constitutional order was at risk, not when some specific issue seemed problematic. It would come into force only when "no other remedy is available," which was not the case in democratic West Germany. And it would never obtain against democratically legitimated policy decisions. That the self-described resisters were implicitly and sometimes explicitly comparing themselves to individuals who had risked their lives against the Nazis seemed to many observers egregiously arrogant.[34]

Violence and nonviolence were the context for the crucial BVerfG Brokdorf decision, which strengthened the right to demonstrate as indispensable for democracy. Amid violent clashes with armed demonstrators that marked some anti-reactor demonstrations, militants planned violence at a demonstration scheduled at Brokdorf, site of a planned nuclear plant, for 28 February 1981. Authorities then secured an injunction banning demonstrations anywhere in the village's vicinity from 27 February to 1 March 1981. Protesters appealed that injunction on constitutional grounds; the BVerfG finally ruled on 14 May 1985. If the court had ruled right after the demonstration, when concerns with violent demonstrations were at their peak, it might have proved less receptive. In the meantime, though, four years of peaceful antimissile demonstrations had shifted public opinion. The BVerfG then ruled unanimously that public protest was so indispensable an element in the democratic formation of the political will that a potentially violent minority could not be allowed to deprive a peaceful majority of the right to demonstrate; given the centrality of freedom of expression in a democracy, only extremely narrow limits on demonstrations were permissible and only with clear evidence that violence might occur. And the right to demonstrate was a crucial protection of minority rights. The court did see demonstrations as about intellectual debate, but explicitly stated that individuals had a right to express an opinion simply as an immediate unfolding of their personalities. Even after the 1982 electoral shift to a CDU/FDP coalition, the FDP had refused to support CDU/CSU proposals to amend the criminal code to make it easier to arrest demonstrators; but after this ruling, the CDU/CSU abandoned those proposals.[35]

The FRG remains a representative democracy, but a much more participatory one than it was in the 1950s. That more participatory conception has roots in pre-1968, broad '68, and post-1968 developments. Efforts to introduce plebiscitary or direct-democratic elements have largely failed. The political parties and large, formal interest groups remain central to policy formation. For most commentators, reason and objectivity are still terms of praise in describing political protests, and emotion is often denigrated. Some Germans have always been willing to protest, but in a significant change since the 1960s, citizens' initiatives and popular protests have come to be accepted as legitimate, and perhaps central, elements in democratic governance. Support for both fluctuates, and debate remains about legitimate tactics and goals of public protest, but few Germans now deny that citizens need more avenues of access than voting, political parties, and large, formal interest groups. The presence of multiple nsms whose activism is widely accepted has created a new and much more vibrant political citizenship. The BVerfG ruling in the Brokdorf decision that protest was to promote rational discussion, but that one could protest just to express one's opinion, is both a reaffirmation of the centrality of rational dialogue and a reflection and a legitimation of emotion in public expression. In a reunified Germany, the spontaneity with which protests can develop—e.g., in mass demonstrations against hatred of foreigners in 1993, or anti-immigrant protests and counterdemonstrations against them—reflects the degree to which newer, more participatory conceptions of democracy are taken for granted.

Yet the story has not simply come to some happy ending—History never does. Democratic means are still being deployed against democratic values (e.g., against tolerance, in anti-immigrant protests), and some Germans do continue to question the right to public protest. Minorities still struggle to secure a voice and to protect their rights. Some Germans still favor direct democracy, and the radical-nationalist Alternative for Germany (AfD) party, established in 2013, has revived traditions of a single national interest to be implemented by a popularly elected president. Germany is a stable, participatory democracy—but one can never be sure, in any country, that such attitudes will last.

Michael L. Hughes is professor of history at Wake Forest University. He received his PhD from the University of California, Berkeley. He has published three books (*Paying for the German Inflation*, *Shouldering the Burdens of Defeat*, and *Embracing Democracy in Modern Germany*) and numerous articles and reviews on modern German history.

Notes

1. Michael L. Hughes, *Embracing Democracy in Modern Germany: Political Citizenship and Participation, 1871–2000* (London: Bloomsbury Academic, 2021), 2, 6–8, 23, 25, 57, 76; Ronald J. Ross, *The Failure of Bismarck's Kulturkampf: Catholicism and State Power in Imperial Germany, 1871–1887* (Washington, DC: The Catholic University of American Press, 1998), 56–57, 102–5, 129–56; Belinda Davis, *Home Fires Burning: Food, Politics, and Everyday Life in World War I Berlin* (Chapel Hill: University of North Carolina Press, 2000), 92, 121, 198.
2. Hughes, *Embracing*, 30, 34, 45, 49–53; Gerhard Stoltenberg, *Politische Strömungen im schleswig-holsteinischen Landvolk 1918–1933* (Düsseldorf: Droste Verlag, 1962), 49, 124–25, 128–30, 132–34, 172–78; Udi Greenberg, *The Weimar Century: German Émigrés and the Ideological Foundations of the Cold War* (Princeton, NJ: Princeton University Press, 2014), 133
3. Dieter Grosser, *Vom monarchischen Konstitutionalismus zur parlamentarischen Demokratie* (Den Haag: Martinus Nijhoff, 1970), esp. 3, 14, 207–8, 213–14; Gerhard A. Ritter, *Die deutschen Parteien 1830–1914* (Göttingen: Vandenhoeck & Ruprecht, 1985), 28–30, 85–88; Thomas Mergel, "Dictatorship and Democracy, 1918–1939," in *The Oxford Handbook of Modern German History*, ed. Helmut Walser Smith (Oxford: Oxford University Press, 2011), 427; Karlheinz Niclauß, *Der Weg zum Grundgesetz: Demokratiegründung in Westdeutschland 1945–1949* (Paderborn: Schöningh, 1998), 17, 176–77; Sebastian Ullrich, *Der Weimar-Komplex: Das Scheitern der ersten deutschen Demokratie und die politische Kultur der frühen Bundesrepublik 1945–1959* (Göttingen: Wallenstein Verlag, 2009), 195–97, 232–35, 292, 619.
4. Günther Ebersold, *Mündigkeit: Zur Geschichte eines Begriffs* (Frankfurt a.M.: Peter Lang, 1980), 110–11, 122, passim; Rolf Poscher, "Das Weimarer Wahlrechtsgespenst," in *Weimars lange Schatten—"Weimar" als Argumente nach 1945*, ed. Christoph Gusy (Baden-Baden: Nomos Verlag, 2003), 274–75; Friedrich Karl Fromme, *Von der Weimarer Verfassung zum Bonner Grundgesetz: Die verfassungspolitische Folge-*

rungen des Parlamentarischen Rates und nationalsozialistischer Diktatur (Berlin: Duncker & Humblot, 1999 [1958]), 21–26, 30–31, 38, 48–49, 135–36, 165–69, 191; Niclauß, *Weg zum Grundgesetz*, 181–85, 192–93, 204–9, 213–15.

5. Justin Collings, *Democracy's Guardians: A History of the German Federal Constitutional Court 1951–2001* (Oxford: Oxford University Press, 2015), xxv–xxvi, 3–4, 9–14, 34–37, 60, 73, 79, passim; Karlheinz Niclauß, "Der Parlamentarische Rat und das Bundesverfassungsgericht," in *Das Bundesverfassungsgericht im politischen System*, ed. Robert Chr. van Ooyen and Maring H. W. Möllers (Wiesbaden: Verlag für Sozialwissenschaften, 2006), 121–22.

6. Jürgen Turek, "Demokratie und Staatsbewußtsein: Entwicklung der Politischen Kultur in der Bundesrepublik Deutschland," in *Politische Kultur und deutsche Frage: Materialien zum Staats- und Nationalbewußtsein in der Bundesrepublik Deutschland*, ed. Werner Weidenfeld (Cologne: Verlag Wissenschaft und Politik, 1989), 236–37; Michaela Richter, "From State Culture to Citizen Culture: Political Parties and the Postwar Transformation of Political Culture in Germany," in *The Postwar Transformation of Germany: Democracy, Prosperity, and Nationhood*, ed. John S. Brady, Beverly Crawford, and Sarah Elise Wiliarty (Ann Arbor: University of Michigan Press, 1999), 131–33; Klaus Günther, *Sozialdemokratie und Demokratie 1946–1966: Die SPD und das Problem der Verschränkung innerparteilicher und bundesrepublikanischer Demokratie* (Bonn: Verlag: Neue Gesellschaft, 1979), 48–50, 129, 175, 178–83, 224; Kurt Sontheimer, *Die Adenauer-Ära: Grundlegung der Bundesrepublik* (Munich: dtv, 1991), 96; Ilona K. Klein, *Die Bundesrepublik als Parteienstaat: Zur Mitwirkung der Parteien an der Willensbildung des Volkes 1945–1949* (Frankfurt a.M.: Peter Lang, 1990), 32, 53, 227, 232–33, 274 (quotation); Karlheinz Niclauß, *Kanzlerdemokratie: Regierungsführung von Konrad Adenauer bis Angela Merkel*, 3rd ed. (Wiesbaden: Springer, 2015), 55, 71; Michael L. Hughes, "Restitution and Democracy in Germany after Two World Wars," *Contemporary European History* 4, no. 1 (1994): 9–10, and sources cited there.

7. Deutscher Bundestag, *Stenographische Berichte*, 1. Wahlperiode, 1228; Canan Candemir, "Die Pariser Verträge und die Wiederbewaffnung (1955) als Gegenstand von Protestverhandlungen, insbesondere der Paulskirchen-Bewegung," in *Ordnung und Protest: Eine gesamtdeutsche Protestgeschichte von 1949 bis heute*, ed. Martin Löhnig, Mareike Preisner, and Thomas Schlemmer (Tübingen: Mohr-Siebeck, 2015), 30, 42; Hans Karl Rupp, *Außerparlamentarische Opposition* (Cologne: Pahl-Rugenstein Verlag, 1970), 127, 213–15; Wolfgang Kraushaar, "Ordnung," ibid., 21; Michael Schneider, *Demokratie in Gefahr?* (Bonn: Verlag Neue Gesellschaft, 1986), 133, 144; Michael L. Hughes, "Reason, Emotion, Pressure, Violence: Modes of Demonstration as Conceptions of Political Citizenship in 1960s West Germany," *German History* 30, no. 2 (2012): 222–46.

8. See the articles in Thomas Henne and Arne Riedlinger, eds., *Das Lüth Urteil aus (rechts-) historischer Sicht: Die Konflikt um Veit Harlan und die Grundrechtsjudikatur des Bundesverfassungsgerichts* (Berlin: Berliner Wissenschaftsverlag, 2005); Collings, *Democracy's Guardians*, 54–60.

9. Cf. Hedwig Richter, *Demokratie: Eine deutsche Affäre* (Munich: Beck, 2020), 8–18, passim; Hughes, *Embracing*, 1–6, passim; See also Geoff Eley's chapter in the volume.

10. Nick Thomas, *Protest Movements in 1960s West Germany: A Social History of Dissent and Democracy* (Oxford: Berg, 2003), 49–182; Timothy Scott Brown, *West Germans and the Global Sixties: The Anti-authoritarian Revolt, 1962–1978* (Cambridge: Cambridge University Press, 2013), 85–91, 238, 334–40; Ingo Juchler, *Die Studentenbewegung in den Vereinigten Staaten und der Bundesrepublik Deutschland der sechziger Jahre* (Berlin: Duncker & Humblot, 1996), 270.
11. See Ingrid Gilcher-Holtey's chapter in this volume; see also Gerd-Rainer Horn, *The Spirit of 1968: Rebellion in Western Europe and North America, 1956–1976* (New York: Oxford University Press, 2007), 38–42; Thomas, *Protest Movements*, 98–99, 130–31, 148–59, 184–91; Brown, *West Germans*, 238, 334–40; Martin Klimke, *The Other Alliance: Student Protest in West Germany and the United States in the Global Sixties* (Princeton, NJ: Princeton University Press, 2010), 55–57, 74.
12. Compare the chapter by Friederike Brühöfener in this volume.
13. Kurt Sontheimer, *Zeitwende? Die Bundesrepublik Deutschland zwischen alter und alternativer Politik* (Hamburg: Hoffmann und Campe, 1983), 44, 62–63, 130, 200–201, 257; Todd Michael Goehle, "Challenging Television's Revolution: Media Representations of 1968 Protests in Television and Tabloids," in *Media and Revolt: Strategies and Performances from the 1960s to the Present*, ed. Kathrin Fahlenbrach, Erling Sivertsen, and Rolf Werenskjold (New York: Berghahn Books, 2016), 221, 223–24; Meike Vogel, *Unruhen im Fernsehen: Protestbewegung und öffentlich-rechtliche Berichterstattung in der 1960er Jahren* (Göttingen: Wallstein Verlag, 2010), 48–50, 205–10; Juchler, *Studentenbewegung*, 231–32, 244, 253–55, 391–92; Klimke, *Other Alliance*, 67; Matthew G. Specter, *Habermas: An Intellectual Biography* (Cambridge: Cambridge University Press, 2010), 61, 103, 122–14, 142.
14. Claus Leggewie, "Bloß kein Streit! Über die Sehnsucht nach Harmonie und die anhaltenden Schwierigkeiten demokratischer Streitkultur," in *Demokratische Streitkultur: Theoretsiche Grundpositionen und Handlungsalternativen in Politikfeldern*, ed. Ulrich Sarcinelli (Bonn: Bundeszentrale für politische Bildung, 1990), 55–57; Michael L. Hughes, "Reason, Emotion, Pressure, Violence," *German History* 30, no. 2 (2012), 241 (Agnoli), passim; Frieder Günther, *Denken vom Staat her: Die bundesdeutsche Staatsrechtslehre zwischen Dezisionismus und Integration 1949–1970* (Munich: Oldenbourg, 2004), 13, 235, 237, 241–42; Rolf Zoll, "Einleitung," in *Vom Obrigkeitsstaat zur entgrenzten Politik: Politische Einstellungen und politisches Verhalten in der Bundesrepublik seit der 60er Jahren*, ed. Rolf Zoll (Opladen: Westdeutscher Verlag, 1999), 9.
15. Konrad Jarausch, *After Hitler: Recivilizing Germans, 1945–1995* (New York: Oxford University Press, 2006), 168–69; Horn, *Spirit of 1968*, 156–57, 194–98.
16. Compare contributions by Friedericke Brühöfener, Bernhard Gotto, and Belinda Davis in this volume.
17. Kristina Schulz, *Der lange Atem der Provokation: Die Frauenbewegung in der Bundesrepublik und Frankreich 1968–1976* (Frankfurt: Campus Verlag, 2002), 90–94, 180–85, 190–94, 203–13, 218–25; Birgit Meyer, "Die 'unpolitische' Frau: Politische Partizipation von Frauen oder: Habe Frauen ein anderes Verständnis von Politik?" *APZ*, 1992, B25–26, 8–13; Anders Widfeldt, "Party Membership and Party Representativeness," in *Citizenship and the State*, ed. Hans-Dieter Klingemann and

Dieter Fuchs (Oxford: Oxford University Press, 1995), 148; E. Gene Frankland and Donald Schoonmaker, *Between Protest and Power: The Green Party in Germany* (Boulder, CO: Westview Press, 1992), 108, 112.

18. Hans-Christian Ströbele, "Vorwort," in *Demonstrationsfreiheit: Kampf um ein Bürgerrecht*, ed. Martin Kuscha (Cologne: Presseverlagsanstalt, 1986), 7; Heiko Drescher, "Genese und Hintergründe der Demonstrationsstrafrechtsreform von 1970 unter Berücksichtigung des geschichtlichen Wandels der Demonstrationsformen" (Diss., Heinrich Heine Universität Düsseldorf, 2005), 176–81, 227–28, 245–48, 270–71, passim.

19. Dominick Rigoll, *Staatsschutz in Westdeutschland: Von der Entnazifizierung zur Extremistenabwehr* (Göttingen: Wallstein Verlag, 2013), 9, 60–61, 84, 95–97, 255–58, 281, 295, 305–6, 322–24, 337–47, 353–54, 356–60, 365–66, 372–74, 415, 424, 441, 444, 446–48, 454–56, 472–73; Karin Hanshew, *Terror and Democracy in West Germany* (Cambridge: Cambridge University Press, 2012), 132–33, 145–47; Michael März, *Linker Protest nach dem Deutschen Herbst: Eine Geschichte des linken Spektrums im Schatten des "starken Staates," 1977–1979* (Bielefeld: transcript Verlag, 2012), 81–82, 113–14; Sven Reichart, *Authentizität und Gemeinschaft: Linksalternatives Leben in den siebziger und frühen achtziger Jahren* (Berlin: Suhrkamp, 2014), 209–16; David P. Conradt, "Changing German Political Culture," in *The Civic Culture Revisited*, ed. Gabriel Almond and Sidney Verba (Boston: Little, Brown and Company, 1980), 242–45.

20. Bernd Guggenberger and Udo Kempe, eds., *Bürgerinitiativen und repräsentatives System*, 2nd ed. (Opladen: Westdeutscher Verlag, 1984), passim; Russel Dalton, Manfred Kuechler, and Wilhelm Bürklin, "The Challenge of New Movements," in *Challenging the Political Order: New Social Movements in Western Democracies*, ed. Russel Dalton and Manfred Kuechler (Oxford: Oxford University Press, 1990), 11–12; Helga Grebing, "Demokratie ohne Demokraten? Politisches Denken, Einstellungen und Mentalitäten in der Nachkriegszeit," in *Wie neu war der Neubeginn? Zum deutschen Kontinuitätsproblem nach 1945*, ed. Everhard Holtmann (Erlangen: Universitätsbund, 1989), 9; Stephen Milder, *Greening Democracy: The Anti-nuclear Movement and Political Environmentalism in West Germany and Beyond, 1968–1983* (Cambridge: Cambridge University Press, 2017), 90–91, 105–6, 126–27, 186–88, 237, 245.

21. Winfried Steffani, "Bürgerinitiativen und Gemeinwohl," in Guggenberger and Kempe, *Bürgerinitiativen*, 73–76; Sebastian Haffner, "Die neue Sensibilität des Bürgers," in Guggenberger and Kempe, Bürgerinitiativen, 86–89; Uwe Thayer, "Bürgerinitiativen—Grüne/Alternativen—Parlament und Parteien in der Bundesrepublik," in Guggenberger and Kempe, *Bürgerinitiativen*, 124; Udo Kempf, "Bürgerinitiativen—Der empirische Befund," in Guggenberger and Kempe, *Bürgerinitiativen*, 312–14; Bernd Armbruster and Rainer Leisner, *Bürgerbeteiligung in der Bundesrepublik Deutschland: Zur Freizeitaktivität verschiedener Bevölkerungsgruppen in ausgewählten Beteiligungsfeldern (Kirche, Parteien, Bürgerinitiativen und Vereinen)* (Göttingen: Verlag Otto Schwarz & Co, 1975), 187–88; cf. the chapters and discussion in Kurt H. Biedenkopf and Rüdiger v. Voss, eds., *Staatsführung, Verbandsmacht und innere Souveränität: Von der Rolle der Verbände, Gewerkschaften und Bürgerinitiativen in der Politik* (Stuttgart: Verlag Bonn Aktuell, 1977), passim.

22. Rob Burns and Wilfred van der Will, *Protest and Democracy in West Germany: Extraparliamentary Opposition and the Democratic Agenda* (New York: St. Martin's Press, 1988), 232, 243–46; Sabine von Dirke, *All Power to the Imagination! The West German Counterculture from the Student Movement to the Greens* (Lincoln: University of Nebraska Press, 1997), 106–8, 185–86; Dieter Rucht and Jochen Roose, "Von der Platzbesetzung zum Verhandlungstisch? Zum Wandel von Aktionen und Struktur der Ökologiebewegung," in *Protest in der Bundesrepublik: Strukturen und Entwicklungen*, ed. Dieter Rucht (Frankfurt: Campus Verlag, 2001), 27–70, 201, 203–4; Frankland and Schoonmaker, *Between Protest and Power*, 2, 7, 152. See also the chapter by Freia Anders in this volume.
23. Ronald Inglehart, *The Silent Revolution: Changing Values and Political Styles among Western Publics* (Princeton, NJ: Princeton University Press, 1977), 7, 9, 15, 21–24, 58, 60–61, 72, 97, 294, 298; Frankland and Schoonmaker, *Between Protest and Power*, 54–55, 73–74; Bettina Westle, "Politische Legitimität und politische Partizipation in der Bundesrepublik Deutschland der achtziger Jahren," in *Political Participation and Democracy in Poland and West Germany*, ed. Gerd Meyer and Franciszek Ryxzka (Warsaw: Ośrodek Badań Społecznych, 1991), 87, 99–100, 112; Hans D. Klingemann, "Ideological Conceptualization and Political Action," in Samuel Barnes and Max Kaase, *Political Action: Mass Participation in Five Western Democracies* (Beverly Hills, CA: Sage Publishers, 1979), 345–48, 355–67; Heiner Meulemann, "Wertwandel in der Bundesrepublik zwischen 1950 und 1980: Versuch einer zusammenfassenden Deutung vorliegender Zeitreihen," in *Wirtschaftlicher Wandel, religiöser Wandel und Wertwandel: Folgen für das politische Verhalten in der Bundesrepublik Deutschland*, ed. Dieter Oberndörfer and Karl Schmitt (Berlin: Duncker & Humblot, 1985), 391–411.
24. Karl-Werner Brand, Detlef Büsser, and Dieter Rucht, *Aufbruch in eine andere Gesellschaft: Neue Soziale Bewegungen in der Bundesrepublik*, 2nd ed. (Frankfurt: Campus Verlag, 1984), 183, 202; Dirke, *All Power*, 39–41, 66, 97–98, 160–62; Susanne Schregel, "Konjunktur der Angst: 'Politik der Subjektivität' und 'neue Friedensbewegung,' 1978–1983," in *Angst im Kalten Krieg*, ed. Bernd Greiner et al. (Hamburg: Hamburger Edition, 2009), 500–502, passim; Friederike Brühöfener, "'Angst vor dem Atom': Emotionalität und Politik im Spiegel bundesdeutscher Zeitungen," in *Den Kalten Krieg denken: Beiträge zur sozialen Ideengeschichte seit 1945*, ed. Patrick Bernhard and Holger Nehring (Essen: Klartext, 2014), 285, 292–94; Thomas Balstier, *Straßenprotest: Formen oppositioneller Politik in der Bundesrepublik Deutschland zwischen 1979 und 1989* (Münster: Westfälisches Dampfboot, 1996), 40–41, 51, 54, 224, 228, 238; Kathrina Fahlenbrach, "Protest in Television: Visual Protest on Screen," in Fahlenbrach, Sivertsen, and Werenskjold, *Media and Revolt*, 240–43, passim. Compare contributions by Brühöfener and Gotto in this volume.
25. Hanshew, *Terror*, 82–88, 92–93, 95, 103–4, 106, 174; Balstier, *Straßenprotest*, 65, 107; Werner Lindner, *Jugendprotest seit den fünfziger Jahren: Dissens und kultureller Eigensinn* (Opladen: Leske + Budrich, 1996), 188–91, 205–10, 222–28; Ute Hasenöhrl, "Zivilgesellschaft und ziviler Ungehorsam: Begrenzte Regelverletzungen und Gewaltfreiheit in der bundesdeutschen anti-AKW Bewegung," in *Zivilgesellschaft: National und transnational*, ed. Dieter Gosewinkel (Berlin: edition sigma, 2004), 91–92, 94; Alexander Sedlmaier, "Konsumkritik und politische Gewalt in der links-

alternativen Szene der siebziger Jahre," in *Das Alternative Milieu*, ed. Sven Reichardt and Detlef Siegfried (Göttingen: Wallsten Verlag, 2010), 185–86, passim.

26. Balstier, *Straßenprotest*, 108, 175, 251; Burns and van der Will, *Protest*, 12, 18–19; Matthew Namiroff Lyons, *The Grassroots Network: Radical Nonviolence in the Federal Republic of Germany, 1972–1985* (Western Societies Program, Occasional Paper #20, Center for International Studies, Cornell University, 1988), 23, 41–44; Karl-Heinz Meyer, *Das neue Demonstrations- und Versammlungsrecht*, 2nd ed. (Munich: C. H. Beck, 1986), 3; Tim Warneke, "Aktionsformen und Politikverständnis der Friedensbewegung: Radikaler Humanismus und die Pathosformel des Menschlichen," in Reichardt and Siegfried, *Alternative*, 455; Walter Schmitt Glaeser, *Private Gewalt im politischen Meinungskampf: Zugleich ein Beitrag zur Legitimität des Staates* (Berlin: Duncker & Humblot 1992), 19, 25, 44, 108, 224–25.

27. Sven Reichardt, "Civility, Violence, and Civil Society," in *Civil Society: Berlin Perspectives*, ed. John Keane (New York: Berghahn Books, 2007), 140–44, 159; Hasenöhrl, "Zivilgesellschaft," 84–85, 89–91; Theodor Ebert, "Direkte Aktion in Formaldemokratien," in *Die rebellischen Studenten: Elite der Demokratie oder Vorhut eines linken Faschismus?* ed. Hans Julius Schoeps and Christopher Dannmann (Munich: Bechtle Verlag, 1968), 126–36; Theodor Ebert, *Gewaltfreier Aufstand: Alternative zum Bürgerkrieg*, 3rd ed. (Waldkirch: Waldkircher Verlagesgesellschaft, 1983), passim; Wolfgang Sternstein, *Überall ist Wyhl: Bürgerinitiativen gegen Atomanlagen aus der Arbeit eines Aktionsforschers* (Frankfurt: Haag+Herchen Verlag, 1978), 112, 253; Lyons, *Grassroots*, 4, 17, 25–27, 36, 43, 46–47.

28. Erich Küchenhoff, "Ziviler Ungehorsam als aktiver Verfassungsschutz," in *Widerstand—Protest—Ziviler Ungehorsam*, ed. Manfred Schleker (Sankt Augustin: COMDOK Verlagsabteilung, 1988), 60–61; Werner Birkenmeier, "Bürgerinitiativen im Parteienstaat," in Biedenkopf and Voss, *Staatsführung*, 120, 125, 129; Josef Isensee, "Staatshoheit und Bürgerinitiativen," in Biedenkopf and Voss, *Staatsführung*, 141–42, 148; Balstier, *Straßenprotest*, 61, 127, 178, 225–26, 242; Lyons, *Grassroots*, iv, 23; Karl-Heinz Stamm, *Alternative Öffentlichkeit: Die Erfahrungsproduktion neuer sozialen Bewegungen* (Frankfurt: Campus Verlag, 1988), 154, 192.

29. Lyons, *Grassroots*, 23, 41–42; Balstier, *Straßenprotest*, 61, 225, 307; Arndt Sinn, "Das Nötigungsstrafbarkeit von Protesthandlungen," in Löhnig et al., *Ordnung*, 117–23, 129–30; Josef Isensee, "Widerstand und demokratische Normalität," in *Jurist und Staatsbewußtsein*, ed. Peter Eisenmann (Heidelberg: V. Decker und Müller, 1987), 45; Thomas Blanke and Dieter Sterzel, "Die Entwicklung des Demonstrationsrechts von der Studentenbewegung bis heute," in *Das Demonstrationsrecht*, ed. Sebastian Cobler et al., (Reinbek bei Hamburg: Rowohlt, 1983), 75–76; Glaeser, *Gewalt*, 19, 23, 25, 75–79, 102, 107–10, 222–23, 227.

30. Susanne Schregel, "'Dann sage ich, brich das Gesetz': Recht und Protest im Streit um den NATO-Doppelbeschluss," in Löhnig et al., *Ordnung*, 136–37; Wolf-Dieter Narr et al., "Den eigenen Menschenrechten, nicht dem Staat gehorchen? Von der Freiheit derjenigen, die zivilen Ungehorsam leisten," in *Ziviler Ungehorsam*, ed. Wolf-Dieter Narr et al., 35, 38; Wolf-Dieter Narr, "Gewaltfreier Widerstand um der Demokratie und des Friedens willen," in Cobler et al., *Demonstrationsrecht*, 142, 152, 156, 160–65; Dirke, *All Power*, 107; Dieter Rucht, "Die konstruktive Funk-

tion von Protesten in und für die Zivilgesellschaft," in *Zivilgesellschaft als Geschichte. Studien zum 19. und 20. Jahrhundert*, ed. Ralph Jessen et al. (Wiesbaden: Verlag für Sozialwissenschaft, 2004), 146–47.
31. Lyons, *Grassroots*, iv, 23; Balstier, *Straßenprotest*, 32, 145–46, 241; Michael L. Hughes, "Civil Disobedience in Transnational Perspective: American and West German Anti-Nuclear-Power Protesters, 1975–1982," *Historical Social Research* 39, no. 1 (2014): 242–46.
32. Isensee, "Staatshoheit," 151; Hasenöhrl, "Zivilgesellschaft," 95–96; Isensee, "Widerstand," 43, 45–48; Rupert Scholz, "Demokratie und freiheitlicher Rechtsstaat," in *Demokratische Streitkultur* ed. Ulrich Sarcinelli (Bonn: Bundeszentrale für politische Bildung, 1990), 309–10; Arnold Köpcke-Duttler, "Ziviler Ungehorsam: Einige verfassungsrechtliche Versuche, seiner Behinderung und ihre Kritiker," Narr et al. (eds.), *Ziviler Ungehorsam*, 309–10.
33. Hanshew, *Terror*, 66–67, 70–74, 153; Narr, "Widerstand," 139–40, 143–46, 149–53, 160–67.
34. Hasenöhrl, "Zivilgesellschaft," 96–97; Isensee, "Widerstand," 41–42, 50–52; Martin Borowski, "Protest unter Berufung auf die Gewissensfreiheit," in Löhnig et al., *Ordnung*, 166–68; Bernd Guggenberger, "Die Grenzen des Gehorsams—Widerstandsrecht und atomares Zäsurbewußtsein," in *Neue Soziale Bewegungen in der Bundesrepublik Deutschland*, ed. Roland Roth and Dieter Rucht (Frankfurt: Campus Verlag, 1987), 327–28.
35. Anselm Doering-Manteuffel et al., "Einführung," in *Der Brokdorf-Beschluss des Bundesverfassungsgerichts 1985*, ed. Anselm Doering-Manteuffel et al. (Tübingen: Mohr Siebeck, 2015), 3–4; Oliver Lepsius and Anselm Doering-Manteuffel, "Die Richterpersönlichkeit und ihre protestantische Sozialisation," in Doering-Manteuffel, *Brokdorf-Beschluss*, 167; Auszug, BVerfG 69, 315, in Doering-Manteuffel, *Brokdorf-Beschluss*, 17–55; Martin Kutscha, "Der Kampf um ein Bürgerrecht. Demonstrationsfreiheit in Vergangenheit und Gegenwart," in *Demonstrationsfreiheit: Kampf um ein Bürgerrecht*, ed. Martin Kutscha (Köln: presseverlagsanstalt, 1986), 24–25, 46–47; Klaus Dammann, "Rache des Rechtsstaates—oder Aufbegehren der Akteure," in Kutscha, *Demonstrationsfreiheit*, 167–69; Meyer, *neue Demonstrations- und Versammlungsrecht*, 1–3.

Select Bibliography

Balstier, Thomas. *Straßenprotest: Formen oppositioneller Politik in der Bundesrepublik Deutschland zwischen 1979 und 1989*. Münster: Westfälisches Dampfboot, 1996.
Brown, Timothy Scott. *West Germans and the Global Sixties: The Anti-authoritarian Revolt, 1962–1978*. Cambridge: Cambridge University Press, 2013.
Collings, Justin. *Democracy's Guardians: A History of the German Federal Constitutional Court 1951–2001*. Oxford: Oxford University Press, 2015.
Davis, Belinda. *Home Fires Burning: Food, Politics, and Everyday Life in World War I Berlin*. Chapel Hill: University of North Carolina Press, 2000.
Dirke, Sabine von. *All Power to the Imagination! The West German Counterculture from the Student Movement to the Greens*. Lincoln: University of Nebraska Press, 1997.

Eley, Geoff. *Forging Democracy: The History of the Left in Europe, 1850–2000*. Oxford: Oxford University Press, 2002.

Hughes, Michael L. *Embracing Democracy in Modern Germany: Political Citizenship and Participation, 1871–2000*. London: Bloomsbury Academic, 2021.

Rigoll, Dominick. *Staatsschutz in Westdeutschland: Von der Entnazifizierung zur Extremistenabwehr*. Göttingen: Wallstein Verlag, 2013.

Chapter 3

New Social Movements and the New Role of the Intellectual

From the "'68ers'" Critique (of the Intellectual) to (the Typus of) the "Specific Intellectual"

Ingrid Gilcher-Holtey

Intellectuals play a key role in the construction and also the subversion of conceptualizations of perception, thought, and the classification of the social world. Social movements constitute one site for opening up new spaces of thought and possibility, in which alternative values, norms, and relationship structures can be tested. Did "'68" in West Germany and beyond change the role of intellectuals and their strategies of intervention into the political arena, with implications for social movements going forward? This chapter responds to that question. First, it explores '68 activists' criticisms of the classic "general" or "universal intellectual" as standing outside, aloof from action. These criticisms are examined through examples in France as well as West Germany (FRG). The chapter then moves on to the most substantial section, investigating five characteristics of a new role for intellectuals that emerged in the course of '68, with significant implications going forward. In this context, the chapter introduces the analytical type of the "specific intellectual" developed by the French philosopher Foucault at the beginning of the 1970s and shows the new understanding of the role of the intellectual associated with it, ending with the example of Naomi Klein and the alter-globalization movement.

"When Words Took to the Streets":
Critique of the Classical Universal Intellectual

Paris, 20 May 1968: "Shit, what does he want here? He's a star and we can't have stars here." These are the words Jean-Paul Sartre has to hear as he makes his way to the Sorbonne's large auditorium. At this point, the Sorbonne, Paris's renowned university, has been occupied for a week. Thousands have come to support the occupiers. The students sit everywhere, even in the corridors. The auditorium is overflowing.[1] The words on the way to the lecture hall irritate him. He feels that the New Left movement, which he has always longed for, is hostile to him. This movement, he notes retrospectively, sought intellectuals like him "not as we were."[2] Reaching the auditorium, he explains, "I didn't come to teach, but rather to listen." But, even with this gesture, he fails to meet students' expectations. After all, he refuses to do what he has been asked to do: that is, to make practical suggestions. So, the movement simply passes him by. As he speaks, someone sends him a piece of paper reading: "Sartre, be brief." Sartre persists, convinced, as he later explains, that in May 1968 he was politically trapped "at zero" and in a "provisional ivory tower."[3] In retrospect, he sees as a lasting effect of the '68 movement the challenge to intellectuals like him.

The archetypal "general" or "universal intellectual" in the tradition of Voltaire and Émile Zola, to which Sartre belongs, interferes in the political arena with reference to abstract, universal values (freedom, equality, justice). He practices criticism outside of his professional competence. He appears as a defender of the truth, as an adjudicator of justice and injustice, and as a critic of power.[4] As sociologist Luc Boltanski and historian Elisabeth Claverie have pointed out, three further criteria prefigure the role of the general intellectual, based on Voltaire's intervention in the Calas affair (1762–65) and on Zola's involvement in the Dreyfus affair (1894–1906). These relate, firstly, to the defense of an unjustly accused (ordinary) person; secondly, to the reversal of the roles of accuser and accused, thus representing an accusation of the accuser; and, thirdly, to the reversal of the verdict on the victim and the accuser in the perception of the public.[5] It is the subversion of public opinion that distinguishes the commitment of the universal intellectual. Successful subversion of public opinion is thus analytically linked to the reversal of patterns of perception and in turn to the emergence of a new audience.

What happened to Sartre in May 1968 had been experienced in West Germany already several months earlier, in October 1967, by writers of the Group 47 (Gruppe 47). This renowned literary group, which, since its foundation in 1947, had advanced from the periphery to the center of the literary field, saw itself as the only "real," "anti-authoritarian" opposition in the Federal Republic. However, students of the Socialist German Student Union (SDS), the central group of the '68 movement in the Federal Republic, characterized Group 47 as a "paper tiger," incapable of generating meaningful change. SDS members thus disturbed the annual meeting of Group 47 in October by burning copies of the scurrilous *BILD* newspaper in front of the conference venue and then trying to occupy the hall where the group's readings took place. With their performative, provocative actions, SDS members challenged the writers to support the campaign against Springer, publisher of *BILD*, which they accused of manipulating the public and simultaneously forming a press monopoly. The rebellious students did not know that members of Group 47 had already written a resolution the evening before, in which they had branded the control of 32.7 percent of all German newspapers and magazines by a single publisher as a "threat to the foundations of democracy." In the resolution, they declared that, in future, they would no longer cooperate with any newspaper or magazine in the Springer group. They called on other writers and their publishers to follow this example. The resolution was read out to the SDS protestors. It was in vain, for the group remained a paper tiger to these students. Group 47 member Hans Magnus Enzensberger wrote in *Kursbuch*, the central forum of West Germany's "extraparliamentary opposition" (*extraparlamentarische Opposition*, APO), that the students had through their protest successfully forced the oppositional intelligentsia in Group 47 to the first reckoning of accounts ("zum ersten Kassensturz genötigt") in the organization's twenty years of existence.[6]

But, again, Group 47's move was to little avail. Appeals and manifestos, resolutions and petitions were not enough for the New Left. This protest polarized and divided the world-famous writers' group, which since 1947 had staked its claims in democratizing the mentalities of postwar Germany. Some of the Group 47 writers, including leading playwright Peter Weiss, now joined APO actions themselves. Such different perceptions of the role of literature in the process of social transformation, and different definitions in turn of the tasks and mandate of the intellectual, contributed to the disintegration of Group 47. Indeed, after the SDS's October disturbance, the writers' group never met again. "Once the student movement emerged," Hans Magnus Enzensberger explained, "the group immediately disbanded."[7]

The examples demonstrate: The "universal intellectual," which dominated the intellectual field in France in the 1960s and established itself slowly too in the Federal Republic, is subject to radical criticism in the course of the '68 mobilization. One of the most striking characteristics of intellectuals is the ability to turn the weapon of critique against one another.[8] What is contested among them is not least who and what is a "legitimate" intellectual. Even the deconstruction of the intellectual propagated by postmodern thought continues the struggle over the concept and the "true" role and function of the intellectual. According to French philosopher Régis Debray, the "intellectuel jusqu'au boutiste" (intellectual to the core) is characterized by the refusal to recognize that there are still intellectuals at all.[9] François Lyotard's dictum of the "death" of the intellectual who fulfilled his mission is an example of this.[10] However, in the context of '68, the critique and the self-reflection/self-criticism of intellectuals, as will be shown, leads to the experimental testing of new role models for the figure. The redefinition of the role of the intellectual in the context of the '68 movement is a hitherto unaccentuated consequence of the '68 movement.

The Development and Testing of Alternative Role Models for the Intellectual

What is it that the rebellious students oppose to the classical intellectual? What characterizes the new type of intellectual that the New Left imagined and anticipated? Five characteristics are shown below and illustrated by way of examples.

Enlightenment through Action. The New Left, which initiated the mobilization process of the '68 movements in all Western industrialized countries, followed the maxim to intervene not only with words but also with provocative performative actions in social confrontations and disputes. The New Left relied on the notion of enlightenment through action, on revolutionizing the minds by acting. The counsel of Régis Debray, who set off for Cuba and Bolivia, acted as motivator for action: "To judge an intellectual, it is not enough to examine his thoughts: what makes the difference is the relationship between what he thinks and what he does."[11]

In its action strategies, the New Left draws on techniques of the artistic avant-garde and the anarchist movement. "Without provocation," said Rudi Dutschke, the symbolic figure of the '68 movement in the FRG, "we are not perceived at all." The classic general intellectual was regarded by the young, critical intelligentsia as integrated into the system. Young activists thus doubted and even refuted its relevance, in view of the all-absorbing "consciousness industry."[12] Hans Magnus Enzensberger, member of the inner circle of Group 47, had coined the term. Regarding the consciousness industry as the actual key industry of the twentieth century, he argued that this industry created a new form of exploitation. He already wrote in 1961: "Whoever is master or servant is decided not only by the one who has capital, factories, and weapons, but, the longer it continues, the clearer it becomes, by the one who can control consciousness of others." And, he added: "Material poverty is replaced by nonmaterial impoverishment, which is expressed most clearly in the disappearance of the political possibilities of the individual."[13]

From Enzensberger's point of view, the consciousness industry, aimed at a "cementing of the established rule," thus changed the social role of the intellectual. He cannot practice cultural criticism without precisely making use of the consciousness industry, which in turn aims at criticizing cultural criticism. Thus, he becomes the "accomplice of an industry," the fate of which depended on him, just as he depended on its fate. But the mission of the consciousness industry to cement the established rule was "incompatible" with the intellectual's intended role.[14] The intellectuals were deprived of the radicality of their statements simply by the fact that the consciousness industry absorbed them. In short: intellectuals would be published and swallowed up at the same time.

Enzensberger, who has critically examined the function of the consciousness industry since 1961, is one of the writers in Group 47 who supported the student critique of the group. Although he is not present as students of the SDS chanted "The group is a paper tiger," one of his friends, Chilean student and writer Gaston Salvatore, who was also a close friend of Rudi Dutschke, was among the protesting students. Salvatore confessed at a party in West Berlin that it was "our duty to the world revolution" to unmask Group 47.[15] What then could and should replace the intervention strategies of the general, universal intellectual? Enzensberger made the answer clear in June 1968: "Disturbances in all areas of public life—disturbances of the authoritarian operation, and the formation of counterinstitutions." He described potential disturbances of the consciousness industry that could lead to the building of counterpower as follows: "Deliver swallow deliver swallow: that is the imperative of the market. When writers and readers notice that those who deliver are swallowed, and those who swallow are delivered, this leads to blockages."[16]

With the recourse to counterpower and counterinstitutions, Enzensberger takes up a core element of the transformation strategy of the New Left, which did not focus on conquering power, but rather on changing power and power structures, on building counter-power and counter-institutions. In April 1968, after the assassination attempt on Rudi Dutschke, Enzensberger also intervenes at the protest march to the radio station Free Berlin (Sender Freies Berlin, SFB). He acts as spokesman for the APO in negotiations with the director of the SFB, in order to sue for a one-hour broadcasting slot for the APO in the station's daily program. Looking back, he comments:

Our demand was: We want broadcasting time. The reporting, not only in the press but also on radio and television, was very one-sided. This demand was therefore certainly not illegitimate. But it was notable that an administrator [from the radio station] was prepared to come to a turbulent meeting and try to justify himself there. In a way, it was a reversal of power, even if only for one evening.[17]

In the months that followed, Hans Magnus Enzensberger stopped writing poetry, declined a fellowship from an American university, and left instead for Cuba. He practiced what the German philosopher Walter Benjamin had already considered, that is, the "interruption of the artist's career."[18] Enzensberger regarded the liberation movements in the Global South as a factor with implications too for the future shape of Western democracies. He thus advanced the thesis that the "self-examination" of "left-wing" writers in the Federal Republic had to be oriented toward revolutionary processes in the "Third World."[19]

Jean-Paul Sartre conversely does not interrupt his work. He writes in May 1968 and afterward on his large study of French novelist Gustav Flaubert.[20] But Sartre did also adopt impulses of the movement. If one considers the forms of his interventions as a universal intellectual, one sees that they did change. Sartre does not stop writing or signing manifestos, open letters, and protest statements. However, provocative action, the limited violation of rules, does become part of the repertoire of his intervention strategies. After World War II, Sartre assumes that speaking was a form of action and that words worked "like loaded pistols."[21] But now he accompanies his speaking and writing with action. He tries to create situations that force the public and the government to express their opinions through his actions, such as taking over editorship and distribution of the banned broadly Maoist newspaper *La cause du peuple* in 1970, two years after its founding in May 1968.

As editor of *La cause du peuple*, Sartre thus assumes responsibility for the paper and, despite the minister of the interior's ban on its publication and confiscation of its issues, he distributes the paper himself in the streets of Paris. He thus uses his prestige and reputation as an untouchable intellectual to prevent the government from "suffocating" a revolutionary press organ, and to present officials with a challenge.[22] "I'm the third editor, so arrest me."[23] This is his message to the Gaullist government that succeeded French president Charles de Gaulle. It was the conservative de Gaulle himself who in 1960 had remarked, "You don't arrest Voltaire," in relation to Sartre, on the occasion of the "Manifesto of the 121," intellectuals' open letter against the Algerian War. Sartre thus confronts the government with a choice: "If you arrest me, you will have a political trial on your hands; if you do not arrest me, you will show that the judiciary has a double standard."[24] Indeed Sartre is not arrested or sanctioned. With a pile of banned magazines under his arm, he proclaims in the streets of Paris the need for equality before the law, freedom of the press, and freedom of expression generally, even for members of what he calls a "radical movement." He criticizes the judiciary for acting under pressure from the prosecutor, who is in turn "completely dependent on the executive branch."[25]

This new form of engagement is not easy for him. He wishes, as he explains to his Maoist interlocutors, that he had been confronted with the "radical movement" at the age of fifty and not at sixty-seven. Sartre feels he can only summon up the strength for action, for the active support that is expected of him, to a limited extent.[26] If he does it nevertheless and takes part in political actions, it is not least to keep the radicalizing successor groups of the May Movement, some of which are tending toward terrorism, from going underground. He hopes rather to encourage these groupings to seek coalition with the intelligentsia and to concentrate on the project of creating a counterpublic. This takes shape in the founding of the magazine *Libération* in 1973. As such, Sartre thus redirects activists' energies and fantasies back to the power of words. By 1974, Sartre has stepped down from *Libération*.

Enzensberger, born 1929 and thus twenty-four years younger than Sartre, fares better in these years. Activist students visit him in his West Berlin apartment and don't seem to notice the difference in status or age, only the speed and flawlessness of his sentences. Only in retrospect did the question arise of how indeed he "endured the proximity to so many horribly written leaflets and pamphlets."[27] Enzensberger also particularly seeks contact with Latin American students. He visits Chilean writer Gaston Salvatore in his student residence in order to recruit authors from his circle of friends for a special issue of *Kursbuch*, dedicated to Latin America. He insists on sitting on the floor during the debates and dinner like the Latin American students around him. He rejects the "poet's chair"[28] and thus a prominent position.

If one tries to draw up an interim balance, one can say: ready to support the struggles of social groups and movements not only with words but with deeds, this new type of intellectual gives up the position outside the conflict that distinguishes the universal intellectual. He stands rather on the side of social groups and movements, determined to support their struggles not only with words but also with deeds. He becomes a fellow fighter, a "militant." In this way, examined via its German historical roots, this new intellectual stands in a tradition of activism, a current within literary expressionism that aims to activate "intellectuals" so that they can also be described indeed as "activist intellectuals."[29] The French sociologist Gisèle Sapiro proposes the term *intellectuel contestataire* (rebellious intellectual). The "activist/rebellious" intellectual can act as a lone fighter but tends to engage via groups.[30]

From Lone Warrior to Member of a Collective. The union/joining of intellectuals into groups and collective protest actions is often, as Gisèle Sapiro has pointed out, an expression of a lack of individual symbolic capital. Groups of the historical avant-garde—such as the Dadaists, Surrealists, and literary activists—attempted to overcome this shortcoming through group manifestos and noisy collective protest actions. Their practices, aimed at something new, were characterized by border crossings and other transgressions. Among the transgressions were provocative, performative violations of rules, in order to change the very rules of the rules: "the turning to the attempt to shape unconscious processes and give validity to nonrational structures."[31] The neo-avant-garde of the 1960s, the New Left, and the New Social Movements of the 1970s and beyond (women's, alternative, peace, globalization-critical, etc.) continued the techniques and action strategies of the classical avant-garde. The negation through exaggerated affirmation,[32] such as that propagated by the new women's movement's campaign "I've had an Abortion," is also borrowed from the avant-garde, likewise intervention as a collective.

Thus, the specifically "feminist intellectual" within the New Women's Movement always appeared publicly in the group and insisted on taking the floor. Following the example of the collective working method of the avant-garde, she simultaneously refrained from identifying her individual authorship. With the New Left, from which she detached herself, she still associated herself with reference to a revolutionary subject. She granted women with children the power of definition over the organization of social life. Any proxy policy was rejected. Self-articulation was the maxim.[33] This implied new patterns in the process of consciousness formation: the renunciation of consciousness formation "from outside" and "from above."

From Mediation "from the Outside" to Mediation "to the Outside." The New Left not only rejects the type of the general/universal intellectual but also breaks with the Marxist intellectual in the tradition of Karl Kautsky and Vladimir I. Lenin, who both defined the intellectual as a mediator of consciousness that had to be carried "from outside" into the working class. The New Left ceases to see the proletariat as the sole revolutionary subject. Rather, it identifies new carriers of social change: the "new working class," the liberation movements of the "Third World"; social fringe, subgroups, "vulnerable groups"; and, finally, the young intelligentsia itself. The "activist"/"rebellious" intellectual of the New Left sets himself the goal of communicating their interests, demands, and goals "to the outside." They thus enter into the role of "mediator" (*Vermittler*) of the criteria of perception and evaluation that opposes the dominant principles of division in the social world.[31] Moreover, the intellectual in the tradition of the New Left does not appear with a theoretical claim to interpretation and leadership but rather assumes that the building blocks of a new theory will emerge from the activities of social groups or movements. In contrast to the classical "universal intellectual" in the tradition of Voltaire and Zola, then, this figure does not try to make accusations against injustice by invoking general, abstract value but rather tries to derive and generalize values, patterns of perception, and classification from social struggles themselves. By recording and documenting the goals and demands of social groups and movements, he contributes thereby not only to his self-representation but also to a group's internal self-understanding. Hans Magnus Enzensberger, together with German composer Hans Werner Henze, make clear what this could look like by using the example of their 1970 opera *El Cimmaron* (from the sobriquet for a real-life runaway slave), which tells the story of a slave who liberated himself. Enzensberger and Henze actually visit this slave, who lives in Cuba in 1968, at the age of 108. They reverse the prevailing direction of cultural transfer with their rendition of his life story. They convey the voice of the Third World to the outside and thus set themselves apart from the predominant patterns of the European intellectual.[34]

Jean-Paul Sartre also reverses social roles, to be sure, at the height of the Paris general strike in May 1968, conducting an interview with the then-twenty-three-year-old Daniel Cohn-Bendit, the symbolic figure of the May Movement in France. In the interview, Sartre asks the questions, and Daniel Cohn-Bendit provides the answers. Cohn-Bendit explains to him "the theory of the acting minority," which drives the action forward without directing it from above. Newspapers all over the world reprint the interview. Cohn-Bendit argues to Sartre that the theory of the "directing avant-garde," a Leninist-style vanguard that managed all decision-making from above, must be replaced by this idea. The New Left rejects the intellectual as a guiding and decision-making authority. Participants in the movement see themselves as grassroots-democratic, antiauthoritarian, antiorganizational, and antihierarchical. They believe the mobilization process should start "from below," via small groups that follow the theory of the construction of situations, and the limited violation of rules by breaking rules, with the express aim of changing the very rules of the rules. "What is interesting about your action," Sartre confesses to Cohn-Bendit on 20 May 1968, is that it puts "the imagination in power." "Even your imagination certainly has limits, but you have many more ideas than your fathers had."[35]

Antiauthoritarian action—challenging the rules of the rules—also grew out of avant-garde cultural influences. The journal *Situationistische Internationale* noted in 1959 that whoever constructs "situations" thereby "transforms his own nature at the same time by affecting and transforming external nature through his movement."[36] Antiauthoritarian action, understood as a "permanent learning process of those involved in the action,"[37] was also regarded by the antiauthoritarian New Left in the Federal Republic of Germany as the central factor in generating "moments of ego-strength" and encouraging individuals in the conviction that they could overthrow the system as a whole in future.[38] The antiauthoritarian maxim of action developed a unique dynamic of mobilization. After all, antiauthoritarian action could be carried out from within a multitude of institutions: from the family to the lecture hall to the courtroom. Reaction to provocative actions often revealed what activists suspected, that is, the potential for repression contained in the authoritarian institutions. The combination of individual and collective emancipation strategies—self-realization and self-administration—made the New Left special and attractive.

The construction of situations that speakers of the movement such as Daniel Cohn-Bendit (who was chased by French authorities to West Germany shortly after his interview with Sartre) and Rudi Dutschke admirably master drew the attention of the media to the actors. Within a short time they had become speakers and "stars," "icons" of the movement. The media rushed at them and, with their photos and reports, shaped the image of them in the movement. But the star cult staged by the mass media, now with regard to the two student activists, once more provoked critique of the movement. How do they understand the alternatives?

From "Charismatic Leader" to the Notion of "Temporary Leadership."
Critics within the SDS complain that newspapers and television have long since stopped talking about the larger movement, focusing rather only on Rudi Dutschke. This cult of personality does not fit with the movement's philosophy. "For many, the antiauthoritarian revolutionary was on his way to authoritarian behavior," Dutschke biographer Michaela Karl observed.[39] Dutschke defends himself against the accusation. In November 1967, he declares during the political magazine television show *Monitor* that "the movement had many Dutschkes" and that the antiauthoritarians did not need a chief ideologist. In January 1968 he argues further on the radio station Deutschlandfunk, referring to himself in the third person:

Dutschke is a mouthpiece of the extraparliamentary opposition. But it will not be absorbed into Dutschke, and the gentlemen will soon understand that, and that is also the opportunity of the future, because the movement does not stand or fall with a leader, it stands or falls with the self-activity of the people.[40]

Dutschke then determines to leave the Federal Republic for some time in order to work politically abroad. He wants too to put the guiding idea of a "temporary leadership" into practice, and thus to leave West Berlin. The suitcases are packed and already on their way to Chicago when three shots are fired at Dutschke on 11 April 1968.

Daniel Cohn-Bendit experiences the same challenge to his outstanding position as a symbolic figure of the May Movement. On 24 May, in the Sorbonne, he triumphantly celebrates his return to Paris despite all the border barriers set up by the French state to keep the "German anarchist" away. However, the next day, at a specially convened press conference of the 22 March Movement, he is no longer present. Instead, a collective appears and explains to the waiting journalists: "Cohn-Bendit—that's us." The journalists simply leave.[41] But, for the French activists, the change is critical. French authorities do not keep Cohn-Bendit away—but his fellow activists do.

The Critical Intelligentsia as "Revolutionary Subject." According to émigré political philosopher Hannah Arendt, the New Left is characterized by a "stock of trust in the possibility of changing the world through action" that has not yet been used up. From New York, where Arendt lives at the time, she attentively follows the development of protest movements in all three, the United States, the FRG, and France.[42] In 1968, the historical image of the New Left thus once again reflects the idea of being able to "make history," an idea that, emerging since 1780, has been a central element of modernity. The New Left inscribes itself into this tradition, declaring the young intelligentsia to be a revolutionary subject, convinced that it could accelerate history and set in motion processes of consciousness and mobilization in society. "It was a high feeling," German writer and activist Peter Schneider recalled in retrospect,

> that drove through the streets of Berlin like an intoxicating wind in those months. Everything seemed possible then, especially the impossible—and we, those carried by this wind, felt called by history itself to build another society, according to new rules.[43]

In Paris it was no different: "One lives here as if in a kind of state of intoxication," writes West German sociologist Elisabeth Lenk to her doctoral supervisor Theodor W. Adorno in May 1968.[44] To have occupied the Sorbonne and other universities, the Odéon Theatre in Paris, and also factories, and to have "conquered the word," is compared in Paris with the conquest of the Bastille in 1789.[45]

From Practice to the New Ideal-Typical Role Definition

During all these events, however, one notable observer was not in Paris, nor even in Europe, but far away in Tunis: that is, philosopher Michel Foucault. After the disintegration of the May Movement in France, he took it upon himself to bundle the characteristics of the new type of intellectual that emerged in the course of the activism and abstract them into a figure of the intellectual that quickly became indispensable to the sociology of the intellectual, specifically in consequence of '68: that is, the "specific intellectual." It was only at the beginning of the 1968/69 winter semester that Michel Foucault returned to France, to take up a professorship at the newly founded, experimental University of Paris 8, at Vincennes. As head of the Department of Philosophy, one of the most rebellious departments at Vincennes, he took part in some student demonstrations. But, as possible, he withdrew from the campus to the Bibliothèque Nationale (National Library) and prepared his application for the Collège de France, a highly prestigious, research-based institution in the heart of Paris. "I've had enough of it," he later explained "to be constantly surrounded by half-mad people."[46] According to his biographer Didier Eribon, he had not especially enjoyed close contact with the students at all. But when, through his partner Daniel Defert, students approached him with the request that he stand up for imprisoned Maoist students, he did not fend them off. He was not as committed as the students hope. He did not advocate for their comrades to be recognized as political prisoners. Still, he made the prison conditions of a minority (the 29 Maoists) the concern of the majority.

Michel Foucault and the GIP. Three letters represent the project: GIP (Groupe d'information sur les prisons, Information on Prisons Group). The group becomes a hallmark of the collective enterprise that, centered around Foucault, sparks a movement that can be counted among the successor movements of May '68. It was the GIP that turns the philosophy professor, now indeed at the Collège de France, into a "committed philosopher" (*philosophe engagé*). The group's mission is not to carry out an investigation itself but rather to convey information. Members do not talk about the prisoners but rather encourage the prisoners to speak for themselves. They do not inquire about conditions inside the prison from the outside but rather work to inspire the prisoners to raise questions themselves—thus making subjects out of research objects. The maxim of action "*Parole aux détenus*" ([Give] the word to the prisoners) suits the Maoists, who want to make the imprisonment and accusation of their comrades the starting point of a trial against society.

Parallel to the investigations of the GIP, Foucault now develops his concept of the "specific intellectual," which he distinguishes on the one hand from the universal intellectual, as represented by Jean-Paul Sartre, and on the other from the Marxist intellectual, as embodied by Louis Althusser, Foucault's mentor at the École Normale Supérieure. The specific intellectual, as Foucault defines him, is neither a bearer of general values nor a mediator of class consciousness. Rather, based on his professional competence, he acts as a mediator of information and knowledge, which he makes accessible as part of the broader "information systems."[47] Starting from a concept of power that emphasizes the ubiquity of power relations also outside the state and its apparatuses, Foucault sees the mandate of the intellectual in the 1970s as exposing the power system that blocks the "speaking" and "knowledge" of the workers. Gisèle Sapiro, who created a typology of intellectual interventions, places the "specific intellectuals" in the tradition of the expert of counterpower, who makes his knowledge available not to the rulers but to the ruled, who have been deprived of the means to express themselves.[48] How can such a mandate be obtained, and how can it be exercised?

Naomi Klein and the Anti-/Alterglobalization Movement

The globalization-critical movement, of which Naomi Klein is regarded as a spokeswoman, is a transnational movement, the networks and partial movements of which are not directed against the government of a nation-state but rather against "power-holders in at least one state other than their own or against an international institution, or a multinational economic actor."[49] The movement emerged after the end of the Cold War, parallel to the worldwide liberalization of trade and the global dissemination of new information and communication technologies. Antihierarchical, grassroots-democratic, horizontally organized, and consensus-oriented, the movement does not dislike intellectuals in its ranks but denies them a leading or guiding role.[50] For the majority of globalization critics, the intellectual as a pioneering Marxist party cadre, who celebrated his comeback in the process of the decay of the transnational movement of 1968, is just as much a part of the past as is the universal intellectual.[51] Naomi Klein has taken this cognitive structure of the movement into account in self-descriptions of her own role. She firmly rejects the attribution of being a "pioneer" or "leader" of the movement,[52] or of being a "thought leader" or even a "utopian thinker."[53] As an intellectual, as she explained after the publication of her first book, *No Logo: Taking Aim at the Brand Bullies* (1999), she does not want to present movements with ready-made ideas for solutions but rather intends to "advocate for more space so that people can therefore develop their own solutions."[54] She becomes the spokeswoman for a movement without ever having been commissioned or elected.[55] How does she do that?

Klein spent four years researching the practices of global players and the alternatives of corporate critics before publishing *No Logo*. At that time, she did not have a university degree. Klein had studied English and philosophy but had interrupted her studies, then dropped out, in order to conduct her own research as a freelance journalist. When the manuscript of her study on "global players" was at press, the groups and networks of corporate-critical resistance she visited and interviewed achieved a breakthrough in public perception, through the blockade of the World Trade Organization conference in Seattle, Washington, on 30 November 1999. The spectacular protest actions of the corporate critics, which led to the imposition of a state of emergency in Seattle, prepared the groundwork for the reception of her book, which is then characterized by the *New York Times* as the "Bible of Movement." The British newspaper *The Observer* even calls the book "the new *Capital.*"[56] *Time* magazine ranked *No Logo* among the best one hundred nonfiction books written since 1923. The author becomes the "star of anti-globalisation activists" (*Die Zeit*), although she has never directly taken part in the movement. "Marches depress me. . . . Going for a walk and chanting—I get nothing out of it," she explains in an interview with the *New Yorker* magazine.[57] She knows what she is talking about. As the daughter of opponents of the Vietnam War who left the United States in 1967 and sought refuge in Canada, Naomi Klein, born in 1970, grew up in a home marked by the spirit of the 1968 movement and its forms of action.

Two and a half years after *No Logo* appeared in the United States in 2000 and first gained wide acclaim, she traveled through twenty-two countries, giving lecture after lecture. Now convinced that only social movements could bring about social change, she accepts the challenge of being the movement's spokesperson. In 2002, she published her notes, speeches, and articles together in the book *Fences and Windows: Dispatches from the Front Lines of the Globalization Debate*.[58] She characterizes the collection of texts as a small part of a massive grassroots democratic exchange of information that has encouraged a myriad of people who are not economists, international commercial lawyers or patent experts to participate in the debate about the future of the world economy.[59]

From an analytical point of view, she claims that, based on her expertise, she has given others access to information, made them speak, and thus made the unsaid sayable. Naomi Klein conveys information into the globalization-critical movement as well as information about the movement out to the public. The author of *No Logo* gives a face to the alterglobalization movement that spread rapidly in all Western industrialized countries after the critical events of Seattle and at the same time presents its concerns as extending far beyond national borders.

While criticizing global players, the book itself is published and protected by a global player: Knopf Edition, an imprint of the Bertelsmann Mega-Edition. Its worldwide distribution is promoted by two literary agents from Westword Creative Artists, who successfully got the book published in Danish, Finnish, French, German, Italian, Japanese, Norwegian, Swedish, and Spanish editions, as well as in New Zealand, only a year after its publication in Canada. To date, *No Logo* has been translated into twenty-five languages and has sold over a million copies.

As a bestselling author, Naomi Klein is supported by experienced editors and a small alternative think tank, consisting of members of her family, long-standing academic staff, and experts from the movement critical of globalization. She supports her analyses, as shown also through a second book, *The Shock Doctrine: The Rise of Disaster Capitalism* (2007), by referring to information from human rights organizations, as well as from committees and submovements that work with the movement critical of globalization.

From an analytical point of view, then, Naomi Klein is committed to a "politics of perception," the cognitive subversion of the established order through alternative guiding ideas and principles of order that open up a new worldview.[60] She works collectively but claims sole responsibility for her books. Book awards and honors, including an honorary doctorate in civil law from the University of Halifax in 2007, the Gloria Steinem Chair in Media, Culture, and Feminist Studies at Rutgers University in 2018, and the Outstanding Lifetime Achievement Award for Humanism in Culture (Rushdie Award-Harvard) 2020, show the worldwide recognition Naomi Klein enjoys. As an expert on countervailing power, she interprets the role of the intellectual in the twenty-first century in an innovative, but also obstinate and resistant, way and refutes Lyotard's thesis of the death of the intellectual, for whom it is only a matter of digging the grave. This example shows that the '68 movement and, in turn, the new social movements that followed have contributed to a redefinition of the role of the intellectual in the long term through their critique and alternative models of intervention.

Ingrid Gilcher-Holtey is professor emeritus of contemporary history at Bielefeld University. Her research focuses on the history of intellectuals and the history of the new social movements, in particular the transnational movements of 1968—as well as the history and sociology of the literary field in Germany. Recent publications include the edited volume *A Revolution of Perception? Consequences and Echoes of 1968* and the monograph *1968: Vom Ereignis zum Mythos*.

Notes

1. See Ingrid Gilcher-Holtey, *"Die Phantasie an die Macht": Mai 68 in Frankreich* (Frankfurt a.M.: Suhrkamp, 2001), 9–10. This chapter is a revised version of Ingrid Gilcher-Holtey, "Dekonstruktion und Neudefinition eines Rollenmodells: Von der Intellektuellenkritik der 68er-Bewegung zum Typus des 'spezifischen Intellektuellen,'" in *Warten auf Gordot? Intellektuelle seit den 1960er Jahren*, ed. Ingrid Gilcher-Holtey und Eva Oberloskamp (Oldenbourg: De Gruyter, 2020), 83–100. It appears here with the permission of De Gruyter Oldenbourg.
2. Jean-Paul Sartre et al., *Der Intellektuelle als Revolutionär* (Reinbek: Rowohlt, 1976), 49.
3. Ibid., 50.
4. Ingrid Gilcher-Holtey, "Nachwort," in *Voltair: Die Affäre Calas*, ed. Ingrid Gilcher-Holtey (Berlin: Insel, 2010), 251–94.
5. Luc Boltanski and Elisabeth Claverie, "Affaires, Scandales et Grandes Causes," in *Affaires, Scandales et Grandes Causes: De Socrate à Pinochet*, ed. Luc Boltanski et al. (Paris: Stock 2007), 397.
6. Hans-Magnus Enzensberger, "Berliner Gemeinplätze," *Das Kursbuch* 11 (January 1968): 157.
7. Hans-Magnus Enzensberger, "'Sie hatten nie eine politische Forderung': Ein Gespräch mit dem Schriftsteller Hans Magnus Enzensberger über die Hintergründe der RAF," in *Die RAF und der linke Terrorismus*, ed. Wolfgang Kraushaar (Hamburg: Hamburger Edition, 2006), 2:1407.
8. Maurice Blanchot, *Les intellectuels en question: Ébauche d'une reflexion* (Paris: Fourbis, 1996).
9. Régis Debray, *i.f. suite et fin* (Paris: Gallimard, 2000), 17.
10. François Lyotard, *Das Grabmal des Intellektuellen* (Graz: Passagen Verlag, 1985).
11. Hans-Magnus Enzensberger, "Offener Brief an den Präsidenten der Wesleyan University Mr. Edwin D. Etherington," *Die Zeit*, 31 January 1968, retrieved 24 October 2019 from https://www.zeit.de/1968/09/index.
12. Hans-Magnus Enzensberger, "Bewußtseins-Industrie," in *Einzelheiten I* (Frankfurt a.M.: Suhrkamp 1962).
13. Ibid., 4.

14. Hans-Magnus Enzensberger, "Gemeinplätze die neueste Literatur betreffend," *Das Kursbuch* 15 (November 1968): 188.
15. Hans-Werner Richter, *Briefe*, ed. Sabine Cofalla (Munich: Hanser, 1997), 662f.
16. Enzensberger, "Gemeinplätze," 188.
17. Enzensberger, "Sie hatten nie eine politische Forderung," 1407.
18. Walter Benjamin, "Der Sürrealismus: Die letzte Momentaufnahme der europäischen Intelligenz," in *Gesammelte Schriften*, vol. II/1, ed. Rolf Tiedemann and Hermann Schweppenhäuser (Frankfurt a.M., 1977), 295–310.
19. Hans Magnus Enzensberger, "Klare Entscheidungen und trübe Aussichten: 1967," in Über Hans Magnus Enzensberger, ed. Joachim Schickele (Frankfurt a.m.: Suhrkamp, 1970), 230.
20. Jean-Paul Sartre, *Der Idiot der Familie: Gustave Flaubert 1821–1857*, vols. 1–4 (Reinbek bei Hamburg: Rowohlt, 1977–80).
21. Jean-Paul Sartre, *Was ist Literatur?* (Reinbek bei Hamburg: Rowohlt, 1981), 26.
22. Sartre, *Was ist Literatur?* 26.
23. Jean-Paul Sartre, "Justiz und Staat," in *Plädoyer für die Intellektuellen: Interviews, Artikel; Reden 1950–1973*, ed. Jean-Paul Sartre (Reinbek bei Hamburg: Rowohlt, 1995), 469.
24. Ibid., 469
25. Ibid., 466.
26. Sartre et al., *Der Intellektuelle*, 739.
27. Peter Schneider, "Bildnis eines melancholischen Entdeckers," in *Der Zorn altert, die Ironie ist unsterblich: Über Hans Magnus Enzensberger*, ed. Rainer Wieland (Frankfurt a.M.: Suhrkamp, 1999), 137–45.
28. Gaston Salvatore, "Vom Luxus der Freundschaft," in *Der Zorn altert, die Ironie ist unsterblich: Über Hans Magnus Enzensberger*, ed. Rainer Wieland (Frankfurt a.M.: Suhrkamp, 1999), 131.
29. Ingrid Gilcher-Holtey, "Konkurrenz um den 'wahren' Intellektuellen: Intellektuelle Rollenverständnisse aus zeithistorischer Sicht," in *Intellektuelle in der Bundesrepublik Deutschland, Verschiebungen im politischen Feld der 1960er und 1970er Jahre*, ed. Thomas Kroll and Tilmann Reitz (Göttingen: Vandenhoeck & Ruprecht, 2013), 21–40. Ingrid Gilcher-Holtey, "Der 'spezifische Intellektuelle': Michel Foucault," in *Eingreifendes Denken: Die Wirkungschancen von Intellektuellen* (Weilerswist: Velbrück, 2007), 359–91.
30. Gisèle Sapiro, "Modèles d'intervention politique des intellectuels: Le cas français," *Actes de la recherche en sciences sociales* 1 (2009): 9–31.
31. Ibid., 21.
32. See Bazon Brock, "Affirmation," retrieved 11 June 2019 from https://bazonbrock.de/bazonbrock/themen/affirmation/.
33. Regina-Marina Dackweiler, "Feministische Intellektuelle: Kollektive Gesellschaftskritik und Gesellschaftsutopien der Neuen Frauenbewegung Ende der 1960er Jahre," *Intellektuelle in der Bundesrepublik Deutschland, Verschiebungen im politischen Feld der 1960er und 1970er Jahre*, ed. Thomas Kroll and Tillman Reitz (Göttingen: Vandenhoeck & Ruprecht, 2013), 87–102
34. Hans-Werner Henze, *Reiselieder mit Quinten: Autobiographische Mitteilungen 1926–1995* (Frankfurt a.M.: Fischer, 1996), 312f.

35. Sartre, "Die Phantasie an die Macht." The plural "fathers" refers precisely to the larger group of activists.
36. "Der Sinn im Absterben der Kunst," *Situationistische Internationale* 1 (1959): 82.
37. Rudi Dutschke, *Mein langer Marsch: Reden, Schriften und Tagebücher aus zwanzig Jahren*, ed. Gretchen Dutschke-Klotz et al. (Reinbek bei Hamburg: Rowohlt, 1980), 3.
38. Rudi Dutschke, "Die Widersprüche des Spätkapitalismus, die antiautoritären Studenten und ihr Verhältnis zur Dritten Welt," in *Rebellion der Studenten oder Die neue Opposition*, ed. Uwe Bergmann et al. (Reinbek bei Hamburg: Rowohlt, 1968), 76.
39. Michaela Karl, *Rudi Dutschke: Revolutionär ohne Revolution* (Frankfurt a.M.: Verlag Neue Kritik, 2003), 200.
40. Dutschke, "Die Widersprüche des Spätkapitalismus."
41. Daniel Cohn-Bendit, *Der große Bazar* (Munich: Trikont, 1975), 50; Gilcher-Holtey, *Die Phantasie an die Macht*, 456.
42. Hannah Arendt, *Macht und Gewalt* (Munich: Piper, 1970), 19.
43. Peter Schneider, *Rebellion und Wahn: Mein "68"* (Köln: Kiepenheuer & Witsch, 2008); "Der Sinn im Absterben der Kunst," *Situationistische Internationale* 1 (1959): 78–85.
44. Elisabeth Lenk, "Brief an Theodor W. Adorno: 15. May 1968," in *Das Leben ändern, die Welt verändern: 1968. Dokumente und Berichte*, ed. Lutz Schulenburg (Hamburg: Nautilus, 1978), 211.
45. Michel de Certeau, *La prise de parole: Pour une nouvelle culture* (Paris: Desclée de Brouwer, 1968).
46. Didier Eribon, *Michel Foucault: Eine Biographie* (Frankfurt a.M.: Suhrkamp, 1991), 296.
47. Michel Foucault, "Die politische Funktion des Intellektuellen," in *Dits et Ecrits: Schriften*, vol. 3: *1976–1979*, ed. Daniel Denfert and François Ewald (Frankfurt a.M.: Suhrkamp 2003), 145–63; Ingrid Gilcher-Holtey, "Der 'spezifische Intellektuelle': Michel Foucault," in *Eingreifendes Denken: Die Wirkungschancen von Intellektuellen* (Weilerswist: Velbrück, 2007), 359–91.
48. Sapiro, "Modèles," 28
49. Sidney Tarrow, "Transnational Politics: Contestation and Institutions in International Politics," *Annual Review of Political Science* 4 (2001): 11
50. Steffen Vogel, *Abtritt der Avantgarde? Die Demokratisierung des Intellektuellen in der globalisierungskritischen Bewegung* (Marburg: Tectum, 2012): 107.
51. David Graeber, "The Twilight of Vangardism," in *Possibilities: Essays on Hierarchy, Rebellion and Desire* (Oakland, CA: AK Press, 2007), 301–12.
52. Naomi Klein, "Keine Macht den Marken! Naomi Klein im Gespräch mit Claudia Riedel," *Die Zeit* (15 March 2001), retrieved 10 June 2019 from https://www.zeit.de/2001/12/200112 aussehen_no_lo.xml.
53. Larissa MacFarquhar, "Outside Agitator: Naomi Klein and the New Left," *New Yorker*, 8 December 2008, retrieved 10 June 2019 from https://www.newyorker.com/magazine/2008/12/08/outside-agitator.
54. Naomi Klein, "Die Folterkeller der Globalisierung: Naomi Klein im Gespräch mit Thomas Fischermann," *Die Zeit*, 7 September 2007, retrieved 10 June 2019 from https://www.zeit.de/online/2007/37/naomi-klein-interview.

55. Ingrid Gilcher-Holtey, "Naomi Klein & Co: Intellektuelle in der Globalisierungskritischen Bewegung," *Eingreifende Denkerinnen: Weibliche Intellektuelle 20. und 21. Jahrhundert*, ed. Ingrid Gilcher-Holtey (Tübingen: Mohr Siebeck, 2015), 213–28
56. Klein, "Keine Macht den Marken!"
57. MacFarquhar, "Outside Agitator."
58. Noami Klein, Über Zäune und Mauern: *Berichte von der Globalisierungsfront* (Frankfurt a.M.: Fischer, 2003); original English edition: *Fences and Windows: Dispatches from the Front Lines of the Globalization Debate* (New York: Picador, 2003), 13.
59. Klein, Über Zäune und Mauern, 16–17.
60. Pierre Bourdieu, *Meditationen: Zur Kritik der scholastischen Vernunft* (Frankfurt a.M. Suhrkamp, 2001), 237–38.

Select Bibliography

Arendt, Hannah. *Macht und Gewalt*. München: Piper, 1970.

Benjamin, Walter. "Der Sürrealismus, Die letzte Momentaufnahme der europäischen Intelligenz." In *Gesammelte Schriften*, vol. II/1, ed. Rolf Tiedemann and Hermann Schweppenhäuser, 295–310. Frankfurt a.M.: Suhrkamp, 1977.

Blanchot, Maurice. *Les intellectuels en question. Ébauche d'une réflexion*. Paris: Fourbis, 1996.

Boltanski, Luc, and Elisabeth Claverie. "Affaires, Scandales et Grandes Causes." In *Affaires, Scandales et Grandes Causes: De Socrate à Pinochet*, ed. Luc Boltanski et al., 395–453. Paris: Stock, 2007.

Bourdieu, Pierre. *Meditationen: Zur Kritik der scholastischen Vernunft*. Frankfurt a.M. Suhrkamp, 2001.

Brock, Bazon. "Affirmation." Retrieved 6 November 2009 from https://bazonbrock.de/bazonbrock/themen/affirmation/.

Certeau, Michel de. *La prise de parole: Pour une nouvelle culture*. Paris: Desclée de Brouwer, 1968.

Cohn-Bendit, Daniel. *Der große Bazar*. München: Trikont, 1975.

Dackweiler, Regina-Marina. "Feministische Intellektuelle: Kollektive Gesellschaftskritik und Gesellschaftsutopien der Neuen Frauenbewegung Ende der 1960er Jahre." In *Intellektuelle in der Bundesrepublik Deutschland, Verschiebungen im politischen Feld der 1960er und 1970er Jahre*, ed. Thomas Kroll and Tillman Reitz, 87–102. Göttingen: Vandenhoeck & Ruprecht, 2013.

———. "Bewußtseins-Industrie." In *Einzelheiten I*, 1–7. Frankfurt a.M.: Suhrkamp 1962.

———. "Berliner Gemeinplätze." In *Das Kursbuch* 11 (January 1968): 151–69.

———. Offener Brief an den Präsidenten der Wesleyan University Mr. Edwin D. Etherington. 31 January 1968. In Über Hans Magnus Enzensberger, ed. Joachim Schickel, 233–238. Frankfurt a.M.: Suhrkamp, 1970. Retrieved 24 October 2019 from https://www.zeit.de/1968/09/index.

———. "Gemeinplätze die neueste Literatur betreffend." In *Das Kursbuch* 15 (November 1968): 187–97.

———. "Klare Entscheidungen und trübe Aussichten: 1967." In Über Hans Magnus Enzensberger, ed. Joachim Schickel, 225–332. Frankfurt a.M.: Suhrkamp, 1970.

———. "'Sie hatten nie eine politische Forderung': Ein Gespräch mit dem Schriftsteller Hans Magnus Enzensberger über die Hintergründe der RAF." In ed. *Die RAF und der linke Terrorismus*, edited by Wolfgang Kraushaar, 2:1392–411. Hamburg: Hamburger Edition, 2006.

Debray, Régis. *i.f. suite et fin*. Paris: Gallimard, 2000.

Dutschke, Rudi. "Die Widersprüche des Spätkapitalismus, die antiautoritären Studenten und ihr Verhältnis zur Dritten Welt." In *Rebellion der Studenten oder Die neue Opposition*, ed. Uwe Bergmann et al., 33–93. Reinbek bei Hamburg: Rowohlt, 1968.

———. Rede in Baden-Baden, Deutschlandfun. 5th January 1968. Cited in Michaela Karl, *Rudi Dutschke: Revolutionär ohne Revolution*, 201. Frankfurt a.M.: Verlag Neue Kritik, 2003.

———. *Mein langer Marsch: Reden, Schriften und Tagebücher aus zwanzig Jahren*. Edited by Gretchen Dutschke-Klotz et al. Reinbek bei Hamburg: Rowohlt, 1980.

Eribon, Didier. *Michel Foucault: Eine Biographie*. Frankfurt a.M.: Suhrkamp, 1991.

Foucault, Michel. "Die politische Funktion des Intellektuellen." In *Dits et Ecrits: Schriften*. Vol. 3: *1976–1979*, edited by Daniel Denfert and François Ewald, 145–63. Frankfurt a.M.: Suhrkamp, 2003.

Gilcher-Holtey, Ingrid. *"Die Phantasie an die Macht": Mai 68 in Frankreich*. 2nd ed. Frankfurt a.M.: Suhrkamp, 2001.

———. "Der 'spezifische Intellektuelle': Michel Foucault." In *Eingreifendes Denken: Die Wirkungschancen von Intellektuellen*, 359–91. Weilerswist: Velbrück, 2007.

———. "Nachwort." In *Voltair: Die Affäre Calas*, edited by Ingrid Gilcher-Holtey, 251–94. Berlin: Insel, 2010.

———. "Konkurrenz um den 'wahren' Intellektuellen: Intellektuelle Rollenverständnisse aus zeithistorischer Sicht." In *Intellektuelle in der Bundesrepublik Deutschland, Verschiebungen im politischen Feld der 1960er und 1970er Jahre*, edited by Thomas Kroll and Tilmann Reitz, 21–40. Göttingen: Vandenhoeck & Ruprecht, 2013.

———. "Naomi Klein & Co: Intellektuelle in der Globalisierungskritischen Bewegung." In *Eingreifende Denkerinnen: Weibliche Intellektuelle 20. und 21. Jahrhundert*, edited by Ingrid Gilcher-Holtey, 213–28. Tübingen: Mohr Siebeck, 2015.

Graeber, David. "The Twilight of Vangardism." In *Possibilities: Essays on Hierarchy, Rebellion and Desire*, 301–12. Oakland, CA: AK Press, 2007.

Henze, Hans-Werner. *Reiselieder mit Quinten: Autobiographische Mitteilungen 1926–1995*. Frankfurt a.M.: Fischer, 1996.

Karl, Michaela. *Rudi Dutschke: Revolutionär ohne Revolution*. Frankfurt a.M.: Verlag Neue Kritik, 2003.

Klein, Naomi. "Keine Macht den Marken! Naomi Klein im Gespräch mit Claudia Riedel." In *Die Zeit*, 15 March 2001. Retrieved 10 June 2019 from https://www.zeit.de/2001/12/200112 aussehen_no_lo.xml.

———. *Über Zäune und Mauern: Berichte von der Globalisierungsfront*, Frankfurt a.M.: Fischer, 2003. Original English edition: *Fences and Windows: Dispatches from the Front Lines of the Globalization Debate*. New York: Picador, 2002.

———. "Die Folterkeller der Globalisierung: Naomi Klein im Gespräch mit Thomas Fischermann." In *Die Zeit*, 7 September 2007. Retrieved 10 June 2019 from https://www.zeit.de/online/2007/37/naomi-klein-interview.

Kroll, Thomas, and Tillmann Reitz, eds. *Intellektuelle in der Bundesrepublik Deutschland, Verschiebungen im politischen Feld der 1960er und 1970er Jahre*. Göttingen: Vandenhoeck & Ruprecht, 2013.

Lenk, Elisabeth. "Brief an Theodor W. Adorno: 15. May 1968." In *Das Leben ändern, die Welt verändern: 1968. Dokumente und Berichte*, edited by Lutz Schulenburg, 211–13. Hamburg: Nautilus, 1978.

Lyotard, François. *Das Grabmal des Intellektuellen*. Graz: Passagen Verlag, 1985.

MacFarquhar, Larissa. "Outside Agitator: Naomi Klein and the New Left." *New Yorker*, 8 December 2008. Retrieved 10 June 2019 from https://www.newyorker.com/magazine/2008/12/08/outside-agitator.

Rammstedt, Otthein. *Soziale Bewegungen*. Frankfurt a.M.: Suhrkamp, 1978.

Richter, Hans-Werner. *Briefe*. Edited by Sabine Cofalla. München: Hanser, 1997.

Salvatore, Gaston. "Vom Luxus der Freundschaft." In *Der Zorn altert, die Ironie ist unsterblich: Über Hans Magnus Enzensberger*, edited by Rainer Wieland, 130–36. Frankfurt a.M.: Suhrkamp, 1999.

Sapiro, Gisèle. "Modèles d'intervention politique des intelectuels: Le cas français." In *Actes de la recherche en sciences sociales* 1 (2009): 9–31.

Sartre, Jean-Paul. "'Die Phantasie an die Macht': Jean-Paul Sartre; Ein Gespräch mit Daniel Cohn-Bendit." 1968. Retrieved 29 May 2019 from https://www.zeit.de/1968/22/die-phantasie-an-die-macht.

———. *Der Idiot der Familie: Gustave Flaubert 1821–1857*, vols. 1–4. Reinbek bei Hamburg: Rowohlt, 1977–80.

———. *Was ist Literatur?* Reinbek bei Hamburg: Rowohlt, 1981.

———. "Justiz und Staat." In *Plädoyer für die Intellektuellen: Interviews, Artikel; Reden 1950–1973*, edited by Jean Paul Sartre, 457–79. Reinbek bei Hamburg: Rowohlt, 1995.

Sartre, Jean-Paul, et al. *Der Intellektuelle als Revolutionär*. Reinbek: Rowohlt, 1976.

Schneider, Peter. "Bildnis eines melancholischen Entdeckers." In *Der Zorn altert, die Ironie ist unsterblich: Über Hans Magnus Enzensberger*, edited by Rainer Wieland, 137–45. Frankfurt a.M.: Suhrkamp, 1999.

———. *Rebellion und Wahn: Mein "68."* Köln: Kiepenheuer & Witsch, 2008.

Situationistische Internationale. "Der Sinn im Absterben der Kunst." In *Situationistische Internationale* 1 (1959): 78–85.

Tarrow, Sidney. "Transnational Politics: Contestation and Institutions in International Politics." *Annual Review of Political Science* 4 (2001): 1–20.

Vogel, Steffen. *Abtritt der Avantgarde? Die Demokratisierung des Intellektuellen in der globalisierungskritischen Bewegung*. Marburg: Tectum, 2012.

Chapter 4

Fighting with Feelings

Experiences of Protest and Emotional Practices in the Autonomous West German Women's Movement during the 1970s and 1980s

Bernhard Gotto

Half a century after the beginning of the second wave of the women's liberation movement, there seems to be no doubt that feminists' collective protest and action fundamentally changed West German society. In many recent accounts of German history after World War II, an impressive list of outcomes is attributed to the women's movement, at least in the long run. Feminists challenged the status and the self-perception of women and men; they introduced the issue of gender inequality to the political agenda; they extended the scope of the political by blurring the distinction between "public" and "private"; and they transformed the political and organizational culture in political parties and trade unions, as well as in other societal formations.[1] Recently, Frank Biess has drawn attention to another change that is closely related to the women's movement. Feminism accelerated the transformation of West German emotional culture because it enforced emotional expressivity as a cultural norm.[2] Biess draws on the enormous success of a book by Verena Stefan, who outlined a new female subjectivity in her novel *Häutungen*. When the book was published, however, it was sharply criticized by Gabriele Goettle and Brigitte Claassen, the editors of the Berlin feminist magazine *Die Schwarze Botin*, for this very reason: "tons of junky sentimental feelings" would not help the women's liberation.[3]

While in retrospect the emotional impact of the women's movement on West German society constitutes one of its historical achievements, it was highly controversial among feminists how feelings should influence their political project. This chapter traces back autonomous feminists' discussions about their feelings and how they practiced them. Unquestionably, the importance of emotional politics for the entire alternative left in West Germany cannot be overestimated. Joachim Häberlen and Sven Reichardt demonstrated in landmark studies that countercultural identity and political activity in the alternative milieu were essentially determined by emotions.[4] For this reason, this chapter focuses on the autonomous feminist movement, because, besides independence from men and state institutions, a particular emotional style was its distinguishing feature. However, autonomous feminism was not strictly segregated from traditional women's movement groups; feminists "defined and practiced autonomy in wide-ranging ways."[5]

From the mid-1970s onward, the various currents of the women's movement increasingly took on a life of their own. Following Ilse Lenz, a "phase of awareness and articulation (1968–1975)" was followed by a "phase of pluralization and consolidation (1976–1980)"; similarly, Myra Marx Ferree contrasts the "autonomous feminist mobilization 1968–1978" with the "women's project movement, 1975–1985."[6] More recent studies, on the other hand, emphasize that despite the many fractures and divisions, certain practices and themes, such as women's bodies, linked different groups and actors.[7] Emotions and emotional practices may have had a similar effect.

Hence, the main question of this chapter is, to what extent did feelings have an integrating or dividing effect in the period between the mid-1970s and the mid-1980s? The first section analyzes the emotional norms applicable to autonomous feminism. It argues that the feminist emotional regime—this means, according to William Reddy, "the set of normative emotions and the official rituals, practices, and emotives, that express and inculcate them"[8]—promoted a profound emotional transformation in order to liberate women. The second section focuses on functions of emotion for the political practice of the autonomous women's movement. It examines how feminists discussed their emotions as a measurement of the feminist movement's condition. The third section centers on emotional practices that autonomous feminists employed in their day-to-day political activities. It argues that these practices served to counter the contradictions and setbacks that autonomous feminists experienced. This chapter thus examines both continuities and ruptures in feminist practices after 1968 and explores the extent to which women practiced the personal as political.

Feeling like a Feminist

Each woman who joined a local feminist group in West Germany in the 1970s and 1980s learned to reevaluate herself and society. She discovered that the private sphere was political, that her personal experiences of sexism, discrimination, and violence resulted from overall patriarchal oppression. She became familiar with various strands of feminist theory. Most importantly, she learned that she could act against oppression and that change began with each individual woman.

Feelings played a central role, and emotion work—the act of altering emotional experience and expression in degree or quality[9]—became a key technique of feminist initiation. The right way to feel was crucial for two reasons: first, because feelings belonged to the realm of the private. The women's movement challenged this attribution with the slogan "the personal is political."[10] In addition, feelings were part of the gender character that conveyed social and cultural inferiority. From a feminist point of view, emotional distress resulted therefore from the patriarchal oppression that they criticized. Second, the self figured as a starting point and the target of political activism.[11] Inspired by ideas of a New Left, many activist women "set themselves as both the agents and subjects of change."[12] This focus on the self went far beyond the women's liberation movement.[13] An unprecedented revaluation of subjectivity and emotions was evident throughout the alternative milieu, encompassing some three or four million mostly young people sharing a common countercultural lifestyle.[14] The deliberate, almost ceaseless engagement with one's own feelings gained more and more importance from the mid-1960s, even in many segments of the larger society.[15] But only the alternative left set up a "political project of emotional transformation."[16]

Feminist women shared some of the emotional assumptions of the broader alternative left. The common ground was suffering: like most leftists, feminist women felt emotionally damaged by capitalism. To overcome boredom, fear, and loneliness, it was necessary to speak out negative feelings. But this was only the first step on the path of emotional healing. Admitting, exploring, and practicing feelings was the supreme norm, a norm that produced significant pressure for quite a few leftists.[17]

Feminist women developed their own version of this emotional regime. It was shaped by a double distinction. On the one hand, feminists demarcated themselves from leftist men, denouncing the latter's machismo as a prolongation of patriarchal oppression.[18] Leftist men, in fact, used certain emotional attributions to subordinate women in gender-mixed groups. The famous "cut the cock off" pamphlet of the Frankfurt "Chicks' Council" (*Weiberrat*) identified such discriminatory labels in November 1968. If women did not conform to an inferior role, they were considered to be "frustrated, hysterical, uptight, asexual, lesbian, frigid . . . , hard, virile, sharp, bitchy."[19] Many activist women had to struggle against the stereotype of the frustrated women's libber.[20] The stereotype claimed that women committed themselves politically in order to compensate for their unsatisfied sexual desires. In contrast, the feminist emotional self was based on a self-determined sexuality.[21] Consequently, women's self-descriptions included embrace of sexual pleasure, tenderness, exuberance, and joy.

On the other hand, feminists designated themselves as a counterimage to the common stereotype of female emotional qualities. Feminists claimed to be the opposite of the gentle, empathetic, selfless, and reserved beings into which patriarchy had deformed women. Attitudes with masculine connotations, such as nonchalance and self-assurance, were regarded as evidence of an advanced feminist consciousness. Especially in the autonomous women's groups, anger and rage were considered appropriate sentiments.[22] In the US women's lib movement and beyond, the "close association between feminism and anger is embodied in the 'angry feminist.'"[23] This attitude, however, was reserved by feminists for the patriarchal outside world. Within the feminist scene, women were to be treated like sisters. Feminists should express solidarity, warmth, and tenderness to their sisters. The claim "sisterhood is powerful" even made this a prerequisite for successful political action.

There were two types of experiences that profoundly affected the emotional regime of women engaging in local women's circles: consciousness raising (CR) groups and the euphoria of the earliest days of activism. Both forms occurred mostly at the onset of feminist trajectories. CR groups emerged in West Germany starting in the early 1970s, but the idea originated in the American women's movement. Kathie Sarachild had presented the concept on 27 November 1968 at the First National Women's Liberation Conference outside Chicago. Emotional work was at its center: "We always stay in touch with our feelings. . . . In our groups, let's share our feelings and pool them. Let's let ourselves go and see where our feelings lead us. Our feelings will lead us to ideas and then to new action."[24] Especially "negative" feelings should be addressed and worked on in the groups: dissatisfaction, feelings of inferiority, humiliation, fear, and isolation. By sharing their feelings, the women were to learn that they were not to blame for such feelings, but also that their emotional suffering stemmed from patriarchal oppression. Moreover, women practiced the "correct" emotional response. Group members would experience encouragement and comfort. In place of low spirits and discouragement, women substituted anger and self-confidence. Numerous reports in the local women's newspapers show that the desired effects actually occurred.[25] Participants reported that their self-confidence had increased, and they felt relieved. Some went through phases of vehement rage, which they attributed to their new feminist consciousness. Of course, women also had bad experiences with CR groups.[26] Some women felt pressured by the guided self-revelation; conversely, frequent speakers discouraged the silent ones from speaking up. Some groups faded away because their members felt that talking about feelings was a stagnant process; others broke up because of internal differences. But for many early stage feminists, CR groups helped them in "aligning their own lives with the politics of Women's Liberation in order to lead increasingly authentic lives as movement members."[27]

It is impossible to quantify how many women found the CR groups a positive experience and how many did not emerge from them strengthened and with renewed political zeal. But, either way, the groups set feelings as a standard for integrating women into the feminist project. Women learned that their feelings were an indicator of the state of patriarchal society. They learned that they were a means of empowerment to change that condition. And they realized that their feelings also revealed something about the movement to which they were committed.

In CR groups, participants sought to purposively change their feelings in order to develop a new feminist self. They reinforced, moderated, or altered feelings using communicative and bodily practices designed to achieve this goal. In contrast, the enthusiasm of the beginning was not a result of a therapeutic intervention. The euphoria of the new beginning grew out of experience. Of course, the first encounter with the women's movement was not always encouraging. Some women who tried to join a women's group felt rejected and complained about disinterest in their participation.[28] But most of the women described their first steps as feminists as a transition into a wonderful new world.

The accounts of women whose career in the movement had just begun give revealing insights into their emotional state during their first weeks of engagement. They portrayed themselves as hopeful, enthusiastic, filled with vigor, and ready for action. After her first visit to the women's center of Göttingen, a woman wrote: "I have a feeling that I cannot describe in words, that I have not had for a long time. I am so happy that I finally came to the women's center."[29] Another woman in Coburg, a small town in Bavaria at the border with the German Democratic Republic, described her excitement after she had set up a feminist group: "I went home with the wonderful feeling that I am strong and can achieve anything that I intend to do."[30] In Heidelberg, a woman experienced the same delight during a "take back the night" demonstration: "I could scream, shout, whatever I wanted. I felt free! Just hug every woman!"[31]

The reports of gushy enthusiasm sometimes read like love letters. Certainly they were sincere, for shy, timid, or lonely women could experience a personal breakthrough due to their political activity. But, at the same time, these sources show how a feminist was "supposed to" feel. Their authors thus aligned themselves with the emotional regime of the women's movement.

Conflicting Experiences

In the April 1977 issue of the Hamburg-based women's magazine *Frauenzeitung des Frauenzentrums Hamburg*, two feminists complained about the attitude of some "sisters." Identified only by their first names, Heimke and Dorothea claimed to represent the thoughts and feelings of many feminists in Hamburg who had been active in that women's center for years. These women were, Heimke and Dorothea claimed, increasingly uneasy concerning the habits of fellow campaigners who had joined the women's center only recently. Heimke and Dorothea claimed a "greater sensibility" toward patriarchal oppression than the so-called "new women" because they had been involved in feminist activism for a much longer time. The more "experienced" women criticized those who had joined more recently because the latter were still living with men, lacked interest in exploring feminist theory, and did not fully engage in the fight for legalizing abortion. Moreover, the women who were active longer were tired of explaining trivial problems they had discussed many times before. Heimke and Dorothea remarked that their radical approach unsettled and repelled their "new" sisters of late, while, for their part, the "old women" felt "upset, frustrated, and disappointed."[32] That some of the fresh feminists still adopted "male norms," they concluded, hampered the progression of all toward an autonomous way of life.

The two women quoted above represented a group within the Hamburg feminist scene. But their observations and complaints were not specific to Hamburg. Other women also voiced them, in Berlin, Frankfurt, Freiburg, Cologne, and elsewhere.[33] In Frankfurt, after the first "take back the night" march in 1976, there was a clash of opposing experiences: while one participant praised the "closeness, warmth, trust" she had felt, another participant confronted her with her "aggressions and depressions," arguing that the demonstration was just a petty event.[34] Likewise, in many West German local feminist networks and organizations (women's centers often linked the various local initiatives), two groupings confronted each other, identifying themselves as "old" and "new" women. The boundary between them did not run along different feminist ideologies or—as far as the sources provide information about this—generations as defined by age cohort. What separated them were different experiences that led to divergent emotional evaluations. They were thus two "emotional communities," according to Barbara Rosenwein's terminology.[35] The magazine article was part of a debate that took place among different members and groups of the West German women's movement from the mid-1970s to the mid-1980s. The debate focused on changes within the women's movement, on the possibility of changing the society, and on the question of what it meant to be a "true" feminist. A pronounced strain of that debate concerned an alleged decline in the movement. Many of the "old" women claimed that the solidarity among women in the movement had shrunk; they saw signs of fragmentation and depoliticization, and they missed the overall will to challenge the patriarchal system. From this perspective, the women's movement was powerless, aimless, harmless, and even "rotten."[36]

These articles provoked prompt reactions. In Hamburg, several feminists who felt concerned by its sharp criticism retaliated with letters to the magazine editors published in the following issue.[37] One of them included a cartoon of two women facing each other, labeled respectively as "old" and "new." When the second tries to engage in critical discussion, the first replies by hammering the head of her opponent. The pain inflicted is not portrayed (as is usual in many comic strips) as stars around her head but rather as Venus symbols (see Figure 4.1).

Activists in other cities, including Munich, Göttingen, and Frankfurt, who also identified themselves as "new" women responded in a similar way. The authors reproached the older feminists as nostalgic and narrow-minded. They criticized their style of discussion as destructive and labeled their complaints as a sign of self-pity and sluggishness.[38] "New" women claimed that they had no intention of "clean[ing] up the spider webs in their old castles."[39] To some of them, the pioneer women even seemed like "grannies of the extra-parliamentary opposition,"[40] as one feminist in Hannover put it in 1986.

Historical research has often interpreted these conflicts as a clash of generations: the "founding mothers," born between 1940 and 1948, collided with the "project initiators," who were born in the mid-1950s.[41] The women

Figure 4.1. Conflicting Experiences. Source: FMT Z 125, Frauenzeitung des Frauenzentrum Hamburg, Nr. 12/13, Mai/June 1977, 9.

of the first generation, many of whom had participated in the protest movement of "1968," organized the first women's groups, magazines, and rallies; they got the campaign against the ban on abortion up and running; and they developed the basic strains of feministic theory. They dominated the movement until a new generation of women took the helm. These younger feminists in turn called for action with a significant, immediate impact on their lives and on society. They engaged in projects such as shelters for battered women, rape crisis centers, women's health clinics, antiauthoritarian childcare centers, and feminist bookstores. Although the sources evaluated in this chapter do not reveal much about the background of the feminists, it seems, however, that the age difference between "old" and "new" women did not place them in different generations. Many of those who deplored what they perceived as decline referred to themselves as "old fighter against § 218," "long-serving feminist" or "long-standing activist in the women's center."[42] They had in common that they had joined the movement years ago. But that did not necessarily mean that they were physically older than the so-called "new" women—there were some women who had found their way to the movement beyond the age of forty and were thus even older than other women who had been involved in the movement for ten years or more.[43] Their mismatch was not due to their age but grew out of the duration of their engagement. They differed in experience, and that difference affected their expectations for the future, their perception of the movement as a political force, and their emotional mindset being a part of it.

Much of the criticism of "old" women of the movement suggests that they had lost their initial enthusiasm—and that they yearned to get it back. In her analysis of the "rotten" movement in 1980, Marion, who had started her feminist career Mannheim in 1975, looked back to her early days of engagement. She remembered great solidarity, optimism, and enthusiasm. Against this background, the present situation seemed sober and gloomy, especially as, in Mannheim, the women's center had closed down as fewer and fewer women attended the meetings.[44] In the same issue of the local women's magazine, another feminist, Gisela, also highlighted this deterioration:

> A lot has changed in recent times; weariness and resignation are spreading. Solidarity has diminished: we no longer embrace each other because being together and doing things together brings us so much joy. The commitment of the women to each other has diminished; the euphoria, the feeling of happiness of the first women's festival, the first women's demonstration can no longer be created, despite all efforts.[45]

Similarly, some members of a women's group in Bremen that had dissolved in 1977 recalled their hopeful beginnings three years earlier: "We wanted to do something against the discrimination of women, although we did not know how. . . . But it was an awesome feeling when 30 women gathered to get personal and societal changes started. Very strong!"[46] Margot Poppenhusen is another example of a so-called "old woman." Born in 1939, she joined the Freiburg Women's Group in 1973. Three years later, she established the first women's center in Freiburg. In 1982 she cofounded the first Freiburg women's newspaper and remained on the editorial board until the journal ceased publication in 1990. In 1976/77 she participated in the first autonomous women's seminars at the sociological institute of the Freiburg University, and in 1977 she became involved with the first autonomous women's department in the student council. For three years she collaborated in the initiative for an equal opportunity office at the Freiburg city council. Later she worked as a freelance author and wrote a history of the women's movement in Freiburg. When she traced back its history for an article in 1983, however, she characterized earlier ambitions as "utopian" and visionary: "Which woman dares to dream of visions like this today? Oh, how modest we have become!"[47]

"Modesty" appeared here as a symptom of crisis, as did "weariness" and "resignation." It is striking how strongly allegedly collective feelings were present in the disputes between "old" and "new" women. Feminists who criticized a decline of the women's movement substantiated their analysis with observations about other feminists' emotional state. Some considered that heartiness, empathy, and solidarity among women in the movement had waned. But less "sisterhood" inevitably meant less political power. "We have become quite docile toward men's society and somewhat rough in dealing with ourselves," a Frankfurt feminist named Christa commented in 1976.[48] One year later, a Frankfurt group stated that optimism and verve had been lost and that the relationships of women in the movement had diminished in intensity. "In the movement's daily routine, coldness draws in,"[49] their analysis concluded. In the emotional regime of the alternative left, coldness was associated with the capitalist state, as were fear, boredom, and loneliness.[50] In the critical self-reflection of feminists, such negative feelings, supposedly common among feminists, served as alarm signals.

Such depictions bear a strong resemblance to the emotional atrophy that feminists attributed to patriarchy. Resignation, apathy, and coldness had been targeted by women in CR groups. If such feelings surfaced years later among feminists who had been committed to women's liberation for years, this was bound to seem like a final victory for patriarchy.

Another strand of criticism directed at the women's movement also claimed a change in the feminist emotional regime. The main argument here was that women in the movement were too concerned with their feelings. According to this view, a "new inwardness" and a "femininity mania" revealed a dangerous emotionalization of the women's movement. Emotions substituted for politics; the focus on the "authentic self" replaced the struggle to change society.[51] Some very prominent feminists supported this criticism, notably the editors of the two most influential feminist magazines in West Germany: Sibylle Plogstedt of *Courage* and Alice Schwarzer of *Emma*. In 1981, Schwarzer identified "sticky emotion," the "persistence in emotions," and the "retreat into the ghetto of 'femininity'" as signs that counterrevolution had broken out in the ranks of the women's movement.[52] Ilse Kokula, one of the leading LGBT activists in West Germany, ridiculed this tendency in a 1979 article about a seminar that centered on how women could become happy: "It was a really sweet atmosphere, like a girls' boarding school."[53]

Both versions of feminist criticism toward the women's movement were based on supposed collective feelings. Such descriptions were not mere fiction, but they generalized emotional currents that gripped only certain feminists. The sources evaluated in this chapter reveal a very heterogeneous emotional landscape. Joy and disappointment, anger and timidity, hope and discouragement, affection and aggression—all these feelings were expressed by feminists in different places at the same time. Even each individual feminist went through a continuous roller coaster of emotions. An anonymous writer for a Bremen women's magazine confessed in 1976: "Sometimes I feel ecstatic and free and like a 'New Woman,' and sometimes I feel terribly discouraged or frightened, or the same person I started out as a long, long time ago."[54]

Feminists who used supposedly prevailing emotions to criticize tendencies in the women's movement therefore resorted to a common rhetorical strategy. They produced a certain emotional knowledge[55] in order to derive conclusions for the overall direction of the women's movement. Their emotional knowledge served as a tool in the disputes about the "right" feminism: the latter required an appropriate way of feeling. However, this only reinforced emotional norms that had already excluded certain women in the CR groups.

Yet the criticism of supposed emotional aberrations can also be interpreted as an attempt to integrate the women's movement as an emotional community. During the period covered by this chapter, different currents and groups in the West German women's movement parted ways. Disintegration and fragmentation were an ongoing theme of feminist self-reflection.[56] Common sentiments thus appeared as a remaining bond that united the many different "sisters." However, the numerous disputes among feminists about the appropriate way to feel prove that stable emotional communities did not exist even across larger segments of the women's movement or at the local level. Yet emotions as a political object were indeed a common feature across the movement. Just like the focus on the body Jane Freeland has pinpointed as a unifying issue, feelings were "both a conduit for the 'discovery' and a site for the practice" of a feminist subjectivity.[57]

Emotional Work

The preoccupation with feelings went beyond incessantly addressing feminists' own sensitivities and arguing about emotional norms. Feminists talked and wrote about their feelings constantly, but they also worked incessantly to model their feelings along perceived prescribed patterns. Emotion work was both a communicative and a physical process. According to Monique Scheer and Pascal Eitler, emotional practices can be conceived as "practices involving the self (as body and mind), language, material artifacts, the environment, and other people." According to this approach, four practices can be distinguished—mobilizing, naming, communicating, and regulating emotion.[58] The last section of this chapter focuses on bodily practices of emotion that feminists employed in their everyday lives. These practices aimed to establish conformity and belonging, following the feminist emotional regime. By doing so, activists sought to experience the women's movement and to perceive themselves as part of it. At the same time, these practices provided a remedy against the many contradictions and setbacks in the movement's daily routine.

Especially important practices were forms of physical touch. The longing for tenderness and closeness was widespread throughout the alternative left. Among "sisters" in the women's movement, affectionate interaction was the norm. But even feminists treated each other harshly, dismissively, and with hostility. All the more important were gestures of affection. "Firmly in a row, embraced by women, I feel strong," was how one participant in a demonstration described the effect of physical closeness. Tangibly feeling connected to other feminists boosted her self-confidence, and as a result, the demonstration was a success for her.[59] Conversely, successful political actions facilitated physical intimacy. A young woman who had agitated at her school against homosexual discrimination received a lot of positive feedback in response. As a result, a few female friends flung their arms around her neck. This "spontaneous emotionality" of her classmates helped her to feel that her message against discrimination was well received.[60] The attempt to combine physical closeness with political activity was not always successful. In some groups, women refused the request to engage in bodily contact. "I can't do this on command, fondling someone," one woman justified her restraint.[61] Others denounced "the casual gentleness of women in greetings and farewells" as hypocrisy.[62] Most important, the conflicts between lesbian and heterosexual feminists had a great impact on how closeness and tenderness affected women. Physical contact was therefore an ambivalent practice that could create cohesion but also destroy it.

Similarly, crying had an ambivalent effect on feminists. Tears could express despair and helplessness, both feelings that a woman liberated from patriarchal oppression should presumably have left behind. Nevertheless, feminists also cried. The problem was that crying could seem like a reversion to the state of mind of an oppressed woman. The situation was even worse if patriarchy was not to blame for the tears but rather the women's movement itself. In this case, some contemporary feminists argued, the tears documented not personal weakness but the failure of the women's movement. In many autonomous women's projects, excessive demands and dashed hopes led to tearful confrontations. Those projects were supposed to fulfill the feminist utopia of a self-determined life but often produced new constraints for the women working there.[63] Sigrid Fronius, who in 1968 had been the first woman to chair the student council at the Free University of Berlin, was a member of the editorial board of the Berlin feminist magazine *Courage*. She had worked there since the first issue, in 1976. After a little more than a year, Fronius described her day-to-day work as exploitation and complained of in-fighting and intrigue among the editors. She described the atmosphere during editorial meetings as "howling, shouting, and denial." Another editor in turn criticized Fronius, saying she could no longer stand her whining.[64] Fronius herself also regarded the situation as unacceptable and left the editorial office. Obviously, crying as an emotional practice in this case conveyed a reproach to the other feminists in the editorial office. As a result, it was hardly possible to verbalize feelings and thereby change them. Liz Wieskerstrauch, who worked at the Bremen autonomous women's shelter, also described this correlation. She and her coworkers were so overburdened that they could no longer resolve the conflicts in the women's shelter team through discussion. "Feelings are only recognizable in tears, screaming, laughing, and dancing," she wrote in 1979.[65] Crying as a physical emotional practice therefore actually conflicted with communicating emotions.

Bodily emotional practices were widespread as a means to mobilize feelings; these practices ranked high in the feminist emotional regime. During political events and demonstrations, participants chanted to encourage themselves. They shouted to express their anger. And they danced at the numerous parties that feminists organized exclusively for women. Many reports show that these emotional practices achieved the desired effect. For example, lesbian activists preparing an information booth in the Hamburg city center memorized songs by the rock group Flying Lesbians to empower each other. The women then sang these songs, "a bit tentatively at first, then louder and louder." One participant described that, as a result, she no longer minded the unfriendly stares of people passing by. She sang along "as loudly and convincingly as I could," and her mood became increasingly euphoric.[66] Especially in the "take back the night" demonstrations directed against sexualized violence, shouting was an emotional practice that "yielded feelings of collective strength, free from fear."[67] Participants put on makeup, dressed up as witches, sang, danced, screamed, and shrieked, as one feminist described one such demonstration in Berlin in 1978.[68] But such emotional practices did not always achieve their goal. Small setbacks could undo the feeling of strength, for instance, if the demonstrating women allowed themselves to be intimidated by a policeman—or if their chanting sounded too timid.[69] There was only a small step from mobilizing anger to feeling ridiculed, and emotional practices could quickly fail.

Jochen Häberlen has characterized those practices as the hallmarks of "disruptive moments." Their unplanned, spontaneous quality distinguishes them from the ongoing emotional work in therapeutic settings such as the CR groups, which aimed to change feelings in the long run. Disruptive moments came and went quickly; they were "a momentary spark." Feelings of exuberance were also "exceptional."[70] The sources evaluated for this chapter confirm this analysis. In particular, the parties that women organized for women were able to achieve this effect. After one party in Cologne, an enthusiastic feminist named Brigitte wrote: "IT WAS!!! SIMPLY!!! AWESOME. ... I felt at times that, after a long dry spell and period of frustration, I had finally reached the fantastic oasis I always dreamed of, where everything happens only by, through and with women."[71] An anonymous woman in Mannheim felt the same way about a celebration after a "Take back the night" demonstration. This demonstration itself had disappointed her, but the subsequent party in a women's pub boosted her again: "I have rarely felt so comfortable in a pub as I did that night, and it gave me strength that we are many after all, if only somewhere; that we are united when we are together, and have fun, feel exuberance and tenderness. And, actually, we need much more frequent opportunities to feel this."[72] This feminist had felt the ideal of the autonomous women's movement at the party. Crucially, she experienced an emotional alignment between herself and the women's movement. Although such moments passed quickly, they confirmed that the goals and promises of the women's movement could be reached.

Conclusion

Emotions were a factor in the autonomous women's movement of the 1970s and 1980s that separated feminists more often than it united them. Even in the quite tight local networks of the autonomous women's movement, common feelings frequently could not bridge the many antagonisms. It is remarkable in this context that similar emotional practices still evolved in many cities to produce a distinctive emotional regime. CR groups existed in almost every place where autonomous feminist circles organized, and they followed more or less the same emotional program. Although many accounts show that women readily learned new regulations of feeling, similar problems also emerged almost everywhere, because the new emotional codes constricted and excluded nonconforming women. CR groups were therefore a "transformative" but also "ambivalent practice."[73] CR groups did, however, establish emotion as a standard by which the success of feminist engagement could be measured. As divergent as opinions could be about how a feminist should feel, feminists agreed that their emotions revealed the state of their political project. Two different emotional communities faced each other, often referred to as "old" and "new" women, respectively. They differed in the way different feminists experienced their political activity and the feelings it triggered in them. Although these two emotional communities can be traced in several cities, they were connected to each other only very loosely. Locally too, however, the different emotional worlds separated autonomous feminists from one another. As a result, there were feelings of powerlessness and isolation, which were reflected in a discourse about a supposed decline of the women's movement. Against such impressions, autonomous feminists often employed bodily emotional practices. These achieved only limited success because they enabled feminists to feel the unity between the autonomous self and the autonomous women's movement only for brief moments. But they boosted activists' motivation to continue believing in the success of their political project.

Bernhard Gotto is Research Fellow at the Institut für Zeitgeschichte München-Berlin and lecturer at the Ludwig-Maximilians-Universität Munich. His fields of interests include the social history of the Nazi dictatorship, the history of democracy, gender history, and the history of social movements. Recently, he has published *Enttäuschung in der Demokratie: Erfahrung und Deu-*

tung von politischem Engagement in der Bundesrepublik Deutschland während der 1970er und 1980er Jahre (2018), *Unwelcome Participation: Ostracizing Public Protest in the Second Half of the Twentieth Century* in Moving the Social: Journal of Social History and the History of Social Movements 66 (2021), ed. with Sabine Mecking, and *Verwaltungskultur, Diktaturerfahrung und Demokratie im 20. Jahrhundert. Das bayerische Finanzministerium von 1919 bis 1979* (2026).

Notes

1. See Hans Ullrich Wehler, *Deutsche Gesellschaftsgeschichte, Bd. 5: Bundesrepublik und DDR 1949–1990* (Munich: Beck 2008), 171; Eckart Conze, *Die Suche nach Sicherheit: Eine Geschichte der Bundesrepublik Deutschland von 1949 bis in die Gegenwart* (Munich: Siedler, 2009), 546; Ulrich Herbert, *Geschichte Deutschlands im 20. Jahrhundert* (Munich: Beck 2014), 861; more skeptical: Philipp Gassert, *Bewegte Gesellschaft: Deutsche Protestgeschichte seit 1945* (Stuttgart: W. Kohlhammer 2018), 144–45; Kristina Schulz, "Introduction: A Success Without Impact? Case Studies from the Women's Liberations Movements in Europe," in *The Women's Liberation Movement: Impacts and Outcomes*, ed. Kristina Schulz (New York: Berghahn Books, 2018), 1–14.
2. Frank Biess, *German Angst: Fear and Democracy in the Federal Republic of Germany* (Oxford: Oxford University Press, 2020), 261. See too the contribution by Friederike Brühöfener in this volume; also that of Belinda Davis.
3. Brigitte Classen and Gabriele Goettle, "*Häutungen*—eine Verwechslung von Anemone und Amazone," *Courage* 1 (1976): 45–46; Brigitte Classen and Gabriele Goettle, "Schleim oder nicht Schleim," *Die Schwarze Botin* 1 (1976): 4–5, in *Die neue Frauenbewegung in Deutschland: Abschied vom kleinen Unterschied; Eine Quellensammlung*, ed. Ilse Lenz (Wiesbaden: Verlag für Sozialwissenschaften, 2008), 116–18, 117. Cf. *Die Schwarze Botin: Ästhetik, Kritik, Polemik, Satire 1976–1980*, ed, Vojin Saša Vukadinović (Göttingen: Wallstein, 2020).
4. Joachim C. Häberlen, *The Emotional Politics of the Alternative Left: West Germany, 1968–1984* (Cambridge: Cambridge University Press, 2018); Sven Reichardt, *Authentizität und Gemeinschaft: Linksalternatives Leben in den siebziger und frühen achtziger Jahren* (Frankfurt a.M.: Suhrkamp, 2014).
5. Sarah E. Summers, "Finding Feminism: Rethinking Activism in the West German New Women's Movement of the 1970s and 1980s," in *Gendering Post-1945 German History: Entanglements*, ed. Karen Hagemann, Donna Harsch, and Friederike Brühöfener (New York: Berghahn Books, 2019), 187.
6. See Ilse Lenz, "Die unendliche Geschichte? Zur Entwicklung und den Transformationen der Neuen Frauenbewegung in Deutschland," in Lenz, *Die neue Frauenbewegung in Deutschland*, 26; Myra Marx Ferree, *Varieties of Feminism: German Gender Politics in Global Perspective* (Stanford, CA: Stanford University Press, 2012), 53 and 83.
7. Jane Freeland, "Women's Bodies and Feminist Subjectivities in West Germany," in *The Politics of Authenticity: Countercultures and Radical Movements across the Iron*

Curtain, 1968–1989, ed. Joachim C. Häberlen, Mark Keck-Szajbel, and Kate Mahoney (New York: Berghahn Books, 2019), 131–50.
8. William M. Reddy, *The Navigation of Feeling: A Framework for the History of Emotions* (Cambridge: Cambridge University Press, 2001), 129.
9. Arlie Russell Hochschild, "Emotion Work, Feeling Rules, and Social Structure," *American Journal of Sociology* 85, no. 3 (November 1979): 551–75.
10. Sara Evans, *Personal Politics: The Roots of Women's Liberation in the Civil Rights Movement and the New Left* (New York: Knopf, 1979), 102–21. On the origin of the slogan, see Deborah Siegel, *Sisterhood, Interrupted: From Radical Women to Grrls Gone Wild* (New York: Palgrave Macmillan, 2007), 24–34.
11. *Changing the World, Changing Oneself: Political Protest and Collective Identities in West Germany and the U.S. in the 1960s and 1970s*, ed. Belinda Davis, Wilfred Mausbach, Martin Klimke, and Carla MacDougall (New York: Berghahn Books, 2010).
12. Belinda Davis, "Redefining the Political: The Gender of Activism in Grassroots Movements of the 1960s to 1980s," in Hagemann, Harsch, and Brühöfener, *Gendering Post-1945 German History*, 207–28, 213; see also Imke Schmincke, "Von der Politisierung des Privatlebens zum neuen Frauenbewusstsein: Körperpolitik und Subjektivierung von Weiblichkeit in der Neuen Frauenbewegung Westdeutschlands," in *Zeitgeschichte als Geschlechtergeschichte: Neue Perspektiven auf die Bundesrepublik*, ed. Julia Paulus, Eva-Maria Silies, and Kerstin Wolff (Frankfurt a.M.: Campus 2012), 297–317.
13. See Häberlen, *Emotional Politics*, 7–13; Jens Elberfeld, "Befreiung des Subjekts, Management des Selbst: Therapeutisierungsprozesse im deutschsprachigen Raum seit den 1960er Jahren," in *Zeitgeschichte des Selbst: Therapeutisierung—Politisierung—Emotionalisierung*, ed. Pascal Eitler and Jens Elberfeld (Bielefeld: transcript 2015), 49–83; Reichardt, *Authentizität und Gemeinschaft*; *Das beratene Selbst: Zur Genealogie der Therapeutisierung in den "langen" Siebzigern*, ed. Sabine Maasen, Jens Elberfeld, Pascal Eitler, and Maik Tändler (Bielefeld: transcript 2011).
14. Sven Reichardt and Detlef Siegfried, "Das Alternative Milieu: Konturen einer Lebensform," in *Das Alternative Milieu: Antibürgerlicher Lebensstil und linke Politik in der Bundesrepublik Deutschland und Europa 1968–1983*, ed. Sven Reichardt and Detlef Siegfried (Göttingen: Wallstein 2010), 9–24.
15. Pascal Eitler and Jens Elberfeld, "Von der Gesellschaftsgeschichte zur Zeitgeschichte des Selbst—und zurück," in Eitler and Elberfeld, *Zeitgeschichte des Selbst*, 27.
16. Häberlen, *Emotional Politics*, 170.
17. Häberlen, *Emotional Politics*, 160–65; Reichardt, *Authentizität und Gemeinschaft*, 887–88.
18. Stefanie Pilzweger, *Männlichkeit zwischen Gefühl und Revolution: Eine Emotionsgeschichte der bundesdeutschen 68er-Bewegung* (Bielefeld: transcript, 2015), 278–85; Summers, "Finding Feminism," 188.
19. "Rechenschaftsbericht des Weiberrats der Gruppe Frankfurt," in Lenz, *Die neue Frauenbewegung in Deutschland*, 64–65.
20. See Bernhard Gotto, *Enttäuschung in der Demokratie: Erfahrung und Deutung von politischem Engagement in der Bundesrepublik Deutschland in den 1970er und 1980er Jahren* (Munich: Walter de Gruyter, 2018), 123–25.

21. Cf. Freeland, "Women's Bodies"; Andrea Bührmann, *Das authentische Geschlecht: Die Sexualitätsdebatte der Neuen Frauenbewegung und die Foucaultsche Machtanalyse* (Münster: Westfälisches Dampfboot, 1995).
22. Cf. Ute Frevert, *Emotions in History: Lost and Found* (Budapest: Central European University Press, 2012), 140–41; Elisabeth Zellmer, *Töchter der Revolte? Frauenbewegung und Feminismus der 1970er-Jahre in München* (Munich: De Gruyter Oldenbourg 2011), 186; Häberlen, *Emotional Politics*, 209.
23. Carly Guest, *Becoming Feminist: Narratives and Memoirs* (London: Palgrave Macmillan, 2016), 127. Cf. Cheryl Hercus, "Identity, Emotion, and Feminist Collective Action," *Gender and Society* 13 (1999): 34–55, 39–41; Mary Holmes, "Feeling Beyond Rules: Politicizing the Sociology of Emotion and Anger in Feminist Politics," *European Journal of Social Theory* 7 (2004): 209–27, 216; Barbara Tomlinson, *Feminism and Affect at the Scene of Argument: Beyond the Trope of the Angry Feminist* (Philadelphia: Temple University Press, 2010).
24. Kathie Sarachild, "A Program for Feminist 'Consciousness Raising'," in *Women's Liberation: Notes from the Second Year; Major Writings of the Radical Feminists* (New York: n.p., 1970), 78–80, retrieved 14 July 2021 from https://womenwhatistobedone.files.wordpress.com/2013/09/notes-from-the-second-year-a-program-for-feminist-consciousness-raising.pdf.
25. See Gotto, *Enttäuschung in der Demokratie*, 126–28; regarding the English and the Scottish WLM see Kate Mahoney, "The Political, Emotional, and Therapeutic: Narratives of Consciousness-Raising and Authenticity in the English Women's Liberation Movement," in Häberlen, Keck-Szajbel, and Mahoney, *Politics of Authenticity*, 65–88, 71–72; Sarah Browne, *The Women's Liberation Movement in Scotland* (Manchester: Manchester University Press, 2013), 45–62.
26. Ibid., 77–78; Gotto, *Enttäuschung in der Demokratie*, 128–29.
27. Mahoney, "Political, Emotional, and Therapeutic," 72.
28. Archiv of the *FrauenMediaTurm* Cologne (FMT) Z 152, Anja, "Brief an die Frauengruppe," in *Grete: Nürnberger Frauenzeitung*, Nr. 1, 1976, 24–25; FMT Z 159, Anonymous letter of a "somewhat disappointed woman" to the *Frauenladen* Saarbrücken, in *Lila Distel: Saarbrücker Frauenzeitung*, Nr. 8, March/April 1980, 24–25; FMT Z 212, "Kurzhaarschnitt und lila Latzhose," in *Lila Lotta: Bonner Frauenzeitung mit Kölner Seiten* 5, Nr. 5, Mai 1985, 29–33, 32.
29. FMT Z 182, Ulrike, "Erfahrungen von neuen ♀en", in *Frauenzeitung* Göttingen, Nr. 1, 1977, 4–5. In Berlin, women felt likewise after their first visit to the women's center: Cristina Perincioli, *Berlin wird feministisch: Das Beste, was von der 68er Bewegung blieb* (Berlin: Querverlag, 2015), 89–90.
30. FMT Z 154, Mechthild Kock, "Frauen in Coburg", in *Kratzbürste: Nürnberger Frauenzeitung*, Nr. 4, September 1978, 26–27, 27.
31. FMT Z 129, [account of a "Walpurgis night" (the night from 30 April to 1 May) demonstration in Heidelberg], in *Heidelberger Frauenzeitung*, Nr. 2, June 1977, 21–25, 22. The author had learned about the "take back the night" protest demonstrations during a women's conference in Munich. The American women's liberation movement had developed the concept since 1973; see Ferree, *Varieties*, 90.

32. FMT Z 125, Heimke and Dorothea, "&?!£$(•) %/ßÆŒØ œœø aèèôüñ£$(•) %/?f," in *Frauenzeitung des Frauenzentrums Hamburg*, Nr. 11, April 1977, 4–6. The headline symbolizes barriers of communication between the two groups.
33. For example, FMT Z 116, Martina, ". . . und Feministin fragt sich in diesem Zusammenhang, ob sie denn noch richtig tickt," in *Frauen wißt ihr schon . . . Frankfurter Frauenzeitung*, Nr. 10, 9 February 1977, 8–10; FMT Z 129, [Evaluation of a questionnaire about the Heidelberg Women's Center], in *Heidelberger Frauenzeitung*, Nr. 3, January 1978, 12–14; FMT Z 106, "Zur Beratungsdiskussion im Frauenzentum," in *Tango Feminista* Nr. 4, Juni 1979, 8–11; FMT Z 135, "Das Frauenzentrum ein Mythos?" in *Kölner Frauenzeitung*, Nr. 4, June/July 1980, 3–5; Ursula Bouczek and Nena Helfferich, "Das Netz wird immer enger: Frauenbewegung und Politik," in: Archive of social movements, Freiburg (ASBF), *Freiburger Frauenzeitung* Nr. 1, 1982, 15–18.
34. FMT Z 116, Hilde: "Impressionen zur Nacht-Demo," in *Frauen wißt ihr schon . . . Frankfurter Frauenzeitung*, Nr. 6, 13 September 1976, 4; FMT Z 116, Heike: Impressionen zur Nacht-Demo, in *Frauen wißt ihr schon . . . Frankfurter Frauenzeitung*, Nr. 8, 3 November 1976, 21–22.
35. Barbara H. Rosenwein, "Worrying about Emotions in History," *American Historical Review* 107 (2002): 821–45.
36. FMT Z 142, Marion, "Die traurige Geschichte der Verrottung des Frauenzentrums Mannheim," in *Lila Klatschmohn: Emanzenblatt Mannheim-Ludwigshafen*, Nr. 8, June/July 1980, 8–10.
37. FMT Z 125, Christiane, "Betr.: ß6&7rnáÖc . . . von Heimke und Dorothea in Heft 11," in *Frauenzeitung des Frauenzentrums Hamburg*, Nr. 12/13, Mai/June 1977, 7; Barbara, "Leserinnenbrief an Heimke und Dorothea," ibid., 8–9; Karin, "Leserinnenbrief," ibid., 16.
38. FMT Z 116, Hilde, "Sind wir noch zu retten???" in: *Frauen wißt ihr schon . . . Frankfurter Frauenzeitung*, Nr. 6, 13 September 1976, 5; Archive of the Institut für Zeitgeschichte Munich-Berlin (IfZ) ED 899/19, Anita, "Über die Entwicklung der Münchner Frauenbewegung. Versuch einer Bilanz 1979," in *Münchner Frauenzeitung*, February 1980, 10–11.
39. Andrea, "Der große Aufschwung in kleinen Anfängen," in ASBF, *Freiburger Frauenzeitung* Nr. 2/3, February 1983, 3.
40. FMT Z 137, Wiebke Nimmer, "Frauenbewegung—wo?" in: *autoxa: Hannoversche Frauenzeitung*, Nr. 3, June 1986, 27–28, 27.
41. See Irene Stoehr, "Gründerinnen—Macherinnen—Konsumentinnen? Generationenprobleme in der Frauenbewegung der 1990er Jahre," in *Konkurrenz & Kooperation: Frauen im Zwiespalt?* ed. Ilse Modelmog and Ulrike Gräßel (Münster: LIT Verlag, 1995), 91–115; Ute Gerhard, "Nachfolge in der Frauenbewegung: Generationen und sozialer Wandel" [2006], in *Die bewegte Frau: Feministische Perspektiven auf historische und aktuelle Gleichberechtigungsprozesse*, ed. Katrin Pittius, Kathleen Kollewe, and Eva Fuchslocher (Münster: Westfälisches Dampfboot, 2013), 23–40. For the women's liberation movement in the United States, see Nancy Whittier, *Feminist Generations: The Persistence of the Radical Women's Movement* (Philadelphia: Temple University Press, 1995). A critical assessment of the generational interpretation is provided by Christine Thon, *Frauenbewegung im Wandel: Eine Studie* über

Geschlechtergenerationen in biographischen Erzählungen (Bielefeld: Transcript, 2008), 57–62.
42. Nena Helfferich, "Ein Brief betreffs §218 und Kinderkriegen," in ASBF, *Freiburger Frauenzeitung* Nr. 1, 1982, 12–13 ("old fighter"); Marion of Mannheim (see note 36—"long serving feminist").
43. Barbara Mahrt, "Mit 40 zur Frauenbewegung? Statt Resignation—Entwicklung!" in *Frauenjahrbuch '76*, ed. Jahrbuchgruppe des Münchner Frauenzentrums (Munich, 1976), 16–21; Anke Wolf-Graaf, "Im Gegenschritt," in *Schwesternstreit: Von den heimlichen und unheimlichen Auseinandersetzungen zwischen Frauen*, ed. Birgit Cramon-Daiber et al. (Reinbek: Rowohlt, 1983), 121–53, esp. 128 and 141.
44. Cf. note 36.
45. FMT Z 142, Gisela, "Feminismus ist die Theorie—arbeiten mit Frauen ist die Praxis," in *Lila Klatschmohn. Emanzenblatt Mannheim-Ludwigshafen*, Nr. 8, June/July 1980, 5–7, 5.
46. FMT Z 102, "das ende und der neuanfang unserer frauengruppe—aufgearbeitet, überlegt und aufgeschrieben von erika, urte, kristine (ehemalige aus der stadtteilgruppe walle)," in *Frauenzeitung Bremen* Nr. 5, 1977, 46–55, 47.
47. Margot Poppenhusen, "Geschichte der Freiburger Frauenbewegung, Teil II," in ASBF, *Freiburger Frauenzeitung* Nr. 2/3, February 1983, 23–25, 24. Cf. Margot Poppenhusen, *Viel bewegt—nichts verrückt? 20 Jahre Frauenbewegung in Freiburg 1972–1992* (Freiburg i. Br.: J. Fritz, 1992).
48. FMT Z 116, Christa, "Ein ganz anderes Verhältnis zum eigenen Körper und zum Frau-Sein," in *Frauen wißt ihr schon . . . Frankfurter Frauenzeitung*, Nr. 8, 3 November 1976, 24–25.
49. FMT Z 102, "Beitrag der Frankfurter Repressionsgruppe," in *Frauenzeitung Bremen* Nr. 3, April 1977, 29–31.
50. Häberlen, *Emotional Politics*, 123–66; Reichardt, *Authentizität und Gemeinschaft*, 195–202.
51. Some recent scholars have followed this interpretation, see Imke Schmincke, "Von der Befreiung der Frau zur Befreiung des Selbst: Eine kritische Analyse der Befreiungssemantik in der (neuen) Frauenbewegung," in Eitler and Elberfeld, *Zeitgeschichte des Selbst*, 217–37; Reichardt, *Authentizität und Gemeinschaft*, 613.
52. Alice Schwarzer, "Wie geht es weiter? Die neue Frauenbewegung, 9. und letzte Folge," *Emma* 5 (1981), no. 10: 32–35; cf. Gotto, *Enttäuschung in der Demokratie*, 168–73.
53. Ilse Kokula, "Vierte Sommeruniversität für Frauen: Übers Glücklichwerden," *Courage* 4 (1979), no. 11: 4–8, 8.
54. FMT Z 102, Frauenhausfest in Kassel, November 1976, in: *Frauenzeitung Bremen* Nr. 2, Januar 1977, 5–6.
55. Häberlen, *Emotional Politics*, 155; cf. Ute Frevert, "Emotional Knowledge: Modern Developments," in *Emotional Lexicons: Continuity and Change in the Vocabulary of Feeling 1700–2000*, ed. Ute Frevert et al. (Oxford: Oxford University Press, 2014), 260–73.
56. Cf. Eva-Maria Silies, "Ein, zwei, viele Bewegungen? Die Diversität der neuen Frauenbewegung in den 1970er Jahren in der Bundesrepublik," in *Linksalternatives Milieu und Neue Soziale Bewegungen in den 1970er Jahren*, ed. Cordia Baumann, Sebastian Gehrig, and Nicolas Büchse (Heidelberg: Winter Verlag 2010), 87–106.

57. Freeland, "Women's Bodies," 145.
58. Pascal Eitler and Monique Scheer, "Are Emotions a Kind of Practice (and Is That What Makes Them Have a History)? A Bourdieuian Approach to Understanding Emotion," *History and Theory* 51 (2012): 193–220, 193.
59. Cf. note 31.
60. FMT Z 116, Bärbel Doelter, "An unserer Schule ist was los—Aktion gegen Chauvinisten," 12.12.1976, in *Frauen wißt ihr schon . . . Frankfurter Frauenzeitung*, Nr. 10, 9 February 1977, 18–20.
61. Häberlen, *Emotional Politics*, 169.
62. FMT Z 102, "Von den Grenzen der Solidarität oder wie ursprünglich Gemeintes eine Sinnentleerung erfährt," in *Frauenzeitung Bremen* Nr. 5, 1977, 28.
63. Cf. Ferree, *Varieties*, 84–94; Reichardt, *Authentizität und Gemeinschaft*, 319–50; Gotto, *Enttäuschung in der Demokratie*, 139–44; Gisela Notz, *Warum flog die Tomate? Die autonomen Frauenbewegungen der Siebzigerjahre* (Neu-Ulm: AG-SPAK-Bücher 2006), 52–55; Sibylle Plogstedt, *Frauenbetriebe: Vom Kollektiv zur Einzelunternehmerin* (Königstein: Ulrike Helmer Verlag, 2006).
64. Frauenforschungs-, Bildungs- und Informationszentrum Berlin (FFBIZ) B Rep. 400 Berlin 20.11. d, Internal statement [of Sigrid Fronius, october 1977]. An extract of this paper was published in *Courage* 2 (1977), Nr. 2, 52–53. Cf. Sigrid Fronius, "Als Frau stand ich nicht unter dem Zwang, jemand sein zu müssen," in *Die 68erinnen: Porträt einer rebellischen Frauengeneration*, ed. Ute Kätzel (Berlin: Rowohlt, 2002), 21–39.
65. FMT Z 104, Liz Wieskerstrauch, "Über die Schwierigkeit, von Konflikten in Frauengruppen zu berichten," in *Gesche. Frauenzeitung aus Bremen*, Nr. 3, June/July 1979, 5–6.
66. FMT Z 125, Sybille: Lesbeninfostand, in: *Frauenzeitung des Frauenzentrums Hamburg*, Nr. 1, June 1976, S. 18–22.
67. Häberlen, *Emotional Politics*, 214.
68. FMT Z 106, "Frauen erobern sich die Nacht zurück?" in *Tango Feminista* Nr. 1, 1978, 15.
69. FMT Z 135, Gisela Thönes and Ute Küppersbusch, "Leserinnenbrief," in *Kölner Frauenzeitung*, Nr. 4, June/July 1980, 25–26.
70. Häberlen, *Emotional Politics*, 206–8.
71. FMT Z 135, Brigitte, "Frauenfest," in *Kölner Frauenzeitung*, Nr. 2, January/February 1980, 4–5.
72. FMT Z 142, "Zur Walpurgisnacht-Demo . . . ," in: *Lila Klatschmohn: Emanzenblatt Mannheim-Ludwigshafen*, Nr. 2, June 1979, 22.
73. Häberlen, *Emotional Politics*, 206.

Select Bibliography

Ferree, Myra Marx. *Varieties of Feminism: German Gender Politics in Global Perspective.* Stanford, CA: Stanford University Press, 2012.
Freeland, Jane. "Women's Bodies and Feminist Subjectivities in West Germany." In *The Politics of Authenticity: Countercultures and Radical Movements across the Iron Cur-*

tain, 1968–1989, edited by Joachim C. Häberlen, Mark Keck-Szajbel, and Kate Mahoney, 131–50. New York: Berghahn Books, 2019.

Gotto, Bernhard. *Enttäuschung in der Demokratie: Erfahrung und Deutung von politischem Engagement in der Bundesrepublik Deutschland in den 1970er und 1980er Jahren.* Munich: Walter de Gruyter, 2018.

Häberlen, Joachim C. *The Emotional Politics of the Alternative Left: West Germany, 1968–1984.* Cambridge: Cambridge University Press, 2018.

Lenz, Ilse, ed. *Die neue Frauenbewegung in Deutschland: Abschied vom kleinen Unterschied; Eine Quellensammlung.* Wiesbaden: VS Verlag für Sozialwissenschaften, 2008.

Reichardt, Sven. *Authentizität und Gemeinschaft: Linksalternatives Leben in den siebziger und frühen achtziger Jahren.* Frankfurt a.M.: Suhrkamp, 2014.

Zellmer, Elisabeth. *Töchter der Revolte? Frauenbewegung und Feminismus der 1970er-Jahre in München.* Munich: De Gruyter Oldenbourg, 2011.

Part II
"Start Where You Are"

Chapter 5

"Break Down the Violence in a Place Where It Is Vulnerable"

The Urban '68 and Its Aftermath—Expert Critique, "Tenant Campaigns," and Squatter Movements

Freia Anders

The "right to the city"—a universal right to affordable housing—is currently being demanded in large cities all over the world.[1] Rising rents and housing prices have made it difficult, not only for low-income households but also for members of the middle class, to find affordable housing. There is no end in sight. A neoliberalization of housing policy, which allegedly began in the mid-1980s, is blamed for the current escalation of this problem. However, the "new housing issue" is by no means new. The issue has merely returned to the political agenda. Its historical dimension is occasionally noticed by those who seek solutions to these problems in tenant initiatives, local authorities, or research institutes.[2] Reawakened concerns include considerations of alternative forms of housing and ownership as well as demands for the socialization of living space or the expropriation of real estate companies. Issues of housing and collective material interests in urban settings were continuously relevant throughout the twentieth century, but the urban movements that emerged around '68 and thereafter took them up with particular intensity.

Historical accounts of past social conflicts over the complex issue of housing as a commodity—as reflected in informal housing, squatting, and rent strikes—are often a mere appendage to research on poverty, migration, urban development, and social movements. Such research typically focuses on current disputes, advocating legal regulations as the primary solution, emphasizing self-help strategies, or adopting a particular aesthetic "framing."[3] Hence observers are quick to interpret squatting in the cities of the Global North as part of the repertoire of subcultures and youth movements, often without sufficiently considering the context of urban crises. The approving label "political" squatting is frequently bestowed on countercultural aspects and identities. It suggests that the free spaces created by "political" squatters are alternatives to neoliberal market logic, which are then—sometimes even by left-wing researchers and activists—positioned against those squatters who acted "only" on account of their precarious situation.[4]

As early as the 1970s, "new" social movement theory, which developed in interaction with these movements, expressed an influential (self-)critique of the Left. According to this line of reasoning, the Left had come to focus predominantly on postmaterialist themes, thus neglecting the social question.[5] This critique lives on in claims that squatter movements replaced class-based forms of organization with forms centered on local identity, thus creating the necessary preconditions for this movement's co-optation by the "neoliberal project."[6] This interpretation is fed by the social and local heterogeneity of urban movements and by the pressure in academia to find something "new" or "surprising," which has repeatedly been achieved by pointing out that movements' goals have grown beyond a narrow understanding of the social question. A historical perspective, however, reveals that such a one-sided interpretation does not do these movements justice. A focus on the collective and political aspects of material interests in urban settings highlights the importance of micro and day-to-day perspectives in fueling social movements. Local politics and "start where you are" approaches promised political opportunities and returns that seemed unachievable at the national level, especially when activists considered the fate of older social movements. With his analytical focus on movements for youth centers, David Templin has highlighted the specific spatial needs and demands of young people, and the conflicts resulting from these, in urban, semiurban, and rural settings.[7] A look at West German housing struggles reveals how the social reappropriation of the resource "city" helped to transcend identity politics by creating a unifying continuity around the social question despite the ups and downs of movement cycles between '68 and 1981. This focus on living conditions overlaps with the various contemporary projects of transforming and optimizing the self, which is the subject of Belinda Davis's chapter in this volume. But the collective and communal nature of the living conditions that were at stake for the urban activists analyzed in this chapter tied activists' struggles all the more explicitly to material politics and issues of distributive justice.

'68–'81

Urban movements, including the "struggle for a different city," are for the most part still lacunae within the historiography on the "'68" era in the

Federal Republic of Germany (FRG). In contrast to the women's or environmental movements, they are rarely considered as movements emerging from '68. Yet, movements from France's May 1968 to the Prague Spring—as Peter Birke points out—cannot be isolated from the question of what "the city" meant for the respective activists.[8] In his 1968 work *Le Droit à la ville* (*The Right to the City*), the oft-quoted philosopher Henri Lefebvre drew attention to the connection between urban development and revolt. Beginning in the early 1970s, the sociologist Manuel Castells developed building blocks for a theory of urban movements based on questions of collective consumption, work that was quickly translated into the major European languages.[9] By the early 1960s, academic criticism of urban planning and modern housing construction had already received extensive impulses from the United States.[10] In 1966, the utopian potential of transforming urban spaces was demonstrated by the Dutch Provos in the anarchist manifestations and reform concepts that they labeled "White Plans." In Switzerland, the '68 movement reached its peak in the Globus riots, a dispute over the use of a former department store building in Zurich that the Globus company wanted to make its new headquarters. Swiss activists demanded that this very expensive piece of real estate in the middle of Zurich become an autonomous youth center instead.[11] The ensuing street fights in June 1968 were among the most militant conflicts Switzerland had ever experienced, long before the "Züri brännt" (Zurich is burning) events in May 1980. The latter were the prelude to the "1980s" movements throughout Western Europe, reaching their 1981 peak in conflicts over squatting, which were, however, often framed as youth movements.[12]

In the FRG, massive militant clashes between squatters and the state caused considerable political unrest in the early 1980s. The ensuing political and legal discourses mainly focused on questions of legitimacy and justification of political violence, regarding property damage, resistance to state authority or breach of the peace on the part of movement activists, and the state's physical use of power in evictions and arrests. Contemporary surveys showed that the protests met with considerable acceptance among the population due to the enduringly dramatic housing shortage. In 1981, it was assumed that 45 percent of the "young generation" sympathized with the protests.[13] Politicians and social scientists nevertheless expressed surprise at the conflict's violent development. It had been hoped that a parliamentarization of social movements via the newly founded Green Party would lead to a pacification of the conflicts of the 1970s. The opposing parties' recourse to violence was interpreted in different ways. Authors who understood the squatting movement primarily as part of a youth revolt interpreted the radicalization of protest as a symptom of the age-specific temperament of the protesters, an identity crisis aggravated by the "dramatic deterioration" of the young generation's "prospects for the future."[14] Others saw the government's "policing" reaction to the conflict as a reason why protest actions had taken on a dynamic of their own, diverging from their actual goals of protesting housing shortages and restructuring, leading to a "peculiar dialectic of marginalization and militancy."[15] By framing these movements merely as alternative, citizen-initiative, or self-help movements, German social movement research—often leaving violent aspects aside, treating them separately, or looking at them only from a sociopsychological perspective—has helped to obfuscate the specific potential for violence inherent in conflicts over urban space.[16] Only more recent studies that treat the history of squatting in the early 1980s comparatively have taken up ideas from the beginnings of urban movement research, which already saw urban conflicts as international concomitants of Fordist urban politics in the transition to neoliberalism.[17] Studies on the emergence of an "alternative milieu," on the formation of antiauthoritarian *Sponti* and autonomist movements, and on protests against "regimes of provision" have meanwhile drawn a detailed picture of the squatter waves of the early 1970s and early 1980s without neglecting their specific potential for violence.[18] Nevertheless, the squatting waves from 1970 to 1974 and from 1980 to 1983 still appear strangely isolated from each other as eruptive crisis situations. The following two sections outline how tenant campaigns and rent strikes took up impulses from the critical urban theory of the 1960s and thereby constituted an element of continuity that connected the peaks of movement activity.

From the Beginnings of Academic Critique to Tenant Campaigns

During the 1960s, it became apparent that the state instruments developed after 1945 were unable to solve housing problems sufficiently. Government support of home ownership and investment in social housing during the 1950s had only partially relieved housing shortages. A 1968 study by the IG Metall (Industrial Union of Metalworkers) found that there were still some 850,000 households living in barracks and makeshift homes.[19] Relative prosperity had negative effects, as well: urban sprawl, increased commuting, and social segregation, including "social trouble spots." Moreover, the state increasingly shifted its obligations into the hands of the market. Between 1960 and 1980, subsidies for social housing were reduced by more than two-thirds, and tenant protection was deregulated.[20] For the majority of the population, housing became the central factor in cost of living increases between 1962 and 1975.[21] Rising property prices and construction costs made living in city centers a privilege, while growing real estate speculation accelerated the decline of districts close to the inner city.[22] The lack of affordable housing and, above all, the shortcomings in urban quality of life, commonly attributed to urban planning, were starting points for a critique of the city around '68.

Since the late 1950s, social scientists came to regard the reconstruction and expansion of cities with unease, with talk of the "destruction of urbanity," "organized urban demolition," the "murdered city," and "inhumane dormitory towns."[23] This discourse became popularized in part by the book *Die Unwirtlichkeit unserer Städte: Anstiftung zum Unfrieden* (The inhospitality of our cities: A deliberate provocation) by the psychoanalyst Alexander Mitscherlich, who combined the growing criticism of monotonous living conditions and urban sprawl with a critique of the state and society by highlighting connections between the built environment, democratic deficits, and sociopsychological distortions: "Man becomes what the city makes him, and vice versa."[24] Unlike many of his academic contemporaries, Mitscherlich considered restrictions on the right to land ownership indispensable. He had been a direct eyewitness to how Frankfurt, under Social Democratic leadership since the early 1960s, developed into the economic metropolis of the Federal Republic, accompanied by an initial wave of displacement of the resident population from inner-city districts and a "sudden increase in commuting."[25] This period also marked the beginning of resistance to certain characteristics of modern urban development. In 1964, the Schutzgemeinschaft Wohngebiet Holzhausen (Association for the Protection of the Residential Area Holzhausen) mobilized more than one thousand signatories in a petition against a plan to build high-rise buildings in the middle of Wilhelmine-era districts, which was nevertheless ratified in 1965. There was, however, no major "upheaval" during that period, even after Frankfurt eliminated rent control in July 1965.[26]

The first to switch to direct political action were the Frankfurt Provos, who were in close contact with their Amsterdam counterparts in the mid-1960s. The Frankfurt group consisted mainly of young people whose lifestyle was oriented toward "dropping out," but who were also leaning toward the Socialist German Student Union (SDS). In 1967, the Provos, initially supported by the city's youth welfare office as a "resocialization project," planned to expand their meeting facilities. When the project failed, they called for the ruins of Frankfurt's opera house to be converted into a "self-administrated communications center."[27] The demand for this symbolic and highly contested location hit a nerve among the city's elites. The reconstruction of the *Old Opera* building was the declared aim of Frankfurt's oldest registered citizens' initiative, the Aktionsgemeinschaft Opernhaus Frankfurt am Main e.V. (Action Group Opera Frankfurt on the Main), which had been founded by dignitaries of the Frankfurt bourgeoisie in 1964. The following year, Rudi Arndt (Social Democratic Party of Germany, SPD), Hesse's minister of economics and later Frankfurt's mayor, caused an outrage when he suggested demolishing the ruin.[28] The Provos' (symbolic) appropriation of public space through direct action brought them into conflict with the police and potential allies, a pattern that would repeat itself in future housing protests. When the Provos graffitied the Sigmund Freund Institute, Mitscherlich, its director, responded with criminal charges.[29]

With the expansion of the protest movement, academic circles within the New Left increasingly took up the issue of urban space. Although criticism of functionalist urban planning was widely shared, divergent approaches to the problem quickly crystallized. These divergences were driven by the question of whether reforms in the urban environment actually helped stabilize the functionalist system or whether small-scale changes would bring about tangible improvements in the living conditions of city dwellers that would ultimately change the system.[30] The urban sociologist Heide Berndt, Mitscherlich's assistant and an SDS member since 1963, interpreted urban building methods as a reflection of the social context in which they occurred. In an article published in the Frankfurt School-inspired journal *Das Argument* in 1967, she focused on the aesthetics of urban planning, which, she argued, had deteriorated into "functionally structured and loosely arranged barracks."[31] Her postdoctoral thesis of 1968 attributed this approach to a "conservative . . . concept of society among urban planners."[32] In the same year and together with other Mitscherlich students, she published a collection of essays titled *Architektur als Ideologie* (Architecture as ideology). Her historical analysis formed the basis for a critique of urban planning's macrostructures, demonstrating how social relationships were expressed in spatial structuring and the forms of construction that went with it. Referring to Marcuse, Berndt condemned the "one-dimensional aesthetic" of architecture resulting from "monopolistic usage demands" and functional rationalism, which led to the deformation of human perception and to the "one-dimensionality" of the human being.[33] This addressed the fundamental issue of alienated forms of life, which would gain great significance for the intellectual orientation of parts of the post-'68 Left and the "alternative milieu" emerging from it.

Berndt attempted to figure out the potential of a different architecture and urban development, in which aesthetics simultaneously "make one conscious of one's demands for new forms of social coexistence."[34] But the assumption implied therein, that a better society could result from planning and construction of better spaces, was rejected by other architecture critics.

Differences arose within the working group Architektur und Gesellschaft (Architecture and Society), which had been formed in late 1967 within the framework of the Critical University at Technical University (TU) Berlin. Inspired by Habermas, the initiative relied on cooperation between citizens, politicians, and experts for urban planning, to a certain extent anticipating later models of citizen participation.[35]

"Architecture and Society" was also influenced by a circle of authors associated with the institutionally unattached musician and intellectual Hans G. Helms, the architect and TU lecturer Jörn Janssen, and the SDS activist and later cofounder of the Maoist KPD-AO Peter Neitzke. The group positioned itself in the field by conducting a polemical campaign against both the Mitscherlich students and the established representatives of "organic architecture" associated with Hans Scharoun. Although they too assumed that the "symbolic violence of the architectural institutions" had repercussions for "social subjects" and especially their individual communication,[36] they deployed Marxist theory to rigorously analyze architecture as a result of the conditions of capitalist production. In a historical study, Janssen reflected on housing shortages as a construct developed in the interest of a "market-oriented analysis for housing production."[37] Helms accused the circle's opponents of neglecting the "contradiction between technologically developed spatial design and the naturally grown city,"[38] while Janssen charged that their critical contemporaries ultimately "fit seamlessly into the battle front of the national economics literature on housing since the mid-nineteenth century . . . whose purpose has always been" to "reduce social conflicts to system-immanent, solvable pseudo-problems." The difference "between Left and Right" in the housing issue was reduced "to a question of one's tastes, [a question] which has neither promoted social change nor satisfied hunger."[39] Neitzke also criticized Frankfurt School Critical Theory from this perspective, claiming that its "legacy" promoted resignation.[40] Neitzke and Janssen considered the ultimate priority to be the organization of class struggle: "In the cities devastated by capital, the revolutionary masses will build a socialist society on the basis of the experiences of class struggle."[41] Janssen soon became known beyond Berlin when he, as visiting professor at ETH Zurich (Swiss Federal Institute of Technology) in 1970, attracted the hostility of the conservative press and the interest of the Swiss security authorities because he and his students investigated the socioeconomic conditions—including corruption—under which Ernst Göhner AG built the Sunnebüel prefabricated housing estate in Volketswil.[42] In spite of the ETH's progressive reputation, university management intervened and ended this phase of experimental teaching.[43]

The academic debate was taken up by architecture students who were part of the student movement at technical universities and engineering colleges, protesting the outdated content of their education and provoking a "battle situation," out of which important impulses for the transformation of curricula and the profession emerged.[44] In September 1968, a group of young TU architects, calling themselves "Aktion 507," accepted an invitation of West Berlin's government to take part in the Berliner Bauwochen (Berlin Construction Weeks). They called their contribution "Gegen-Bauwochen" (Counter Construction Weeks). At its center was the exhibition "Diagnosen: Zum Bauen und Wohnen in Berlin" (Diagnoses: On building and living in Berlin). The group's manifesto was imbued with a critique of the capitalist exploitation of the city. This included a sweeping strike against rising rents, speculation, the existing policies of subsidies for social housing construction and competition in public tendering, which led the coming generation of architects to expect a precarious professional future. The manifesto vividly addressed the sociopsychological consequences of modern mass housing.[45] While the official building exhibition took West Berliners by bus to the new development areas to admire the "glimmers of hope for urban planners in half of Europe," Aktion 507 contrasted statements by architects with those of residents of Märkisches Viertel (MV), a "satellite housing estate" in the north of West Berlin where some seventeen thousand housing units were built beginning in 1964. While officials boasted of building "flowers and fairy tales," the MV settlement left the impression of "embrasures, barracks, prison," even among residents who were not necessarily readers of Frankfurt social psychologists. While high-rise architects praised the advantages of "sun and orientation," those living in such places criticized "unbearable noise, stench and drafts." Aktion 507 concluded that the statements of those whom the authorities had "forcibly" resettled from demolition districts reflected their "social isolation," which had now turned into "open aggression."[46] The idea of a concrete mobilization of the people affected by mass housing development got its start here.

The rapid spread of a counter-public promoted exchange between local initiatives that were developing in many cities. In August 1968, the magazine *Was tun?* (What is to be done?), founded by leading members of the SDS, first reported on Munich grassroots groups that sought to "unmask" the politics of the institution "city" to "question the capitalist housing industry."[47] Squatting and rent strikes in London and Milan, which reached their first climax in the summer of 1968, were followed with great interest.[48] With the eventual dissolution of the extraparliamentary opposition (APO), urban criticism broadened further. At the universities, "red cells," such as RotzArch (Rote Zelle Architektur), emerged, which addressed issues of real estate policy and urban renewal in seminars. In addition, ideologically diverse neighborhood grassroots groups developed—ranging from Marxist(-Leninist) to antiauthoritarian to anarchist—in which politicized students sought to close ranks with proletarian youth and pupils. From 1969 onward, the *Märkische Viertel Zeitung* (MVZ), a newspaper published by students of the Berlin College of Education, became the most important organ of the approximately two dozen initiatives in the neighborhood. Among these were the tenants' initiative MV, several *K-Gruppen* (Communist groups) and the so-called "Sonntagsgruppe" (Sunday Group),[49] to which future members of the Red Army Faction (RAF) Ulrike Meinhof, Horst Mahler, and Petra Schelm belonged. The MVZ's reports on unrest in the satellite town brought the newspaper to the attention of the security authorities even before the actions of the RAF caused an uproar.

The newspaper *Socialist Correspondence* (abbreviated *SC-Info*), first published in April 1969 and emerging from the Socialist Club Frankfurt, followed the events in Berlin closely.[50] Addressing developments in Frankfurt's West End and the outrage over the planned construction of a high-rise complex in Rothschild Park, *SC-Info* appealed to "all comrades," not just future architects and urban planners, to "discuss theoretically the role of the housing market as part of organized political violence," to develop a "practice" that "should break down the violence in a place where it is vulnerable." A Home Procurement Project Group outlined a spectrum of causes and perpetrators of this "violence" by denouncing the "brutal speculation of the landlords . . . , the home ownership ideology of the building societies . . . , the policies . . . of the so-called non-profit housing associations and the apparatchiks from SPD and DGB [German Trade Union Confederation]." It was yet unclear, however, to what extent the victims of these constellations at the lower end of the social hierarchy—"indebted home-builders, tenants stuck in their obsolete traditional values in dormitory towns and guest workers, pensioners and students living in demolition properties"—had the potential to merge into a diverse urban movement that could become a successor movement to the APO. Nevertheless, organizers hoped to mobilize tenants in the Gallus quarter, a traditional working-class neighborhood around the freight station, hit particularly hard by urban redevelopment.[51] For the leftists emerging from the antiauthoritarian wing of the APO, questions about which mobilization strategies were appropriate arose. "Tenant campaigns" were considered a means of choice, as they were developing into a socially comprehensive form of political action. Even though an alignment of "student movements" and "working class," which the Left hoped for, remained fragile, the SC project group's strategy appeared to be successful at first.

Glimmers of hope also emerged from West Berlin, where the "Diagnoses" exhibition had drawn attention to MV, a place that appeared to justify political expectations. The suffering of the quarter's inhabitants had been documented. A constant increase in rents, which devoured up to 40 percent of tenants' incomes, frequently caused tenants to fall behind on their payments. By the end of 1969, a wave of forced evictions loomed over the high-rise quarter. Inadequate infrastructure links, which particularly affected children and young people, were a source of constant dissatisfaction. This manifested itself in the occupation of a nearby unused factory building, which had been eyed by activists as a future site for a youth center, following a performance by Hoffmanns Comic Theater on Mayday 1970. The forcible eviction of the occupiers by police caused the activists to consider what strategy was suitable for the political work of the radical Left. Ulrike Meinhof—shortly before she went underground due to being wanted for her role in Andreas Baader's escape from prison—drafted a "strategy paper" in which she attempted to explore the revolutionary potential of those who could not be easily integrated into consumer society: "Moving into the MV also increases the pressure of consumption for the proletarian tenants—new housing . . . cars due to longer commuting distances and poor transit connections . . . the question is . . . who is already so fed up, so impoverished that they have no choice but to take up the struggle." According to Meinhof, these were families with many children threatened with eviction and the "sub-proletarian youth," for whom everyday conflicts "with Gesobau [a municipal housing company] and its property managers, with the police, with their neighbors" were unavoidable. The fundamental problem standing in the way of political mobilization in the MV was the challenge of transcending the isolation of a single-issue movement. This included, on the one hand, overcoming the "skepticism of the comrades who live in the quarter . . . toward those who live . . . in the city" and, on the other hand, the need to link the housing struggles with uprisings in the factories and the ongoing protests against "US imperialism" in Vietnam.[52] Ultimately, her idea was to stimulate cross-movement mobilization.

It was equally difficult to organize residents and their material needs in redevelopment areas. When extensive demolition began in Kreuzberg in 1968, there was initially little protest. Following examples of US slum clearing, West Berlin's government had passed a program in 1963 that designated large, old inner-city areas in Kreuzberg, Neukölln, Schöneberg, Tiergarten, and Wedding as redevelopment areas. Objections to these concrete plans for Berlin's transformation did not originally come from the Left. Although the planning concept by TU professor Fritz Eggeling represented a compromise in comparison to the competing proposals advocating total demolition of the area, it still envisaged replacing many old buildings with new ones. Opposition came from his colleague Peter Koller,[53] a former Nazi architect and creator of the "Stadt des KdF-Wagens" (the future Wolfsburg).

For Koller, demolition and new construction meant destroying social structures and wasting public money. However, gradual reconstruction, which was to become the dominant approach in the 1980s, was still considered backward-looking at the time.[54]

With the Büro für Stadtsanierung und soziale Arbeit (Office for Urban Redevelopment and Social Work), which was founded by students of architecture and urban planning on 1 May 1969, architectural criticism broke new ground beyond the university. The office was to become a model for grassroots, neighborhood offices, which to this day consult tenants on rental issues in many cities and ultimately help to create "careful urban renewal." Through detailed surveys of the population, activists attempted to gain an overview of housing conditions and commercial structures. Handing out leaflets and performing street theater, they built public awareness among architects and residents regarding the "anti-resident aspects" of the destruction of Kreuzberg. Members traveled to London to hear about rent strikes and squatting as models for leftist strategies.[55] Inspired by the American approach of advocacy planning, they saw their own task in "counterplanning as a concrete utopia . . . encompassing the overall context of living conditions . . . : apartments, care facilities and public utilities, workplaces in factories, retail structure."[56] Latent competition arose with the Maoist KPD-ML, which had meanwhile also taken up the issue. The latter organized residents' meetings, encouraged by the emerging protests against the closure of Bethanien Hospital, in which they successfully awakened memories of the interwar period when the German Communist Party (KPD) had been a major political force in Kreuzberg.[57] However, the outcome that the Left had hoped for did not materialize: the residents of the blocks earmarked for demolition did not join together in a "collective refusal to leave." As a result, many activists withdrew back into the academic world.[58]

It was equally difficult to realize the protests' potential in Frankfurt. In the autumn of 1970, an activist group calling itself Socialist Aid considered a "campaign against the real estate brokers" and drew inspiration from London. On invitation, London activist Peter Polish reported on how social workers had initiated squats for homeless families, a model that had been successful since the mid-1960s.[59] A similar approach was already practiced in Frankfurt's first squats in September 1970, when activists of the action group Westend invited homeless people to squat at Eppsteiner Straße 47.[60] A different approach—more focused on agitation—was taken by the district group Roter Gallus (Red Gallus), cofounded in the spring of 1970 by former SDS chair Karl Dietrich Wolff, which brought together student "Red Cells" and the Black Panther Solidarity Group. Explicitly understanding itself as an experiment in "socialist practice" that sought to grasp the "living conditions of the proletariat outside the factory," the Gallus group hoped that "concentration" on this "relatively 'homogeneous' proletarian" quarter would lead to a "longer-term" connection between factory and neighborhood work. Among others, it cooperated with the factory project group Revolutionärer Kampf (Revolutionary Struggle).[61] The everyday practice of the Red Gallus group focused on public relations and legal assistance. The neighborhood group's lawyers offered tenants support in applying for rent subsidies. In late June 1970, they organized the first "tenant protest," which passed a resolution to persuade the housing company Hellerhof AG to retract a planned 30 percent rent increase. The campaign was accompanied by the newspaper *Roter Gallus*, which, starting in July 1970, was distributed with a print run of twenty thousand copies. The concept of the activist group was to offer itself to residents as a self-help organization, like the MVZ: "Here the residents can address conflicts . . . police assaults on young people, forced evictions from flats, exploitative piecework in factories."[62] They used a particular political language to distinguish themselves from both bourgeois and social democratic circles. Their critique was primarily aimed at the Frankfurt Social Democrats, who only protested "extreme individual cases," although these were "inconceivable without the general climate of speculation on the construction market and the price hikes." With reference to the demands for "lower rents" and "decent housing" by FIAT workers in Italy, Red Gallus criticized the "temporary rent freeze" demanded by the DGB.[63] They kept their distance, however, from the simultaneously developing criticism of the destruction of the "residential character" of the Westend, as expressed by the AG Westend (AGW), founded in April 1968. In the context of their first involvement with squatting, the AGW called for a demonstration in October 1970, protesting the "destruction of housing, devastation of the cityscape, urban depopulation [and] rent profiteering." Red Gallus did not see the AGW's calls for the "democratization" of municipal administration and the development of alternatives to urban planning as real solutions to the more deep-rooted plight. These groups all worked to highlight the collective—and thus political—character of individuals' material needs in urban settings. Nonetheless, ideological and tactical differences often superseded shared outlooks.

The grassroots work in the neighborhoods was controversial from the beginning. It was criticized by part of the SC editorial staff, the Kommunistische Gruppe (Communist Group), stating that this work ultimately had a "social democratic" character instead of a "radical political approach," especially since it lacked a starting point in the sphere of production. It merely continued a "tradition of [performing a] 'social movement'" in which "anticapitalist consciousness is never more than moral indignation in the guise of socialist slogans." The "inner logic of tenant agitation," which under the aforementioned conditions "must result either in social aid or in putschist 'street actions,'" corresponds more to the model of a tenants' association.[64] Nonetheless, even such a "social democratic" association seemed to have little success at this point. The future squatter and writer Ulrike Heider reports that the group's "agitational-political house calls" found little sympathy among the residents of the working-class district, who seemed "poorer, but also more petty-bourgeois than expected"; only the "lumpenproletariat" was responsive to the idea of a rent strike.[65]

Although doubts arose among leftists about these approaches, and some, succumbing to revolutionary impatience, already favored retreat, broad coalitions involving grassroots neighborhood groups, independent Communist groups, the German Communist Party (DKP), churches, trade unions, migrant workers, and lower middle-class residents did emerge in many cities from 1970 onward. A vehement urban critique was also articulated from within the governing SPD, and the Young Socialists often worked closely with the emerging initiatives. In October 1970, the German Tenants' Association called for a nationwide protest rally for the first time in its history. The Düsseldorf daily newspaper *Rheinische Post* displayed ambivalent sympathies for the burgeoning movement, being particularly concerned that those negatively affected by the housing situation would grow to believe that even "illegal" actions were legitimate forms of protest:

> What Rudi Dutschke hoped for in vain, what the SDS never succeeded in doing is currently being accomplished almost effortlessly by protesting students: the applause of citizens, the solidarity of workers, employees and civil servants. . . . More alarming, however, is the widespread feeling among many tenants that they can legitimately violate the law because they are morally in the right. Yesterday, for example, 50 tenants of the municipal housing association in Weiden (Upper Palatinate) went on a payment strike. Their rents had been increased by 20 percent.[66]

Rent strikes took the form of refusing to accept increases in the basic rent or, with the oil price crisis of 1973, the immense increases in utility costs. These rent strikes became a form of protest in many large and medium-sized towns and cities and spread throughout the country, being taken up by the tenants of the large housing associations in new buildings as well as by migrant workers (and their families) who lived in company housing or under particularly precarious conditions in dilapidated old buildings. After initial successes of the rent strikes, however, legal means of protest indeed became largely exhausted, leading to a decline in the mid-1970s.

Rent Strikes in Student Residences

Students remained an important link between an academic critique of urban planning policy, tenant protest in nonprofit housing, and squatters. A first wave of rent strikes in student residence halls started around 1969. Residents demanded greater say and tried to resist house rules and the rigid regulation of their daily lives by administrators. Students at the Kirchliche Hochschule Berlin, a theological university, denied entrance to nonstudent home inspectors and declared that they no longer wanted to pay their rent to the "authoritarian residence management."[67] At a Frankfurt student residence that had a reputation for being a center of left-wing agitation, residents reneged on the house rules, claimed authority over the allocation of rooms, and rejected rent increases. Their example was taken up elsewhere.[68] In the early 1970s, student housing shortages were a prevalent problem due to the growing number of students, but also to the loss of cheap housing resulting from the ubiquitous policy of destroying old buildings. This became a central theme of the student press and of the left-wing papers of the *K-Gruppen*, which were widespread at universities, in neighborhood groups, and in factories. Protests turned against makeshift accommodations that student tenants had to put up with and misappropriations of student housing. In Darmstadt, students occupied an empty floor of a university building. Bonn students spent nights in lecture halls, and Hanover students refused to allow their living spaces to be converted into offices.[69] In Marburg, students tried to go beyond their halls of residence and to make connections with other critics of housing policy by filing rent extortion lawsuits.[70]

Rent strikes in student residences became a common practice nationwide. Interregional "rent strike" networks developed.[71] A red "S" (for strike) appeared in student housing windows across the country, affecting both universities and technical colleges.[72] These strikes continued throughout the 1970s and were far from over at the end of the decade when the cities saw a resurgence of squatting. The wave of payment refusals reached its peak in 1973/74, when housing firms tried to balance out dramatically increased utility costs incurred from the oil crisis by increasing students' rent. Simultaneously, what might be called a second student movement took place, with protests directed against legislation emerging in the context of the Higher Education Framework Act and, above all, advocating an improvement of students' social situation. In January 1974, forty thousand students took to the streets in Bonn. They demanded an adjustment of student loans to cover inflation and an increase in the parental income threshold that would make more students eligible for student loans.[73]

One of the most protracted rent strikes in student halls of residence took place in Aachen between 1972 and 1977. Since the early 1960s, the RWTH Aachen had developed into the largest technical university in West Germany, with about 17,000 enrolled students in 1973. As early as 1971, resident students had protested a rent increase from 80 to 95 DM, but they had quickly capitulated. Nonetheless, in April 1972, when the board of the *Studentenwerk* (a nonprofit organization for student affairs) tried once again to raise the rent—this time from 95 to 115 DM—and also to change rental contracts so that it would no longer be necessary to receive signed approval for rent increases, the general assembly of Aachen student residences spoke out against the decision. This time, the proclamation was a complete success. Already in early July 1972, the newspaper of the Aachen AStA (General Students' Committee) announced that 89.6 percent of residents had joined the rent strike. A rent of more than 100 DM corresponded to more than a quarter of the loan granted to needy students under the Federal Education Assistance Act (BAföG) to cover their living costs. Under the slogan "Fighting the social *numerus clausus*," the Gemeinsamer Ausschuss (Joint Committee, GA) of residence halls demanded "replacing the principle of cost-covering with that of social sustainability" and the "inclusion of students in social housing."[74] The GA drafted a rent support agreement, according to which the state and the university would pledge joint-responsibility for the operating costs of student housing. The Studentenwerk lost the complicated legal process that ensued. Both parties rejected the court's settlement option, which would have delayed the rent increase until March 1973. In response, the court dismissed the payment summons and eviction suits issued by the Studentenwerk and ordered it to pay the court costs.[75] In addition, the court challenged the Studentenwerk's accounting practices, which led to the dismissal of its managing director and a state audit of its accounts.

The Aachen conflict quickly escalated into a dispute between the striking students, the Studentenwerk, and the state of North Rhine-Westphalia. With the argument that residential students were privileged per se, the state insisted on rents that covered all costs and obtained a court order to intervene in the proceedings. The students rejected a compromise proposal from the Ministry of Science that would have limited the rent increase to 105 DM, arguing that the increase was not tied to the rates of the Federal Education Assistance Act. The state responded in January 1974 by threatening to block all subsidies flowing through the Studentenwerk. When new notices of dismissal began arriving in February, the strike spread further. The state reacted with a legislative reform, which transformed the independent Studentenwerk into a public institution and legally anchored the link between state subsidies and cost recovery. The students succeeded in delaying the transfer of the Studentenwerk's assets to the new institution by renewed legal action and by mobilizing a blocking minority on the association's board. In the long legal dispute, the students had to accept serious service restrictions, such as limited water and reduced cleaning services, and ultimately they had to put up with the changed legal situation. However, the long delay to the rent increases and the district court's dismissal of the evictions were partial successes. There was hope that the Aachen struggle would serve as an "example" for other groups suffering from "rent hikes" and housing shortage.

For students living in residence halls in North Rhine-Westphalia, the course of the Aachen conflict was a decisive impulse. Already in January 1973, a first meeting of student rent strike committees took place in Cologne. The Coordinating Committee of the Rent Strikers NRW, founded in November 1974, succeeded early the following year in drafting a unifying set of demands including the formula that students were to pay no more than 15 to 25 percent of their student loans for rent.[76] The national press was well-disposed toward the students and recorded the partial legal successes as a "defeat" for SPD minister of science Johannes Rau, who again found himself at the center of disputes during student rent strikes in Münster and Düsseldorf.

Even after settlement of the Aachen conflict in 1977, rent strikes persisted, especially under the SPD government in North Rhine-Westphalia.[77] As late as 1978, the *Bochumer Volksblatt* published a series on rent strikes, and the local student paper *Gegendruck* reported on a strike that had been going on in a residence hall for married students and students with families since 1973.[78] In Münster, strikers and squatters, some of whom had been active since 1972, continued to cooperate with each other in their fight for adequate student housing, sometimes very successfully.[79] When a nationwide "squatters' meeting" took place in Münster in late March 1981, forcible evictions had become a common experience for tenant activists in halls of residence. The meeting once more put squatting onto the political agenda alongside wider issues such as housing shortage and real estate "speculation." At the end of the meeting, an observer who was close to the DKP again highlighted the material interests that were at the heart of violent conflicts: "The 'rioters' were those who refused to be defeated come what may . . . [those who continued] with often unprecedented courage . . . to fight for better housing and living conditions."[80]

Conclusion

The independent urban movements that developed within the cross-movement structures of the 1970s and 1980s, including student movements, women's movements, and movements against large-scale infrastructure projects, spread far beyond the famous squats in the protest strongholds of Frankfurt and Berlin. This is shown by a host of protest campaigns: rent strikes, initiatives for the preservation of architectural heritage (from the medieval buildings of Lüneburg to the miners' housing estates in the Ruhr), initiatives for the reallocation of buildings as youth and cultural centers or childcare facilities, not to mention initiatives against road construction projects or the increase of public transport fares. Protest increasingly broadened from academic trailblazers to the directly affected. The nonparliamentary left-wing opposition around and after '68—including district base groups, *Spontis*, *K-Gruppen*, and later autonomists—was an important factor in this process. For them, housing struggles were an integral part of their social critique and a continuous field of action. With the aim of expanding the class struggle in the factory to include the reproductive sphere, these groups developed mutual alliances in their efforts to mobilize tenants of mass housing projects while frequently seeking their ideological or tactical distance from potential fellow campaigners. They supported and got involved in migrants' rent strikes and numerous rent payment refusal protests in student residence halls. Although these housing struggles reflect the fragmentation of the Left, they simultaneously reveal the connections that held together the broader movement milieus of the 1970s and 1980s. New constellations and alliances emerged amid struggles to preserve old neighborhoods, despite the substandard conditions prevailing there during the 1960s and 1970s. These new cooperations were supported by the surge of interest in countercultural ways of life and by a trenchant critique of the traditional family model.[81] The driving force behind all of this, however, were tangible material interests: affordable housing, a decent quality of life in urban spaces, and not least the (re)distribution of public goods—issues that have hardly lost their relevance over the past fifty years.

Freia Anders is a lecturer in history at Johannes Gutenberg University Mainz, and was a research fellow at Bielefeld University from 2004–2012. Her publications include *Public Goods versus Economic Interests: Global Perspectives on the History of Squatting* (Routledge, 2017), coedited with A. Sedlmaier, and *Strafjustiz im Sudetengau 1938–1945* (Oldenbourg, 2008).

Notes

1. The author would like to thank Rolf Engelke for his generous comments on Frankfurt history, including the provision of an unpublished manuscript: *Eine chronologische Materialsammlung (1962–1975/76) zu urbanen Kämpfen: Umkämpfte Stadtentwicklung—Mietstreiks—Hausbesetzungen—"Häuserkampf"* (November 2019); also see Engelke, "'Häuserkampf'—Urbane Kämpfe in Frankfurt 1970–74," in *Dieses Haus ist besetzt! Frankfurter Häuserkampf 1970–1974*, ed. Frankfurter Archiv der Revolte (Frankfurt a.M., 2020), 92–103.
2. Barbara Schönig, "Sechs Thesen: Zur wieder mal 'neuen' Wohnungsfrage; Plädoyer für ein interdisziplinäres Gespräch," in *Wohnraum für alle?! Perspektiven auf Planung, Politik und Architektur*, ed. Barbara Schönig, Justin Kadi, and Sebastian Schipper (Bielefeld: transcript, 2017), 11–27.
3. Freia Anders and Alexander Sedlmaier, eds., "Introduction," in *Public Goods versus Economic Interests: Global Perspectives on the History of Squatting* (New York: Routledge, 2017), 3–7.
4. Squatting Europe Kollective, *The Squatters' Movement in Europe: Commons and Autonomy as Alternatives to Capitalism* (London: Verso 2014), 3.
5. Daniel Schmidt, "In Freiräumen leben: Hausbesetzungen und Hausbesetzer in der Bundesrepublik Deutschland (1970–1982)," in *Radikalismus und politische Reformen*, ed. Duco Hellema, Friso Wielenga, and Markus Wilp (Münster: Waxmann, 2012), 133; critical with contemporary references, see Margit Mayer, "Städtische soziale Bewegungen," in *Die sozialen Bewegungen in Deutschland seit 1945: Ein Handbuch*, ed. Roland Roth and Dieter Rucht (Frankfurt a.M.: Campus, 2008), 305.
6. Lisa Vollmer, "Mieter_innenproteste von den 1960er bis in die 1980er Jahre in der BRD: Von der Klassenallianz zur Aufspaltung und Einhegung ins neoliberale Projekt," *sub/urban* 6, nos. 2/3 (2018): 174.
7. David Templin, *Freizeit ohne Kontrolle: Die Jugendzentrumsbewegung in der Bundesrepublik der 1970er Jahre* (Göttingen: Wallstein, 2015); also see his chapter in this volume.
8. Peter Birke, "Diese merkwürdige, zerklüftete Landschaft: Anmerkungen zur 'Stadt in der Revolte,'" *Sozial.Geschichte Online* 6 (2011): 28–62.
9. *Luttes urbaines et pouvoir politique* (Paris: Maspéro, 1973); German, English and Spanish version 1974/75.
10. Christopher Klemek, *The Transatlantic Collapse of Urban Renewal: Postwar Urbanism from New York to Berlin* (Chicago: University of Chicago Press, 2011), 90–92.
11. Alexander Sedlmaier, *Consumption and Violence: Radical Protest in Cold-War West Germany* (Ann Arbor: University of Michigan Press, 2014), 205.
12. Bart van der Steen and Knud Andresen, eds., *A European Youth Revolt: European Perspectives on Youth Protest and Social Movements in the 1980s* (London: Palgrave, 2016).
13. Thomas Würtenberger, *Zeitgeist und Recht* (Tübingen: Mohr Siebeck, 1991, 2nd edition), 143.
14. Karl-Werner Brandt, Detlef Büsser, and Dieter Rucht, *Aufbruch in eine andere Gesellschaft: Neue soziale Bewegungen in der Bundesrepublik* (Frankfurt a.M.: Campus, 1983), 203.

15. Matthias Manrique, *Marginalisierung und Militanz: Jugendliche Bewegungsmilieus im Aufruhr* (Frankfurt a.M.: Campus, 1992), 101, 218.
16. Freia Anders, "Wohnraum, Freiraum, Widerstand: Die Formierung der Autonomen in den Konflikten um Hausbesetzungen Anfang der achtziger Jahre," in *Das alternative Milieu: Unkonventionelle Lebensentwürfe und linke Politik in der Bundesrepublik Deutschland und Westeuropa 1968–1983*, ed. Sven Reichardt and Detlef Siegfried (Göttingen: Wallstein, 2010), 475.
17. Armin Kuhn, *Vom Häuserkampf zur neoliberalen Stadt: Besetzungsbewegungen in Berlin und Barcelona* (Münster: Westfälisches Dampfboot, 2014), 41–44.
18. Sven Reichardt, *Authentizität und Gemeinschaft: Linksalternatives Leben in den siebziger und frühen achtziger Jahren* (Berlin: Suhrkamp, 2014), 498–570; Freia Anders and Alexander Sedlmaier, "Squatting Means to Destroy the Capitalist Plan in the Urban Quarters: Spontis, Autonomists and the Struggles over Public Commodities (1970–1983)," in *Cities Contested: Urban Politics, Heritage, and Social Movements in Italy and West Germany in the 1970s*, ed. Martin Baumeister, Bruno Bonomo, and Dieter Schott (Frankfurt a.M.: Campus, 2017), 195–211; Sebastian Kasper, *Spontis: Eine Geschichte antiautoritärer Linker im roten Jahrzehnt* (Münster: Unrast, 2019), 83–96; Sedlmaier, *Consumption and Violence*, 205–31.
19. *Metall* 2 (1968), quoted in Projektbereich Infrastrukturplanung und Sozialpolitik, "Städtewesen und Wohnungsbau," *SC-Info* 16, 10 October 1969, 8. This and other journals and leaflets, if not stated otherwise, are taken from the online archives of Dietmar Kesten and Jürgen Schröder, *Materialien zur Analyse von Opposition* (MAO), https://www.mao-projekt.de/.
20. Björn Egner, "Wohnungspolitik seit 1945," *Aus Politik und Zeitgeschichte*, nos. 20/21 (2014): 14–16.
21. Adalbert Evers and Juan Rodriguez-Lores, "Hausbesetzung und Mietstreik: Zur Selbstorganisation der städtischen Bevölkerung," *Das Werk: Architektur und Kunst* 62, no. 3 (1975): 287.
22. Rainer Neef, "Die Bedeutung des Grundbesitzes in den Städten," *Kursbuch* 27 (1972): 32–57.
23. Bernhard Schäfers, "Leitbilder der Stadtentwicklung in der Bundesrepublik Deutschland," in *Soziologie und Gesellschaftsentwicklung: Aufsätze 1966–1996*, ed. Bernhard Schäfers (Frankfurt a.M.: Suhrkamp, 1996), 319–22.
24. Alexander Mitscherlich: *Die Unwirtlichkeit unserer Städte: Anstiftung zum Unfrieden* (Frankfurt a.M.: Suhrkamp, 1965), 16.
25. Ernst Stracke, *Stadtzerstörung und Stadtteilkampf in Frankfurt am Main* (Cologne: Pahl-Rugenstein, 1980), 33–37.
26. Engelke, *Materialsammlung*, 8.
27. Detlef Siegfried, *Time Is on My Side: Konsum und Politik in der westdeutschen Jugendkultur der 60er Jahre* (Göttingen: Wallstein, 2006), 416, 426.
28. Joy Gantevoort, "Nur ein bisschen Dynamit," *Frankfurter Neue Presse*, 22 January 2018.
29. Siegfried, *Time*, 419.
30. Nina Gribat, "Grabenkämpfe um die Kritik am funktionellen Städtebau um 1968: Sozialpsychologische Reformist_innen und marxistische Revoluzzer_innen," *sub\urban* 6 (2018): 181.

31. Heide Berndt, "Der Verlust von Urbanität im Städtebau," *Das Argument*, no. 44 (1967): 286.
32. Heide Berndt, *Das Gesellschaftsbild bei Stadtplanern* (Stuttgart: K. Krämer, 1968).
33. Heide Berndt, "Ist der Funktionalismus eine funktionale Architektur? Soziologische Betrachtung einer architektonischen Kategorie," in *Architektur als Ideologie*, ed. Heide Berndt, Alfred Lorenzer, and Klaus Horn (Frankfurt a.M.: Suhrkamp, 1968), 20, 29, 40ff.
34. Ibid, 42.
35. Nina Gribat, "Selbstorganisiertes und politisches Lernen in der Architektur an der TU Berlin um 1968," in *Vergessene Schulen: Architekturlehre zwischen Reform und Revolte um 1968*, ed. Nina Gribat, Philipp Misselwitz, and Matthias Görlich (Leipzig: Spector Books, 2017), 327.
36. Hans G. Helms, "Die Stadt—Medium der Ausbeutung: Historische Perspektiven des Städtebaus," in *Kapitalistischer Städtebau*, ed. Hans G Helms and Jörn Janssen (Neuwied: Luchterhand, 1971), 24–25.
37. Jörn Janssen, "Sozialismus, Sozialpolitik und Wohnungsnot," in ibid., 67.
38. Helms, "Stadt," 27.
39. Janssen, "Sozialismus," 79, 91.
40. Peter Neitzke, "Die Agenten der Kulturkritik isolieren! Anweisung zum richtigen Verständnis von Schriften, die nur Verwirrung stiften," in *Kapitalistischer Städtebau*, ed. Helms and Janssen, 163.
41. Ibid., 165.
42. Autorenkollektiv der Architekturabteilung der ETH Zürich, *Göhnerswil: Architektur im Kapitalismus* (Zürich: Verlagsgenossenschaft, 1971).
43. Anne Kockelkorn, "Ein Gespräch über Wohnungsfragen, Hochschulintrigen und einen Meister aus Italien: Zürich 1971," *Candide: Journal for Architectural Knowledge* 7, no. 10 (2013): 113.
44. Gribat et al., *Vergessene Schulen*, 7, 244–48.
45. Faksimile in ibid., 111–14.
46. Quoted in "Städtebau West-Berlin: Slums verschoben," *Der Spiegel* 37, 9 September 1968. On MV, see Christiane Reinecke, "Am Rande der Gesellschaft? Das Märkische Viertel—eine West-Berliner Großsiedlung und ihre Darstellung als urbane Problemzone," *Zeithistorische Forschungen* 11, no. 2 (2014): https://zeithistorische-forschungen.de/2-2014/5095.
47. The magazine's imprint mentions Günter Amendt, Peter Brandt, Rudi Dutschke, Gaston Salvatore, and Christian Semler.
48. Thomas Schmitz-Bender and Helge Sommerrock, "Organisierung der Unorganisierten! Basisgruppen," *Was tun?* 1, August/September 1968.
49. Andreas Hüttner and Azozomox, "Von Blumen und Märchen: Stadtteilorganisierung im Märkischen Viertel," in *Mieterkämpfe vom Kaiserreich bis heute: Das Beispiel Berlin*, ed. Philipp Mattern (Berlin: Bertz+Fischer, 2018), 67, 71.
50. Rudolph Bauer, "Entlarvt den Sozialstaat!" *SC-Info* 7, 5 July 1969.
51. *SC-Info* 1, 19 April 1969, quoted in Engelke, *Materialsammlung*, 4.
52. Ulrike Meinhof, "Strategiepapier MV," in *'Jetzt reden wir': Betroffene des Märkischen Viertels*, ed. Johannes Beck (Reinbek: Rowohlt, 1975), quoted in *trend.infopartisan* 8 (2013): http://www.trend.infopartisan.net/trd0813/t070813.html. On the integral

position of "consumption" in Meinhof's political thought see Sedlmaier, *Consumption and Violence*, 101–33.
53. Marcel Glaser, "Peter Koller (1907–1996): Stadtplaner in Diktatur und Demokratie; Eine Biographie," in *Lebensreform um 1900 und Alternativmilieu um 1980: Kontinuitäten und Brüche in Milieus der gesellschaftlichen Selbstreflexion im frühen und späten 20. Jahrhundert*, ed. Detlef Siegfried and David Templin (Göttingen: Wallstein, 2019), 327–30.
54. Jürgen Enkemann, "Von der Abrisssanierung zur behutsamen Stadterneuerung: Kontroversen um die West-Berliner Stadtplanung der 1960er und 1970er Jahre," in Mattern, *Mieterkämpfe*, 45.
55. Büro für Stadtsanierung und soziale Arbeit: *Sanierung—für wen?* (Berlin, 1970/1971).
56. Helga Fassbinder, "Gegen-Planung," *Bauwelt* 48 (1983): 351–54.
57. Leaflet, "Hände weg von Bethanien! Nr. 4," Berlin [1969].
58. Fassbinder, "Gegen-Planung," 354.
59. "Kurzprotokoll über die Arbeitskonferenz der Sozialistischen Hilfe," *SC-Info* 21, 15 November 1969, 17–18; on London, see John Davis: "'The Most Fun I've Ever Had . . .'? Squatting in England in the 1970s," in Anders and Sedlmaier, *Public Goods*, 237.
60. Engelke, "Häuserkampf," 96.
61. Stadtteilgruppe Gallus, "Bericht der Stadtteilgruppe Gallus," *SC-Info* 48/49, 15 June 1970, 23–25; Engelke, *Materialsammlung*, 6.
62. *Roter Gallus* 1, 1 July 1970, quoted ibid., 6.
63. *Roter Gallus* 2, 20 September 1970, quoted ibid., 8.
64. KG, "Agitation und Propaganda in der aktuellen Klassenkampfsituation," *SC* 52/53, July 1970.
65. Ulrike Heider, *Keine Ruhe nach dem Sturm* (Hamburg: Rogner & Bernhard, 2001), 99–100.
66. *Rheinische Post*, 30 September 1970, quoted in Volker Rekittke and Klaus Martin Becker, *Politische Aktionen gegen Wohnungsnot und Umstrukturierung und die HausbesetzerInnenbewegung in Düsseldorf von 1972 bis heute* (Düsseldorf University 1995), https://archiv.squat.net/duesseldorf/Index.html, Fn. 427.
67. Tobias Sarx, *Reform, Revolution oder Stillstand? Die 68er-Bewegung an den Evangelisch-Theologischen Fakultäten Marburg, Bochum und an der Kirchlichen Hochschule Berlin* (Stuttgart: Kohlhammer, 2018), 322–24.
68. Heider, *Keine Ruhe*, 112–14, 159–64.
69. *Hannoversche Studentenzeitung* 8, no. 52, 1 November 1971, 1.
70. Leaflet [Marburg], "Mietwucherklagen: Caritative Aktion oder Ansatzpunkt für pol. Bewegung?" *AStA-Info Extra*, 18 October 1973.
71. [FH Clausthal-Zellerfeld], "Mietstreiks in CLZ," *Kommunistische Arbeiter Nachrichten*, no. 3, June/July 1973, 5; leaflet [Marburg], "Beitrag zum Sozialkampf—Mietstreik im Vilmarhaus!!!" 28 January 1974; [Hamburg], "Senat will Abbruch der Mietverweigerung erzwingen," *Rote Presse* 4, 29 April 1975, 5; [Berlin], "Mietstreik in der Keithstr.," *Kommunistische Hochschulzeitung* 5, 22 May 1974, 5.
72. "Rotes 'S' an der Fensterscheibe. Mietstreik in Kölner Studentenwohnheimen," *Hochschulfront Extra*, 12 December 1973, 9.

73. Freia Anders, "'Die Universität ist nicht mehr en vogue': Die JGU in den 1970er-Jahren," in *75 Jahre Johannes Gutenberg-Universität Mainz: Universität in der demokratischen Gesellschaft* (Regensburg: Schnell+Steiner, 2021), 90–108, 104.
74. Hochschulgruppen der RWTH Aachen, GA, *3 Jahre 1972–1975... Mietstreik. Dokumentation Nr. 3*, February 1975, 3–5.
75. "Prozeß gewonnen—was nun?" *Aachener Studentenzeitung* 20, 9 May 1973, 1–2, 6.
76. "Protokoll des Koordinierungsausschusses," 17 November 1974, GA, 14, 69.
77. *Aachener Studentenzeitung* 18, 17 October 1977, 12.
78. "Bochumer Initiativen informieren," *Bochumer Volksblatt* 12, March 1978, 5; "Marmor, Stein und Eisen bricht—Aber unser Mietstreik nicht!" *Gegendruck. Zeitungsprojekt an der RUB* 2, no. 5, June 1978, 5–6.
79. "Frauenstraße 24: Zwangsversteigert!"; "Mietstreik-Informationstag im Wilhelmskamp," *Asta-Info: Informationen des Asta der Universität Münster* 61, 6 February 1976, 1; "Zwangsräumungen verhindert. Wohnheim besetzt," *Asta-Info*, 28 October 1977, 1.
80. Wilfried Reckert, "Lieber Instandbesetzen als Kaputtbesitzen," *Jugendpolitische Blätter* [Dortmund], May 1981.
81. Siegfried, *Time*, 646.

Select Bibliography

Anders, Freia, and Alexander Sedlmaier, eds. *Public Goods versus Economic Interests: Global Perspectives on the History of Squatting*. New York: Routledge, 2017.

Gribat, Nina, Philipp Misselwitz, and Matthias Görlich, eds. *Vergessene Schulen: Architekturlehre zwischen Reform und Revolte um 1968*. Leipzig: Spector Books, 2017.

Klemek, Christopher. *The Transatlantic Collapse of Urban Renewal: Postwar Urbanism from New York to Berlin*. Chicago: University of Chicago Press, 2011.

Mayer, Margit. "Städtische soziale Bewegungen." In *Die sozialen Bewegungen in Deutschland seit 1945: Ein Handbuch*, edited by Roland Roth and Dieter Rucht, 294–318. Frankfurt a.M.: Campus, 2008.

Sedlmaier, Alexander. *Consumption and Violence: Radical Protest in Cold-War West Germany*. Ann Arbor: University of Michigan Press, 2014.

Vollmer, Lisa. "Mieter_innenproteste von den 1960er bis in die 1980er Jahre in der BRD: Von der Klassenallianz zur Aufspaltung und Einhegung ins neoliberale Projekt." *sub/urban* 6, nos. 2/3 (2018): 137–48.

Chapter 6

Running Over Trees in Germany

Social Movements and the US Army, 1975–85

Adam R. Seipp

For a week in September 1984, a carnival of protest descended on Fulda and other communities in eastern Hessen. Thousands of protestors, many of them young, followed by the German and international press, held a series of events they called "Rock Against Maneuvers." The occasion was Operation Flinker Igel, the latest iteration of the annual NATO fall maneuvers. For NATO forces, and particularly the US Army, this was an opportunity to show off a range of operational and technological innovations that promised to give the West an insurmountable advantage over their more numerous Eastern Bloc foes. For a broad and diffuse network of activists in the Federal Republic, this moment was an opportunity to show their ability to mobilize and to at least hinder NATO efforts. For both sides, the central focus was a swath of land in Osthessen known as the Fulda Gap.[1]

After a week of maneuvering and demonstrating, neither side made their case particularly convincingly. More than 250,000 NATO troops put on a dramatic display in Bavaria and Hessen. Bad weather made the tracks of 10,000 armored vehicles particularly destructive to farmland. Six servicemen died in accidents, and maneuver damages totaled more than $10 million. Politicians in Wiesbaden, Munich, and Bonn complained loudly, and one American journalist wondered about the extent of "psychological damage wrought by a military invasion of this extraordinarily orderly society."[2]

On the other hand, protestors proved able to generate more light than heat with their demonstrations. They certainly attracted considerable attention, but numbers were far lower than organizers wanted. The proposed human chain, which was to have linked several local communities, fell short of expectations. The protest's organizers, the Arbeitsgruppe Aktionsherbst 84, hoped for 110,000 demonstrators across the region. Only about one-third of that number showed up.³ The chain had, one unsympathetic German journalist wrote, "Fulda Gaps of its own."⁴ The demonstrations in Osthessen point to the possibilities and the challenges confronting an assertive but inchoate coalition of German activists who arrayed against the continued military buildup in their country.

An examination of the relationship between German activists and the US military in the 1970s and 1980s can tell us much about the broader political transformations in the Federal Republic during these pivotal years. The American presence was large, economically important, and spread through much the southern and central parts of the country. American forces had rights in the Federal Republic as part of a web of international agreements dating from the postwar founding period. Bases and maneuvers were explicitly transnational in scope and legal authority but were also embedded into local communities and local contexts. As the other chapters in this volume stress, activism in the post-1968 context needs to be understood at the juncture of the transnational and the local.⁵ In this way, the story of how activists confronted the American presence, and how the Americans responded, is an important and illustrative example of the wider phenomenon.

This chapter is about what I will call the "antimilitarization" movement in the Federal Republic of Germany (FRG) in the late 1970s and early 1980s. This movement is often overshadowed in existing literature by the enormous public campaign against the stationing of new-generation missiles in the FRG. Both are often grouped under the umbrella term *Friedensbewegung*, or "peace movement."⁶ The two were certainly related, but they were also quite distinct and sometimes competed with each other over membership, goals, and tactics. There was also a substantial difference in German public opinion on the missile modernization program and the continued deployment of American forces in the country. While around 50 percent of the FRG's population opposed or expressed serious reservations about the deployment of next-generation missiles, about 70 percent consistently indicated support for a continued American military presence in the country.⁷ If we take the Krefeld Appeal of 1983 as a document expressing a minimal consensus among the members of the peace movement, we can see this quite clearly. There is no reference in the Appeal to conventional weapons per se. The antimilitarization movement had to operate in a relatively limited political space.

Four points need to be made about this movement and its public role. First, antimilitarization was a highly diffuse movement that merged long-lasting local concerns with national and transnational organizing strategies and concerns. Second, antimilitarization drew from a tradition of grievance and protest dating back to the 1950s and the early period of the foreign military presence in a semi-sovereign Federal Republic. Third, the antimilitarization movement emerged in tandem with the post-Vietnam modernization of NATO forces, and particularly the US Army. The "Second Cold War," a renewed military buildup following a decade of détente, created new sites of conflict on German soil. The Americans, aware that they needed the cooperation of German society, made substantial efforts to accommodate at least some of the antimilitarization movement's demands. Finally, the antimilitarization movement's tactics evolved in response to the successes of the antimissile campaign but were also quite limited because of the narrow parameters of their argument.

Recent scholarship on social movements in the FRG has been rich in empirical and theoretical insights. A series of edited volumes and monographs has vastly expanded our understanding of the transnational German environmental movement and of the vast peace movement.[8] The citizen activism of the 1970s is now firmly embedded in the history of a plural, prosperous Federal Republic. Scholars have productively explored the close linkages between the growing environmental movement and other calls for political change within the Cold War context.[9] Several recent studies have asked us to consider the important role of fear in shaping the politics of the Bonn Republic and for contextualizing the nuclear fears of the late Cold War within the history of a state founded as an imperiled Cold War borderland in the shadow of defeat and disaster in 1945.[10] Susanne Schregel, in her excellent 2011 study, draws attention to the "turn to local" in German peace activism during this period.[11] Schregel's work is particularly significant here because of the importance that she places on activism targeting conventional weapons and other military installations in the FRG.

This chapter argues that the antimilitarization movement, and the peace movement of the late 1970s and early 1980s more broadly, needs to be examined in an explicitly transnational context. The antimilitarization movement had its origins in three distinct developments. First was the changing character of the American military presence in the FRG after 1975. Second was the development of a robust and grassroots environmental movement in the FRG during that decade. Finally, the movement drew many of its issues and impulses from a long-standing set of conflicts between Germans and Americans over the use the physical space of the Federal Republic. These debates, which began in the late 1940s and early 1950s over the system of requisitioning that the Americans used to build their base archipelago, were far more than the sum of their parts. These were arguments about the nature of the FRG's sovereignty. The system of agreements and treaties that bound the FRG to the NATO alliance created a *system of modulated sovereignty*. In this sovereignty system, the formal Westphalian sovereignty of the FRG may have been embedded in international law after 1955, but Germans experienced sovereignty quite differently.[12]

In the FRG, sovereignty as lived experience varied widely, depending on where one lived. Almost 6 percent of the FRG's territory was under some form of military control or administration.[13] The majority of this territory, larger than the Saarland, was held by foreign military forces. Special economic and legal arrangements extended far beyond these pockets of land to the roads, apartment buildings, shops, and entertainment districts of the FRG's cities and towns. At the Cold War's height in the early 1980s, more than one hundred thousand Germans worked directly for foreign military forces, about half of those for the Americans.[14] For these workers, the limits of German sovereignty were an everyday reality. They woke up in the morning as full citizens of the FRG, gave up some of those rights when they entered their workplace, then resumed them at the end of their shift.[15] The American presence in the FRG mattered a tremendous amount to the everyday life of its citizens and others living there. The history of the Federal Republic, including its endogenous social conflicts and movements, cannot be understood without integrating the history of NATO forces who spent decades there.

The American military presence in the Federal Republic was enormous throughout the post-1950 period, but it dipped considerably under the pressures of Vietnam and the cost-cutting measures of the 1970s. The total number of American military personnel, civilians, and dependents dropped below four hundred thousand in 1968 and did not return to that level until 1978.[16] At the same time, the army struggled with serious challenges in its barracks in West Germany, including rampant drug use, low morale, and deeply entrenched racism.[17] Germans witnessed this state of affairs up close, since hundreds of thousands of citizens of the Federal Republic worked for, lived near, or otherwise interacted with American forces on a near-daily basis. The German press widely covered the army's agonies in the 1970s. Stories in the popular press highlighted the depths of the problems but also increasingly praised the Americans for at least trying to do something about them.[18]

Historians of the US Army have long argued that the disaster of Vietnam led to a series of profound reforms in doctrine, manpower policy, and technology that began to turn the army around.[19] These transformations matter in the story of the army in West Germany because they happened in full view of a German population that was itself very different than the broader public of the early 1960s. The US Army "returned" to Germany after 1975, but they found a very different Germany. This chapter attempts to consider both of these transformations together, as integrated and entangled developments.

The US Army of the late 1970s and early 1980s rolled out an astonishing array of new technology, including vastly improved armored vehicles, missile systems, and helicopters. Mammoth M1-Abrams battle tanks tore up rural roads across Germany, while Apache attack helicopters flew at all hours of the night. These were familiar problems in Germany, but they now accelerated considerably in intensity.[20] The new weapons systems required larger and more concentrated training exercises and facilities, including ever-larger nighttime exercises that reliably infuriated local sensibilities. An American report focusing on protests against nighttime helicopter training sardonically noted that

> it would be preferable to conduct aviation operations in such a way as to permit all citizens to enjoy their evenings, weekends, and holidays without the aircraft noise annoyance; however, since there is no assurance that a potential aggressor would respect this preference, the only alternative was to continue to meet current training and operational requirements.[21]

Maneuvers, and the damages that they caused, had been a source of problems between foreign forces and Germans since the 1950s.[22] Probably no other aspect of German-American relations at the local level caused more friction on a consistent basis. American forces trained next to and among the German population, so any expansion of training schedules necessarily exacerbated existing tensions. With the return of the Americans, maneuvers vastly increased in size and scope. By one estimate, the fall 1984 NATO maneuvers were the largest military exercise in Western Europe since the Normandy landings.[23] These maneuvers were increasing not only in size but also in the level of security required. As fears of protest groups and potentially violent organizations like the Red Army Faction (RAF) escalated, armed soldiers and German police now protected maneuver sites. An American officer conceded that this uptick in maneuvers only aggravated the "growing defense weariness on the part of the German population."[24]

Along with the technology came new doctrine, beginning with "Active Defense" in 1976 and the science fiction–sounding "AirLand Battle" in 1982.[25] Both doctrines called for an aggressive posture calculated to stop a Warsaw Pact armored offensive by breaking up the waves of "follow-on forces" expected to attack after the initial thrust into the FRG. AirLand Battle, in particular, seemed to call for the concentration of vast amounts of firepower behind the initial front and extending deep into East Germany (GDR) and Czechoslovakia. In a 1983 article in *Military Review*, two officers with considerable experience in West Germany wrote that such a conflict would feature "high volumes of fire and lack of a clear forward line of [*sic*] own troops."[26]

For Germans already skeptical of the increasingly aggressive posture of the Americans, AirLand Battle seemed to be a confirmation of the growing gulf between American strategic thinking and German attitudes toward issues of war and peace. It can be safely said that no American military manual has been as much read and discussed outside of the US Army as have the successive iterations of the Army Field Manual 100-5 (Operations), published in 1976 and 1982. FM 100-5 consists of hundreds of pages of dense, turgid text.[27] It is therefore all the more remarkable to find German editions of these manuals, some of which simply reprinted the English-language text. In the archives of the Green Party are copies of many of these manuals, including substantial annotation. It is quite clear that German activists were paying close and careful attention to what the US Army was planning in the Federal Republic.[28] The party's Bundestag delegation published an edited collection of documents on the new American doctrines, which they argued represented "the efforts of the US and NATO to decisively improve their 'conventional' warfare capability in Europe and elsewhere, but also stand for an immense military buildup and an increasing danger of war."[29]

The protest group Arbeitsgruppe Aktionsherbst 84's manifesto quoted extensively from FM 100-5. Its authors even read the Lynch and Bloxham article from *Military Review* quoted above. To these activists, the fact that the Americans enacted their new doctrines on German soil reduced the FRG's sovereignty and made their state complicit in American aggression. "This is not about the 'misuse' of Central Europe by ominous Superpowers, but rather the hard-nosed military and economic interests, into which the Federal Republic is fully integrated with the United States, despite small differences."[30]

The Bundeswehr actively tried to counter antimilitary sentiment. General Adalbert von der Recke visited with students at the University of Heidelberg to talk about the doctrine. He met a hostile reception. Students accused him of speaking in platitudes and "empty phrases" about security and the balance of power. Von der Recke tried to assure his audience that AirLand Battle was American doctrine, not NATO doctrine. German forces would not embrace the offensive-mindedness of the concept. The students were unmoved.[31]

This strategic context is critical to understanding the growing and increasingly vocal antimilitarization movement. Grassroots problems and conflicts between German communities and Americans languished in the early 1970s as the American presence declined and attention focused on issues like the conflict in Vietnam and the Offset Agreements. However, the return of

American forces in the country now reenergized old debates. The rise of citizens' interest groups in the FRG contributed to a blending of local concerns with national and international organizing.

Throughout the 1970s, a series of confrontations took place in and around garrison communities in the FRG over the actual or reported storage of chemical weapons by the Americans. In Baden-Württemberg, significant public protests began in 1969 over rumors of nerve agents being stored near Mannheim.[32] National media, most notably *Der Spiegel*, picked up the story and consistently reported on chemical weapons issues over the course of the 1970s. US Army Europe (USAREUR) headquarters in Heidelberg maintained a consistent policy of measured response to these accusations. They acknowledged that chemical weapons made up part of the American arsenal but would not comment on the location of these or any other agents. German antimilitarization activists consistently pointed to the 1954 Brussels Agreement, in which the FRG formally pledged to neither manufacture nor store chemical weapons. USAREUR asserted the claim that the weapons were in American custody under relevant NATO agreements.[33] This rather narrow technical argument actually pointed to a very substantive point of disagreement over the nature of German sovereignty. The Mannheim City Council passed yearly resolutions demanding information from USAREUR, which the Americans simply ignored. Activists from local antimilitarization organizations argued that these weapons were being stored "on German Federal property" and that the Americans were treating the FRG as if it had "reduced sovereignty."[34]

The nerve gas issue featured regularly in the Landtag, where a coalition of Green and SPD delegates used questions about American weapons to castigate the state government. During a particularly contentious session in 1980, the state's finance minister asserted that this was "not a topic for the Landtag of Baden-Württemberg" but rather a matter for negotiation between the Americans, NATO, and the federal government. He was promptly shouted down with calls of "Occupying Power!"[35]

The nerve gas dispute dovetailed perfectly with another long-running argument in the Mannheim area, this one over the American use of the Käfertaler Wald. This stretch of forest outside the city housed an American training facility since the 1950s, but it was also a critical source of the city's drinking water. Locals hated the noise of tank training and feared contamination of drinking water with oil and other toxins. The nerve gas question only exacerbated local anxieties. By 1980, local farmers and activists had been protesting against American use of the forest for thirty years.[36] The newly energized citizen groups of the 1970s and the nascent Green Party now attached themselves to a far older protest tradition in a region densely packed with foreign bases. "Many Germans," wrote a Darmstadt journalist in 1980, "have long assumed that they couldn't do anything to push back against" the Americans when they had complaints.[37] This was clearly changing.

The city archives in Mannheim have considerable documentation from citizens' groups of the late 1970s, collected under the umbrella of the early history of the Green Party in the area. These records show an interesting relationship between the proto-Greens and the American military presence. In some ways, it is surprising how little the American presence shows up in the records of these movements. There is a great deal of conversation about industry, water quality, and particularly the debate over nuclear power. To the extent that security issues arise, it was generally in the context of platitudes about the need for German nonalignment (*Blockfreiheit*) and the subsequent removal of all foreign troops from the FRG and GDR.[38]

However, there were groups in this orbit who explicitly or implicitly connected the environmental issues at their core with the American presence. The Bürgeraktion Umweltschutz Rhein-Neckar (BURN), a group formed primarily to protest against the nuclear power plant at Biblis, regularly spoke out against the noise, smoke, and pollutants generated by American activities in the region. "The mentality of the German population has changed recently," BURN wrote threateningly to the local American commander in 1975, "when unreasonable risks or burdens are imposed, spectacular incidents may occur in response."[39] The Americans alerted local authorities, who assured them that BURN was a small splinter group whose leadership was embroiled in factional disputes among themselves.

The intellectual connection between environmental issues and the American presence was increasingly clear. Pollutants generated by military activity did not respect the demarcation of the FRG's sovereign territory but moved through the storm drains, streams, and skies that connected foreign armies with the German population. Antimilitarization activists could point to a linkage between German soil, which was being polluted by tracked vehicles and unexploded ordnance, and German soil as a legal entity on which Germans exerted visibly limited sovereign rights. In its manifesto for elections in 1980, the Stadjugendring Mannheim asserted that "two world wars have begun on German soil. The FRG therefore has a special moral responsibility for the complete dismantling of arsenals around the world." At the same time, places like the Käfertaler Wald must be "protected for public use" and kept out of the hands of military forces.[40]

The Americans proved willing to listen on environmental matters, largely because they did not have a choice. Facing political pressure from the Federal Republic and the states, as well as from civil society organizations,

USAREUR began to take tentative steps toward abating some of the most visible environmental problems. USAREUR filed an annual environmental plan starting in 1976, but it did not involve much German input. While many at USAREUR recognized the extent of environmental problems, there were serious structural impediments toward fixing them. In 1980, there were at least 100 million DM worth of cleanup projects in Hessen alone. While USAREUR agreed in principle to try to remediate them, the fall in the dollar's value in the 1970s made this prohibitively expensive.[41]

By the early 1980s, USAREUR actively solicited German advice and began to include German officials and experts in planning. In September 1982, USAREUR sponsored a major conference in Heidelberg that included representatives from the *Länder* in which Americans operated. Much of the conference was taken up with pleasantries and effusive expressions from all sides that things should improve. However, this is also tangible evidence in the notes taken by representatives of the Hessian Ministry of Agriculture that the Americans were now taking German activist groups and public opinion seriously. USAREUR designed a training exercise for officers involving the fictional village of "Green" (*Grün*), near which the Americans hoped to build a small installation. "It is likely the townspeople will be very active during planning of the facility to ensure its impacts on the surrounding environment and the quality of life in their town will be minimized." Junior officers taking part in the exercise needed to consider ways to convince townspeople that the new installation would be minimally invasive. USAREUR also issued orders that applied only to Germany that directed commanders at all levels to "cooperate with host nation officials in protecting the natural environment and in mitigating environmental impacts, consistent with the military situation."[42]

The newfound concern with environmental matters did not necessarily stem from altruism. American commanders were keenly aware that they were operating in a political environment in which mistakes or oversights could have serious consequences for USAREUR and its mission. Before the Return of Forces to Germany (REFORGER) maneuvers in 1984, USAREUR commanding general Glenn Otis sent a directive to senior commanders reminding them that "Germans are understandably sensitive to any activity harmful to their physical environment. This sensitivity has both intensified and become highly politicized in recent years. Politically active environmentalists now exist in virtually every community. Participants in REFORGER must bear in mind that any unnecessary environmental damage will not go unnoticed and could well serve as the basis of political attacks detrimental to US interests."[43]

Officers were supposed to pass this message on to ordinary soldiers. A pamphlet distributed to personnel preparing for maneuvers made these points quite plainly:

> "But, look," you say, "I'm in the US Army. I'm supposed to soldier. We've got a mission in USAREUR and it's not cleaning up someone else's pollution, is it?" Well, you're only partially right. We have a mission to defend our country and to support NATO. Our mission is important to preserve society—our way of life. But remember, society—the people around us, their homes, and their culture—are also part of the environment. Our role requires us to be more than good soldiers. We also have a responsibility to be good guests in our host country—partners in a common effort. . . . Have you ever seen someone use a tank to push a tree over just to hear it snap or to show the vehicle's strength? That driver is being just plain dumb![44]

Officers also needed to work closely with German officials to avoid the possibility of embarrassing or disruptive protests. Heidelberg was to be immediately informed "in the event an organized effort is mounted by an environmental activist group (eg 'Bundesverband Bürgerinitiativen Umweltschutz e.V' in the FRG) which is demonstrating or protesting against a USAREUR activity which is impacting, has the potential or may be perceived as having potential for impacting environmental quality and/or interfering with normal social and/or economic pursuits."[45]

Domestic politicians were also subject to criticism if they appeared too close to the Americans. Senior German officials made regular confidence-building visits to American bases, which became sites of protest. In 1982, *Bundespräsident* Karl Carstens visited the Second Armored Division in Garlstedt. He received a raft of letters from local groups, urging him to cancel his visit, or to at least plan a stop in nearby communities to hear about opposition to American training activities. He eventually decided to fly into the base by helicopter. German domestic intelligence reported that a coalition of environmental, antiwar, and leftist groups from Bremen planned to disrupt the visit by blockading the base or releasing balloons with aluminum strips to prevent his helicopter from landing. A flyer posted near the base read, "Once again we see the unconditional solidarity of our leaders with the 'Protective Power USA' (*Schutzmacht USA*)"[46] On the day of the visit, a robust German and American police presence kept the small number of demonstrators back from the perimeter, and Carstens's arrival went unhindered.

In his memoirs, Colin Powell tells a story about his experiences as commander of the US V Corps in the mid-1980s. An ambitious group of

German activists broke into a tank training facility in the Third Armored Division's area, where they planted one hundred saplings. The base commander reported to Powell that he planned to knock down the trees. Powell ordered him to dig them up and hold an "Earth Day–type" replanting ceremony in a nearby housing area. He noted with some satisfaction that the local Green Party declined an invitation to attend the event. Powell, who came to West Germany for the first time as a young second lieutenant in 1958, absorbed an important lesson about the changing climate of the FRG. "One does not casually run over trees in Germany."[47]

The intense focus on the militarization of the German landscape in the early 1980s resulted in a remarkable literary genre: the military guidebook. The first few years of the decade saw a flurry of publications across several genres intended to inform German readers of what was going on in their country. These texts included atlases, photo encyclopedias, and travel guides.[48] Historians have written about this genre, but generally in the context of the missile debate. Benjamin Ziemann recently observed that these guides emerged from "efforts to gather and extrapolate more detailed knowledge" about nuclear weapons.[49] This is true, but it is also worth noting that the vast bulk of these volumes had nothing to do with nuclear weapons per se. They provided a granular accounting of military installations in the FRG (and, to some extent, the GDR), often accompanied by photos and technical specifications for weapons systems. These books were both the result of a wave of citizen journalism and an encouragement for others to be better observers of military activities and facilities.

A range of publishers, from commercial presses to political parties, produced these studies. Several authors were associated with the newly founded Institute for Peace Policy (Institut für Friedenspolitik) in Starnberg, including its enigmatic founder, Alfred Mechtersheimer.[50] One of the most ambitious manifestations of these efforts, which included data on the GDR, began with a foreword by Petra Kelly that encapsulated the hopes behind this raft of publications. "Our country is covered with military facilities and there is hardly a place where militarization is not noticeable. We will no longer withhold this information! We will no longer allow anything that concerns our security to be declared 'classified' anymore."[51]

These books shared a common ideological perspective: that the FRG lacked core components of sovereignty that allowed foreign military forces to act at will within German space. In their *Militarization Atlas of the Federal Republic*, Mechtersheimer and his colleague Peter Barth opened the book with the claim that "the citizen of the FRG lives in an over-militarized, occupied, and battle-ready country. He is a resident of 'Battlefield Federal Republic of Germany.'"[52] The core of their claim lay in the distance between "citizen" (*Bürger*) and "resident" (*Bewohner*). Because the FRG lacked the sovereignty to determine or ensure the rights of those legally resident within its territory, German citizens were not, functionally, citizens. They were residents in their own country. Even if the Cold War ended and Germany reunited, they argued, it was not clear if the "network of contractual obligations and commitments" that bound the FRG to its allies would allow the government to insist on the departure of foreign troops. Germany was, therefore, in a sovereignty trap.[53] The documents that the Federal Republic signed in the 1950s that permitted the FRG to emerge as a sovereign state also kept it from being a fully sovereign state.

The answer, according to these critics, lay partly in education. Germans simply did not know enough to recognize the "militarization of everyday life" going on around them. This phrase appeared frequently in critical commentary on the foreign troop issue, and particularly with regard to the Americans.[54] Authors and journalists wrote these exposés to encourage Germans to keep a critical eye out for maneuvers, installations, and possible risks to the environment from military activity.

Nowhere in Germany did these concerns seem more pressing than in eastern Hessen. There, in the space internationally known as the Fulda Gap, the American V Corps faced the Soviet Eighth Guards Army. If West Germany was the centerpiece of the army's rebuilding efforts, the Fulda Gap was the centerpiece of the army's activities in Germany. The unit shielding the gap, the "Black Horse" of the Eleventh Armored Cavalry Regiment, came directly from Vietnam and attempted to convey an attitude of aggressive readiness. The army brought VIP visitors from around the world to Point Alpha near Fulda, where press officers were supposed to begin briefings with the words, "My unit will kill the first Russian tank that crosses the border."[55]

The centrality of the Fulda Gap to NATO and the Americans was not at all lost on German critics. In 1981, a CBS News report from the US Army Command and General Staff College at Fort Leavenworth recorded the existence of a scale model of the village of Hattenbach, which American planners assumed would be at or near ground zero of World War III. The footage was not shown in Germany, but it was in Austria, and word quickly got back to the region.[56] In the early 1980s, a coalition of local and nonlocal antimilitarization groups began to focus on Osthessen as a place from which to raise wider awareness of the growing American presence in the country.

In addition to staging protests on the roads outside of American installations, protestors staged regular tours of the region for visitors from across the country. The West Berlin–based journalist Paul Kohl took such a tour in 1983 while working on a radio documentary on the Fulda Gap. Kohl recalled driving into a Security Zone, a perimeter around a base where Americans reserve the right to limit activities:

> So far, German law applies. Apparently, a few hundred meters we leave the territory of the Federal Republic, because on the gate it reads: "Violations are punishable according to the laws of the United States and/or the Federal Republic of Germany." In the Federal Republic, US law applies in certain areas. Did someone abandon the word sovereignty? Yes, they abandoned it.[57]

One of the other discussion items on the tour was a remarkable Cold War artifact: a board game called *Fulda Gap*, produced in the United States and only available in Germany through American PX stores.[58] *Fulda Gap*, one of many similar war games then popular in the United States, simulated the outbreak of a conventional war in Germany. The game board is a village-level map of Osthessen. As Kohl's tour guide said, "What happens to the population in this country—not a word in the rules of the game. This is one of the many points where the game and reality are identical. You can forget the population."[59]

The guide also read directly from the English-language rulebook, which included text like, "After all, *Fulda Gap* is designed to be an enjoyable experience. . . . The biggest question in an unfought war is just how effective the combination of weapons, tactics, training, doctrine, etc. will be for each army. Unfortunately, the only way to find out for certain is to fight the war"[60] This blithe lack of concern infuriated critics, who saw the board game, Air-Land Battle, and the growing American presence in the FRG as parts of a wider crisis.

While Kohl toured American facilities in the Fulda Gap, there were growing signs that Germans could and would mobilize against rural bases. In 1983, several dozen protestors began camping outside the Pershing II base on the Mutlanger Heide in Baden-Württemberg. The number of peace protests across the FRG peaked in that year, with 9,237. Significantly, German authorities tended to allow protests outside of American facilities to proceed with minimal police interference, driven in part by American concerns about public image.[61] The small action groups spearheading the Fulda Gap protests clearly saw this as a propitious moment to try something larger.

These groups eventually formed a coalition called the Arbeitsgruppe Aktionsherbst 84, which attempted to mobilize public outrage over the continuing militarization of the Fulda Gap. The *Arbeitsgruppe* planned an ambitious program of what they described as *Manöverbehinderung*, an effort to make it difficult for NATO—and particularly American—forces to conduct training exercises. They argued that the Americans were illegitimately using German territory to prepare for aggressive war, stipulating that this was a distinct issue from the debate over missile modernization. Gertrud Schilling, a newly elected Green delegate in Hessen's Landtag, and her colleague Priska Hinz wrote the *Arbeitsgruppe*'s press release (as of April 2022, Hinz is Hessen's environment minister):

> It has become clear to a broader public that it is not just about rockets, but about the militarization of a vast region with all of the weapons that are stored there. An offensive American military doctrine, in place since 1982, the so-called AirLand-Battle doctrine, stipulates that "the enemy" should be "destroyed" deep in his own territory before he starts an attack or enters the western area. The starting point and focus for such a battle—according to the Americans—should be Osthessen.[62]

At the national level, discussions about interfering with maneuvers split the Green Party leadership in an ugly and public way. While some, notably Annemarie Borgmann, enthusiastically supported the effort, others expressed strong reservations. A group from within the party but including activists from elsewhere in the peace movement, led by former soldiers Gert Bastian and Helmuth Priess, criticized the planned demonstrations on a number of fronts. There were real risks of physical harm to demonstrators, the targets were young American volunteers and not policymakers, and the connection between Fall maneuvers and an abstract strategic concept like AirLand Battle would not be clear to demonstrators or the media.[63] Despite the passion of some organizers, the Fall demonstrations lacked a clear sense of purpose or direction.

Protestors hoped to at least partially block roads and to cause enough uncertainty to prevent troops from accomplishing the goals of the exercise. That, along with the promise of live music and fun in Fulda, might bring enough protestors to this rural region. Police counted forty-two demonstrations in the region during the first weekend of the protests. Germans risked arrest by crossing into American-controlled areas. Some painted trees and buildings in bright colors, while others released balloons with the words "unilateral disarmament" written on them in various languages.

Almost immediately, the organizers received an entirely unexpected political gift. Lieutenant General Robert Wetzel, commander of V Corps, vented his spleen at the inconvenience to some sympathetic reporters. He told the press that a peaceful society like Germany should not tolerate "criminals and anarchists" and suggested that local communities might want to see these "groups of vandals" punished under the law. Wetzel's clumsy intervention, and particularly the suggestion that American officers might influence German law enforcement, struck critics as inappropriate. "This is not Central America," complained the speaker of Hessen's Landtag.[64] The state's interior minister, Horst Winterstein (SPD), commented that Germany "is not a vassal of Washington." While NATO tanks maneuvered and protestors moved across the Hessian landscape, Landtag delegates slung insults at each other over the Winterstein affair. Holger Börner, the state's Minister-minister-President, issued a decidedly unenthusiastic rebuke of his minister, saying simply that "we can only preserve the freedom of our country in cooperation with our American allies."[65]

Wetzel's comments energized speakers and participants. Alfred Mechtersheimer told his audience that the general had violated the duties of a guest and should be sent home. "Today, Moscow threatens your freedom. Washington threatens your lives!"[66] Another activist told a reporter that the general's remarks represented "a political victory for the Action Week that we could not have dreamed of before."[67] Such victories proved hard to come by. Sparse crowds and lack of coordination limited the visual impact of the protests, along with the ability to actually slow NATO maneuver plans.

The protesters faced a series of challenges in their choice of location. Aside from Fulda, there was no obvious geographic center to the region that might serve as a locus of organizing. The *Arbeitsgruppe* set up five "peace camps" near American installations from Hanau northeast to Fulda, but these were too far apart to communicate effectively. The plan to build a human chain, clearly inspired by the massive effort the previous year that linked four hundred thousand protestors between Stuttgart and Neu-Ulm, proved impossible, given distances and the lower-than-anticipated turnout.

Local communities did not offer much support for the protestors, which undercut the protest organizer's claim to represent public anxieties in the region. Much of the surrounding countryside was deeply politically conservative, including the constituency of the ferociously anticommunist and pro-military CDU grandee Alfred Dregger. Most local farmers and town dwellers wanted nothing to do with the protests. "What you can't change," remarked a farmer's wife, "you should leave alone." Another farmer, living on the edge of the American training area of Wildflecken, referenced his own dispossession at the hands of the Nazi state when they first built a training facility in the region in the late 1930s.[68] "As long as they are shooting in there," he said as he pointed to the edge of the training area, "they aren't shooting out here."[69]

Even organizers and supporters of the event had to concede that the results were mixed at best. Gertrud Schilling told a reporter that the premise of the protests likely limited its success. *Manöverbehinderung*, obstruction of maneuvers, proved to be a tough sell because the target was simply too diffuse. Protests against a particular weapons system, like the Pershing II, clearly had more potential for large-scale mobilization. These protests, Schilling acknowledged, targeted "the everyday nature of military installations."[70] In a region that benefited, if not always cheerfully, from the presence of these substantial military forces, there was little appetite for the kinds of protests that filled the streets of Bonn or Mutlangen.

Green Party leadership grudgingly acknowledged that they had overreached in the Fall of 1984. Many party activists were exhausted after the intense protests of the previous year. It is not surprising that some started to lose heart. A few weeks after the demonstrations, Antje Vollmer urged movement activists to move past a "bitter" and disappointing few months to keep up the fight "in Mutlangen, in Wildflecken . . . ," that is, against AirLand Battle and missile modernization, at the same time.[71] This would not be easy.

The antimilitarization movement in the Federal Republic did not end with the disappointing results of the Fall 1984 demonstrations, but these events probably represent the high point of the movement's activities. Within a few years, the Cold War context changed dramatically, and the story of the foreign military presence in the FRG changed with it. A decade after the protests of 1984, many of the facilities at the center of those actions no longer existed, and the villages of Osthessen ceased to lie in the likely path of World War III.

The antimilitarization movement reflected the changes in German society and in the Cold War security architecture over the last two decades of that conflict. Friction between garrison communities and the enormous foreign military presence in the FRG had been endemic since the aftermath of World War II. The FRG's legal and diplomatic entrée into the NATO alliance was based on the tacit acceptance of an unusual sovereignty regime in which German citizens regularly confronted the limits of the state's power to exercise meaningful control over its own territory. For the Americans, the dominant NATO partner in military terms but linked to Europe by a long supply line, relations with German society had long been a crucial element in maintaining their ability to project power across the Atlantic. As German civil society grew more assertive, if less cohesive, under the strains and upheavals of the 1970s, groups mobilized to question the existing sovereignty regime. By challenging American hegemony, these diffuse groups and organizations asserted a vision of a new, meaningfully democratic Germany.

Adam R. Seipp is Professor of History and Associate Dean for Graduate Studies in the College of Arts and Sciences at Texas A&M University. He is the author or editor of several books, including *Strangers in the Wild Place: Refugees, Americans, and a German Town, 1945–1952* and *Modern Germany in Transatlantic Perspective* (with Michael Meng).

Notes

1. The term "Fulda Gap" was used regularly by the Americans beginning in the 1960s, but it did not enter common German usage until the late 1970s. Germans generally used the English-language name. When it was rendered into German, the words *Lücke, Senke,* or *Bresche* were used interchangeably.
2. Walter Pincus, "War Games Wreak Havoc in West Germany," *Washington Post*, 24 September 1984.
3. Hans-Helmut Kohl, "Beim Point Alpha begegnen sich die Blöcke," *Frankfurter Rundschau*, 1 October 1984.
4. Georg Paul Hefty, "Fulda-Gap—Die Lücke zwischen Erwartung und Wirklichkeit," *FAZ*, 1 October 1984.
5. Compare particularly the chapters by David Spreen, Christian Helm, and Julia Ault in this volume.
6. On this broader peace movement, see contributions by Friederike Brühöfener in this volume.
7. Elisabeth Noelle-Neumann and Edgar Piel, eds., *Allensbacher Jahrbuch Der Demoskopie, 1978–1983*, vol. 8 (Munich: K. G. Saur, 1983); Wolfgang Krieger, "Security through Deterrence? German-American Security Relations, 1945–1968," in *The United States and Germany in the Era of the Cold War, 1958–1990*, ed. Detlef Junker (Cambridge: Cambridge University Press, 2004), 121.
8. This is a very substantial literature. Important contributions include Belinda Davis, "What's Left? Popular Political Participation in Postwar Europe," *American Historical Review* 113, no. 2 (2008); an excellent set of essays on this specific topic is summarized in Christoph Becker-Schaum et al., "Introduction," in *The Nuclear Crisis: The Arms Race, Cold War Anxiety, and the German Peace Movement of the 1980s*, ed. Christoph Becker-Schaum et al. (New York: Berghahn Books, 2016).
9. Silke Mende and Birgit Metzger, "Eco-Pacifism: The Environmental Movement as a Source for the Peace Movement," Christoph Becker-Schaum et al., *Nuclear Crisis*; Stephen Milder, *Greening Democracy: The Anti-nuclear Movement and Political Environmentalism in West Germany and Beyond, 1968–1983* (New York: Cambridge University Press, 2016).
10. Benjamin Ziemann, "German Angst? Debating Cold War Anxieties in West Germany, 1945–90," in *Understanding the Imaginary War: Culture, Thought and Nuclear Conflict, 1945–90*, ed. Matthew Grant and Benjamin Ziemann (Manchester: Manchester University Press, 2016); Frank Biess, "Jeder hat eine Chance: Die Zivilschutzkampagnen der 1960er Jahre und die Angstgeschichte der Bundesrepublik," in *Angst im Kalten Krieg*, ed. Bernd Greiner, Christian Th. Müller, and Dierk Walter (Hamburg: Hamburger Edition, 2009).
11. Susanne Schregel, *Der Atomkrieg vor der Wohnungstür: Eine Politikgeschichte der neuen Friedensbewegung in der Bundesrepublik 1970–1985* (Frankfurt a.M.: Campus, 2011).
12. The literature on sovereignty is quite large. For the purposes of this chapter, see especially John Agnew, "Sovereignty Regimes: Territoriality and State Authority in Contemporary World Politics," *Annals of the Association of American Geographers* 95, no. 2 (2005).

13. Peter Barth and Alfred Mechtersheimer, *Militarisierungsatlas der Bundesrepublik* (Darmstadt: Luchterhand Literaturverlag, 1986), 166–67
14. Glenn K Otis, "Speech to Head Works Council, December 13, 1984," (Glenn Otis Papers: US Army Military History Institute, 1984).
15. Adam R. Seipp, "'We Have to Pay the Price': German Workers and the US Army, 1945–1989," *War in History* 26, no. 4 (November 2019): 563–84.
16. Dewey Arthur Browder, "Appendix," in *GIs in Germany: The Social, Economic, Cultural, and Political History of the American Military Presence*, ed. Thomas W. Maulucci Jr. and Detlef Junker (New York: Cambridge University Press, 2013).
17. Alexander Vazansky, *An Army in Crisis: Social Conflicts in the United States Army, Europe and 7th Army, 1968–1975* (Lincoln: University of Nebraska Press, 2019).
18. An excellent example was Spiegel's extensive 1972 report on the state of the Americans in Germany. "Hausmitteilung," *Spiegel* 17 (1972).
19. The specialist literature on this is enormous. A particularly readable version can be found in Frederick W. Kagan, *Finding the Target: The Transformation of American Military Policy* (New York: Encounter Books, 2006).
20. Beratungspunkte for meeting on 27 May 1977. GABAUS. StadtA MA, ISG Allgemeine Verwaltung, 2/1977 1383
21. USAREUR Annual Historical Summary 1973, 8-5. USAREUR Archive, Wiesbaden.
22. Max Plassmann, "Manöverschäden und die deutsch-amerikanische Bezihungen in der Pfalz (1951–1955)," *Militärgeschichtliche Mitteilungen* 56, no. 2 (1997).
23. Barth and Mechtersheimer, *Militarisierungsatlas der Bundesrepublik*, 121.
24. Herbert E. Koenigsbauer, "USAREUR: Force Readiness and the Maneuver Damage Dilemma" (Carlisle, PA: Army War College, 1983), 12.
25. Benjamin M. Jensen, *Forging the Sword: Doctrinal Change in the US Army* (Stanford, CA: Stanford University Press, 2016), 46–59.
26. William R. Lynch III and Garth T Bloxham, "Training in the 8th Infantry Division (Mechanized)," *Military Review* (September 1983).
27. The 1982 edition of FM 100-5 can be found on the website of the Army's Combined Arms Research Library: http://cgsc.cdmhost.com/cdm/ref/collection/p4013 coll9/id/48.
28. Annemarie Borgmann's files are noteworthy in this regard. See Archiv Grünes Gedächtnis (hereafter AGG) B.II.1 1994.
29. Die Grünen im Bundestag, "Angriff als Verteidigung: Airland Battle, Airland Battle 2000 und Rogers Plan" (1984).
30. Undated broadsheet pamphlet, written by Sebastian Wertmüller. HHStAW 2016/1, 397.
31. "Germany and the Euromissile Debate," *International Journal* 40, no. 1 (1984/85).
32. "Erneuter Protest gegen Nervengas," *Rhine-Necker-Zeitung*, 20 August 1969.
33. Annual Historical Review (1982–83), 38. USAREUR Archive.
34. Roland Pott, "Bundesregierung Deckt Giftgaslager," *Rhein-Neckar-Zeitung*, 16 May 1982. "Gegen Giftgas!" ed. Mannheimer Arbeiterkreis für Frieden und Abrüstung (StAMA, NL Nikitopoulos, 3/1995_002201982).
35. "Plenarprotokoll, Landtag Von Baden-Wuerttemberg, 11. Sitzung" (Stuttgart: Haus des Landtages, 1980).

36. "Das sollte im siebten Besatzungsjahre unmöglich sein," *Mannheimer Morgen*, 16 May 1951; "Panzerstrasse Sandhofen/Kaefertaler Wald" (StAMA 48/1997_02041971).
37. Rüdiger Börner, "Verbündete, Panzer und Natur," *Darmstädter Echo*, 22 March 1980.
38. Program of the AUD (Aktionsgemeinschaft unabhäniger Deutscher) based in Munich. This copy belonged to Kreisverband Esslingen-Göppingen. StadtA MA, ISG Nichtstädtische Bestände, 46/1993 189.
39. Letter to Public Affairs Office, Taylor Barracks, from Bürgeraktion Umweltschutz Rhein-Neckar, 14 April 1975. StadtA MA, ISG Dezernatsregistratur, 8/1993 189.
40. Leitlinien zu den Wahlen, 1980. Stadtjugendring Mannheim. StadtA MA, ISG Nichtstädtische Bestände, 46/1993 189.
41. Börner, "Verbündete, Panzer und Natur."
42. Records of USAREUR Environmental Program Managers' Workshop, Berchtesgaden, September 1982. HHStAW 509, 4917.
43. USAREUR Annual Historical Review (1984), 281. USAREUR Archive.
44. Pamphlet, "The Soldier and the USAREUR Environment," HHStAW 509, 4917.
45. Records USAREUR Environmental Program Managers' Workshop.
46. Memo of 1 June 1982 in Bundesarchiv Koblenz, B 122/24529.
47. Colin Powell and Joseph E. Persico, *My American Journey* (New York: Random House, 1995), 323.
48. There are lots of examples, including Barth and Mechtersheimer, *Militarisierungsatlas der Bundesrepublik*. Barbara Dietrich and Eric Schmidt-Eenboom, *Der Militarisierte Frieden: Studie der Militarisierung der Rhine-Main Region* (Starnberg: Forschungsinstitut für Friedenspolitik, 1982); Barth and Mechtersheimer, *Militarisierungsatlas der Bundesrepublik*; Knut Krusewitz, *Umweltkrieg: Militär, Ökologie und Gesellschaft* (Königstein: Athenäum, 1985); Burkhard Luber, *Militäratlas von Flensburg bis Dresden: 3000 Daten zur Militarisierung der BRD und DDR* (Dortmund: Die Grünen, 1986).
49. Ziemann, "German Angst?" 128.
50. Mechtersheimer later drifted toward right-wing extremism, highlighting perhaps the blurriness of the ideological edges of some components of anti-American sentiment in Germany since 1968.
51. Luber, *Militäratlas*, 8.
52. Barth and Mechtersheimer, *Militarisierungsatlas der Bundesrepublik*, 7.
53. Ibid., 14.
54. Luber, *Militäratlas*, 13.
55. Roger Cirillo, "The Defense of Highway 84: Recollections of the Commander, B Troop, 11th Armored Cavalry Regiment, 1978–1980," in *Fulda Gap: Battlefield of the Cold War Alliances*, ed. Dieter Krüger and Volker Bausch (Lanham, MD: Rowman and Littlefield, 2017), 121.
56. Ziemann, "German Angst?" 129. The mayor of Hattenbach reportedly said that he was not bothered by the lack of coverage because "one would not tell a pig in advance that it is going to be slaughtered."
57. Paul Kohl, *Fulda Gap: Eine Reportage über die Militarisierung in Deutschland* (Göttingen: edition herodot, 1984).
58. This game is now a collector's item. You can see something of it, and the vast complexity of its rules, at https://boardgamegeek.com/boardgame/4235/fulda-gap.
59. Kohl, *Fulda Gap*.

60. Ibid., 63.
61. Michael Sturm, "The Police," in *The Nuclear Crisis: The Arms Race, Cold War Anxiety, and the German Peace Movement of the 1980s*, ed. Christoph Becker-Schaum et al. (New York: Berghahn Books, 2016), 278.
62. Press release, 2 October 1984, HHStAW 2016/1, 397.
63. The exchange of letters can be found in AGG B II.1, 4589.
64. "US-Militärs zurechtgewiesen," *Tageszeitung*, 29 September 1984.
65. Minister Winterstein ein Vasall Moskaus, *FAZ*, 1 October 1984.
66. Hefty, "Fulda-Gap."
67. Kohl, "Beim Point Alpha," 20.
68. Adam R. Seipp, *Strangers in the Wild Place: Refugees, Americans, and a German Town, 1945–1952* (Bloomington: Indiana University Press, 2013).
69. Hefty, "Fulda-Gap."
70. Kohl, "Beim Point Alpha," 53.
71. Text of speech in AGG, B.II 1 1976 (1).

Select Bibliography

Becker-Schaum, Christoph, et al. "Introduction." In *The Nuclear Crisis: The Arms Race, Cold War Anxiety, and the German Peace Movement of the 1980s*, edited by Christoph Becker-Schaum et al., 1–36. New York: Berghahn Books, 2016.

Biess, Frank. "Jeder hat eine Chance: Die Zivilschutzkampagnen der 1960er Jahre und die Angstgeschichte der Bundesrepublik." In *Angst im Kalten Krieg*, edited by Bernd Greiner, Christian Th. Müller, and Dierk Walter. Hamburg: Hamburger Edition, 2009.

Davis, Belinda. "What's Left? Popular Political Participation in Postwar Europe." *American Historical Review* 113, no. 2 (2008).

Jensen, Benjamin M. *Forging the Sword: Doctrinal Change in the Us Army*. Stanford, CA: Stanford University Press, 2016.

Milder, Stephen. *Greening Democracy: The Anti-nuclear Movement and Political Environmentalism in West Germany and Beyond, 1968–1983*. New York: Cambridge University Press, 2016.

Schregel, Susanne. *Der Atomkrieg vor der Wohnungstür: Eine Politikgeschichte der neuen Friedensbewegung in der Bundesrepublik 1970–1985*. Frankfurt a.M.: Campus, 2011.

Seipp, Adam R. "'We Have to Pay the Price': German Workers and the US Army, 1945–1989." *War in History* 26, no. 4 (November 2019): 563–84.

Sturm, Michael. "The Police." In *The Nuclear Crisis: The Arms Race, Cold War Anxiety, and the German Peace Movement of the 1980s*, edited by Christoph Becker-Schaum et al., 274–89. New York: Berghahn Books, 2016.

Vazansky, Alexander. *An Army in Crisis: Social Conflicts in the United States Army, Europe and 7th Army, 1968–1975*. Lincoln: University of Nebraska Press, 2019.

Ziemann, Benjamin. "German Angst? Debating Cold War Anxieties in West Germany, 1945–90." In *Understanding the Imaginary War: Culture, Thought and Nuclear Conflict, 1945–90*, edited by Matthew Grant and Benjamin Ziemann, 1–29. Manchester: Manchester University Press, 2016.

Chapter 7

Radical Change Close to Home

Transforming the Self and Relations
in West German Alternative Politics

Belinda Davis

The year 1968 in West Germany was—as in many locales—marked by the highest hopes for "revolutionary" change, but also by the deepest despair, prompted by unrelenting and often physically dangerous attacks against "extraparliamentary" activists and the attendant perceived dissipation and dissolution of a broad movement.[1] By the end of 1968, West German activists found the verdict unassailably clear: the chance for any imminent "revolution" had passed. Yet the profound disappointments surrounding the year and its outcome were not without their own great, even radical, effects. The chasm between what activists sought and what transpired contributed to an ultimately productive rethinking of the timeline and also of possible sites of change. Activists' work in the years following 1968, often far removed from the streets, offers some of the era's most important lessons, too often lost in emplotments of breakdown and crisis, and a retreat from popular politics altogether, except in violent and/or dogmatic manifestations. The hackneyed phrase "the personal is political" bears further reexamination, moreover, beyond still-dominant liberal narratives of the post-'68 period.

Regularly chased from the streets and other public venues, many activists in West Germany looked for means of change literally closer to home. "Living communities" (*Wohngemeinschaften*, WGs), or group houses, were by the late 1960s already commonplace, products of necessity of the early postwar period and earlier still. They had counterparts across Europe and beyond, including in the squatting movement. They offered more than just a practical and affordable form of shelter: they were a response too to other "everyday needs." WGs burgeoned by the late 1960s as a key site of experiments with the politics of everyday life. Political WGs were nowhere more commonplace relative to the larger population than in West Germany; there were at least tens of thousands of them from the early 1970s to the early 1980s.[2] They spread across West German cities (especially though not exclusively in poorer districts, and where buildings were often damaged or run down); they existed too in small towns—and in the form of rural communes.[3] WGs offered sites for radical alternatives to the most intimate relationships, for activists seeking a total integration of life and "politics."[4] They provided space for fresh forms of political process, allowing for transformed theoretical convictions and means of practice. Some questioned these practices as utopian self-ghettoization from mainstream society.[5] Paradoxical relations with state officials, as well as with the broader public, challenged just how insulated activists could be through the 1970s and into the 1980s, even insofar as they wanted to be.[6] Moreover, WGs were nodal points for the extraordinary efflorescence of the activism of the new social movements (antinuclear, environmental, feminist, and, later, peace), enabling entirely new forms of political organization. Collectively, they created a fabric of communications and action of increasingly dense weave. They were sources of "basis work," consisting of everything from novel modes of childrearing and schooling to building semiautonomous economies, often around squatted cultural-political centers and workshops, clinics, and bookstores. A premier lesson of these experiments was both a philosophical and practical one about the nature of change, a lesson radical in nature.

Living Together, Not Alone

In this chapter, I use the biographies of contemporary West German activists as a lens for a brief analysis of this phenomenon. The case of Hubert, a teenager in Hannover, is a telling one.[7] Hannover was itself a liberal city of half a million in Lower Saxony, situated squarely between the more prominent bastions of "extraparliamentary" politics, West Berlin and Frankfurt. Born in 1952, Hubert left his family at a tender seventeen to ply his early politics in experimental living spaces, first in WGs, then in a squatted independent youth center (*Unabhängiges Jugendzentrum*, UJZ), one of the offshoots to which WGs gave rise.[8] Hubert's initial move at seventeen reflected paradoxes of the postwar era. Though Hubert grew up in a working-class neighborhood, his father insisted that Hubert take advantage of postwar social openings to attend *Gymnasium* (college preparatory school) starting at age eleven, where he found fellow pupils particularly interested in "politics." In his oral history, Hubert claimed to have felt alienated, "distant" from his parents as a child, and at the same time "too close" to them physically at home. As he came to think about sex, "which one certainly never addresses at home at all," he began to chafe at his "cramped living quarters," which prohibited his "try[ing] out" sexual activity.

This in itself sounds like a commonplace of modern puberty. Yet specifics of the period contributed to a particular politics. Those raised up in the postwar decades sought to live both more and less "alone." The postwar housing emergency meant that many young people grew up sleeping in a room with many brothers and sisters, and even with one or both parents and/or other adults.[9] This was in itself not necessarily a fundamental problem for youth who had not known any different; nor was it rare in many times and places. Yet the ambivalence toward and even the antipathy of many to family ties is little surprise, in a Federal Republic in which relations in the family—nuclear and otherwise—could be poisonous. The Nazi past and its ongoing effects, psychological and otherwise, was a piece of these poisonous relations, as they were of self-questioning among activists. Polls in the 1950s and 1960s revealed that West Germans associated "family" ever less with notions of an "emotional homeland," of a "community of solidarity." On the contrary, West Germans of all ages felt far more able to depend on friends than on family in this period.[10] Officials and societal scions celebrated the virtues of the nuclear family. Yet, from the war era into the 1970s, the nuclear family ideal either failed to correspond to lived experience or conversely represented little positive experience for many family members.

This sense crossed paths with the politics of "'60s activists." The experimental living Kommune 2, established in 1967, declared in a lengthy publication documenting their living experiment that the nuclear family had indeed never been sufficient to the range of human needs.[11] All the more in postwar than in Nazi Germany, Kommune members saw family life as a site of "total control," contributing to a "growing emotional impoverishment," producing children unable to communicate or even understand their needs. Living collectives like their own were intended to open up "a liberating social communication."[12] In the event, residents found that WGs broadly could offer the "feeling of belonging and security," protection from "social isolation and loneliness," even as they constituted a retreat from mainstream contemporary family life.[13] As Susanne T. described her own first WG, "That *was* my family."[14] Hundreds of thousands began to follow members of Kommune 2 and other radical living communities in viewing WGs not just as an affordable alternative to the nuclear family or to living alone but also as a springboard "to revolutionize and politicize the everyday," linking politics with the most intimate spheres of life.[15] At another time and place, Hubert might have just gritted his teeth until he could move to an apprenticeship or higher education at eighteen or nineteen. At this moment, discussion at Hubert's school evinced in him the sense that "everything was possible," even in the dismaying aftermath of 1968. So, when in 1969 a group of local students and others invited him to live in their WG—even as he completed high school—the seventeen-year-old jumped at the chance.

For some of the most engaged activists of the 1960s, however, such ideas were not welcomed from the start.[16] While attending West Berlin's Free University (FU), Klaus Hartung lived in a WG in 1964 with other members of the SDS, the (West) German Socialist Student Union. The intent was both to hold down costs and to facilitate ongoing discussion of SDS political actions beyond formal assemblies. Yet the FU SDS board member found himself fully unprepared for the meeting of the political and the private when fellow activist Rainer Langhans moved into the WG for a time. The "rather neurotic" Langhans wanted to talk with his housemates about problems with his girlfriend and other personal concerns.[17] Hartung feared not only distraction from the group's more conventional political efforts; Langhans's practices were also prospectively embarrassing for these "rational functionaries of the SDS. This self-exposure bared us too. It brought us under suspicion: that completely personal motives underlay our political activity, that we went out in the street for Vietnam because we also were [sexually] frustrated."[18] When Rainer Langhans later joined Kommune 1, a political and living collective still more publicly challenging than Kommune 2, Langhans's "neurosis was out in public. It was the uprising of the aggrieved (*Geschädigten*, also damaged)," who "made public their plight." But, Hartung later acknowledged, he too came to understand this linkage between politics and the most intimate aspects of life as representing a new kind of revolution. This was not a distraction from but rather a "totalization of politics"—and not moreover a totalization as Nazis had viewed it but a positive form. "The intervention of Kommune 1 intensified once and for all the contradiction in dividing 'doing politics' and the everyday." This was central to constituting an "antiauthoritarian movement" that was both broad and enduring: in 1989, he claimed at the moment of his reflections, "the shock waves could be felt still, now as earlier." This was one piece of the radical change that both inspired and emerged with the widespread practice of these living and political communities.

The beginnings of this radical politics of private life came coincident with and as a piece of the ravaging disappointments of 1968. As hundreds of thousands felt chased from the public expression of politics, sites like WGs offered both an exciting and relatively protected locus of political thinking and experimentation.[19] The potential radical nature of these "personal politics" was not lost on less sympathetic West Germans. Hartung saw widespread public "hate" telegraphed across the "bourgeois press." In Frankfurt, the Social Democratic–affiliated newspaper *Kommunalzeitung* trumpeted in late 1968 that WGs were all secret dens of "pimping, orgies, and drug trade," a predictably lurid assortment of charges.[20] But Hartung suspected the real concern was the "revolutionary explosive power precisely in the collective expression of individual misery. . . ."[21] Members of Kommune 2 also opined that officials and others did understand "the collective form of living itself as a political act," evidenced "in their grotesque reaction to the communes, [and in] the violence of the system and its methods of repression. . . ."[22] Increasing official penetration of private space through the 1970s took place under the guise of guilt by association for the small number of cases of activist violence. Nonetheless, overall, these experiments transpired in relative peace—once groups could find landlords who would rent to them, or a building they could squat. Some contemporary activists perceived conversely that this sort of retreat to the interior was actually a sign of how little a threat of radical change activists posed, particularly after Kommune 1, Kommune 2, and other better-known such experiments folded by the dawn of the new decade.

How Radical Were WGs?

Yet the demise of the Kommunes was not in itself a sign of failure. One of the critical lessons of this period was precisely the need for a constant renewal of effort, as one experiment served its purpose, leading to the next, producing a critical new vision of what change looked like and how to produce it.[23] Members of Kommunes 1 and 2, for example, saw their "revolution of the bourgeois self" above all as a means to create of themselves a revolutionary vanguard, by which they would render themselves able to connect the more conventionally recognized political struggles of peoples in Southeast Asia and in Latin America to Europeans, acting as the agents of the former in Europe. Conversely, WGs, and the larger "alternative" communities they built, came to see transformation of the self and of social, psychological, economic, and cultural relations with others as an increasingly meaningful end in itself. It related to larger visions of change within West Germany—as a piece of continued close ties to those outside the country. But, as to developing themselves as a revolutionary vanguard, activists increasingly rejected such visions as caught up in the modernist theory that had already demonstrated its bankruptcy for understanding change in the present. This was no easy acceptance that one simply could not enact collective, widespread, and radical change. The move beyond the thinking of the Kommunes was itself a sign of change taking place at a deeper level still, concerning the episteme of modern political thought. This constituted an expressly political as well as cultural transformation; it argued against any easy differentiation between the two.

Thus, terrifying for many West Germans who looked on, the politicization of everyday life—and the bringing of the everyday to politics—was electrifying for others. So it was that, in 1969, the seventeen-year-old Hubert entered his first WG with little clear idea except that of "pursu[ing] a *different* life, at all events." Pursuing difference, challenging expectations, was the starting point. Hubert's experience highlights how WGs functioned as laboratories for social relations. "The exciting thing was actually the everyday. So, that a person was all at once different from at home, where one [was] with one's parents or with one's brother. [There] were completely different people there, with respectively varied interests." It was not just new people. WG residents left the discomforts of home to find individuals (still) less like themselves, with whom they could work to form and develop "equitable and compassionate" bonds, in an "effort to revolutionize bourgeois individuality."[24] This was a critical means to "liberate everyday life" broadly, "living together without pressure to perform, frustration, and fear," through "countermodels."[25] It became part of a larger project for Hubert, one of a broad fording of boundaries (*Grenzüberschreitungen*): boundaries among individuals, and those separating out discrete familial and societal roles; those dividing a day into "work," "free time," "home life," and, if at all, "politics." It was such boundaries that uncomfortably squeezed individuals into fractured identities or those assumed by others: into memberships in one party, or demographic, or political belief or another. It was out of these experiments in turn that contemporary activists came to challenge notions of a "productive society" (*Leistungsgesellschaft*), concerning jobs that, at the latest following the recession of the 1973–74 OPEC oil embargo—and a ban on the hiring of "radicals"—seemed in any case few and far between. Thus, the 1978 "Tunix" (Do Nothin') festival and set of workshops in West Berlin, only the best known of such projects, drew a crowd of nearly twenty thousand.

How radical were WGs in practice? Reaching out beyond one's own family was, to be sure, a normal part of modern "bourgeois individuation" among young people. In the event, members of Hubert's WG and of many others found themselves reproducing timeworn roles and patterns in their new, chosen "families." Hubert himself really appreciated "how the people treated one another" in his own WG in 1969, especially "across age divisions. There were fifty-year-olds there, there were also really young people like me." At the same time, Hubert acknowledged, house members treated him tenderly, as the "baby" of the house. This was not only because of his age but also because he represented the "working-class historical subject" in the eyes of some of his housemates, Hubert wryly conjectured. Like Hubert,

Manfred D., born in 1956, played the "little brother" in the WG he joined in 1977. For Manfred, this became a problem. The two older members of the WG "were a bit like the parents," harping on whether the bathroom had been cleaned well enough or whether someone had left hair in the bathtub.[26] He and other WG members finally decided they had to throw these "parents" out of the WG. Of course, leaving the "parents" behind was as conventional as it got, even if it was something slightly different to throw *them* out. Yet such descriptions challenge the charges of many older activists in the West German case that it was younger people—the "new generation" of activists after 1968—who adopted dogmatic stances, whether concerning historical materialism or standards of cleanliness.

More important, to point to the regular deep conflicts in WGs, even their frequent dissolution and reorganization, and, as rehearsals of childhood fantasies or as failed experiments misunderstands the way change took place in WGs: as a process of a laborious working through—and often remaking—meaning. How clean was it important to be, and how should disparate views be reconciled? Did household order represent residual fetishes of fascism or care for the WG community? This questioning itself was central to WG life and politics. WG life was not an event with a finite end: it was rather a challenge to notions of radical change as coming necessarily through evenemental politics. The very process of working through such issues, of questioning the most basic assumptions, was a central component of the larger experimentation; whether or not an individual WG lasted for any length of time was not. Members of Kommune 2 castigated the "old-fashioned" (*altväterlich*, literally, old-father-like) notions of the former SDS authorities. The great expectations that were aroused above all in young comrades (*Genossen*) have certainly been miserably disappointed."[27] Yet by the time of Kommune 2's 1969 report on their experiment, the Kommune itself had already dissolved. It was from this very point, through the publication, that Kommune 2's experiment took on its greatest significance.

Like divisions across age, those across gender were another regular source of rancor in WGs—and a fillip for further questioning, debate, and transformation of practice at all levels.[28] Here again, this was a personal issue and more, inseparable from "politics." In the renowned film *Der subjektive Faktor*, activist filmmaker Helke Sander's protagonist Anni is pushed along with other women into the role of making coffee for the men during a political meeting in the living room.[29] Together in the kitchen, the women prepare the coffee—and then come up with practical, politically significant solutions to the childcare problem, reflecting their own, immediate concern, and one preventing them from engaging politically. In contrast, as Sander depicts it, the men in the living room continue their esoteric and ultimately unproductive discussion regarding how best to represent Viet Cong interests in West Berlin and best "make revolution in [their] own land." This too bespoke a transformation from notions of "revolutionary vanguardism" to fresh ideas of producing radical change.[30]

In the context of gender all the more than of age, "housekeeping" broadly conceived constituted a thorny landscape of everyday politics in WGs. Notices to "please sit while peeing" decorated the walls of WGs across West Germany, as women signaled to men that splashing the toilet seat created both more cleaning work and an unpleasant experience for those who had to sit on the seat. This was an issue of trying to understand the perspective of others at the most fundamental level. It could also be a matter of challenging conventional practices. Volker T. remembered the tissue of issues from the "other side," still smarting a little, it seemed:

> One lived together, one ate, drank, cooked, tried to make it all happen. Of course there were permanent conflicts, yes, regarding cleaning, and who didn't clean the toilet again, who had to go shopping, and so on. . . . But it was a part of our . . . process of left socialization, yes, that one had to solve these problems too, and that . . . that there was something like solidarity and a feeling of responsibility and so on. . . .[31]

Volker laughed humorlessly as he described the truly remarkable scene of a female housemate standing over him in the early 1970s, emphasizing that "it's not clean yet, you have to get back to it!" He made a direct comparison to his experience cleaning toilets during his military service, under a watchful officer's eye. "It was rather women in the WGs who set the standards, so to speak. Yes. So, how often cleaning took place and how clean it must be." He repeated this last point three times, betraying the power the memory still held over him. "So, WGs tried to organize themselves so that each, regardless of whether woman or man," bore responsibility.

Remaking Meaning to Remake Relationships

How much of this actually transformed mores, and relations? Notwithstanding Volker's evident enduring discomfort with the presumption of particular standards, many male interview subjects spoke of learning to cook and clean in this way as a badge of honor: a mark of their own transformation through WGs, to both independence and interdependence, as such a hallmark of the "revolution of everyday life." Activist and later German foreign minister

Joschka Fischer saw it explicitly as an important example of the everyday realization of the women's movement: "it was a real resocialization, a second socialization" for him, after growing up with his two sisters doing all the housework at home. "It was an unbelievably *painful* resocialization," taking years, he emphasized. But it was "successful in the end." It was also for him a key form of personal "liberation" across genders. "The transformation in gender relations thus played a very, very large role, retrospectively also a great gain for us men, because, when I think of my father, who," without his mother, "was completely incapable of surviving. . . ." By contrast, Fischer "cooked myself, cleaned myself, did everything myself." Robert G. found it likewise an "emancipatory act": "one wanted to get away from these petite bourgeois kitchen practices," such as only women cooking in the home.[32] Robert and a male housemate who had spent part of his life in Italy considered it their "calling" not only to take on the cooking in their WG but also to introduce their housemates to dishes from around the world.[33] Many perceived the changes moreover as going further still. Robert connected to his own transformation the preparation and then collective eating of food, sociability always accompanied by lively political debate. "So it was both in a broad and also in a narrower sense even somehow emancipatory, as if it tapped a life world (*Lebenswelt*) in me that was previously completely unknown, that was completely new." It was nothing like the home he came from, where the evening often comprised a lecture from his widowed father.

The WG and women's movements were intimately entangled; WGs were a crucible for reworking gender as other relations. But that men began to cook and even clean was what advocates of the "bourgeois" women's movement and others have long claimed for the period, to be sure. The most powerful result of these intense interactions and struggles, played out over thousands of WGs and other households across West Germany, did not lie in men's learning to cook and clean, nor even in women's introspection concerning particular standards of cleanliness, where they came from, and what they meant. In West Germany, the more "radical" wing of the women's movement was associated with "difference feminism," often described as celebrating women's cultural and even biological differences with men.[34] In consequence of these living experiments, however, activists came overwhelmingly to reject generalities and essentialisms even on the basis of gender, a perceived limiting case of "who one was." Activists came to see such generalizations as defying the purpose of these projects in the politics of everyday life: both prejudging others by one category or another and failing to recognize the possibilities of individual change and growth. Sigrid T. saw cleaning as one locus through which to pursue "more justice and also another relationship between men and women": "that the men should also wash the steps." But she emphasized in her narration the individual nature of the "cleanliness" question: "I also threw a woman out once, because she never ever did housework here. . . . We live together, and it also has to be taken care of together. But in principle I am 'for' neither man nor woman."[35] Conversely, between her boyfriend and her, there was "no problem. He could cook and also clean," and did so more often than she.

This challenge to identity politics questioned the presumptions of some contemporary feminists in other ways too. Women discovered that living only with other women did not preclude these encounters. In an all-women's WG in West Berlin in 1978, Wiebke S. recalled, "naturally there were conflicts," but not usually over politics, or over the fact that there were "singles and lesbians and heteros" living together. Rather, they were "more about order. . . . More about . . . soap that was somehow lying wrong."[36] Of course, even if Wiebke didn't explicitly acknowledge it as part of the issue, what did it mean that soap was lying "wrong"? But, Wiebke quickly learned, living and working together with just women itself guaranteed no personal or political success. Likewise, in the early 1980s, Andreas of the Bahnhof Street WG in Bonn expressed his annoyance at "clichés" implied in an outsider's query regarding the roles of "men" and "women" in WGs. He was not some "average" man and did not care to be pigeonholed as such.[37] His own concern for the WG indeed was to see more "care" work in a broad sense: that all members take the WG itself seriously as a collective commitment, at the formal biweekly meeting and dinner, through the emotional as well as physical work of the WG, and through the development of relations with the others in the house.[38] This was about the transformation of the individual as a member of a community. He saw himself as such as a guardian of—as putting in the care work for—this tiny community, as a part of larger society.

Challenging normative heterosexuality was also for Wiebke, as for many within the radical feminist movement, closely related to contemporary living experiments. Yet, for the teenaged Hubert, living together with women who were not blood relations was an especial attraction of the WG. This did not preclude experimentation with "difference" in intimate relations. "Most interesting of all for me," Hubert recalled, "was girls. Yes, I really said that." Hubert's first great love was a WG housemate, "a university student, I was very proud of it, because she was simply much older than me, and so on." WGs provided and normalized the space he had sought while living in his parents' home, to "try out" sex and couples relationships more broadly. Such partners often reflected WGs' trademark diversity. Eighteen-year-old Tulla R. found her own first "serious relationship" with a member of her WG in working-class West Berlin: a laborer and autodidact whose different political thinking was for her a source of constant stimulation.[39] At the same time, contemporary notions that communes and WGs were sites of "promiscuous" sex and group orgies were almost entirely the fantasies of fear (and otherwise) of those outside the broad movement. This applied even to the original "Horror Kommune," as Kommune 1 cofounder Dagmar Seehuber Przytulla noted drily. In regard to sexuality at least, Kommune members all fundamentally wound up imitating their parents—despite the "psychoterror sessions" they undertook together.[40]

Yet WGs did raise critical questions concerning conventional couples' relationships and practices altogether. Tulla loved her housemate qua boyfriend. Soon, however, their relationship pushed both partners to leave for separate WGs. WGs first developed in part as a means to leave home without the pressure of developing one's own "narrow couple's relationship" and then, marrying.[41] Thus, Martin of the Bahnhof Street WG found it a problem "when some couple" in a WG "only speaks in terms of 'we,' and the individual person seems to totally disappear."[42] In the event, WG members often discouraged couples relationships in WGs altogether. Karl W. quipped that there was an "incest taboo" in many WGs: none of the members could live in the same WG as their sexual partners. Such relations were often "deadly for the general climate."[43] When Karl's two housemates in one Hamburg WG became romantically involved, "they created a common front against me," leaving relations a far cry from "equitable." WG residents often found living apart from their romantic interest better for them as well. Residing in separate WGs "helped the relation" with Karl's own partner, avoiding the "conflicts that normally arise in *Wohngemeinschaften*," such as "'Why is the couch so dirty?' Or 'Why haven't you washed the dishes yet?' . . ."

This commonplace WG practice was more challenging to prevailing mores than Karl's facetious characterization might suggest. When feminist literary critic Eve Sedgwick wrote in the late 1980s about her experience living in an intimate and caring relationship with someone not her sexual partner, who lived elsewhere, it was considered a breakthrough in queer sexuality and life practices.[44] Such experiments were a mainstay of West German WG life by the 1970s. WGs challenged the nature of one's most intimate relations in many ways, not only dividing up these ties conventionally focused on a single other person, in a single cohabited space, but also "downgrading" the importance of the couple's relationship altogether. Members of Martin R.'s WG in Munich agreed that it was important to be able to "come home" to talk about one's relationship—and everything else—with "many discussion partners." In the Bonn WG, the latter was always Karin's first "emotional backup. When something is going on," bad or good, "I always think first about the WG" to discuss, to find support, to celebrate. This was "very different" from "couples' relationships." The latter often constituted a low priority among commitments for WG residents. Karin had no interest in marriage—or children—because of the "ten to fifteen years" of her life she had already spent caring for her younger siblings. Housemate Andreas and his girlfriend both prioritized their respective WGs; his girlfriend also seemed to depend on her WG and other adults to help her with parenting her young child.[45] Andreas's parents assumed the WG was just a "transitional phase" for him. Critically, "change" was the presumed norm in this politics of everyday life. Yet, of all possible futures, Andreas did not envision necessarily settling into a nuclear family at any point.

This experimentation in moving away from the heterosexual couple, the sexual couple, and the couple altogether, as the core of the social and societal unit, drew on the same sources as the "sexual revolution," conventionally understood—and was arguably both more radical and lasting in terms of effect. "Neurotic" SDS member and founding member of Kommune 1 Rainer Langhans proclaimed, along with many contemporary social scientists, that West Germans had a "sex hang-up," an "intercourse hang-up." So, Kommunards determined, "we'll go after all these hang-ups, so that life can be freer. That was our revolution that we wanted. The revolution of the everyday, this whole hang-up." Langhans described his own relationship with Kommune cofounder Dieter Kunzelmann. "We were a fantastic 'married couple' [*Ehepaar*], a fantastic couple, which complemented itself in every respect, and was unbelievably effective." Langhans did not thereby reveal unknown sexual predilections or relations, or any kind of "exclusive" couples' relations at all. Rather, he thereby followed contemporary transformations in disaggregating the relation between sexuality, eroticism, intimacy, and the single partner, exploding the package of conventional associations. He also offered insight into the very erotics of the WG, again, entirely aside from physical sexual acts. Langhans argued that it was the dominant boulevard newspaper *BILD* that turned such discussions "into the scandalous phrase 'whoever screws the same person twice belongs to the Establishment.'" Initially, SDS members and other activists outside the Kommune were furious with this representation, which seemed to delegitimate their "politics," just as Klaus Hartung had feared. But, Kommunards responded, "'no, this is politics.'"[46] It was economics, too, Langhans averred, deeper than those of an imagined proletarian revolution. It was this that Klaus Hartung himself came to appreciate by the 1980s.

Rethinking Political Organization

With the proliferation of WGs throughout the 1970s, WG members, then, often lived apart from lovers. Such lovers contributed in fact to the connective tissue among WGs: they joined the "team" of "friends of the WG" (*Hausfreunde-Riege*).⁴⁷ Lovers and friends, political workmates from the range of settings, activities, and groupings: all helped join personal and political sites together explicitly in a way often unrecognized in the institutional organization of earlier times. It was through this means that all the WGs in Hannover were "networked," as Norbert T. described: drawn together via a dense web of relations that permitted steady contact and communications.⁴⁸ The regular change in housemates, and dissolution and reconstitution of WGs, only reinforced this phenomenon. Tulla recalled how, socially as otherwise, "one visited from one WG to the next. There were these famous parties, with cheap wine and noodle salad. Between WG and WG. Saturdays were always these big parties, where one stood around and talked." On principle, WGs tended to follow an "open-door" policy: those identifying generally with the broad movement were welcomed, for a meal and a discussion, for a short or even often a longer stay.⁴⁹ It was for such reasons that WGs often designated a room for guests who might visit, despite interest in keeping costs down. High schoolers like Norbert T. in Hannover might move in—or just pop in for an evening political meeting. Runaway youth spent days or weeks in a WG. This attitude challenged fixity, it kept things in flux, and, at the same time, it further developed connections among people and groupings. Everyone was in a sense "related"; despite constantly changing living circumstances, everyone who opted in to the broad community was "findable." This constituted yet another politico-cultural transformation, in the structures of modern political organization, along with political identities.

More than this: in these self-made living communities, these activists' embrace of difference, characteristic from the earliest days of the movement, played a prominent role.⁵⁰ In Tübingen, just as Tulla had described in West Berlin, Kerstin D.'s WG and women's center was "also an open house. Everyone could come. We had parties. . . . We could invite everybody, everyone could bring someone. One was really generous, everyone was invited to eat, and we always had something to drink, and so on." But it was more than just a chance to come together, to "network," and to demonstrate that one was not "petit bourgeois." The experience allowed everyone to "grow" through their encounters. Hubert recalled his own excitement in his first WG, when political artists and literary figures came to visit, still more of a type he had never before encountered. "So there was always something happening, if you will, and indeed in spheres that I never even knew from home. That was the most important for me." Visitors frequently came too from abroad, in this way also generating ever broader and more diverse political networks and political ideas. Such visits consolidated the sense of a very broad movement and, simultaneously, WG members incorporated or rejected ideas and practices that visitors brought with them.

To be sure, this embrace began already with the broad '68 movement. A critical aspect of that movement was a serious, personal engagement with those from elsewhere, at many levels.[51] Many ethnic German activists in the movement were initially inspired by hanging out casually with foreigners (predominantly but not exclusively foreign students) whose concentrated, collective housing in dorms and even "villages" of non-Germans in turn gave Germans ideas about sites of living and acting politically.[52] Close work in West Berlin between renowned transplanted activists East German Rudi Dutschke and Chilean Gaston Salvatore represented only one among millions of points of contact across borders in the broader movement, but it offers an intriguing case in point, when in 1967 Salvatore responded to Dutschke's pleas to translate Che Guevara's "Message to the Tricontinental" (concerning the creation of "Two, Three Vietnams") into German. The middle-class Salvatore recalled humorously his own confrontation with Dutschke's outwardly quite conventional living space, an apartment he shared with his new wife, American activist Gretchen Dutschke-Klotz. Inside, however, "unwashed dishes have piled up in the sink. Bits of food are stuck to them and are starting to turn green. The plates stink. I start to wash up," until Dutschke returned to the room with an ancient typewriter, urging Gaston to begin translating.[53] Dutschke and his wife may have already by that time transcended "bourgeois" concerns for cleanliness, but the scene was evidently a fillip to some kind of thought on Salvatore's own part. These exchanges remained a critical element of the movement into the 1970s and 1980s.

WGs were central sites of political as well as other forms of heterogeneity, moreover. They offer a nuanced alternative perspective to commonplace characterizations of West German extraparliamentary political life in the 1970s as increasingly sectarian.[54] Well-known figure in the "Paris May" Daniel Cohn-Bendit claimed that, in contrast with rising alternative political stratification in France, West Germany offered an opportunity to thrive in the broad "political other": the endless "multitude of subgroups" working in great proximity, permitting him in turn to "define his [own] everyday life differently."[55] The differences of political perspective made WG life "exciting," if also frequently frustrating. Karl W. recalled an exemplary case: one of his WGs that was "really great in atmosphere, even if there were many of these massive 'fractional' differences. There were people who were KPD, others who were in the Spartacus group"—that is, Maoists and those who adhered more closely to the GDR, normally considered the fiercest enemies. In that WG, they shared only a common political foe in the fiercely antiauthoritarian *Spontis*—which is how Karl himself identified, he recalled, laughing. At home, these individuals talked, argued, and shared ideas with each other endlessly; Karl stayed in the apartment a full two years. Conversely, Hubert humorously described problems in an all-*Sponti* WG he moved into. "Group time" was always a chance affair in the WG. "Everyone was glad to see one another, when everyone was there. But it was precisely so antiauthoritarian that absolutely no group pressure developed." This made it difficult to plan for collective activities. Naturally, this was in itself a highly relevant topic of discussion: the relation of group pressure and other constraints on individual "freedom" to political efficacy; and the relation of WGs as a unit of political thinking and learning to action in or out of the group.

Karl's two years in his one WG was a long stretch in any single communal home—even if other house members had changed around him. The frequent adding or subtracting of a house member, the entire dissolution of a WG, became a critical part of movement life. Indeed, a defining characteristic of WGs was specifically their kaleidoscopic character, over time as well as at a single moment, as a new perspective, an additional person, or ongoing discussions among members turned WGs around.[56] This was a frequently painful aspect of the experience, but it was consistent with activists' initial approach to WGs: embracing difference rather than seeking out the comfort of the familiar. The paradoxical comfort of impermanency in this most intimate of settings offered its own lessons, not least in terms of prefigurative politics more broadly. Each WG was an exciting new experiment to be carefully examined as well as cared for—until it was no longer workable. This changeability was one of the very ways in which alternative culture was to prefigure mainstream change.

The very experience of living in WGs exponentially reinforced the sense that change was not only the norm but something to seek at every level. Karin of Bahnhof Street noted, "I have no fixed picture of myself, of what I want to do. In my utopias"—the plural emphasizing the very changing nature of her political vision—"I always swing between one way of life, like the one here, and something completely different." The plural, personalized, even ironic form of "utopias" bespeaks the challenge of WG experiences to totalizing political visions altogether.[57] It wasn't just that Karin had not yet found her perfect way of life, that Hubert had not yet identified the right WG, or that Tulla still sought the correct political theory. It was whether there was any such thing, any "end of history." In a seminal collection of experiment reports concerning the "emancipation of everyday life," Frank Böckelmann wrote already in 1970 that "countermodels of living together and fulfilling needs . . . are no prognoses. . . . They don't purport that their realization is imperative and inevitable [*unumgänglich*], and they don't incorporate all the developing tendencies. They are to be provocations to think, and to recognize the paralyzing gravitational force of the status quo as arbitrary. They don't mean to distract, but rather to make one unsatisfied."[58]

In this extraordinary provocation, Böckelmann thus warned against putting too much faith in any single effort—and against seeking an "ultimate" transformation, an idea that was highly constraining instead of liberating. There was and would be no single right way that had simply eluded activists to date: it was about a new way of understanding—and acting on—change. Following the examples of Böckelmann, Kommune 2, and others, participants in WGs and other "life experiments" across West Germany took on the mantle of turning their experiences into demonstration projects, so that those across the broader movement could learn from the findings of one another. The answer was in the continual blossoming of the variety of experiments, simultaneous and serial, drawing on the last, but only as useful, through continued recounting and sharing of efforts. Contrary to seeking an end point, one should expect to always question, learn from others, and then still push for something that seemed better. This formed part of a radical epistemological change, a broad, onsite corollary to and expansion of some of the contemporary work and of what was soon to come concerning postmodern understandings.[59] New strategies of pursuing change constituted new ways of understanding how change takes place—and arguably challenging the terms of modern politics altogether. It reflected a sense that individuals and groups were always actively making and remaking their societies, in fundamental ways.

Conclusion

Alternative living experiments played a significant political role throughout the 1970s and beyond, not exclusively but especially in West Germany. They were a powerful enactment precisely of the ever-greater challenge to more formalized political organization. They were exemplary of the broader movement's character: comprising a self-identified "left" in the widest sense; constituting "politics" too with the blurriest of borders. This intense work did not "ultimately" displace the role of hegemonic politics, though it contributed to bringing what were at least temporarily new kinds of party politics to the fore, in a form straddling parliamentary and movement activism.[60] The limits of change at these levels continues to serve as a source of disappointment for some erstwhile activists. Yet I argue for the truly radical forms of rethinking that emerged from experiments like WGs that came especially in the aftermath of "'68," both drawing on and responding to immediately preceding as well as longer-past alternative political practices. "Revolutionary" aspects of this thought—including what constitutes politics and how to produce radical change—continue to influence and reshape thinking across decades. The remarkable recent transformation of views of gender identity as essential and fixed, and increasingly mainstream challenges to couples' relationships, in addition to groupings like Black Lives Matter and Occupy: these are some notable ongoing results of the kind of work of rethinking that took place behind the doors of WGs as well as elsewhere. There are also limits to individuals' willingness to actively continue such experimentation, such purposive willingness to change and make change. Joschka Fischer claimed in my 2007 interview with him that his self-transformation within the WG was "successful in the end." Klaus Hartung claimed in 1989 that "the shock waves could be felt still": but how much are they still felt now? Is there willingness—and ability—still to put in the enormous time and energy such experiments took? One lesson of these early activists was that "success" was always qualified, always limited: but this did not make it a failure. Change might be faster or slower at times, unconnected to the level of radicality. But the work toward change was never done—for good or ill. These activists' lessons might continue to serve us today—indeed, as we begin to see new breakthroughs in fundamental ways of thinking clearly connected with ongoing, radical work.

Belinda Davis, professor of History at Rutgers University, is author or co-editor of five books, including *The Inner Life of Politics: Grassroots Activism in West Germany, 1962-1983* (Cambridge, 2026); and, ed. with M. Klimke, C. MacDougall, and W. Mausbach, *Changing the World, Changing Oneself: Political Protest and Transnational Identities in 1960s/70s, West Germany and the U.S.* (Berghahn, 2010, 2012). Her current book project is entitled "Apartheid Planet: An Environmental History of Europe and European Reach from 1500."

Notes

1. This contribution is a shortened and lightly revised version of Belinda Davis, "What's in a Revolution? '68 and Its Aftermath in West Germany," in *Global 1968: Cultural Revolutions in Europe and Latin America*, ed. A. James McAdams and Anthony P. Monta (Notre Dame: University of Notre Dame Press, 2021), 230–57; it is included here with permission of the University of Notre Dame Press.
2. Compare Herrad Schenk, *Wir leben zusammen nicht allein: Wohngemeinschaften heute* (Köln: Kiepenheuer und Witsch, 1984); also Sven Reichardt, *Authentizität und Gemeinschaft: Linksalternatives Leben in den siebziger und frühen achtziger Jahren* (Berlin: Suhrkamp, 2014).
3. Reichardt, *Authentizität*, 459–87.

4. See Dieter Duhm, *Der Mensch ist anders* (Lampertheim: TIP, 1975); compare Reichardt, *Authentizität und Gemeinschaft*; also Joachim C. Häberlen, *The Emotional Politics of the Alternative Left: West Germany, 1968–1984* (Cambridge 2018), 30–75; Belinda Davis, *The Inner Life of Politics: "Extraparliamentary" Activism in West Germany, 1962–1983* (Cambridge: Cambridge, forthcoming).
5. Compare Wolfgang Kraushaar, *Autonomie oder Getto?* (Frankfurt: Verlag Neue Kritik, 1978).
6. Compare, e.g., Sabine Jauer, "Autonome Frauenhäuser: Weiter ohne Staatsknete," *Die wöchentliche Courage* 9, no. 16 (1984), 5; Robert Stephens, *Germans on Drugs: The Complications of Modernization in Hamburg* (Ann Arbor: University of Michigan Press, 2007).
7. Hubert R., interview with author, 7 July 2004.
8. On this youth center and its expansive activities, Heiko Geiling, *Das andere Hannover: Jugendkultur zwischen Rebellion und Integration in der Grosstadt* (Hannover: Offizin, 1996); David Templin, *Freizeit ohne Kontrollen: Die Jugendzentrumsbewegung in der Bundesrepublik der 1970er Jahre* (Göttingen: Wallstein, 2015); also Davis, *Inner Life*. On autonomous life and squatting particularly, compare Freia Anders and David Templin in this volume.
9. Compare Richard Birkefeld et al., *Mit 17. Jugendliche in Hannover 1900 bis heute* (Hannover: Historisches Museum, 1997), 113–4ff.
10. See Renate Köcher, "Lebensverhältnisse 1951–2001: Ein Rückblick mit Daten des Allensbacher Archivs," in *Fünfzig Jahre nach Weinheim: Empirische Markt- und Sozialforschung gestern, heute, morgen*, ed. Heinz Sahner (Baden-Baden: Nomos Verlagsgesellschaft, 2002), 59–73, 62.
11. Kommune 2, *Versuch der Revolutionierung des bürgerlichen Individuums: Kollektives Leben mit politischer Arbeit verbinden* (Berlin: Oberbaumverlag, 1969), 17–18.
12. See ibid., 8; also Helmut Kentler, in *Pardon* 5 (5/69), 43.
13. Schenk, *Wir leben*, 17.
14. Susanne T., interview with author, 26 July 2005.
15. Kommune 2, *Versuch*.
16. Schenk, *Wir leben*, 10.
17. Klaus Hartung, "Küchenarbeit," in *CheShahShit*, ed. E. Siepmann et al. (Berlin: Elefanten, 1989), 103.
18. Ibid. Hartung seems to refer to the apocryphal story that Kommune 1 cofounder Dieter Kunzelmann had claimed that he couldn't worry about Vietnam when he was having trouble with his orgasm.
19. Compare Belinda Davis, "Jenseits von Terror und Rückzug: Die Suche nach politischem Raum und Verhandlungsstrategien in der BRD der 70er Jahre," in *Terrorismus in der Bundesrepublik: Medien, Staat und Subkulturen in den 1970er Jahren*, ed. H.-G. Haupt et al. (Frankfurt a.M.: Campus, 2006), 154–86.
20. Cited by "William Tell," in Daniel Cohn-Bendit, *Der große Basar* (Munich: Trikont, 1975), 112.
21. Hartung, "Küchenarbeit," 103.
22. Kommune 2, *Versuch*, 8.
23. Compare Geoff Eley in this volume.
24. Schenk, *Wir leben*.

25. Frank Böckelmann, *Befreiung des Alltags: Modelle eines Zusammenlebens ohne Leistungsdruck, Frustration und Angst* (Munich: Rogner & Bernhard, 1970), frontispiece.
26. Compare Bernhard Gotto's chapter in this volume.
27. Kommune 2, *Versuch*, 23.
28. Cf. Timothy S. Brown, *West Germany and the Global Sixties* (Cambridge: Cambridge University Press, 2013).
29. *Der subjective Faktor*, dir. Helke Sander (1981).
30. However, "glocal" politics remained critical in WGs; compare contributions on "Solidarities" in this book.
31. Volker T., interview with author, 28 June 2004.
32. Joschka Fischer., interview with author, 26 October 2006.
33. Robert G., interview with author, 15 July 2004.
34. Compare Kristin Schulz, *Der lange Atem der Provokation: Die Frauenbewegung in der Bundesrepublik und in Frankreich 1968–1976* (Frankfurt a.M.: Campus, 2002).
35. Sigrid T., interview with author, 28 July 2005.
36. Wiebke S., interview with author, 18 July 2005.
37. Schenk, *Wir leben*, 46.
38. Ibid., 45.
39. Tulla R., interview with author, 19 July 2005.
40. Dagmar Przytulla, "Niemand ahnte, dass wir in ziemlich verklemmter Haufen waren," in *Die 68erinnen: Porträt einer rebellischen Frauengeneration*, ed. Ute Kätzel (Berlin: Rowohlt, 2002), 201–18, 206.
41. Schenk, *Wir leben*, 10.
42. Ibid., 33.
43. Ibid., 48.
44. Eve Koslowsky Sedgwick, *Epistemology of the Closet* (Berkeley: University of California Press, 1990).
45. Schenk, *Wir Leben*, 44–45.
46. Hartung, "Küchenarbeit."
47. Kommune 2, *Versuch*, 33.
48. Norbert T., interview with author, 14 July 2005.
49. Compare the infamous "guest towel" in *Taxi zum Klo*, dir. Frank Ripploh (1981).
50. Compare, e.g., Belinda Davis, "A Whole World Opening Up: Transcultural Contact, Difference, and the Politicization of 'New Left' Activists," in Davis et al., *Changing the World*, 255–73.
51. Compare too examples in *Unter dem Pflaster ist der Strand*, dir. Helma Sanders-Brahms (1975); also Quinn Slobodian, *Foreign Front: Third World Politics in Sixties West Germany* (Durham: Duke UP, 2012).
52. Davis, *Inner Life*.
53. Cited in *Foreign Front*, 75; also Rudi Dutschke: "If This Had Been Latin America."
54. See chapters by David Templin and Craig Griffiths in this volume.
55. Cohn-Bendit, *Der große Basar*, 103, 105.
56. Compare Stephen Milder's chapter in this volume.
57. Compare Friedericke Brühöfener's chapter in this volume.
58. Böckelmann, *Befreiung*, frontispiece.
59. Compare Ingrid Gilcher-Holtey's chapter in this volume.

60. Compare, e.g., Konrad Jarausch and Stephen Milder, eds., "Creating Participatory Democracy: Green Politics in Germany since 1983," special issue of *German Politics and Society* (Winter 2015).

Select Bibliography

Böckelmann, Frank. *Befreiung des Alltags: Modelle eines Zusammenlebens ohne Leistungsdruck, Frustration und Angst.* Munich: Rogner & Bernhard, 1970.

Davis, Belinda, *The Inner Life of Politics: "Extraparliamentary" Activism in West Germany, 1962–1983.* Cambridge: Cambridge University Press, forthcoming.

Davis, Belinda, et al., eds. *Changing the World, Changing Oneself: Political Protest and Transnational Identities in 1960s/70s, West Germany and the U.S.* New York: Berghahn Books, 2010.

Geiling, Heiko. *Das andere Hannover: Jugendkultur zwischen Rebellion und Integration in der Großstadt.* Hannover: Offizin, 1996.

Häberlen, Joachim. *The Emotional Politics of the Alternative Left: West Germany, 1968–1984.* Cambridge: Cambridge University Press, 2018.

Kommune 2. *Versuch der Revolutionierung des bürgerlichen Individuums: Kollektives Leben mit politischer Arbeit verbinden.* Berlin: Oberbaumverlag, 1969.

Reichardt, Sven. *Authentizität und Gemeinschaft: Linksalternatives Leben in den siebziger und frühen achtziger Jahren.* Berlin: Suhrkamp, 2014.

Rübner, Hartmut. *"Die Solidarität organisieren": Konzepte, Praxis und Resonanz linker Bewegung nach 1968.* Berlin: Plattner, 2012.

Schenk, Herrad. *Wir leben zusammen nicht allein: Wohngemeinschaften heute.* Köln: Kiepenheuer und Witsch, 1984.

Siegfried, Detlef, and Sven Reichardt, eds. *Das Alternative Milieu: Antibürgerlicher Lebensstil und linke Politik in Der Bundesrepublik Deutschland und Europa 1968–1983.* Göttingen: Wallstein, 2010.

Chapter 8

Changing the World for the Better
Women Activists' Redefinitions of Identities, Relationships, and Society

Friederike Brühöfener

"What's wrong with the reunited Germans? Are they really all slackers, sissies, softened by 40 years of peace in Central Europe?" asked *Der Spiegel* in 1991.[1] The German newsmagazine felt compelled to address this question because of German peace activists protesting the Iraq War and soldiers of the German army (Bundeswehr) filing applications for conscientious objection, alongside international criticism that condemned Germans as "cowards." According to *Der Spiegel*, one explanation for this behavior could be found in the history of the Bundeswehr. Since the Bundeswehr had been established as a defense force that could count on NATO's backing, West German soldiers were only trained in "work and adventure, camaraderie and mutual support." Despite some attempts by conservative traditionalists to rehabilitate the image of the "forceful fighter," *Der Spiegel* argued, German society had come to see the military as a peaceful "vocational school" for young men. The overall rejection of military might and ferocity that the newsmagazine described was, however, not limited to the history of the Bundeswehr. Rather, *Der Spiegel* noted, the military both reflected and fitted neatly into German society, because the population rejoiced in having "manly bravery and honor, fatherland and courage, appear only as footnotes in history books."[2]

The newsmagazine's article points to several interrelated developments in (West) Germany's post-1945 history that have attracted scholarly attention in the last decades. In the wake of World War II, scholarship suggests, West Germany embarked on a path from a "culture of war" toward a "culture of peace."[3] Although the Federal Republic of Germany established and maintained a sizable military force and upheld the practice of compulsory military service for men, large segments of West German society came to embrace attitudes and social practices that no longer treasured military norms or accepted war as a means to solve international conflicts. As scholars have highlighted, this cultural change was accompanied by a reevaluation of masculinity. The belief in the military as a palladium for socially accepted male behavior, which defined much of German history prior to 1945, gradually retreated into the background.[4] Whereas the military was still perceived as a "good pedagogical institution" for young men in the 1950s and in 1960s, by the 1970s large segments of West German society had come to negate the military as an organization that would properly socialize young men. Other institutions—most importantly paid compulsory community service (*Zivildienst*)—increasingly overshadowed it.[5]

Historical research indicates that the arguments and actions of activists affiliated with the New Left, as well as the new social movements that expanded in the 1970s and 1980s, helped sustain West Germany's changing mentality.[6] A number of activist women and female politicians, this chapter maintains, who were affiliated with the new peace movement, the environmental movement, and the second-wave women's movement not only represented this overall shift but actively and vocally contributed to it. Building in part on practices and rhetorical strategies that developed already in the 1960s, West German activist women publicly envisioned and pushed for alternative models of society, modes of human interactions, and concepts of masculinity. Denouncing nuclear threats and warfare as a state's legitimate means to ensure self-preservation, many activists condemned the military as an institution that created uncaring, violent, and depraved men. These oppressive masculinities ran counter to activists' visions of an affectionate society, a vision that for many included men who embraced individual freedom, peacefulness, and sensibility.

Aimed at changing the world for the better, women activists' demands were also embedded in and reflected the growing importance that emotions and the personal well-being of the individual assumed in West Germany during the 1970s and 1980s.[7] This emphasis on emotions and "the self" led some activists to develop alternative societal concepts and to challenge commonly held assumptions about the gendered nature of emotions. Central to the goals of many activists who sought to facilitate fundamental social and political change was the alteration of how people engaged with each other, their emotions, and society as a whole. In particular, they questioned the attribution of emotions and feelings based on the perceived differences between the sexes.

To show this, this chapter follows Alberto Melucci's suggestion that the new social movements of the 1970s and 1980s should be analyzed as a "network of groups and individuals sharing a conflictual culture and a 'collective identity.'"[8] Studying the speeches, writings, and publications of a diverse group of women, including Michaela von Freyhold, Petra Kelly, and Dorothee Sölle, the chapter emphasizes that many women gave voice to a shared "moral utopianism"[9] that intertwined both domestic and international issues. Although these women were by no means uniform in their agendas, thoughts, and arguments, and though they represented a multitude of oftentimes conflicting ideas about political activism, much of their criticism of the international Cold War politics of the 1970s and 1980s focused especially on nuclear "fantasies" and the posturing of male world leaders. As they criticized Cold War politicians, activist women furthermore connected the fraught international situation to problems and conflicts inherent in West German society. Drawing on a potpourri of personal experiences, convictions, and spiritual belief systems, they criticized the state of contemporary social relations, specifically the flawed relations between the sexes, as directly related to Cold War politics.

"Make Love, Not War": Activists' Dystopias and Utopias in the 1970s and 1980s

In 1982, the feminist, peace activist, and scholar Michaela von Freyhold raised the question: "Women against war, but how?"[10] Published as an essay in the pacifist reader *Frauen für den Frieden* (Women for Peace), Freyhold's answer closely linked gender, emotions, and the body. Like many of her fellow campaigners, Freyhold, who at the time was professor of sociology at the University of Bremen, emphasized the gendered nature of modern states, politics, and warfare. "War," she argued, was still "a giant male fantasy" even though, "in reality," it had lost all its romantic appeal. For the sociologist, society's approval of the ongoing nuclear arms race was infused with "notions of violence" and subjugation. These ideas and behaviors, she argued, were the result of a "sick and sickening relationship between man and woman, an inability to love." While men viewed war as an "unbridled adventure" that allowed them to act on their aggressions, women associated war with violence. According to Freyhold, contemporary Cold War society was defined by an emotional and bodily "coldness between people" that fed "secret fantasies of destruction and death wishes."[11] As she described the early 1980s as a modern-day dystopia, Freyhold also offered suggestions on how people and societies could overcome this desperate situation. To dismantle this "nuclear apparatus of annihilation" and create a world of love in which people could be "soft and vulnerable and open," Freyhold maintained, a broad and radical social movement was necessary. Women who were willing to take up the "fight against the man" on every societal and political level were vital for the success of this movement.[12]

Freyhold's concerns about society's emotional emptiness and bodily deficiencies should not be mistaken for meaningless buzzwords. Rather, they were fundamental to her and many other activists' understanding of what was wrong with the world in general and the Federal Republic in particular. As Belinda Davis's research has shown, Michaela von Freyhold's arguments reflect the opinions and rhetorical strategies of many women activists who engaged in the widespread peace and ecological protests as well as feminist activism in the 1970s and 1980s.[13] During those decades, campaigners such as Freyhold had numerous reasons to call for open protest and demonstrations. On a national level, for instance, many West Germans—activists or not—were concerned about their governments' eagerness to expand the Federal Republic's use of nuclear energy for both military and civilian purposes. Under the leadership of chancellors Willy Brandt (1969–74) and Helmut Schmidt (1974–82), the Federal Republic saw an expansion of plans to build new nuclear reactors and reprocessing plants for atomic waste on West German soil. The implementation of the chancellors' energy polices led to an explosion of antinuclear protest in various parts of the country, including the Badensian village of Wyhl, where in 1975 protesters occupied the construction site for a massive nuclear reactor.[14] The antinuclear protest that developed in the mid-1970s very much influenced the wave of protests that swept the Federal Republic of Germany in the early 1980s.

Then, in 1978 and 1979, Schmidt's minister of defense, Hans Apel, and the parliamentary ombudsman of the armed forces, Karl-Wilhelm Berkhan, made headlines by proposing the recruitment of women for military services. Although SPD politician and former minister of defense George Leber had already in 1975 granted female volunteers access to the Bundeswehr's Medical Corps as doctors and pharmacists with officers' rank, their proposals went a step further. Apel especially pushed for the recruitment of "girls and women" into almost all areas of the Bundeswehr.[15] Even though the minister made the proposal in light of the Bundeswehr's growing recruitment crisis, he also attempted to portray it as proof that Helmut Schmidt's government supported women's equality and emancipation. Apel stated that the recruitment of women into the Bundeswehr provided a great opportunity to "break up the last bastion of men."[16] The minister's arguments led to a lengthy and intense public dispute that was very much dominated by feminist and women peace activists. Women's dismay over Apel's suggestions was aggravated partly because Alice Schwarzer, who had become one of the most prominent figures of West Germany's new women's movement, argued in the popular feminist magazine *Emma* that if women wanted to be fully emancipated, they had to serve in the Bundeswehr alongside men. Even though Schwarzer emphasized that if she "were a man" she too "would be a conscientious objector," her statement infuriated many.[17]

Apel's proposal coincided with heightened tensions on the international stage, and Chancellor Helmut Schmidt was at the forefront of those developments. Mainly in reaction to the Soviet Union's decision to upgrade its nuclear arsenal by deploying new SS-20 intermediate-range missiles, Schmidt argued that an arms buildup by NATO powers was necessary in order to restore the "political and military equilibrium." After intense negotiations among the alliance's foreign and defense ministers, NATO threatened on 12 December 1979 to modernize its own weaponry with new intermediate-range missiles, even as it pursued arms reduction negotiations with the Warsaw Pact. When Soviet troops invaded Afghanistan less than two weeks later, the prospect of successful negotiations and arms reduction was all but obliterated. Moreover, the international political climate continued to be marred by tensions, in large part because the United States and the Federal Republic of Germany elected two men in the early 1980s who were willing to uphold the principles of NATO's double-track decision. Both Ronald Reagan, who became president in January 1981, and Helmut Kohl, who became chancellor following a vote of no confidence against Helmut Schmidt in the fall of 1982, embraced the belief that NATO had to modernize its weaponry, since all nuclear disarmament negotiations had proven unsuccessful.[18] Kohl's pro-deployment policy was fiercely opposed by West Germany's Greens and Social Democrats, who, in the wake of Schmidt's loss of the chancellorship, performed a political turnaround and largely abandoned NATO's policies. Nonetheless, the stationing of missiles on West German soil commenced in December 1983, following an affirmative parliamentary vote the month before.[19]

The tense international situation prompted peace activism in West Germany and other European countries to grow in an extraordinary manner. Between 1980 and 1984, an unprecedented number of groups and individuals took to the streets of West German towns and cities to campaign against NATO politics and the stationing of any rockets or missiles that could be used for nuclear warfare. One of the first protests that drew record numbers of participants was the demonstration in the West German capital of Bonn in October 1981. That month roughly 300,000 citizens came together at the Bonner Hofgarten to voice their dissent. Already four months earlier, activists had used the German Protestant Church Congress in Hamburg to rally against NATO politics. Now, demonstrations continued into 1982, accompanying Ronald Reagan's visit to West Germany. In addition to attending the NATO Council summit in Bonn, Reagan traveled to West Berlin on 11 June 1982. The visit of the US president drew about 350,000 protesters. Further, throughout 1983, "millions of citizens"[20] sustained the collective effort to challenge international Cold War politics by participating in various protest campaigns against the stationing of missiles on German soil. Armed with posters and pamphlets, activists blockaded the access routes and entrances to US military bases on which the nuclear weapons were to be installed.

Activist women were vital and successful participants in this new peace movement, which brought together numerous groups and organizations from different social, cultural, and political backgrounds. As historian Reinhild Kreis emphasizes, they "covered all ages, professions, and religions, they came from urban as well as rural areas, and displayed a wide range of political orientations."[21] The *Frauenwiderstandscamp* (women's resistance camp) in the mountainous region of the Hunsrück, in Rhineland-Palatinate, exemplifies this. Between 1983 and 1993, the Hunsrück was an important site of peace activism, because NATO's double-track decision included the plan to station ninety-six cruise missiles in that area. Activists started organizing "peace weeks," an "easter peace [bike] tour," as well as "easter marches" in reaction to NATO's decision.[22] In June 1983, the first women's resistance camp was established in the Hunsrück. Activist women who participated in the protest camp were geographically, socially, politically, and spiritually diverse. Yet, even though the women of the *Widerstandscamp* were far from homogenous, many agreed that NATO's double-track decision was the "fatal expression of militarism and sexism."[23] Unified and driven by this interpretation of Cold War politics, they offered successful resistance for eleven years.

As the Hunsrück example indicates, many women who engaged in the 1980s protests closely linked the nuclear threat and the "atomic behavior" of contemporary world leaders to issues of gender. Engaging in a broad analysis of societal and political structures that perpetuated women's oppression, activists rejected the "male principle and power relations."[24] In particular, the argument that the country's population just needed to behave rationally, detached, and emotionless, an argument perpetuated by male politicians, military leaders, scientists, and operators of nuclear reactors, rubbed many the wrong way. In a lengthy essay, titled "150,000 Deaths and Political Utopias," the well-known feminist writer, film director, and activist Helke Sander argued that the public call for more rationality very much resembled a common criticism—"Don't be so emotional!"[25]—that men tended to level at women during disputes in their everyday lives. In her essay, which was published in the 1986 edited collection *Kein Wunderland für Alice? Frauenutopien* (*No Wonderland for Alice? Women's Utopias*)[26] Sander maintained that there was "no sensible reason to not react emotionally." Yet, even two years after nuclear disaster in Chernobyl, male politicians and scientists were somehow more afraid of a "hysterical woman on television" than a nuclear reactor releasing radioactive gases far and wide. Convinced that "emotionality and expertise could definitely be combined," Sanders saw no reason for women or anybody else to be impressed by "men's internalized militarism," which for her included "the hiding of feelings" and the mistake to confuse "being unmoved [*Unberührtheit*] with objectivity."[27] In light of the dangers of the nuclear threat, it was more important than ever to question and challenge male experts. This kind of engagement with the traditional notion that cool, calculated objectivity and rationality were superior to any form of emotions and emotionality reflects a broader trend in German society and, especially, leftist activism at the time. In the 1970s, as Joachim Häberlen and other scholars have pointed out, contemporaries "reimagined politics as a struggle against the domination of rationality." Blaming "capitalism for 'damaging' their personalities," they instead emphasized the importance of "developing and expressing feelings."[28]

To overcome the "fatal tendencies of men's alliances," many activist women sought to develop different counternarratives and alternative emotional practices. After all, as Antje Vollmer, Protestant pastor and politician of Die Grünen, observed in 1986, "Men's phantasies fill voluminous volumes of books," and even the genre of utopian novels is dominated by men. Yet, women's utopias were nowhere to be found.[29] Vollmer's colleague, the ardent peace activist and founding member of the West German Green Party, Petra Kelly, penned a new narrative in an elaborate essay published in her book *Fighting for Hope* (*Um Hoffnung Kämpfen: Gewaltfrei für eine Zukunft*). In this essay, titled "For an Erotic Society" ("Für eine Erotische Gesellschaft"), she called for a new appreciation of subjectivity and emotions. For Kelly, it was time that people and society became both "affectionate and subversive." She argued that in the "nuclear, militarized world" of the Cold War, human relationships were "permeated by distrust, fear, and insecurity."[30] This lack of hope, love, and security not only polluted national and international politics but also contaminated people's intimate practices. According to Kelly, "interactions between the sexes" were reduced to "pure sexuality" and "coital acrobatics" aimed at one's own satisfaction. If activists truly wanted to change how society and politics functioned, love had to be "integrated into all areas" of life. Only then could the "societal powers of isolation and division and hostility" be overcome.[31] Petra Kelly's publication and her reasoning in particular was part of a larger trend among leftist thinkers and activists who "envisioned and tried to practice a radically different form of sexuality" that did not adhere to the "genital supremacy."[32]

While calling for "free sexuality and emancipation," an argument that had been prominent among proponents of the New Left in the 1960s, Kelly also implicitly criticized those of the 1960s student and broader extraparliamentary opposition (APO). For her, they were too "penis-focused" and prone to relegate women to passivity. "Men, even the progressive ones," she argued, had been raised to be physically dominant and to "measure their virility by the size of their penis and the frequency of their ejaculation." In contrast to this male-dominated and male-focused world, Kelly envisioned an "erotic, nonviolent, and loving society" in which people were "affectionate, erotic human beings" who had learned how to truly love each other.[33] As she wanted society to move beyond the common tendency to see any sexual union as "penis-related," Kelly built on a criticism that had already developed among activists of the new women's movement in the mid- to late 1970s and that continued to concern feminists in the 1980s.[34] During the international "feminist sex debates" of the 1970s, women activists such as the American Kate Millett demanded the renunciation of social structures that overrated penile significance and subjugated women as sexual objects.[35] Many female campaigners who were involved in the student-based protests of the New Left also criticized their male counterparts for ignoring or belittling the emancipatory demands of women. In late 1968, Helke Sander had famously delivered a scathing speech at a congress of the Socialist German Student League (SDS), in which she chastised the men of the SDS as "blockheads" who neither understood nor cared about women's needs and demands.[36]

Kelly's arguments represented the political agenda and opinions of many feminist, peace, and ecological activists who opposed the nuclear policies of Helmut Schmidt, Helmut Kohl, and other Western leaders for different but often related reasons. In the wake of NATO's double-track decision, the articulation of emotions became an important element of political engagement and activism. Instead of hiding their fears, women as well as their male counterparts who participated in large and small protest rallies all over West Germany visibly displayed them on picket signs, bearing such phrases as "I am afraid" or "We are afraid."[37] They also articulated them in pamphlets, essays, and books, as well as in letters sent to members of the West German government and Bundestag. Whether it was the arms race between the United States and the Soviet Union, the constant "improvement of weapons systems,"[38] or "America's matter-of-fact calculations and theories," for many protesters admitting one's fears was a sign of superior human qualities and sensibilities that governments west of the Iron Curtain had to take seriously.[39] The articulation of one's "fear of nuclear war" was not only the expression of a person's immediate feelings, but it was also seen as a useful method to counter the cold rationalities of governments, nuclear scientists, and militarists.[40]

The sentiments and the ways in which activists displayed them in the early 1980s did not come out of the blue. Rather, they reflected and were part of a broader development that Frank Biess has described as the emergence of a "therapeutic society" (*therapeutische Gesellschaft*).[41] During the 1970s, many West Germans associated with the Left-alternative milieu embraced a "culture of self-reflection," which was supposed to help them "sharpen" their "awareness of the self's aggressive and potentially (self)destructive impulses." One of the main goals for those who embraced this trend was to "maximize life happiness" as well as to learn how to articulate emotions, in particular fears.[42] These therapeutic foci also included new approaches to sexuality. Sex therapy that was practiced around 1980 aimed at the development of an "affectionate-sensitive sexual attitude" that considered the desires of both partners.[43] To a certain extent, this increased emphasis on the self, subjectivity, and emotions also led contemporaries to question what they considered the traditional "male view of life." Analyzing the esoteric-religious circles associated with the "New Age" movement, Pascal Eitler shows that some members of the movement advocated for the creation of a "new man." This new type of man was seen as central to overcoming the coldness, rationality, hierarchies, violence, and aggressiveness of the "old life." Although this "new men" would always remain "a man," he was supposed to free his "soft core" and "(re)discover" his "own feelings"[44]

Men's Societies of the "Old Age": Activists' Criticism of the Bundestag and the Bundeswehr

The new appreciation of individual emotions did not only shape the ideological self-conception and political practices of the New Left; it also fundamentally influenced the rhetoric and actions of West German peace and environmental activists.[45] As they developed visions of a new, peaceful world that was free from destructive male aggression and violence, and, instead, populated by a new type of emotional, affectionate human activist, they also identified numerous obstacles, places, and individuals that prevented them from reaching their goals. Most prominently, they identified the men in power as a hindrance and as representatives of the "old age." Contemporaries identified the United States and, in particular, Ronald Reagan's government as the main perpetrator who endangered world peace and people's emotional well-being. Many campaigners who took the streets in the 1980s publicly stated that they were not afraid of "the Russians" but rather the politics of the

United States and their NATO allies: they portrayed the United States and the American government as "aggressive and crazy with power."[46]

In addition to foreign NATO leaders, national politicians seemed to represent the not yet bygone era of old notions of masculinity as well. Remembering her experience as a parliamentarian of the Bundestag in her 1984 publication . . . *und wehret euch täglich! Bonn—ein grünes Tagebuch* (. . . *and resist daily! Bonn—A Green diary*), the theologian and member of the Green Party Antje Vollmer described the West German parliament as a "men's society through and through," which included Chancellor Helmut Kohl, former chancellor Helmut Schmidt, and Vice Chancellor Hans-Dietrich Genscher. According to her, some of these men, who personified the "manly ideal of our mothers' generation," looked quite "gray," "artificially tanned" [*höhensonnengebräunt*], and "smug."[47] Considering herself a "postwar woman" who was raised by a "generation of unknowingly emancipated" and strong mothers, Vollmer lamented that she and her female colleagues had to deal with a "generation of men who considers women's strength as loss of power, as dependence and oppression."[48] Because they still remembered the "aggressive and omnipotent" roles that men had acquired during Fascism, today's men fought against emancipated women with the "full severity of the newly oppressed." As she recalled the public interest in Waltraud Schoppe's famous 1983 Bundestag speech, in which fellow Green parliamentarian Schoppe controversially tackled Paragraph 218—the so-called *Abtreibungsparagraph* §218 (abortion law)—and accused men of "negligent penetration," Vollmer noted that men not only defined West Germany's norms of morality but also determined "the style in which affections and sensuality can be exchanged."[49] Because those men were still fundamentally in power, the societal change that Vollmer and many others desired seemed very difficult to achieve. Furthermore, revolutionary women who longed for emancipation also could not count on the New Left, socialist students, or even the Green Party. In her speech at the 1988 congress of the Socialist German Students' League (SDS), Vollmer accused the "men of the SDS" to have reacted to their female comrades' fight for emancipation by combining "revolt and machismo." Continuing Helke Sander's 1968 argument, Vollmer criticized the "leftist macho man" who became the dominant masculine ideal in the SDS and who wholeheartedly ignored the needs and wants of his female colleagues.[50]

To be sure, the congruence of arguments should not suggest that activist women constituted one happily unified group that unanimously embraced each other's ideas, actions, and agendas. Over the course of the 1970s and 1980s, West Germany's women's movement, for instance, became increasingly diverse as different strands of feminist activism developed.[51] While contentious topics such as revision of §218 revealed diverse understandings and approaches to women's bodily autonomy,[52] campaigners also disagreed on how to pursue their emancipatory goals. Most notably, activists' opinions diverged on whether an autonomous approach to the many problems that women faced would prove more successful than harnessing the powers of party and parliamentary politics. The tensions between "project- and party-based ideas of feminist strategy" increased over the course of the 1980s,[53] especially as the newly founded West German Green Party, which had integrated not only ecological and pacifist but also emancipatory and feminist issues into its party platform, entered the Bundestag. The ascension of Die Grünen and the party's entry into the Bundestag also revealed fractures in the ways that activists and politicians identified themselves and related to the different but connected social movements. In addition to personal animosities, the party's structure, practices, and actions throughout the 1980s revealed considerable strife between some of the female politicians who were, to varying degrees, affiliated with the feminist movement.[54]

Still, the obvious disagreements and contestations notwithstanding, many ecological and feminist movements agreed that the military apparatus in general and the Bundeswehr in particular posed one of the biggest threats to their hopes and dreams. Probing the mechanisms of the Cold War, many peace and feminist activists criticized the Bundeswehr as the premier institution to produce these threatening and destructive masculinities they despised. The early 1980s saw an increased production of pamphlets, brochures, magazine articles, and anthologies in which peace and feminist activists portrayed the Bundeswehr as an institution that not only destroyed men as men but also jeopardized any normal human relationships. While many recalled the mutilated and broken men who returned after World War II, others emphasized the experiences of men who had served or were currently serving in the West German Bundeswehr. In these stories, military service was not depicted as a rite of passage that turned boys into real men but rather as an institution that "humiliated" and "dehumanized" men and as a result created "hate" and "barbarity."[49]

One important publication that enabled activists to publish their concerns was the anarchist-pacifist magazine *graswurzelrevolution*. In its October/November 1979 edition, for example, *graswurzelrevolution* published a speech that Dorothee Sölle had given at an event in Hamburg titled "Women into the Bundeswehr?—No Thanks!"[55] At the time of the publication, Sölle was an accomplished and internationally known scholar of literature and theologian who represented the new "leftist *Protest*antism" ("Links*protest*antismus").[56] Arguing that the madness of the arms race militarized brains, endangered peace, and caused hunger, Sölle propagated a "theology of love" that emphasized categories such as trust, friendship, and solidarity as well equal rights for men and women.[57] In her speech, the activist theologian argued that young men who served in the Bundeswehr experienced a "lack of dignity," and lived through a "rehearsal of alcoholism, of petty crime, as well as a system of command and obedience." For her, this "hierarchical system," which "even the most sensitive among them" could not escape, did not correspond to the educational ideal that she and other activists held dear.[58]

To overcome the threat the military system posed, some activists also called on both men and women to fight together. According to Petra Kelly, women lived "more and more free from traditional norms and paradigms" in the "new free space" that was the ecology and peace movement. In contrast, many men had not yet been afforded this luxury. Therefore, women activists not only had to fight against women's integration into the Bundeswehr, but they had to collaborate with their "brothers and sisters in the movement against war service."[59] For Kelly, this was essential, because men, not just women, had to "see the bigger picture, the overall problem that concerns us all, women, children and men." Only "when men themselves reject violence and warfare," she argued, was it possible to take the next step in the overall movement "against the nuclear state, against the increasing militarization."[60]

As women activists foregrounded the Bundeswehr as the place where men and women would fall victim to state-sanctioned brutalization and dehumanization, they continued a form of criticism that some anti-Wehrdienst activists, peace activists, and intellectuals of the "New Left" had begun to level at the Bundeswehr already in the 1960s and 1970s. As Patrick Bernhard shows, in the mid- to late 1960s a number of APO organizations took up the "battle against the Bundeswehr" and military service during those years.[61] Peace activists like those participating in the Campaign for Democracy and Demilitarization and the German Peace Union (Deutsche Friedens Union or DFU) collaborated with organizations of different foci, such as the Social Democratic University Union (Sozialdemokratischer Hochschulbund or SHB). Even though these groups had very different political motives, pursued diverse agendas, and oftentimes fought against each other, together they questioned the legitimacy of Bundeswehr and military service.

To be sure, APO groups pursued diverse methods of protest, which built on different notions of masculinity. For instance, while members of the German section of the War Resisters' International called on West German men to file for conscientious objection as soon as they received the draft call, many other activists disagreed. Rudi Dutschke called on his fellow male activists who were truly "strong enough" to enter the military as recruits to "weaken" the Bundeswehr from within.[62] At the same time, several groups expressed concerns about the violent male behavior that military life produced. In 1969, the Cologne section of the extraparliamentary Republican Club (Republikanische Club) distributed a short leaflet that juxtaposed violent notions of military masculinity with an irenic ideal of masculinity.[63] The leaflet informed girls that, if their boyfriends went into the Bundeswehr, the military leadership would force them to learn and practice the act of killing.[64] As a result, the "tenderness" that girls had experienced at the hands of their boyfriends would soon turn into "brutality." In juxtaposing a sensitive civilian masculinity of a loving boyfriend with a violent military masculinity, the leaflet assumed that its female readership would want to prevent this vision from becoming reality. Using slogans from the American peace protests against the Vietnam War, it asked the "girl" to remember that "love is always better than war."

Of course, the convictions and arguments of feminist and peace activists should not be understood as a mere copying of arguments developed by organizations in the 1960s. Yet some of the practices and rhetoric of that era offered an important starting point for activists in the 1980s and beyond. For instance, in light of Germany's reunification and the possible expansion of compulsory military service, activists once more highlighted how military service in the Bundeswehr corrupted West German men. According to peace and anti-Wehrpflicht activists in Berlin, who engaged and grappled "with our role as men" and with the workings of "our patriarchal society," there were "a thousand reasons" to oppose military service and the Bundeswehr. Constituting the most brutal and "fundamental pillar of patriarchal rule," the military taught men aggressiveness, "sexism and chauvinism." [65]

As the military's hierarchy and command structure prevented the development of any "individual subjectivity," men only acquired "abilities and inabilities" such as discipline, blind obedience, and the hardening of their bodies, which they needed to "rule and survive men's hierarchy." This was particularly problematic, because men went to the Bundeswehr at an age when they were "unsure, insecure about their life philosophies, also in terms of their sexuality." Yet as the Bundeswehr broke them "psychologically and physically," those men learned to control themselves and learned that they "must not show any fear, any pain, or any sorrow." Those who required the human needs such as affection, empathy, or warmth, were, feminist activists argued, "softies," "faggots," and "chicks."[66] They were discriminated against and bullied. Instead of being themselves and content masters of their own autonomous and peaceful lives, activists asserted, men became both the victims and perpetrators of state-sanctioned violence. As such, the practices and customs of the Bundeswehr and, for that matter, any other military institution or system undermined the irenic version of the world that peace, environmental, and feminist activists of the 1970s and 1980s envisioned.

Conclusion

Utopian and dystopian projections of society and life flourished during the two decades that followed the cultural and political upheavals of '68. These projections emerged alongside the growing focus on healthy emotions and the personal well-being of the individual that developed especially among segments of the Left-alternative milieu. Women activists affiliated with the women's, peace, and environmental movements, which expanded in the 1970s and 1980s, were vital agents. While warning against destructive powers of Cold War warriors who, with their misconceived, destructive ideas of manly and nuclear power, would push the world into an even bleaker future, if not to the point of destruction, activists also formulated new ideals of masculinity. Even though they surely represented a diverse group of individuals whose personalities, political priorities, and actions diverged and occasionally clashed, the women discussed in this chapter thus shared certain moral imperatives.

As they provided their contemporaries with alternative versions of human interaction as well as visions of a livable and sustainable future, women propagated these ideals vocally and publicly. The examples discussed here show that women used both informal and formal channels of political expressions to undermine traditional understandings and "limits of legitimate political participation" and behavior.[67] Moreover, if their methods can be understood as contributing to the postwar process of increased democratization through new forms of popular politics,[68] then their messages can likewise have sustained the rethinking of emotional norms and practices in postwar Germany.

Friederike Brühöfener is Professor of History at San Jose State University, where she also serves as Assistant Vice Provost for Faculty Excellence and Teaching Innovation. She is the co-editor, together with Karen Hagemann and Donna Harsch, of *Gendering Post-1945 German History: Entanglements*, published by Berghahn Books in 2019.

Notes

1. "Den Ernstfall nicht gewagt," *Der Spiegel* 7, 11 February 1991, 18–21a.
2. "Den Ernstfall nicht wagen," 21a.
3. See, for example, Thomas Kühne, "'Friedenskultur,' Zeitgeschichte und Historische Friedensforschung," in *Von der Kriegskultur zur Friedenskultur? Zum Mentalitätswandel in Deutschland seit 1945*, ed. Thomas Kühne (Hamburg: LIT, 2000), 13–33. See also Wolfram Wette, "Kann man aus der Geschichte lernen? Historische Friedensfor-

schung," in *Friedens- und Konfliktforschung in Deutschland: Eine Bestandsaufnahme*, ed. Ulrich Eckern, Leonie Herwartz-Emden, and Rainer-Olaf Schultze (Wiesbaden: VS Verlag, 2004), 83–97.
4. See, for example, Till von Rahden, "Sanfte Vaterschaft und Demokratie in der frühen Bundesrepublik," in *Männer mit "Makel": Männlichkeiten und gesellschaftlicher Wandel in der Bundesrepublik Deutschland*, ed. Bernhard Gotto and Elke Seefried (Munich: De Gruyter Oldenbourg, 2017), 142–56.
5. See Heinrich J. Bartjes, *Der Zivildienst als Sozialisationsinstanz: Theoretische und empirische Annäherungen* (Weinheim: Juventa-Verlag, 1996); Heinrich J. Bartjes, "Der Zivildienst als die moderne 'Schule der Nation'?" in *Von der Kriegskultur zur Friedenskultur? Zum Mentalitätswandel in Deutschland seit 1945*, ed. Thomas Kühne (Hamburg: LIT, 2000), 130–45; Patrick Bernhard, *Zivildienst zwischen Reform und Revolte: Eine bundesdeutsche Institution im gesellschaftlichen Wandel 1961–1982* (Munich: Oldenbourg, 2005).
6. For a short overview, see Silke Mende and Birgit Metzger, "Eco-Pacifism: The Environmental Movement and a Source for the Peace Movement," in *The Nuclear Crisis: The Arms Race, Cold War Anxiety, and the German Peace Movement of the 1980s*, ed. Christoph Becker Schaum et al. (New York: Berghahn Books, 2016), 119–37. For a related discussion, see also Bernhard Gotto's chapter in this volume.
7. For the growing body of scholarship that looks at societies and political activism through the lens of the history of emotions, see, for example, Sabine Maasen, Jens Elberfeld, Pascal Eitler, and Maik Tändler, eds., *Das beratene Selbst: Zur Genealogie der Therapeutisierung in den "langen" Siebzigern* (Bielefeld: Transkript Verlag, 2011); Sven Reichardt, *Authentizität und Gemeinschaft: Linksalternatives Leben in den siebziger und frühen achtziger Jahren* (Berlin: Suhrkamp Verlag, 2014); Joachim C. Häberlen, *The Emotional Politics of the Alternative Left: West Germany, 1968–1984* (Cambridge: Cambridge University Press, 2018); Frank Biess, *German Angst: Fear and Democracy in the Federal Republic of Germany* (Oxford: Oxford University Press, 2020).
8. Alberto Melucci, "The Symbolic Challenge of Contemporary Movements," *Social Research* 52, no. 4, Social Movements (1985): 798–99.
9. Melucci, "Symbolic Challenge," 803.
10. Michaela von Freyhold, "Frauen gegen Krieg, aber wie?" in *Frauen für den Frieden: Analysen Dokumente und Aktionen aus der Friedensbewegung*, ed. Eva Quistorp (Frankfurt a.M.: päd.-extra-Buchverlag, 1982), 47–53.
11. Ibid., 48.
12. Ibid., 51–52.
13. Belinda Davis, "The Gender of War and Peace: Rhetoric in the West German Peace Movement of the Early 1980s," *Mitteilungsblatt des Instituts für Soziale Bewgungen* 32 (2004): 99–130; Belinda Davis, "'Women's Strength and Crazy Male Power': Gendered Language in the West German Peace Movement of the 1980s," in *Frieden, Gewalt, Geschlecht: Friedens- und Konfliktforschung als Geschlechterforschung*, ed. Jennifer Davy, Karen Hagemann, and Ute Kätzel (Essen: Klartext, 2005), 244–65.
14. For the development of antinuclear protest in West Germany and the significance of Wyhl, see, for example, Stephen Milder, *Greening Democracy: The Anti-nuclear Movement and Political Environmentalism in West Germany and Beyond, 1968–1983*

(New York: Cambridge University Press, 2017). See further: Jens Ivo Engels, *Naturpolitik in der Bundesrepublik: Ideen und politische Verhaltensstile in Naturschutz und Umweltbewegung 1950–1980* (Paderborn: Verlag Ferdinand Schöningh, 2006); Johann Vollmer, "Vom 'Denkmal des mündigen Bürgers' zur Besetzungsromantik: Die Grenzen symbolischer Politik in der frühen Anti- AKW-Bewegung," in *Bürgersinn mit Weltgefühl: Politische Moral und solidarischer Protest in den sechziger und siebziger Jahren*, ed. Habbo Knoch (Göttingen: Wallstein Verlag, 2007), 271–293.

15. Davis, "Gender"; Jens-Reiner Ahrens, "Verzögerte Anpassung und radikaler Wandel: Zum parlamentarischen Diskurs über Frauen in den Streikräften seit Gründung der Bundeswehr," in *Frauen im Militär: Empirische Befunde zur Integration der Streikräfte*, ed. Jens-Reiner Ahrens, Maja Apelt, and Christiane Bender (Wiesbaden: VS Verlag, 2005), 32–44; Friederike Brühöfener, "Between Flintenweib and Stewardess: Putting West German Women into Military Uniforms, 1960s–1970s," *Women's History: The Journal of The Women's History Network* 2, no. 12 (2019): 19–26.
16. Swantje Kraake, *Frauen zur Bundeswehr: Analyse und Verlauf einer Diskussion* (Frankfurt a.M.: Lang, 1992), 177–78.
17. Alice Schwarzer, "Frauen ins Militär?" *Emma*, June 1978, retrieved 30 August 2021 from https://www.emma.de/lesesaal. For an analysis of the discussion, see Davis, "Gender." See also Myra Marx Ferree, *Varieties of Feminism: German Gender Politics in Global Perspective* (Stanford, CA: Stanford University Press, 2012), 104–6.
18. For a history of the Cold War and its different phases, see Bernd Stöver, *Der Kalte Krieg, 1947–1991: Geschichte eines Radikalen Zeitalters* (Munich: Beck, 2007), 402–242. For a discussion of the double-track decision, see the chapters "The NATO Double-Track Decision: Genesis and Implementation," by Tim Geiger and "NATO's Double-Track Decision and East-West German Relation," by Hermann Wentker, in Schaum, *Nuclear Crisis*, 52–69 and 154–72.
19. Judith Michel, *Willy Brandts Amerikabild und -Politik 1933–1992* (Göttingen: Vandenhoeck & Ruprecht, 2010), 472. See also Andreas Wirsching, *Abschied vom Provisorium, 1982–1990* (Munich: Deutsche Verlags-Anstalt, 2006), 90–100.
20. "Kinder des Lichts, Kinder der Finsternis," *Der Spiegel* 42, 17 October 1983, 30. See, Rob Burns and Wilfried van der Will, *Protest and Democracy in West Germany: Extra-parliamentary Opposition and the Democratic Agenda* (London: Macmillan Press, 1988), 219.
21. Reinhild Kreis, "'Men Build Missiles': The Women's Peace Movement," in Schaum, *Nuclear Crisis*, 292.
22. Ilona Scheidle, "Das Frauenwiderstandscamp im Hunsrück (1983–1993): Lesbische Frauen für Frieden, gegen Krieg und Männergewalt," in *Frauen und Frieden? Zuschreibungen—Kämpfe—Verhinderungen*, ed. Franziska Dunkel and Corinna Schneider (Opladen: Budrich, 2015), 117–44.
23. Scheidle, "Das Frauenwiderstandscamp," 130.
24. Birgit Meyer, "Viel bewegt—auch viel erreicht? Frauengeschichte und Frauenbewegung in der Bundesrepublik," *Blätter für deutsche und internationale Politik* 34 (1989): 832–42; Davis, "Gender," 112–21.
25. Helke Sander, "150 000 Deaths and Political Utopias," in *Kein Wunderland für Alice? Frauenutopien*, ed. Antje Vollmer (Hamburg: Konkret Literatur Verlag, 1986), 98–99.

26. Antje Vollmer, ed. *Kein Wunderland für Alice? Frauenutopien* (Hamburg: Konkret Literatur Verlag, 1986).
27. Sander, "150 000 Deaths," 99. See a similar criticism by Dorothee Sölle in *The Arms Race Kills Even without War* (Philadelphia: Fortress Press, 1982), 26–27.
28. Häberlen, *Emotional Politics*, 170–174.
29. Antje Vollmer, "Vorwort," in Vollmer, *Kein Wunderland für Alice?*
30. Petra Kelly, "Für eine Erotische Gesellschaft," printed in Petra Kelly, *Um Hoffnung Kämpfen: Gewaltfrei für eine Zukunft* (Cologne: Lamuv, 1983), 169. See further Davis, "Gender," 123. See also Stephen Milder and Friederike Brühöfener, "Petra Kelly: A Green Leader out of Place?" in *German Female Leadership: From Maria Antonia of Saxony to Angela Merkel*, ed. Elizabeth Krimmer and Patricia Simpson (Rochester, NY: Camden House, 2019), 281–300.
31. Kelly, "Für eine Erotische Gesellschaft," 170.
32. Joachim C. Häberlen, "Feeling Like a Child: Dreams and Practices of Sexuality in the West German Alternative Left during the Long 1970s," *Journal of the History of Sexuality* 25, no. 2 (2016): 222–23.
33. Kelly, "Für eine Erotische Gesellschaft."
34. Häberlen, "Feeling Like a Child," 242–43.
35. See, for example, Ilse Lenz, *Die Neue Frauenbewegung in Deutschland: Abschied vom kleinen Unterschied; Eine Quellensammlung* (Wiesbaden: Springer, 2008), 100; Belinda Davis, "Redefining the Political: The Gender of Activism in Grassroots Movements of the 1960s to 1980s," in *Gendering Post-1945 German History: Entanglements*, ed. Karen Hagemann, Donna Harsch, and Friederike Brühöfener (New York: Berghahn Books, 2018), 207–28. For a contemporary critique, see Häberlen, "Feeling Like a Child," 242–43.
36. The full German text of Sander's speech is printed in Lenz, *Die Neue Frauenbewegung*, 57f.
37. See Friederike Brühöfener, "Politics of Emotions: Journalistic Reflections on the Emotionality of the West German Peace Movement, 1979–1984," *German Politics & Society* 33, no. 4 (December 2015): 97–111.
38. Petra Kelly, *Um Hoffnung Kämpfen: Gewaltfrei für eine Zukunft* (Cologne: Lamuv Taschenbuch, 1983), 119.
39. Margot Steinbicker, "Meine Angst! Deine Angst?" in *taubenschlag: Die Zeitschrift der Duisburger Friedensinitiativen* 1, no. 2 (1982): 42, reprinted in *Frieden und Friedensbewegung in Deutschland 1892–1992*, ed. Karlheinz Lipp, Reinhold Lütgemeier-Davin, and Holger Nehring (Essen: Klartext, 2010), 363.
40. See Brühöfener, "Politics of Emotions. See further, Susanne Schregel, "Konjunktur der Angst: 'Politik der Subjektivität' und 'neue Friedensbewegung,' 1979–1983," in *Angst im Kalten Krieg*, ed. Bernd Greiner, Christian Th. Müller, and Dierk Walter (Hamburg: HIS Verlag, 2009), 508–15; Brühöfener, "Politics of Emotions."
41. Frank Biess, "Die Sensibilisierung des Subjekts: Angst und 'Neue Subjektivität,'" in den 1970er Jahren," *Werkstatt Geschichte* 49 (2008): 51–71.
42. Biess, "Die Sensibilisierung," 52 and 68. See also, Pascal Eitler "'Angst ist eine Lüge': Emotion und Religion im 'New Age,'" Webportal *Geschichte der Gefühle: Einblicke in die Forschung*, Oktober 2013, DOI: 10.14280/08241.3, retrieved 30 August 2021 from https://www.history-of-emotions.mpg.de/texte/angst-ist-eine-luege; Sven Rei-

chardt, "Is 'Warmth' a Mode of Social Behaviour? Considerations on a Cultural History of the Left-Alternative Milieu from the Late 1960s to the Mid 1980s," *BEHEMOTH: A Journal on Civilisation*, no. 2 (2010): 84–99.
43. Annika Wellmann, "Instruktionen für ein sensitives Selbst: Sexualtherapie und Zärtlichkeitsregime um 1980," in *Das beratene Selbst: Zur Genealogie der Therapeutisierung in den "langen" Siebzigern*, ed. Sabine Maasen, Jens Elberfeld, Pascal Eitler, and Maik Tändler (Bielefeld: Transcript, 2011), 185–204.
44. Pascal Eitler, "Der 'Neue Mann' des 'New Age': Emotion und Religion in der Bundesrepublik Deutschland 1970–1990," in *Die Präsenz der Gefühle: Männlichkeit und Emotion in der Moderne*, ed. Manuel Borutta and Nina Verheyen (Bielefeld: Transcript, 2010), 287–94.
45. See for example, Albrecht Weisker, "Powered by Emotion? Affektive Aspekte in der westdeutschen Kernenergiedebatte zwischen Technikvertrauen und Apokalypseangst," in *Natur- und Umweltschutz nach 1945: Konzepte, Konflikte, Kompetenzen*, ed. Franz-Josef Brüggemeier and Jens Ivo Engels (Frankfurt a.M.: Campus, 2005), 203–21; Judith Michel, "'Die Angst kann lehren, sich zu wehren': Der Angstdiskurs der westdeutschen Friedensbewegung in den 1980er Jahren," *Tel Aviver Jahrbuch für deutsche Geschichte* 38 (2010): 246–69. See also Susanne Schregel, *Der Atomkrieg vor der Wohnungstür: Eine Politikgeschichte der neuen Friedensbewegung in der Bundesrepublik 1970–1985* (Frankfurt a.M.: Campus, 2011); Häberlen, *Emotional Politics*; Biess, *German Angst*.
46. Davis, "Gender," 112. See also, Belinda Davis, "Europe Is a Peaceful Woman, America Is a War-Mongering Man? The 1980s Peace Movement in NATO-Allied Europe," Themenportal *Europäische Geschichte* 2009, retrieved 9 July 2020 from https://www.europa.clio-online.de/searching/id/fdae-1716. Schregel, *Atomkrieg*, 508–11.
47. Antje Vollmer, *. . . und wehret euch täglich! Bonn—ein grünes Tagebuch* (Gütersloh: Gütersloher Verlagshaus, 1984), 33.
48. Vollmer, *Kein Wunderland*, 12.
49. Vollmer, *. . . und wehret euch täglich*, 53.
50. Antje Vollmer, *Die schöne Macht der Vernuft: Aufkünfte über eine Generation* (Berlin: Verlag der Nation, 1991), 97.
51. See Ilse Lenz overview "Viele Frauen finden verschiedene Stimmen," in *Die neue Frauenbewegung in Deutschland: Abschied vom kleinen Unterschied: Eine Quellensammlung* ed. Ilze Lenz (Wiesbaden: Verag für Sozialwissenschaften, 2008), 111–21.
52. Irene Stratenwerth, "Feministischer Familienstreit fand nicht statt," *die tageszeitung* (21 January 1987), 5.
53. Ferree, *Varieties of Feminism*, 111.
54. See for example, the book by Irene Krieger, which offers an at-times-scathing assessment of the Green Party, including individual female politicians, the party's feminist agenda, and the overall feminist movement. Irene Krieger, *Was bleibt von den Grünen* (Hamburg: Konkret Literatur Verlag, 1991), 18–19, 23, 51–93.
55. ". . . aber diese Firma verkauft nicht Seife, sie verkauft TOD . . . ," Beitrag von Dorothee Sölle auf der Hamburger Veranstaltung "Frauen in die Bundeswehr?—Nein Danke!" Am 31. August 1979, *Graswurzelrevolution* 44 (Okt./Nov. 1979), 17–18.
56. Christian A. Widman, "Der 'Links*protest*antismus' und die evangelische Kirchen in den 1960er und 1970er Jahren," in *Linksalternative Milieus und Neue Soziale Bewe-*

gungen in den 1970er Jahren, ed. Cordia Baumann, Sebastian Gehrig, and Nicolas Büchse (Heidelberg: Universitätsverlag Winter, 2011), 211–38; Thomas Kroll, "Der Linksprotestantismus in der Bundesrepublik Deutschland der 1960er und 1970er Jahre: Helmut Gollwitzer, Dorothee Sölle und Jürgen Moltmann," in *Intellektuelle in der Bundesrepublik Deutschland: Verschiebungen im politischen Feld der 1960er und 1970er Jahre*, ed. Thomas Kroll and Tilman Reitz (Göttingen: Vandenhoeck & Ruprecht, 2013), 103–22.

57. Klaus Aschrich, *Theologie schreiben: Dorothee Sölles Weg zu einer Mystik der Befreiung* (Berlin: LIT, 2006), 21; Saskia Richter, "The Protagonists of the Peace Movement," in Schaum, *Nuclear Crisis*, 193; Renate Wind, *Dorothee Soelle: Mystic und Rebell* (Minneapolis: Fortress Press, 2012), 136.
58. ". . . aber diese Firma verkauft nicht Seife." See also Helke Sander, "Über Beziehungen zwischen Liebesverhältnissen und Mittelstreckenraketen," *Courage*, April 1980, 16–29.
59. Kelly, *Um Hoffnung Kämpfen*, 123.
60. Ibid., 123.
61. Bernhard, *Zivildienst zwischen Reform und Revolte*, 124. Nick Thomas, *Protest Movements in 1960s West Germany* (London, 2003), 107–23. See also Alice H. Cooper, *Paradoxes of Peace: German Peace Movement since 1945* (Ann Arbor, 1996), 104–10.
62. Bernhard, *Zivildienst*, 121.
63. For the history of the Republican Clubs see, Timothy Scott Brown, *West Germany and the Global Sixties: The Anti-authoritarian Revolt, 1962–1978* (New York, 2013), 69.
64. The pamphlet is documented in several archives, for example: Archive for Christian Democratic Policy, 08-001, CDU/CSU Fraktion, 376/1.
65. Leaflet "Zucht und Ordnung: Total Verweigern," undated, Archiv Aktiv, Berlin, Ordner: Ordner: Kampagne gegen Wehrpflicht + Zwangsdienst und Militär 1990. See also "Vortrag 'Weg mir der Wehrpflicht' am 2.11.89 in Bremen," Archiv-Aktiv, Kampagne gegen Wehrpflicht + Zwangsdienst und Militär 1990.
66. "Zucht und Ordnung."
67. Belinda Davis, "What's Left? Popular Political Participation in Postwar Europe," *American Historical Review* 113, no. 2 (2008): 370.
68. Stephen Milder and Konrad Jarausch, "Introduction: Renewing Democracy: The Rise of Green Politics in West Germany," *German Politics and Society* 33, no. 4 (2015): 3–24.

Select Bibliography

Biess, Frank. *German Angst: Fear and Democracy in the Federal Republic of Germany*. Oxford: Oxford University Press, 2020.
Davis, Belinda. "'Women's Strength and Crazy Male Power': Gendered Language in the West German Peace Movement of the 1980s." In *Frieden, Gewalt, Geschlecht: Friedens- und Konfliktforschung als Geschlechterforschung*, edited by Jennifer Davy, Karen Hagemann, and Ute Kätzel, 244–65. Essen: Klartext, 2005.
Ferree, Myra Marx. *Varieties of Feminism: German Gender Politics in Global Perspective*. Stanford, CA: Stanford University Press, 2012.

Häberlen, Joachim C. *The Emotional Politics of the Alternative Left West Germany, 1968–1984*. Cambridge: Cambridge University Press, 2018.

Kreis, Reinhild. "'Men Build Missiles': The Women's Peace Movement." In *The Nuclear Crisis: The Arms Race, Cold War Anxiety, and the German Peace Movement of the 1980s*, edited by Christoph Becker-Schaum, 290–305. New York: Berghahn Books, 2016.

Kühne, Thomas. "'Friedenskultur,' Zeitgeschichte und Historische Friedensforschung." In *Von der Kriegskultur zur Friedenskultur? Zum Mentalitätswandel in Deutschland seit 1945*, edited by Thomas Kühne, 13–33. Hamburg: LIT, 2000.

Lenz, Ilse. *Die Neue Frauenbewegung in Deutschland: Abschied vom kleinen Unterschied; Eine Quellensammlung*. Wiesbaden: Springer, 2008.

Melucci, Alberto. "The Symbolic Challenge of Contemporary Movements." *Social Research* 52, no. 4, Social Movements (1985): 789–816.

Milder, Stephen. *Greening Democracy: The Anti-nuclear Movement and Political Environmentalism in West Germany and Beyond, 1968–1983*. New York: Cambridge University Press, 2017.

The Nuclear Crisis: The Arms Race, Cold War Anxiety, and the German Peace Movement of the 1980s, edited by Christoph Becker-Schaum, Philipp Gassert, Martin Klimke, Wilfried Mausbach, and Marianne Zepp. New York: Berghahn Books, 2016.

Chapter 9

From Self-Organization to Self-Management

Paradigms of Social Movements in West Germany from '68 to the Early 1980s

David Templin

For the philosopher of science Wolfgang Krohn, self-organization was a pivotal "paradigm" of the '68 revolt and the movements between 1965 and 1975. From his perspective, it revealed a crisis of societal institutions as well as an upsurge of new, experimental forms, a widening of possibilities, and a rush of do-it-yourself impulses.[1] In fact, we can observe a boom of conceptions and practices of self-organization (*Selbstorganisation*) and self-management (*Selbstverwaltung*) in the context of social movements around '68 and thereafter. Revolutionary visions of a society of self-management flourished when students and workers took to the streets. In the 1970s, thousands of citizens' initiatives emerged, dealing with issues such as ecology, urban restructuring, and social infrastructure. In the second half of the decade, a boom of alternative projects followed, all of which tried to implement a collective form of grassroots organization into daily life.

Social movement researchers fit this development into a pattern of interpretation they characterized as the transition to "new social movements." In contrast to the "old" ones, new social movements were characterized by decentralized organizational structures and loose networks. They aimed at reform and pursued a postmaterialistic agenda with a focus on alternative lifestyles and values such as self-realization. According to these researchers, the new movements' social structural core could be found in the new middle class of well-educated service sector workers.[2]

In this chapter, I review such assumptions. By looking at the concepts and slogans of self-organization and self-management and by following their tracks between the mid-1960s and the early 1980s, I assess their significance for the West German Left and the social movements of these years from the perspective of contemporary history. How did contemporaries frame such conceptions in order to distinguish their political projects from hegemonic lifestyles and institutional structures of capitalist society but also from authoritarian forms of socialism? And can we use concepts such as self-organization as analytical tools to characterize social movements after '68 and to distinguish them from older movements?

In the first three sections of this chapter, I follow the "career" of these terms in the Federal Republic between the mid-1960s and the early 1970s. The first section looks at their role in the '68 revolt, highlighting transnational impulses. The second section, then, focuses on the "debate on organization" around 1969 and the question of how and why different currents of the Left picked up the slogan of self-organization. In the third section, I demonstrate the ambivalent role and fragile nature of practical self-organization by looking at the apprentices' movement (*Lehrlingsbewegung*) between 1968 and 1972/73.

In the fourth through sixth sections, I analyze three aspects of self-organization in the social movements of the 1970s more closely. In the fourth section, I look at the programmatic dimension by which movement actors tried to distance themselves from "heteronomy" (*Fremdbestimmung*) in everyday life while at the same time formulating elements of a concrete utopia. In the fifth section, I turn to the ways in which self-organization functioned as an organizing principle, structuring the work of initiative groups and challenging traditional forms of organization. Finally, in the sixth section, I look at the practical implementation of self-management in alternative projects, where it functioned as a structuring principle in the administration of newly created spaces. Throughout the second half of the chapter, I focus primarily on the youth center initiatives that emerged beginning in 1970/71, which demanded the creation of self-managed youth houses at the local level.

Transnational Impulses: From Workers' Self-Management to Direct Action

In the New Left of the 1960s, activists discussed and promoted the political self-organization of different subjectivities as well as models of workers' self-management. Impulses for such debates came from countries such as Yugoslavia, France, and the United States.

In Yugoslavia, the Communist Party had developed a distinct model of socialism since its break with the Soviet Union in 1948: workers' self-management (*radničko samoupravljanje*, translated into German as *Arbeiterselbstverwaltung*). While the party still controlled the political system, workers' councils managed production at the factory level—at least in theory.³ In the 1960s and 1970s, a group of Yugoslavian Marxists around the magazine *Praxis* propagated the "forgotten idea of self-management" on the international level while at the same time criticizing its realization at home.⁴ However, only few West German activists at this time adopted such ideas.⁵ As Christian Fenner stated in 1973, the student movement was "not primarily oriented toward the Yugoslavian theory of socialism."⁶ Rather, activists were fascinated by developments in China or America.

In Western Europe, the idea of self-management gained most interest in France. Early groups of the emerging New Left, especially Socialisme ou Barbarie, had discussed the idea of self-management (*autogestion*) since the mid-1950s. Influenced by workers' councils in the Hungarian revolt of 1956, Cornelius Castoriadis elaborated on the idea of workers' self-management of production as an alternative to bureaucratic forms of socialism.⁷ Others, such as the philosopher Henri Lefebvre or the Situationist International, picked up on these thoughts as well.⁸ In May 1968, when the student revolt was followed by a general strike and the occupation of factories, *autogestion* became a leading slogan propagated not only by radical students but also by the French Democratic Confederation of Labor (Confédération française démocratique du travail, CFDT). By questioning structures of power and decision-making, the term expressed the antiauthoritarian tendencies of '68, especially in the sphere of production. At the same time, it aimed at a transformation of the whole society.⁹ In an interview translated into German, one French activist characterized self-management as the "path to a classless society."¹⁰

In West Germany, this idea was only hesitantly picked up. In their book *Obsolete Communism: The Left-Wing Alternative*, Daniel Cohn-Bendit, one of the most prominent student radicals during the French May, and his brother Gabriel propagated self-management as a crucial idea. Referring to historical examples as well as recent ones from Algeria, Yugoslavia, and France, the Cohn-Bendits characterized the takeover of factories and social services by workers as "the only true revolutionary act."¹¹ For them, students also practiced self-organization when they met in plenary assemblies, thereby establishing forms of direct democracy in the movement and dissolving "the separation between leading and executing persons."¹²

The antiauthoritarian current of the West German student movement agreed with such ideas. But for these activists, self-organization was more important than the practical self-management of institutions. In July 1967, the student movement's leading figure, Rudi Dutschke, published a plan for a revolutionary transformation of West Berlin. Rejecting not only the parliamentary system but also the idea of the "seizure of power by a group, clique or particular class," he favored the "establishment of new, more humane self-organizations."[13] For Dutschke, self-organization meant small groups of activists joining forces at work and in schools, universities, and churches—thereby avoiding the creation of an "apparatus" and counteracting an assumed manipulation of interests. The "self-organization of own interests and needs" should be the ultimate starting point of revolutionary activities.[14]

The newfound prominence of self-organization points to the idea of "direct action" imported from the civil rights movement and the New Left of the United States in the mid-1960s. Direct action referred to activities ranging from civil disobedience to the foundation of "counter-institutions."[15] When the German SDS activist Michael Vester presented this conception to his organization in 1965, he stressed the role of the affected people ("*Engagement der Betroffenen*") and the importance of subjectivity and personal experiences: "Direct action is in any case a voluntary action of the affected [people] themselves, not by activist minorities who can only play the role of catalysts."[16] With references to the concept of "participatory democracy," but also to anarchism and the idea of workers' self-management, Vester linked direct action to antiauthoritarian ideas of a socialist society. At the same time, as a leftist socialist, he conceded that self-organization could not replace trade unions, which were much more powerful organizations.[17]

The social movements that emerged between 1966 and 1969 fit Vester's concept. Students protested against the situation in schools and universities, "dropouts" formed communes as a new way of cohabitation beyond the nuclear family, and female activists founded childcare centers (*Kinderläden*) as an act of self-help. "Counteruniversities" (*Kritische Universitäten*) with alternative curricula, an idea adopted from the United States, took shape in the course of the movement too.[18] "Collective self-organization" was also a guiding principle of the pupils' movement (*Schülerbewegung*)—even if the impulse to create an umbrella organization for pupils in fact came from the SDS.[19]

Nevertheless, within the West German Left of 1967 and 1968, self-organization remained a vague political concept and was not further elaborated theoretically. However, when the SDS, which had been the organizational center of the revolt, disintegrated in 1969 and many activists began to dismiss their former antiauthoritarian aspirations as "petty bourgeois," the idea of self-organization gained in importance. It provided a counterconcept for those who rejected Marxist-Leninist (ML) party-building projects.

"Party-Building or Self-Organization"? Leftist Debates between 1969 and 1971

In spring 1968, the West Berlin student movement decided to form grassroots groups (*Basisgruppen*) on a district level. These groups, which were intended to reach other parts of the urban population, were part of an organizational conception that favored decentralization.[20] But since the end of 1968, a growing chorus of voices demanded more effective cadre structures, aimed at the rebuilding of a Communist Party. Against such tendencies, which resulted in different ML party projects, other currents of the Left reinforced the idea of self-organization as a counterconcept. In this respect, four currents can be identified: the Young Socialists (Jungsozialisten or Jusos), the Socialist Office (Sozialistisches Büro, SB), the *Spontis*, and a comparatively small political spectrum of anarchists and left-wing communists.

The Young Socialists, as the youth organization of the Social Democratic Party of Germany (SPD), were likely the single organization that had benefited most from the politicization of West German youth. In 1969, it turned leftward by emphasizing Marxist ideas, resulting in increasing conflicts with its parent organization. By developing a so-called "double strategy" for anti-capitalist reforms, the Young Socialists tried to link grassroots activism with parliamentary work. The idea of self-organization played a prominent role in this strategy.[21] Young Socialist activists saw their own role as an initiating one, pushing citizens, wage-earners and young people to organize themselves while trying to ensure "effectivity and continuity" of such groups.[22] At the same time, they also regarded the conception of a "self-organization of the people in all areas" as "an important element of a future democratic socialism."[23] Following this conception, their activists worked in several citizens' initiatives.

In the same year that the Young Socialists shifted to the left, left-wing socialists founded the Socialist Office. Rejecting hierarchical structures or attempts to build a cadre organization, the SB promoted self-organization from the beginning—"especially in the field of production, in companies, offices, schools, municipalities and housing areas."[24] Oskar Negt, a leading SB activist, criticized communist parties for trying to control and discipline spontaneous actions of "the masses."[25] At the same time, he distanced himself from a glorification of spontaneity as an end in itself. The idea of the SB was to connect independent grassroots groups working in different sectors of the economy or on different issues. In the early 1970s, Leninist organizations such as the Communist League (Kommunistischer Bund, KB) nevertheless attacked the group for cultivating a "myth of 'self-organization.'"[26]

More militant in their approach were the *Spontis*, which emerged as a current of the radical Left, especially in university cities, around 1970/71.

Influenced by the Italian Marxist approach of workerism (*operaismo*), with its guiding idea of workers' autonomy, *Sponti* activists began to work in factories in order to get into contact with industrial workers.[27] Rejecting the leading role of trade unions, they tried to support spontaneous workers' protests. Wildcat strikes, which flourished between 1969 and 1973, fit into their vision of the working class acting autonomously. But *Sponti* activists also came to see social struggles in the field of housing, such as a rent strike conducted by migrants in Frankfurt between 1971 and 1973, as an arena of "proletarian self-organization."[28]

While Young Socialists and the SB acknowledged a dialectic of spontaneous self-organization and more structured forms of political organization, anarchists were hostile against political parties and similar forms of organization. For the editorial staff of the magazine *Agit 883* in Berlin as well as the small publishing house MAD in Hamburg, self-organization became the ultimate point of reference in social and political struggles. They regarded it as "the radical negation of every social-democratic and Bolshevik organizational frippery [*Organisationsspielerei*]"[29] and as a "weapon of the suppressed against their powerlessness and an instrument for the realization of a society free from domination."[30] In May 1971, West Berlin anarchists organized a conference commemorating the 1921 Kronstadt uprising. They contrasted the rule of the party with the "self-reliant class movement of the proletariat," which expressed itself in the power of workers' councils. By focusing on Kronstadt, these anarchists intended to take a stand against the flourishing Marxist-Leninist party projects: "Let's fight everything that oppresses self-organization!!!" they declared in their announcement of the conference.[31]

Despite "factory interventions," the relationship between the New Left and struggles at the workplaces remained comparatively weak in West Germany. Nevertheless, the very existence of an apprentices' movement contradicts the thesis that '68 was only an "uprising of the young intelligentsia."[32] A closer look at this movement offers insights into the ambivalent meaning of self-organization in its practical realization between powerful institutional actors and groups of the "old" and "new" Left.

Between Trade Unions and the Far Left: Self-Organization in the Apprentices' Movement

The movement of apprentices, which started in 1968/69, focused on grievances related to vocational training. It was initiated by a heterogenous coalition of SDS students, trade union youth, and the orthodox German Communist Party (Deutsche Kommunistische Partei, DKP). The movement linked a common criticism of the "exploitation" of apprentices and the call for better vocational training with an antiauthoritarian impulse. With symbolic actions like protests and disturbances, young workers adopted forms of action from the repertoire of the student movement. The protests reached their climax with a large demonstration organized by the Federation of German Trade Unions (Deutscher Gewerkschaftsbund, DGB) against the new Vocational Training Law in June 1969.[33] For 1970, contemporary observers estimated that there were between 150 and 200 apprentice groups in West Germany.[34]

As the protests began, many groups that called themselves "apprentice centers" (*Lehrlingszentren*) took a critical stance toward the unions. Some even considered the unions part of the "establishment." Leading actors such as the Union Students' Group (Gewerkschaftliche Studentengruppe, GSG), a Hamburg group with a left-wing socialist orientation, propagated the "'open' self-organization of the apprentices."[35] From the GSG's perspective, partly autonomous apprentice organizing was necessary to combat the sense of objectification that young workers experienced at the workplace. This conception of self-organization was directed against the trade union apparatus, which the GSG students harshly criticized for its bureaucratic tendencies. "Antiauthoritarian" youth work inside the unions, the GSG maintained, would challenge the power of this bureaucracy. But their project of self-organization was also directed against Marxist-Leninist conceptions of ideological instruction that they considered authoritarian. The apprentice center in Hamburg, founded in 1969 under the name Jour fix and influenced by the GSG, was therefore open for all apprentices, whether they had a membership card of a union or not.[36]

Ultimately, this self-organization did not get beyond the early stages, and the movement disappeared after a few years. There were several reasons for this, one of them related to the fragile nature of its organizational structures. Many apprentice centers had been initiated by left-wing student groups, which predefined their political ideas and forms of action. The transformation of these student circles into tightly structured party projects also had effects on the apprentice groups. Young workers joined new ML organizations as well as the youth organization of the DKP. When these organizations began to propagate the "unity of the working class" and advocated the organization of intergenerational groups at the shop-floor level, the apprentice centers lost important protagonists.[37] Even a GSG student such as Manfred Wilke, a member of the Trotskyist International Marxist Group (Gruppe Internationale Marxisten, GIM), was attacked by his own organization for promoting "self-organization as mere representation of interests," thereby abandoning revolution and rejecting the leading role of the political avant-garde. For Wilke's critics, the promotion of self-organization and its treatment as a political "fetish" turned out to be nothing more than "anticommunist" reformism.[38]

Aside from such disputes within and among left-wing organizations, apprentice centers had to deal with the leadership of the trade unions. Older functionaries were skeptical or even hostile to the new conception of open youth work. From their point of view, it was little more than a gateway for infiltration by the "extreme left" and the manipulation of young workers by students. The strategy of conflict, which groups such as the GSG pursued, contributed to this impression. But the apprentice centers were also responsible for a revitalization of the youth sections of the unions and an activation of their committee work. The result was a situation where more or less autonomous apprentices' organizations no longer seemed to be necessary. Thus, around 1972 many centers dissolved themselves or were liquidated from above.

Looking at the apprentice movement highlights three ways in which self-organization was significant. First, the notion of self-organization played a crucial role in the political empowerment of young workers, revealing the importance of transfers from the student movement promoted by its left-socialist and antiauthoritarian currents. Second, as the close entanglements with the trade unions show, self-organization was also practiced within large institutions and "old social movements." At the same time, however, self-organization proved fragile as an organizational principle because the apprentice groups did not develop political power as independent actors. In fact, it is questionable whether "self-organization" is an accurate description of the actual process, considering the crucial role of student organizers. Third, the movement reveals the extent to which self-organization was also an issue within workplaces. Simplistic divides between "materialistic" and "post-materialistic" orientations do not carry much interpretive weight here. Apprentice groups sought "material" objectives, such as higher training wages, but at the same time demanded the breakup of hierarchies, an end to humiliation at work, and the right of young men to wear long hair. Even if the links between protests in the sphere of production and the New Left were not as strong in West Germany as they were in Southern Europe, it would be wrong to assume that no such links existed.[39]

An "Act of Liberation": Contemporary Perspectives on Self-Organization

The GSG students from Hamburg saw self-organization as an expression of self-empowerment and emancipation from power structures. Other groups shared this pattern of interpretation, attributing to self-organization the power to fundamentally change society. "Release is the self-organization of marginalized youth groups. . . . Release is an instrument in the struggle over emancipation from dependencies of all kinds," the self-help group of young drug addicts, Release Heidelberg, proclaimed at its foundation in 1970.[40] The politicization of crucial needs as a starting point of emancipation and the collective organizing of "affected" people in small groups were core elements of the discourse of self-organization.[41] The new women's movement spoke of "politics in the first person" in order to characterize a political approach based on subjectivity and personal involvement.[42]

Similar viewpoints and ideas flourished in the initiative groups for self-managed youth centers, which began emerging in 1970/71 and could eventually be found in more than fourteen hundred West German municipalities.[43] With their criticism of existing municipal youth houses and their complaint about a general lack of youth facilities, the protagonists of this movement attacked a social reality that they perceived to be determined by others. In 1969, young people from Karlsruhe declared a local tower to be the "first antiauthoritarian youth house." They proclaimed that "the antiauthoritarian youth house is the self-organization of the revolutionary base of the youth. . . . Its foundation is an act of liberation from unbearable dependencies in family, school, youth welfare, and social life per se, young people are subjected to."[44] Their action was a precursor of the youth center movement (*Jugendzentrumsbewegung*). Many more groups followed this line of argumentation in subsequent years—albeit in most cases with less revolutionary pathos. Youth centers were to function as alternatives to conventional facilities. They ought to be open for everyone, "free from authoritarian constraints," with possibilities "for informal conversations" and usable "without notable financial expenditure." The movement's demands were not limited to an increase in the number of facilities. The activists explicitly argued for a "new quality of leisure activities" and an alternative form of organization.[45]

Crucial for the notion of self-management, which turned out to be the guiding concept of the movement (the historian Detlef Siegfried speaks of a "magic formula"[46]), was the intention not to be supervised, patronized, or controlled. "What we want—leisure time without controls" became one of its popular chants. In the early 1970s, the term 'self-management' primarily worked as a programmatic slogan, contributing to the formation of a social movement and legitimizing its demands. Youth center initiatives argued in favor of this idea by emphasizing that those affected by decisions should get to make them. "The decision over what young people need and what they don't need should no longer lie in the hands of those who don't have a clue about the needs of young people," activists from the town of Wiesloch stated.⁴⁷ Quite a few groups related their demand for self-management to the contemporary discourse on democratization.

Guided by antiauthoritarian and Marxist ideas, many activists saw self-management as a starting point for changes in society as a whole. A spokesperson of Baden-Baden's Interest Group Youth Center (Interessengemeinschaft Jugendtreffpunkt) declared in 1971: "If an adolescent can make decisions for himself in a youth house, [then, later] as an apprentice in his workplace[,] he will certainly postulate the demand for codetermination as a natural organization of work . . . !"⁴⁸ Noticeable in this and similar statements is the tremendous political potential attributed to self-management. For the movement, self-organization was not just a means but an end in itself, a concrete and generalizable utopia.

However, not all initiative groups at the time shared such an approach. Self-organization as the association of those directly affected by decisions and their claim to co- or self-determination was also a core element of the broad spectrum of citizens' initiatives (*Bürgerinitiativen*). The number of these initiatives that were dealing with social, urban, and ecological politics on a local level had increased exponentially since 1969/70.⁴⁹ Many citizens' initiatives pushed for reforms rather than a fundamental transformation of society. They looked to self-organization as a corrective to established mechanisms of representative democracy and not as a revolutionary power. In a "handbook for citizens' initiatives," published in 1976, Roland Günter, an activist in the movement against the demolition of workers' settlements in the Ruhr area, and his coauthor Rolf Hasse defined citizens' initiatives as "forms of self-organization . . . which are not yet included in the system of political institutions but complement it. . . ."⁵⁰ But despite, or rather in light of, their moderate approach, these groups revealed how forms of grassroots democracy spread in society after '68 and how they reached social milieus beyond the young protagonists of protest. Activists of the radical Left, on the other hand, registered the "danger [that] every self-organization [might] become a mere citizens' initiative," as Willi Hau from the "Free-Clinic Heidelberg" warned.⁵¹

While collective self-organization, therefore, lost some of its utopian connotations in the course of the 1970s, a related term flourished, especially in the women's movement but also in other alternative groups focusing on subjectivity: self-awareness (*Selbsterfahrung*).⁵² In encounter groups, individuals talked about personal experiences, trying to discover their psychological problems, their needs, and their own "self." While in the beginning closely connected to movement impulses and enhancing reflections on gender roles and power structures, this conception put more emphasis on the individual self than on collective forms of social and political organizing. With the emergence of therapy groups and religious tendencies of the "New Age" (emphasizing self-knowledge [*Selbsterkenntnis*], and self-realization [*Selbstverwirklichung*]), a "psycho boom" took shape in the 1970s, indicating a new regime of subjectivity.[53]

Local Plenaries and Larger Networks: Self-Organization as an Organizational Principle

Self-organization was not just a "slogan of struggle" that referenced ideas about emancipation and the creation of alternative spaces. It also worked as a category referring to crucial organizational principles of the newly emerged social movements. Some scholars even regarded it as a unique feature distinguishing the "new" movements from earlier ones. In one of the first systematic analyses of the movements of the 1970s and early 1980s, the sociologists Karl-Werner Brand, Detlef Büsser, and Dieter Rucht drew the conclusion that

> a constitutive element of the new social movements seems not just to be the rejection of a charismatic leader but, in contrast to the labor movement, the rejection of all forms of organizational hierarchy, the definitive primacy of the principle of self-organization.

They also noted, however, that this principle did "not shape the organizational structures of the new social movements consistently in the same way."[54]

Self-organization implied the idea that people affected by political decisions or belonging to specific groups associated themselves autonomously and represented their interests separately from political parties or large federations. As early as 1970, the Grassroots Group (Basisgruppe) in the Berlin district of Spandau had emphasized that self-liberation should find an expression in the movement's organizational forms. "That means," they explained, "already in our organization, we have to anticipate elements of what we aim for."[55] Such an approach implied organizational structures of an anti-institutional, decentralized, and local type. The plenary assembly served as a central place of decision-making, while subgroups worked on specific tasks. In some cases, initiative groups elected an executive board or a smaller group responsible for representing the initiative in the public.

In the second half of the decade, a complex mesh of structures consisting of local and regional initiatives emerged, an alternative political network with certain nodes. As Brand et al. had already pointed out, self-organization did not mean that larger organizations or party or trade union formations could not be part of these structures. Instead, larger organizations played a new role that was no longer a leading or dominating one. The youth center movement was a prime example of how such political organizations played new, less dominant roles. In many cases—as much as 40 percent, according to a survey from 1974—local Young Socialist groups were responsible for founding a youth center initiative. However, their stimulating role did not correspond to a leading or dominating one inside the movement.[56]

Other political groups had a more ambivalent relationship with the new movements' autonomy. Marxist-Leninist groups attacked the emphasis on self-organization particularly harshly. From their perspective, this guiding principle was an expression of illusionary, petty bourgeois politics. The Communist Youth Federation (Kommunistischer Jugendverband, KJV) of Dortmund criticized *Sponti* tendencies in the local youth center movement in 1974, stating that "with a general 'self-organization' you cannot conduct a class struggle."[57] For ML groups, hierarchical party structures were indispensable. But the KJV also added a further argument against self-organization. Its activists pointed to the fact that "without a tight organization in which representatives are elected and can be controlled . . . a 'secret' bureaucracy will evolve in self-organized structures, leading to some people talking all the time and controlling everything."[58]

The involvement of Marxist-Leninist groups in movement structures based on grassroots democracy often led to conflicts, for example when activists of the "alternative" left accused those from ML groups of instrumentalizing a movement. At the same time, their involvement led to inner contradictions in the ML groups, causing some activists to leave the organizations. It is important not to confuse the programmatic dissociation of these organizations from "self-organization" as a political model with the actual reality within the initiatives. In contrast to the DKP, which favored "codetermination," most ML groups adopted the demand for "self-managed youth centers." Through their practical work in the initiative groups, ML activists actually recognized this grassroots form of organization. Groups of the "Old" as well as the "New" Left therefore were part of self-organized networks of adolescents. In some cases, conflicts ensued from attempts to outvote and take over such structures, while in many others cooperation between different actors worked well.[59]

Nevertheless, communist groups were not the only organizations involved in the emerging alternative networks. In the youth center movement, various larger associations supported the local initiatives with their financial capabilities, infrastructure, and expertise. The examples of the Federal Scout Association (Bund Deutscher Pfadfinder, BDP) and the Socialist Youth of Germany (Sozialistische Jugend Deutschlands, SJD—Die Falken) show that such involvement was not uncontroversial. The federal board of the Falken emphasized in 1975 that "the principle of self-organization . . . [has existed] in the movement of the working-class youth as a matter of course since its emergence." But it nonetheless rejected a separate "self-organization" outside that "movement."[60] While this outlook distanced parts of the Falken from youth center initiatives, the BDP transformed itself through its involvement in alternative networks. In 1979, one of its regional chapters noted that the association had changed its character fundamentally in the course of interaction with youth center initiatives so that it had actually turned into an "organization of the non- or self-organized."[61]

While local groups with a structure based on grassroots democracy appeared as the locus of political work in all these cases, left-wing cadre organizations as well as larger associations with a historical background in older movements participated in the networks around them. Considering the fluid boundaries between "organizations" and "self-organizations" and the crucial role of external impulses or internal hierarchies, self-organization therefore is only partially sufficient as a term to describe a specific mode of organization.

Practices of Self-Management in Alternative Spaces

When female activists started to advise pregnant women and organize abortions abroad in the early 1970s, they regarded this as a practical form of self-help.[62] While "self-help" referred to an activity that immediately improved the situation of people by direct action without waiting for political reforms or a revolutionary transformation, such activities could be institutionalized in the form of "alternative projects." In the second half of the decade, a multitude of such projects emerged, ranging from communication centers, autonomous kindergartens, and women's shelters to rural communes and alternative businesses. In 1980, the number of self-organized projects, collectives, and small businesses was estimated to be 11,500, with some 80,000 people involved.[63] Experimenting with new forms of life and working structures, the creation of alternative spaces based on collectivity posed the challenge of putting the guiding principle of self-management into practice.

To realize self-management and prove its possibility to skeptical authorities, youth center initiatives developed elaborated models of administration. Activists considered the power to make decisions regarding content and program but also the domiciliary right, the choice of social workers, and the disposal of funds as decisive criteria for self-management.[64] An initiative group from Goslar stressed that self-management neither meant "chaos nor lack of plan." By elaborating on the different organizational bodies, the activists intended to show that self-management was not an illusionary utopia.[65] Very few activists questioned the focus on space and its administration. Reflecting on the limits of formal structures, a *Sponti* group from Mannheim argued in 1972: "Even a free and self-managed youth center can only be a prerequisite for self-organization—self-organization as a possibility to work on and cope with our problems."[66]

But the alternative projects of the 1970s/80s also tried to overcome alienation at work and the divisions between working and leisure time as well as between manual and cognitive labor. As an activist with the Workers' Self-Help (Arbeiterselbsthilfe), a group founded in Frankfurt in 1976, explained, "I have no desire to let my life be cut into alienated working and leisure time."[67] The aim of all efforts was no longer a socialist revolution in the future but an "alternative life in the here and now."[68] But even if activists' orientation to the working-class and their hopes for a revolutionary upheaval dwindled, and even if they began to focus on their own niches, they did not abandon visions of another society. The idea was common, as Kristina Schulz observed for the women's movement, that the "new society" could be anticipated in small projects inside the "old" society.[69] The feminist activist Monika Seifert for example had the expectation that the old society finally "at some point . . . just had to throw off its shell."[70] Notions of a more evolutionary transformation therefore spread in these movements and the alternative milieu.

After 1977, at a time when many ML party projects fell into a crisis, advocates of self-organization gained a new hegemony in the (radical) Left. However, practical attempts to realize self-management were far from pure success stories. Activists' experiences at self-managed youth centers demonstrate the difficulties they faced. The establishment of such centers went hand in hand with their integration into structures that the activists had vehemently rejected beforehand. Most municipalities demanded the foundation of an incorporated association by the activists as a prerequisite before providing them a building—a demand that contradicted the self-conception of the initiative groups as a movement of those adolescents who were not organized in associations with fixed memberships. With the conclusion of user contracts, the provision of financial means, and the recruitment of social workers, self-managed youth houses were integrated in the municipal system of youth welfare—their autonomy was therefore relative and based on negotiations over its range and limits.[71] For activists and sympathizing educationalists, the process of institutionalization constituted a danger. However, in the 1970s this institutionalization remained precarious. Recurring conflicts with the authorities erupted, the facilities had to deal with insufficient resources, and self-management remained a crucial point of reference for the active users.[72]

A far bigger challenge for the practical realization of self-management could be found in the gap between activists and the larger groups of regular or sporadic visitors. Vandalism, destruction, and brawls were frequent phenomena that the activists had not expected beforehand.[73] Instead of participating in the structures of self-management, many visitors showed a lack of interest and an open consumerism. In the language of the core groups of the centers, a distinction between "active" and "passive" users soon emerged and was repeatedly reproduced. In 1977, the editors of an anthology on the movement emphasized: "To be part of the active persons means to sacrifice much leisure time (full-time job), to be pushed in the role of an auxiliary social worker, a substitute janitor . . . and you can hardly get away from this."[74]

The gap between activists and allegedly "passive" visitors points to the fact that adolescents from different social backgrounds met in these spaces. Already contemporary observers frequently emphasized the division between students and apprentices, but these observers also noted that both groups came together in the centers.[75] Sven Reichardt has recently shown that the social profile of the left-alternative milieu was one of a "middle-class movement"—with highly educated protagonists and a relatively high level of homogeneity.[76] "Self-management," therefore, was primarily a guiding principle for better educated middle-class members. However, the cases of the apprentices' and the youth center movement also show that a minority of working-class youth participated in this alternative culture.[77]

A few years after the first youth center activists had complained about their role, employees of alternative businesses described similar experiences when they bemoaned their "self-exploitation" based on idealistic motives.[78] Low payment, economic constraints, long working hours, and financial problems showed that these businesses had to compete with others under capitalist market conditions. Some of them could only exist because of government grants. Conflicts erupted inside the collectives, as well.[79] On the basis of such difficult practical experiences, the utopian expectation of the early 1970s that self-management would pave the way toward another society reached its limits. Nevertheless, self-managed spaces as well as businesses continue to exist today, even if there are far fewer of them now than at their heyday in the 1970s and 1980s.[80]

Conclusion

In the 1960s, only small circles of the New Left advocated for the ideas of self-organization and self-management, which worked as guiding political principles and provided a concrete utopia for a society beyond capitalism.

In the years between 1967 and the mid-1970s different currents of the Left promoted self-organization as a strategy of empowerment aimed at the emancipation of the working class as well as other "affected" subjectivities. In the 1970s, self-organization and self-management therefore became part of powerful social movement discourses in the Federal Republic, influencing thousands of citizens' initiatives, grassroots groups, and alternative projects. In the course of the decade, however, the focus shifted toward a self-management of alternative spaces. As a result, the notion lost its connection to ideas about the "autonomy of the working-class" and its revolutionary charge. In the face of the economic crisis and new political trends, but also against the background of first practical experiences with self-management, the utopian surplus slowly disappeared. Contemporary observers depicted processes of institutionalization, professionalization, and incorporation of alternative projects into existing structures. But at the same time, self-management had become "normal." Its protagonists had developed a more pragmatic approach. Those parts of the radical Left that distanced themselves from this pragmatism chose a self-designation as autonomists (*Autonome*) to characterize their more militant approach to politics.[81]

As I have shown in this chapter, we can distinguish between contemporaries' use of terms like "self-organization" as programmatic slogans of struggle, directed against structures of society that were perceived as authoritarian, and an analytical use of those terms intended to describe specific forms of organization. While self-organization points to more decentralized and smaller as well as grassroots-democratic structures compared to traditional organizations such as parties and unions, no clear boundaries between "organizations" and "self-organizations" exist. Many "self-organizations" were in fact founded by external organizers; and large associations, as well as communist cadre groups, were part of "self-organized" structures. As the case of the apprentice protests shows, self-organization also happened within the trade unions and other established institutional actors, thereby contributing to their transformation.

If we look at historical phenomena such as cooperatives or workers' councils, manifestations of self-organization and self-management were not completely new in '68 and thereafter. What was new was the spread of these conceptions, their practical realization in a multitude of different areas of society, and the actors' strong emphasis to distance themselves from traditional forms of organization. This process had impacts on subjectivities and lifestyles. But while the concept of workers' self-management influenced the labor movement to a greater extent in France, self-management was much more fruitful in the alternative milieu in West Germany. Nevertheless, it would be misleading to reduce this trend to a rise of "postmaterialist" orientations in specific social milieus. As the case of the apprentice protests as well as others show, "materialistic" and "idealistic" motivations came together in the movements of the 1970s.[82]

This chapter presents only a rough overview of the "career" of self-organization and self-management and their manifold aspects since the mid-1960s. In the 1980s, the alternative economy further flourished. Periodicals such as *Contraste*, a "magazine for self-management," were founded, and activists thought about the creation of a trademark "made in self-management."[83] In fact, we can assume that these "self-managed" businesses provided new impulses for the transformation of the capitalist economy through their flexible, precarious, and idealistic forms of labor and their emphasis on an activation of the "self."[84] The promotion of self-organization, therefore, also contributed to a new "regime of subjectivity," on which the neoliberal promotion of "self-entrepreneurship" could build in later decades.[85] Future historical research must elaborate on this transformation and the ways it took shape.

David Templin is a research associate at the Institute for Migration Research and Intercultural Studies (IMIS) at the University of Osnabrück. He is currently working on a project on arrival neighborhoods in Hamburg in the twentieth century. His PhD dealt with the history of the youth center movement in West Germany. It was published in 2015 under the title *Freizeit ohne Kontrollen: Die Jugendzentrumsbewegung in der Bundesrepublik der 1970er Jahre* (Wallstein).

Notes

1. Wolfgang Krohn, "Die 1968er Bewegung und das Paradigma der Selbstorganisation," in *Krisen verstehen: Historische und kulturwissenschaftliche Annäherungen*, ed. Thomas Mergel (Frankfurt a.M.: Campus, 2012), 297–313.
2. See, for example, Dieter Rucht, *Modernisierung und neue soziale Bewegungen: Deutschland, Frankreich und USA im Vergleich* (Frankfurt a.M.: Campus, 1994).
3. Boris Kanzleiter, "1968 in Yugoslavia: Student Revolt Between East and West," in *Between Prague Spring and French May: Opposition and Revolt in Europe, 1960–1980*, ed. Martin Klimke, Jacco Pekelder, and Joachim Scharloth (New York: Berghahn Books, 2011), 84–100.
4. Mihailo Marković, *Dialektik der Praxis* (Frankfurt a.M.: Suhrkamp, 1968), 94 (this and subsequent translations are by the author, D.T.). See also Gerson S. Sher, *Praxis: Marxist Criticism and Dissent in Socialist Yugoslavia* (Bloomington: Indiana University Press, 1977), 151–67.
5. For the early 1950s, see Gregor Kritidis, *Linkssozialistische Opposition in der Ära Adenauer: Ein Beitrag zur Frühgeschichte der Bundesrepublik Deutschland* (Hannover: Offizin, 2008), 153–72.

6. Christian Fenner, "Die deutsche Studentenrevolte und das Modell der jugoslawischen Arbeiterselbstverwaltung," in *Marxistische Praxis: Selbstverwirklichung und Selbstorganisation des Menschen in der Gesellschaft*, ed. Ossip K. Flechtheim and Ernesto Grassi (München: Wilhelm Fink, 1973), 175. However, in the 1970s a boom of literature in German language on *Arbeiterselbstverwaltung* in Yugoslavia followed. See, e.g., Herwig Roggemann, *Das Modell der Arbeiterselbstverwaltung in Jugoslawien* (Frankfurt a.M.: EVA, 1970).
7. Andrea Gabler, *Antizipierte Autonomie: Zur Theorie und Praxis der Gruppe "Socialisme ou Barbarie" (1949–1967)* (Hannover: Offizin, 2009), 12–13, 68–70.
8. Ingrid Gilcher-Holtey, *"Die Phantasie an die Macht": Mai 68 in Frankreich* (Frankfurt a.M.: Suhrkamp, 1995), 148–52; Klaus Ronneberger, "Die Frage der Autogestion: Henri Lefebvre, Selbstverwaltung und Partizipation," *analyse & kritik* 550, 21 May 2010.
9. Gilcher-Holtey, *Phantasie*, 303–6, 310, 336; Frank Georgi, "Selbstverwaltung: Aufstieg und Niedergang einer politischen Utopie in Frankreich von den 1968er bis zu den 80er Jahren," in *1968 und die Arbeiter: Studien zum "proletarischen Mai" in Europa*, ed. Bernd Gehrke and Gerd-Rainer Horn (Hamburg: VSA, 2007), 252–74.
10. J. Sauvageot, A. Geismar, and D. Cohn-Bendit, *Aufstand in Paris oder Ist in Frankreich eine Revolution möglich?* (Reinbek: Rowohlt, 1968), 54.
11. The Cohn-Bendits' book was first published in French as *Le gauchisme, remède à la maladie sénile du communism* (Paris: Seuil, 1968) before being translated into German. The reference here is to the German edition. Gabriel and Daniel Cohn-Bendit, *Linksradikalismus: Gewaltkur gegen die Alterskrankheit des Kommunismus* (Reinbek: Rowohlt, 1968), 91.
12. Ibid., 223.
13. Quotes from: Gretchen Dutschke, *Wir hatten ein barbarisches, schönes Leben: Rudi Dutschke; Eine Biographie* (Köln: Kiepenheuer & Witsch, 1996), 144–45, 167.
14. Günter Gaus, *Was bleibt, sind Fragen: Die klassischen Interviews* (Berlin: Ullstein-TB, 2005), 436, 442, 451. For a less prominent activist emphasizing "self-organization" in 1968 as "our [form of] organization," see Lothar Binger, *68 selbstorganisiert & antiautoritär: Die Jahre 1967–1978* (Berlin: self-published, 2018), 64–67.
15. See Michael Schmidtke, *Der Aufbruch der jungen Intelligenz: Die 68er Jahre in der Bundesrepublik und den USA* (Frankfurt a.M.: Campus, 2003).
16. Michael Vester, "Die Strategie der direkten Aktion," *neue kritik* 30, June 1965, 12–20, 13. On Vester's role: Martin Klimke, *The Other Alliance: Student Protest in West Germany and the United States in the Global Sixties* (Princeton, NJ: Princeton University, 2010), 10–39, 52–54.
17. Vester, "Strategie," 14–16.
18. Schmidtke, *Aufbruch*, 225–40; Ben Mercer, *Student Revolt in 1968: France, Italy and West Germany* (Cambridge: Cambridge University Press, 2020), 254–84.
19. Manfred Liebel and Franz Wellendorf, *Schülerselbstbefreiung: Voraussetzung und Chancen der Schülerrebellion* (Frankfurt a.M.: Suhrkamp, 1969); Günter Amendt, ed., *Kinderkreuzzug oder Beginnt die Revolution in den Schulen?* (Reinbek: Rowohlt, 1968).
20. Karl-Heinz Schubert, ed., *Aufbruch zum Proletariat: Dokumente der Basisgruppen* (Berlin: Taifun, 1988). The quote in the headline is from Binger, *68 selbstorganisiert*, 20.

21. Dietmar Süß, "Die Enkel auf den Barrikaden: Jungsozialisten in der SPD in den Siebzigerjahren," *Archiv für Sozialgeschichte* 44 (2004): 67–104; Karsten D. Voigt, "Zur Strategie systemüberwindender Reformen," in *Wege zur veränderten Gesellschaft: Politische Strategien*, ed. Hendrik Bussiek (Frankfurt a.M.: Fischer-TB, 1971), 71–102.
22. Paper for their federal congress in December 1971, quoted in *Der Thesenstreit um "Stamokap": Die Dokumente zur Grundsatzdiskussion der Jungsozialisten* (Reinbek: Rowohlt, 1973), 96; see also ibid., 41, 80.
23. Ibid., 97.
24. *Links* 0, April 1969: 9–12.
25. Oskar Negt, "Nicht nach Köpfen, sondern nach Interessen organisieren!—Aktuelle Fragen der Organisation," *links* 39, December 1972: 9–11.
26. "Der Mythos der 'Selbstorganisation,'" *Arbeiterkampf* 28, May 1973: 8–9.
27. Jan Ole Arps, *Frühschicht: Linke Fabrikintervention in den 70er Jahren* (Berlin and Hamburg: Assoziation A, 2011); Sebastian Kasper, "Unter der Parole 'Kampf gegen die Arbeit!' Die Betriebsintervention der frühen Sponti-Bewegung," *Arbeit—Bewegung—Geschichte* 15, no. 1 (2016): 49–62.
28. Sebastian Kasper, *Spontis: Eine Geschichte antiautoritärer Linker im roten Jahrzehnt* (Münster: edition assemblage, 2019), 83–96; Häuserrat Frankfurt, *Wohnungskampf in Frankfurt* (Munich: Trikont, 1974).
29. *Agit 883* 85, 15 November 1971, 2.
30. Thesen zur Selbstorganisation, *MAD* Sonderheft 2 (1972), quoted in Günter Bartsch, *Anarchismus in Deutschland*, Band II: *1965–1973* (Hannover: Fackelträger, 1973), 369–70.
31. *Agit 883* 80, 11 May 1971, 23. See also Bartsch, *Anarchismus*, 201–5.
32. As the title of the nevertheless convincing study of Schmidtke, *Aufbruch*, suggests.
33. David Templin, *"Lehrzeit—keine Leerzeit!" Die Lehrlingsbewegung in Hamburg 1968–1972* (Munich and Hamburg: Dölling & Galitz, 2012), 23–61; Knud Andresen, *Gebremste Radikalisierung: Die IG Metall und ihre Jugend 1968 bis in die 1980er Jahre* (Göttingen: Wallstein, 2016), 118–53.
34. Reinhard Crusius, *Berufsbildungs- und Jugendpolitik der Gewerkschaft: Struktur und Verlauf bei DGB und einigen Einzelgewerkschaften 1945–1981* (Frankfurt a.M.: Campus, 1982), 172.
35. Reinhard Crusius, Oskar Söhl, and Manfred Wilke, *Praxis und Theorie gewerkschaftlicher Lehrlingspolitik: Dargestellt am Beispiel des Hamburger "Jour Fixe"; Schilderung, Analyse, Dokumente sowie eine umfassende Lehrlingshandbuch-Dokumentation* (Offenbach: Verlag 2000, 1971), 10.
36. Templin, *Lehrzeit*, 40–43, 106–8.
37. Ibid., 88–103, 136–44.
38. Christa, "Selbstorganisation als reine Interessenpolitik," *GIM Hamburg Info*, no. 9 (1971).
39. See Gerd-Rainer Horn, *The Spirit of '68: Rebellion in Western Europe and North America, 1956–1976* (New York: Oxford University Press, 2007), 93–130.
40. Kollektiv Release Heidelberg, *Krankheit† Institution: Dokumente der Unterdrückung eines Versuchs zur Selbstorganisation* (Gießen: edition 2000, 1973), 6.

41. As an attempt at theorization: Rolf Schwendter, *Theorie der Subkultur* (Cologne and Bonn: Kiepenheuer & Witsch, 1971), who spoke of a "self-organization of needs" (*Selbstorganisation der Bedürfnisse*) without defining it in detail.
42. This conception was adopted by *Spontis* and *Autonome*; see Kasper, *Spontis*, 163–64, 169; Sebastian Haunss, *Identität in Bewegung: Prozesse kollektiver Identität bei den Autonomen und in der Schwulenbewegung* (Wiesbaden: VS, 2004), 115–18, 143–44. On such "politics of subjectivity": Joachim C. Häberlen, *The Emotional Politics of the Alternative Left: West Germany, 1968–1984* (Cambridge: Cambridge University Press, 2018), 104–13. Cf. Bernhard Gotto's chapter in this volume.
43. David Templin, *Freizeit ohne Kontrollen: Die Jugendzentrumsbewegung in der Bundesrepublik der 1970er Jahre* (Göttingen: Wallstein, 2015).
44. Archiv Soziale Bewegungen, Freiburg, 6.4.V, "Basler Tor Turm," AUSS/SDS/Roter Turm, "Aufruf zur Gründung des antiautoritären Jugendheims ROTER TURM," 28 March 1969, in *Turmgespräche 15: Antiautoritäres Jugendheim ROTER TURM*, ed. Redaktionskollektiv Roter Turm (Karlsruhe: self-published, 1969), 5–6.
45. Templin, *Freizeit*, 71–86.
46. Detlef Siegfried, *Time Is on My Side: Konsum und Politik in der westdeutschen Jugendkultur der 60er Jahre* (Göttingen: Wallstein, 2006), 660.
47. Private Archive of Herbert Weisbrod-Frey, *Wieslocher Culturnachrichten: Zeitung der Aktion Jugendzentrum in Selbstverwaltung e.V.*, no. 1, June 1974, 5.
48. Südwestrundfunk, Historical Archive (SWR/HA), "FS Nachmittagsprogramm", 29/01089, Jour fix 1, 16 April 1971.
49. Heinz Grossmann, ed., *Bürgerinitiativen: Schritte zur Veränderung?* (Frankfurt a.M.: Fischer, 1971); Peter Cornelius Mayer-Tasch, *Die Bürgerinitiativbewegung: Der aktive Bürger als rechts- und politikwissenschaftliches Problem* (Reinbek: Rowohlt, 1976).
50. Roland Günter and Rolf Hasse, *Handbuch für Bürgerinitiativen: Argumente, Berichte, Erfahrungen* (Westberlin: VSA, 1976), 15.
51. Willi Hau, "Redet nicht nur von Alternativen—Lebt sie," in *Free-Clinic Heidelberg: Alternative Jugendarbeit in Selbstorganisation* (Eschborn/Ts.: Direkt, 1977), 225.
52. Elisabeth Zellmer, *Töchter der Revolte? Frauenbewegung und Feminismus der 1970er Jahre in München* (Munich: Oldenbourg, 2011), 164–72; Ursula Krechel, *Selbsterfahrung und Fremdbestimmung: Bericht aus der Neuen Frauenbewegung* (Darmstadt and Neuwied: Luchterhand, 1975).
53. See Maik Tändler, *Das therapeutische Jahrzehnt: Der Psychoboom in den siebziger Jahren* (Göttingen: Wallstein, 2016). Cf. Bernhard Gotto's chapter in this volume.
54. Karl-Werner Brand, Detlef Büsser, and Dieter Rucht, *Aufbruch in eine andere Gesellschaft: Neue soziale Bewegungen in der Bundesrepublik* (Frankfurt a.M.: Campus, 1984), 247.
55. BG Spandau, "Basis-Gruppen-Arbeits-Bericht," *Agit 883* 60, 14 May 1970, 5.
56. Templin, *Freizeit*, 107–18.
57. *Kämpfende Jugend* (KJV), no. 1, 15 January 1974, 8.
58. Ibid.
59. Templin, *Freizeit*, 118–31.
60. Quoted in Kay Schweigmann-Greve, "'Ein Gespenst geht um in der BRD—das Gespenst der Jugendzentrumsbewegung!': Die SJD—Die Falken und die unabhän-

gige Jugendzentrumsbewegung in den 1970er Jahren," in *Lebensreform um 1900 und Alternativmilieu um 1980: Kontinuitäten und Brüche in Milieus der gesellschaftlichen Selbstreflexion im frühen und späten 20. Jahrhundert*, ed. Detlef Siegfried and David Templin (Göttingen: V&R unipress, 2019), 298.
61. Self-conception of the BDP/BDJ Hessen, February 1979, quoted in David Templin, "Vom Pfadfinderbund zur 'Organisation der Selbstorganisierten': Der Bund Deutscher Pfadfinder (BDP) und die Jugendzentrumsbewegung der 1970er Jahre," in *Avantgarden der Biopolitik: Jugendbewegung, Lebensreform und Strategien biologischer "Aufrüstung,"* ed. Karl Braun, Felix Linzner, and John Khairi-Taraki (Göttingen: V&R unipress, 2017), 200.
62. Zellmer, *Töchter*, 169–72. On the *Selbsthilfebewegung* see Tändler, *Jahrzehnt*, 158–66; Fritz Vilmar and Brigitte Runge, *Auf dem Weg zur Selbsthilfegesellschaft? 40.000 Selbsthilfegruppen: Gesamtüberblick, politische Theorie und Handlungsvorschläge* (Essen: Klartext, 1986).
63. Sven Reichardt, *Authentizität und Gemeinschaft: Linksalternatives Leben in den siebziger und frühen achtziger Jahren* (Berlin: Suhrkamp, 2014), 322–23.
64. Templin, *Freizeit*, 82, 191–93.
65. Archive of the Forschungsstelle für Zeitgeschichte in Hamburg (FZH), 14–9, 59, "Konzept für ein unabhängiges Jugendzentrum," 24 March 1973.
66. Municipal Archive of Mannheim, 3/1981, 647, Selbstorganisation Paradeplatz, SOP-Info II, undated [1972].
67. Quoted in Arndt Neumann, *Kleine geile Firmen: Alternativprojekte zwischen Revolte und Management* (Hamburg: Edition Nautilus, 2008), 21.
68. Sven Reichardt and Detlef Siegfried, "Das Alternative Milieu: Konturen einer Lebensform," in *Das Alternative Milieu: Antibürgerlicher Lebensstil und linke Politik in der Bundesrepublik Deutschland und Europa, 1968–1983*, ed. Sven Reichardt and Detlef Siegfried, 9–24.
69. Kristina Schulz, *Der lange Atem der Provokation: Die Frauenbewegung in der Bundesrepublik und in Frankreich 1968–1976* (Frankfurt a.M.: Campus, 2002), 72.
70. Ibid.
71. Templin, *Freizeit*, 230–33, 281–305.
72. Ibid., 404–515.
73. Ibid., 349–58.
74. Albert Herrenknecht, Wolfgang Hätscher and Stefan Koospal, eds., *Träume, Hoffnungen, Kämpfe… Ein Lesebuch zur Jugendzentrumsbewegung* (Frankfurt a.M.: Jugend und Politik, 1977), 35–36.
75. Templin, *Freizeit*, 87–98, 417–28.
76. Reichardt, *Authentizität*, 271–77, 329–34, 365–70, 467–68.
77. David Templin, "Avantgarde im Klassenkampf oder aufstiegsorientierte Minderheit? Arbeiterjugend in sozialen Bewegungen der späten 1960er und 1970er Jahre," *Arbeit—Bewegung—Geschichte* 17, no. 3 (2018): 39–56.
78. Reichardt, *Authentizität*, 246, 335–37.
79. Neumann, *Firmen*, 28–37.
80. As an overview: Frank Heider, "Selbstverwaltete Betriebe in Deutschland," in *Die sozialen Bewegungen in Deutschland seit 1945: Ein Handbuch*, ed. Roland Roth and Dieter Rucht (Frankfurt a.M.: Campus, 2008), 513–26.

81. Freia Anders, "Wohnraum, Freiraum, Widerstand: Die Formierung der Autonomen in den Konflikten um Hausbesetzungen Anfang der achtziger Jahre," in Reichardt and Siegfried, *Das Alternative Milieu*, 473–98.
82. This was also the case in earlier movements. See Siegfried and Templin, *Lebensreform*, for comparisons of reform movements around 1900 and the alternative milieu of the 1970s.
83. Rolf Schwendter, ed., *Die Mühen der Berge: Grundlegungen zur alternativen Ökonomie*, vols. 1–2 (Munich: AG Spak, 1986).
84. Luc Boltanski and Ève Chiapello, *The New Spirit of Capitalism* (New York: Verso, 2005); Sergio Bologna et al., eds., *Selbstorganisation . . . Transformationsprozesse von Arbeit und sozialem Widerstand im neoliberalen Kapitalismus* (Berlin: Die Buchmacherei, 2007).
85. Detlef Siegfried, "Die Entpolitisierung des Privaten: Subjektkonstruktionen im alternativen Milieu," in *Privatisierung: Idee und Praxis seit den 1970er Jahren*, ed. Norbert Frei and Dietmar Süß (Göttingen: Wallstein, 2012), 124–39; Ulrich Bröckling, *Das unternehmerische Selbst: Soziologie einer Subjektivierungsform* (Frankfurt a.M.: Suhrkamp, 2007).

Select Bibliography

Horn, Gerd-Rainer. *The Spirit of '68: Rebellion in Western Europe and North America, 1956–1976*. New York: Oxford University Press, 2007.

Reichardt, Sven. *Authentizität und Gemeinschaft: Linksalternatives Leben in den siebziger und frühen achtziger Jahren*. Berlin: Suhrkamp, 2014.

Templin, David. *"Lehrzeit—keine Leerzeit!" Die Lehrlingsbewegung in Hamburg 1968–1972*. München and Hamburg: Dölling & Galitz, 2012.

———. *Freizeit ohne Kontrollen: Die Jugendzentrumsbewegung in der Bundesrepublik der 1970er Jahre*. Göttingen: Wallstein, 2015.

Part III
"Learn to Live in Solidarity"

Chapter 10

The Gay Movement in 1970s West Germany

Liberation in Its Multidimensional Context

Craig Griffiths

Perhaps more than any other social movement in the long 1970s, the gay movement has often been pigeonholed as an "exotic" or "single-issue" or merely "cultural" phenomenon, testament to the implicit skepticism in some quarters over its political relevance.* Seeking to differentiate a "left-alternative milieu" from "new social movements," Dieter Rucht categorizes what he refers to as the "coming out of gays and lesbians" as a "cultural-expressive" aspect of the long 1970s, as opposed to its more "political-instrumental" counterparts.[1] In fact, the gay liberation movement, for the most part, was driven forward by activists with a transformational agenda: theirs was no narrow vision of gradually increasing tolerance bit by bit, politely encouraging same-sex desiring men and women out of the closet. Instead of single-issue politics, activists diagnosed homosexual oppression as inseparable from the structural injustice of the capitalist system and hence intimately connected with other forms of social and racial exclusion. In one of the earliest accounts of the West German gay movement, Andreas Pareik, a member of the Homosexual Action West Berlin, titled his work "Struggle for an identity."[2] This struggle for an identity was never only sexual—or only cultural—but always also political. Referring to the gay movement as a "single-issue movement" trivializes and erases the multidirectional form of activists' political and emotional attachments.

This chapter therefore contends that the West German gay movement is best analyzed when placed in its immediate context in the alternative left that developed after '68. I use "alternative left" as a loose placeholder for those diverse movements, groups, and countercultural tendencies to the left of the governing Social Democrats; the alternative left was the 1970s successor to the "New Left" of the late 1960s, which found expression particularly in the student movement and the Socialist German Student League (SDS).[3] The alternative left provided not just ideological influences but also discursive and physical spaces for the gay movement. Rather than the *Öffentlichkeit*, the wider public sphere, gay activists were often more concerned with the left-alternative *Gegenöffentlichkeit*, the counterpublic, with its network of independently produced papers, flyers, and zines, alongside its alternative spaces: bars, cafés, bookshops, grocery stores, housing, and film and theater collectives. It was in these spaces and media that a great deal of queer activist energy was invested in the 1970s, one of the most distinctive features of homosexual politics in this period. Although some groups continued to quietly lobby sympathetic journalists and politicians, this approach of seeking "mainstream" and "respectable" support was more typical of the preceding homophile movement of the 1950s and 1960s ("homophile," which sought to downplay the "sexual" in "homosexual," was the term preferred by many activists before the impact of '68 had made itself felt, and before the partial decriminalization of male homosexuality in 1969).[4]

While activists from across a multitude of social movements in the 1970s sought to collaborate in a broader social justice agenda, this collaboration could never be taken for granted. There was never a moment when all progressive causes and all dreams for a transformed society neatly coalesced in some mutually invigorating feedback loop. Although we can broadly place most gay activists within the contours of the alternative left, this does not mean that unity and solidarity prevailed. The members of the action groups that made up the West German gay movement rarely reached agreement about the best way forward or found consensus over whose cooperation should be prioritized. Moreover, the gay movement could never rest on its laurels. Notions of sexual liberation, "free love," or antiauthoritarianism might spring to mind, but these were not sufficient to anchor the gay movement in the alternative left. To explore the sometimes fraught nature of solidarity, this chapter moves on to examine the so-called *Tuntenstreit* (Queens' Dispute), a strategic debate in the gay movement concerning the political value of drag and gender transgression. All participants in the debate pursued profound change to existing society but sharply disagreed over what exactly this change should consist of, in what manner it should be reached, and whose support should be sought along the way. Some prioritized the socialist revolution, arguing that the gay movement should not only collaborate with the worker's movement but also subordinate itself to the task of economic liberation. Others rejected this reading of liberation, emphasizing instead a politics of personal, individual emancipation as a stepping-stone to working with other forces, especially the women's movement, in a wider struggle against oppression. Notwithstanding their differences, no players in the debate defended a "single-issue" platform. As will be seen, all sides were committed to a "dual militancy," an understanding whereby activists should not restrict themselves to organizing in the gay movement alone.

1968 and the Emergence of the Gay Movement

The gay movement was not part of '68, narrowly defined; this was the case not just in West Germany but throughout Europe and North America.[5] Unlike for second-wave feminism, there was no queer "hurling of tomatoes" in the West German '68. Indeed, when Sigrud Rüder arose from the audience during the SDS conference in September 1968, symbolically launching the women's movement, the ironic target of her well-aimed tomatoes was Hans-Jürgen Krahl, a same-sex desiring man. Whether he found himself unwilling or unable to claim a gay identity, Krahl was simultaneously a participant in and victim of the macho and heteronormative environment of the student movement and the New Left scene.[6]

Chronologically speaking, 1969 was more important than 1968 for the gay movement. Most famously, this was because of Stonewall. Beginning on 28 June 1969, when patrons of the Stonewall Inn on Christopher Street, New York City, defended themselves against a police raid, the Stonewall riots are often credited as the spark that set gay liberation alight: not just in the United States but across the Western world.[7] Gay and lesbian activists marked the first anniversary of the riots in June 1970 with a large demonstration, an event that became an annual one that was subsequently exported around the world, including to Germany, where CSD (Christopher Street Day) parades continue to take place in many cities each June.[8] Notwithstanding this commemorative success story, the most significant development to occur in 1969 for same-sex desiring men in West Germany was actually not Stonewall but homosexual law reform, as the Nazi-era version of paragraph 175 was finally liberalized.[9] This legal reform made it much easier for homosexuals to come together and to come out, and it paved the way for a transformed queer print culture, as glossy monthlies including *him* and *du&ich* immediately appeared in newspaper kiosks across the Federal Republic, even before activist-produced zines and journals emerged onto the scene.[10]

If in 1968 there was not a single group in West Germany providing help and support for homosexuals or agitating for gay rights, by 1980 some fifty-three towns and cities in the Federal Republic were home to such groups, and there were several hundred in total.[11] Clearly, '68—conceived broadly—had quite a lot to do with this transformation, even if there was no *direct* line from '68 to the gay movement.[12] Following women's liberation, gay liberation was at once both a product of and response to the ambiguous sexual politics of 1968. Examples of leftist homophobia and misogyny abound, but that should not blind us to the spaces opened up by '68. As Kristina Schulz notes, the works of the intellectual New Left were important in allowing second-wave feminists to come to see themselves as subjects of change.[13] The most influential intellectual on the new left, Marcuse, had heralded the transformative capacity of the "substratum of the outcasts and the outsiders," having in mind the student and civil rights movements in the United States.[14] It did not take much imagination for gays to place themselves in this category. In a few cases, an adherence to the Frankfurt School and Marcuse was explicitly cited, as with the Rote Schwule Fraktion in Oberhausen.[15] More generally, Marcuse and others offered a theoretical framework that leftists (of all sexualities) could use to justify their abandonment of the working class as the sole revolutionary subject (even if some activists, as will be seen, chose not to take this path).

Gay activists regularly identified the capitalist system as responsible for homosexual oppression. A case in point was the Homosexual Action West Berlin (HAW). As the group's statement of founding principles, written in 1971, put it:

> The discrimination of homosexuals cannot be separated from the conditions of the emergence and development of capitalism. . . . We see in the oppression of homosexuality just one case of the general oppression of sexuality, which serves the security of political and economic power.[16]

Homosexual and pederast activist Peter Schult, meanwhile, argued that while homosexuality per se was not revolutionary, the homosexual who learned from his oppression and connected this with the broader social order ceased to be merely a gay man but instead belonged to the camp of the oppressed.[17]

This kind of understanding offered homosexuals a potential cachet as righteous victims of an oppressive order, which goes some way to explaining why the gay movement "rediscovered" the pink triangle—an insignia invented by the Nazis to categorize homosexual men in the concentration camps—and turned this into a symbol of gay liberation.[18] Recapitulating a trend from the student movement, this understanding also bequeathed activists in the gay movement a somewhat avant-garde role within the wider homosexual population, making them responsible for lifting their fellow queers from the depths of their ostensible false consciousness. Accordingly, Martin Dannecker, a leading member of the Frankfurt-based Red Cell Gay (RotZSchwul), came up with the following inventive slogan on the occasion of West Germany's first demonstration by gays and lesbians, in Münster in April 1972: "Brothers and sisters, whether queer or not, fighting capitalism is a duty we've got" (*Brüder und Schwester, warm oder nicht, Kapitalismus bekämpfen ist unsere Pflicht*).[19]

The *Tuntenstreit*

In June 1973 the HAW organized an international six-day gathering attended by both gay and lesbian activists.[20] By this point, gays and lesbians in the HAW tended to organize separately, although the HAW women's group did not formally depart and rename itself the Lesbian Action Centre (LAZ) until January 1975.[21] The gathering in June 1973 was the gay movement's second "Pentecost meeting" (*Pfingsttreffen*), an occasion when activists from different regions would come together over the long weekend marked by a public holiday in Germany, a tradition taken from the workers' movement. Organized under the slogan "The oppression of homosexuality is only a particular case of the general oppression of sexuality," the week included a public information stand, workshops, films, street theater, and fêtes before culminating in a demonstration in central Berlin.[22] During this demonstration, some of the French and Italian activists, in drag, refused to stay in the main body of the march and danced around in the surrounding streets, chanting slogans and interacting with passersby.[23] Reporting in brief on the demonstration under the title "March of the Eye Shadow," the tabloid *BILD* commented that "some of the participants had full beards and wore long dresses, eye shadow and blue nail varnish."[24]

As the informal minutes of heated discussions that took place after the demonstration reveal, some West German activists reacted with anger to what had transpired.[25] Comments included that the appearance and behavior of the *Tunten* was unpolitical, that as they did not wear drag in the workplace their behavior at the demonstration was as exotic as the Easter Bunny or Father Christmas, and that the demonstration had been made into a carnival for the voyeurism of passersby. *Tunten*, along with their supporters, responded by criticizing the conformism of other demonstrators, with one (French) activist decrying this "typically German militaristic behavior."[26] Controversy also raged about who could and should call themselves a *Tunte*. These were the opening salvos in what became known as the *Tuntenstreit*, one of the most acrimonious episodes in the history of the 1970s gay movement.[27]

Tunten can be loosely translated as "queens" or "fairies": the term "gender fuck" is more suitable than "transgender," though both are anachronistic when applied to the 1970s. Carsten Balzer, investigating the differences between *Tunten* and drag queens, has argued that *Tunten* reject straightforward female impersonation in favor of adopting elements of effeminate dress, style, speech, and mannerism and acting them out in theatrical, "grotesque," or "trashy" ways.[28] This performative critique of gender norms was a signal feature of the *Tuntenstreit*. West German *Tunten* in this debate therefore roughly map onto the proponents of "political drag" or "radical drag" in Britain, of "faggotry" in the United States, or can be compared to the so-called *gazolines* in the Homosexual Revolutionary Action Front in France.[29] It is not possible, however, to make hard and fast distinctions between different identity categories. The *Tuntenstreit* saw complex interactions of sexual, gender and political identity. Some who called themselves *Tunten* adopted this category only briefly or used it only at certain times. Other activists occasionally called into question whether this made them *Tunten* at all, for instance demarcating between "real" and "student" *Tunten*.[30] Confusing this further, gay male activists routinely adopted female aliases, including those who were in fact antagonistic to *Tunten*.

Carsten Balzer argues that in the 1970s the label of *Tunte* was resignified, previously having been used mainly as a slur term by those "outside of the community."[31] However, fundamental to the politicization of *Tunten* within the gay movement was a growing consciousness of the discriminatory attitudes held not just by heterosexuals but also by other gay men. This had been clearly articulated as early as November 1971 in the HAW's founding document:

> Whoever, in either his appearance or behavior, does not conform to the ideal of the normal man, is considered a *Tunte*, and everyone can easily find someone else who seems *tuntiger* than himself [more of a *Tunte* than himself] and whom he can make into the object of his aggression instead of demonstrating solidarity with him against social discrimination.[32]

The theoretical interpretation of this hatred of *Tunten* was provided by Reimut Reiche and Martin Dannecker in their sociological study *The Ordinary Homosexual*; this collaboration between Reiche, the erstwhile SDS leader, and Dannecker, the cofounder of Red Cell Gay, is another example of the interconnectedness of the alternative left. According to the authors, West Germany's gay men were suffering from a "collective neurosis," evidenced primarily by their views towards *Tunten*.[33] In response to the leading question, "When homosexuals are discussed in public, it is often especially effeminate types who are mentioned: would you please briefly describe what you think about so-called *Tunten*?" 76 percent of respondents expressed a negative opinion, ranging from aggression and disgust to complaints that *Tunten* made relations between gays and straights more difficult. The authors argued that this was an example of homosexuals projecting their guilt onto *Tunten*, blaming their effeminacy for the homophobia that they, the "normal" homosexuals, had to face.[34]

If the debates during and after the June 1973 demonstration are anything to go by, gay activists were by no means immune to the rejection of gender transgression that prevailed in the gay scene at large. Seeking to challenge these discriminatory attitudes, *Tunten* within the HAW soon coalesced into a single "feminist" caucus, cementing this process with their Feminists' Paper (*Feministenpapier*), a programmatic document setting out what was termed "male feminism" and the feminists' understanding of emancipation.[35] It is not clear if all members of the HAW's "male feminist" group wore drag, or how often, when, or where they did so. A member of the group, Andreas, credited the French demonstrators with awakening many West German *Tunten* out of their "Sleeping Beauty–esque self-oppression." He subsequently wore drag for the first time during the discussion after the demonstration and in public at the HAW's information stand in central Berlin.[36] For Andreas, this was a revelatory experiment: "I realized that I have many more possibilities to love, to live, to express myself than these guys, these blokes in their suits, who were really trembling in front of me. Oh, it was great!"[37]

In their Feminists' Paper, the male feminists argued that the HAW and the gay movement at large must concentrate on working with the women's movement in challenging gender oppression, since this oppression predated the advent of capitalism: "The first class oppression is the oppression of women through men!"[38] Within this context, adopting drag was seen as one means for gay men to demonstrate their commitment to undermining the gender norms seen as responsible for this oppression. This argument was developed, while also reaching a wider audience, in an article titled "Die Homosexualität in uns" (The homosexuality in us), originally published in 1974 in the leftist journal *Kursbuch*. The five authors, all of whom identified as HAW feminists, argued that fixed gender norms were the root cause of the oppression of homosexuality and that feminists, in drag, could call these norms into question:

> The specific approach of male feminism, to appear wearing makeup, "feminine," or with the Pink Triangle, is *one* means and at the same

time a necessity for gay men of rupturing the imposed division between private and public, a division that has become second nature.³⁹

Not all activists agreed. Published a few months after the Feminists' Paper, an article written by the HAW's teachers' group discussed the particularities of engaging with school pupils, youth clubs, colleagues, and parents. The authors stressed their "fundamental sympathy" with the feminists but wrote that it was impossible for them to adopt a feminist stance—understood as wearing makeup and drag—in their public work or outreach (Öffentlichkeitsarbeit). They called on the feminists to restrict themselves to "sensibly limited fields of activity, in which, with the agreement of the whole HAW, they can act in a mediated way."⁴⁰ As "total feminism" could not possibly be "classified" or "digested" by the general public, this approach should only be considered when previous efforts had been made to open up "possibilities for understanding."⁴¹

The notion that effeminate homosexuals should keep their gender transgression hidden away from the public sphere is of long currency, dating back at least to the so-called "masculinist" wing of the homosexual rights movement in Imperial Germany and the Weimar Republic.⁴² Concerns over potentially damaging interactions with the general public undoubtedly remained, and in this sense the rejection of *Tunten* on the part of some gay activists in the 1970s is an example of continuation from earlier traditions of homosexual politics. For example, adopting gender-normative dress and appearance was a key tenet of the "respectability" insisted upon by leaders of the homophile movement in the 1950s and 1960s.⁴³ In the 1970s, this concern over respectability narrowed, since activists generally had more specific audiences rather than the public at large in mind. The HAW teachers' group mentioned a public specific to their work: children, parents, and teachers. Yet, significantly, they also stated that demonstrations and meetings with leftist groups were not appropriate occasions for drag.⁴⁴

Indeed, those who rejected drag during the *Tuntenstreit* were primarily motivated by their desire to gain support either from the working class or from the left-alternative (counter)public. These remained two different audiences, even if the predominantly middle-class activists who set out to build a counterpublic hoped to win working-class involvement. Back in 1967, the SDS passed a resolution calling for the creation of an "enlightening counterpublic" (*aufklärende Gegenöffentlichkeit*) to break "the dictatorship of the manipulators."⁴⁵ This leftist counterpublic was seen by some theorists as the prototype for a future "proletarian public sphere."⁴⁶ In the discussions after the demonstration in June 1973, one activist had argued that the working class should be the only addressee of the gay movement. Engaging with this constituency was so difficult, according to the activist, because "we always comprehend emancipation as a private act of liberation." He admitted that reciprocal solidarity was not yet in evidence but maintained that "we just have to struggle on with stubborn persistence, not through shocking actions which ultimately remain private and harmless."[47]

This "stubborn persistence" belonged to the strategy of double or twin-track membership (*Doppelmitgliedschaft*), whereby gay activists were to organize not just in gay action groups but also in other leftist organizations. The PSA, the "plenary of socialist working groups in the HAW," put forward its view of double membership in October 1972. While the HAW should advocate "necessary reforms," the organization could not itself lead a socialist struggle, as gayness was not a "class feature."[48] This position was developed in an article published in *Problems of Class Struggle* in 1974, written in response to the aforementioned "Die Homosexualität in uns." The article's pseudonymous authors, both members of the HAW, criticized homophobia in leftist organizations but classified the oppression of homosexuality as merely a "special" or "additional" oppression (*Sonderunterdrückung*).[49] They urged homosexuals to recognize their majority position as exploited workers and aim for a gradual integration of the homosexual movement into the workers' movement. Other activists were warned against a potential "relapse to an unpolitical self-understanding [with] the adoption of fashionable bourgeois ideologies" rather than a "consistently socialist orientation."[50]

Another member of the HAW, meanwhile, denounced the "exotic bunch of *Tunten*" as a "new spawning of upper-class bluster," serving only as a distraction from "actual" problems, which were socioeconomic in nature.[51] Manfred Herzer, coauthor of the article in *Problems of Class Struggle*, left the HAW in 1974 to join the General Homosexual Committee (AHA).[52] Herzer explained his decision in an open letter sarcastically titled "Es lebe der Feminismus!" (Long live feminism!), in which the male feminists were castigated as a "clique of bohemians and petite bourgeoisie [*Spießer*] gone wild."[53] In a subsequent coauthored article in the Marxist journal *Das Argument*, Herzer—this time without a pseudonym—expanded his critique of the "unpolitical" nature of drag by connecting this "faux-radical" protest pose to a faulty understanding of emancipation.[54] Class, not gender, was presented as central category of analysis. Herzer and his coauthor argued that "polarity between gender roles" could probably be abolished within capitalism without calling into question the forces that sustained the capitalist system: "It would however be absurd to mistake these processes for emancipation, which can only be understood as liberation from exploitation and class rule."[55] In this light, the male feminists were to blame not only for confusing private affairs with collective emancipation but also for hindering this collective emancipation by alienating the only force capable of bringing it about, the working class.

It is unclear whether activists actually experienced negative reactions from the working class regarding drag. The *fear* of a hostile—or indifferent—reaction, however, was certainly salient. This fear may have been inherited from the late 1960s. According to Reimut Reiche, the largely unenthusiastic reception of the student movement by the general population may have been down to perceptions of student protesters as being scruffy and licentious and having long hair, characteristics that were supposedly alien to the working class.[56] Several erstwhile members of the HAW, including Manfred Herzer, were also activists in the Socialist Unity Party of West Berlin (SEW), the West Berlin chapter of the German Communist Party (DKP), which was funded by the East German state. This may have made them especially eager to avoid any impression that homosexuals were given to bourgeois tendencies, since according to one discourse in the GDR, sexual acts between men were not only unmanly but also un-proletarian.[57]

The allegiance of the DKP was not typical of the West German left, but several Communist groups (*K-Gruppen*) did share this party's attempt to return to the proletariat as the only acceptable revolutionary subject. As part of this mission, activists were encouraged to marry and to dress more formally; discussion of homosexuality, and indeed sexuality more generally, was not encouraged.[58] When Marxist-Leninist members of the Homosexual Action Bremen wrote to the Communist League of West Germany (KBW) in 1974, a spokesman replied that in the KBW's view, homosexuality might not occur in a postrevolutionary society and that homosexual action groups were reformist in nature and as such counterrevolutionary.[59] This was hardly an auspicious climate for gay activists, yet it is clear that some of those activists worked very hard to reconcile their sexuality with their political belongings. As the *Tuntenstreit* shows, it was not only the "antiauthoritarian" or "*Sponti*" aspects of the alternative left that appealed to members of the gay movement (though these were the parts of the alternative left in which sex, sexuality, and gender presentation were more prominently discussed).[60] A capacious understanding of "alternative left," including the *K-Gruppen* and the likes of the DKP, serves to underline the diverse and conflicting approaches and affiliations in post-'68 leftist activism, queer or otherwise.[61]

The male feminists, unlike Manfred Herzer or the Marxist-Leninists in the Homosexual Action Bremen, had little time for the *K-Gruppen*. The caucus did not oppose forms of leftist solidarity—such as taking part in a demonstration against the war in Vietnam—but argued that the gay movement must renew its support for personal emancipation. Rather than being hidden in large groups of people, the first emancipatory step for each activist should be an affirmation of their own homosexuality.[62] The male feminists stressed that in the gay movement's rush to prove itself to the left, to demonstrate that it had the "right" politics—such as taking part in *de rigueur* demonstrations, joining annual 1 May rallies, or collecting donations for imprisoned leftists—their specific position as gay men was being lost. They argued that while the gay movement *should* articulate an anti-capitalist stance, its task was also to focus on the oppression faced by homosexuals—and women—whether that occurred in wider society or within leftist circles. Therefore, a struggle on two fronts was deemed necessary, against capitalism but also against the social situation of oppressed groups; any approach that did not combine both struggles was doomed to failure.[63]

In other words, while the male feminists opposed the specific understanding of double membership supported by their adversaries—since it seemed to imply a political devaluation of the significance of homosexual oppression—they, too, were committed to a model of "dual militancy," not absolute autonomy or "single-issue politics."[64] The terms "special oppression" and "secondary contradiction" (*Nebenwiderspruch*), both used in the course of the *Tuntenstreit* to stress the primacy of class struggle, had been employed previously by some student movement leaders to downplay the gender oppression thematized by the women's movement.[65] In criticizing what they perceived as the unquestioned masculinity of other gay activists, the male feminists were consciously treading in the footsteps of women's movement activists who had critiqued the masculinity and misogyny on the part of male student movement leaders.

However, there is little evidence that the male feminists enjoyed much success in seeking support from other (female) feminists. Male feminist drag did not lead to a successful reorientation of the gay movement toward second-wave feminism. Lesbians within the HAW, for example, do not seem to have offered any support to the male feminist group, instead criticizing what they understood as the orientation of male feminists toward a traditional image of women.[66] One lesbian activist who attended the 1973 gathering came away with the impression that *Tunten* saw themselves as women and as victims of the oppression of women. This saddened her, as she took it as evidence that these gay men no longer had "any identity whatsoever."[67] Others were not convinced that gay men had anything to offer feminism, since they were not women. This was the perspective adopted by the author of an article in the gay movement journal *Emanzipation* in 1977, who added that the male feminists should confess their "unpolitical enjoyment of grotesque-theatrical performances."[68] While gays and lesbians tended to organize separately even before the *Tuntenstreit*, the debate did little to bridge these latent divides, as lesbians continued to work much more closely with and in the women's movement than with gay men.[69] In the West German context, it is difficult to talk of a common gay *and* lesbian movement until the 1990s.[70]

Between Public and Counterpublic

At stake in the question of how interconnected the left-alternative movements, networks, and spaces were after '68 is more than merely the matter of what activists thought about other causes. By comprehending the gay movement as a "single-issue" struggle, we fail to capture something foundational to the identities of gay activists. Victoria Hesford argues that the public sphere should be considered "a malleable discursive space in which groups do not simply articulate established positions but actually come into being through their dialogical interactions with others."[71] Similarly, Nancy Fraser contends that public spheres are not just about deliberation but are also "arenas for the formation and enactment of public identities."[72] Gay activists were of course members of the wider public sphere in West Germany, alongside everyone else living in the Federal Republic. They sought to gain enough publicity in order to stand a chance of influencing public opinion, to challenge popular public (mis)conceptions about homosexuality, to seek to change policy. At the same time, gay activists were part of a gay public. They addressed other members of this gay public, not least because this was the most likely pool of "recruits" for the movement. But members of the gay movement actually spent more of their time during the 1970s addressing another arena: the left-alternative public, which they themselves belonged to. Oscillating from public to counterpublic involved not just a question of who to address but of who gay activists were. Implicated in all three of these spheres, how activists negotiated these poles would shape not only the course of the gay movement but its members' very identities as gay activists.[73]

Action forms are a case in point. Elsewhere in this volume, Bernhard Gotto shows how second-wave feminists, despite the sexism they endured, "transferred their repertoire of action to a great extent from the '68 protest movement." Models of civil disobedience, sit-ins and street theater jostled with other forms of action that long predated '68, including open letters and demonstrations.[74] Gay activists followed in these footsteps, organizing protests and public information stalls, often as part of, or to coincide with, wider feminist or leftist concerns (for example, on annual 1 May rallies). More inventive actions included the effort of activists in Bielefeld, who rented a city tram for a few hours, from which they would jauntily serenade passersby, or the delivery of the enormous papier-mâché phallus that the *Brühwarm* theater collective delivered into the audience during their performances.[75] These types of actions, or spectacles, owed much to the influence of situationism, even if this was rarely explicitly cited by activists.[76] Sometimes, the threads of inspiration were more direct. It is not possible to imagine the spectacular public action undertaken in October 1978, when 682 gay men outed themselves to the millions of readers of the *Stern* magazine, without the prior performance conducted by feminists in June 1971, when 374 women declared on the front cover of the same magazine that they had had an abortion.[77]

Several scholars have described how in the 1970s feminists established a network of bookshops, publishers, meeting places, women's centers, and rape crisis centers: for Fraser a "feminist subaltern counterpublic" and for Dagmar Herzog a "female-centred public countersphere."[78] The gay movement followed suit. The movement's first national journals were founded in 1975 (*Emanzipation* and *Schwuchtel*), as was the *Rosa Winkel Verlag* (Pink Triangle Press). In 1978, the gay bookshop *Prinz Eisenherz* opened in West Berlin.[79] *Brühwarm*, the movement's first theater collective, staged its inaugural play in 1976.[80] Again learning from the women's movement, many gay activists took part in "consciousness-raising" (*Selbsterfahrung*) groups to explore their fears, overcome loneliness, and to build a sense of solidarity.[81] These consciousness-raising groups laid a foundation for the subsequent development of telephone helplines, which in turn gave rise to the "self-help" groups that proliferated after the onset of HIV/AIDS.[82] Groups in Dortmund, Frankfurt, Munich, West Berlin, and elsewhere opened their own centers or cafés. Signposting the intention to reach a wider public than solely gay activists, these were often called "communication centers."[83]

Given the less-than-rosy relationship between the commercial gay press and the gay movement, the left-alternative press offered activists a crucial alternative avenue, allowing gay groups in Nuremberg, Frankfurt, Munich, West Berlin, and Heidelberg to present themselves to readers of *ID*, *Pflasterstrand*, *Blatt*, *Info-BUG*, *Carlo Sponti*, and many others.[84] Student unions, dominated by leftist parties in the 1970s, often provided the rooms where gay groups held their meetings. The student union in Aachen covered the legal costs of the "Society for Sexual Reform" (GSR), one of West Germany's most discreetly named gay action groups, in its effort to overturn the banning of its information stall by the city council.[85] As we have seen, articles in the leftist journals *Probleme des Klassenkampfs*, *Kursbuch*, and *Das Argument* were central in launching the *Tuntenstreit*. Yet this was not merely a case of taking what was on offer. Gay activists did not just seek to appeal to other movements on the alternative left but were very much part of that post-'68 alternative left. In this way, tactical considerations cannot be considered as divorced from activist subjectivities.[86]

Although the alternative left provided both models and inspiration for the construction of alternative publics, gay activist initiatives were also sometimes informed by a sense of exasperation with leftist attitudes. The editors of *Schwuchtel* expressed their frustration with homophobic attitudes on the left, declaring that "whoever is made an outsider by this society remains an outsider among leftists too."[87] An article in the first issue expressed the journal's rationale: "Us gays continue to occupy the lowest rung of the human value ladder in the Federal Republic. Therefore no one will champion our cause if we fail to create a public ourselves."[88] Paul Seidenberg, one of the 682 men who outed themselves in the *Stern* special, specifically cited his membership of the German Communist Party (DKP) in the feature.[89] This did not please party functionaries, who accused him of exhibitionism; Seidenberg ultimately left the party in 1980.[90] Equally, as we have seen, several gay activists in the HAW persevered in the SEW, and there was an active caucus of gay members in the Communist League (KB), who compiled various articles concerning homosexuality for the KB's newspaper, *Arbeiterkampf*.[91] Examining gay movement debates in detail therefore reveals the ideological diversity of gay left thought, which was as broad, complex, and conflicting as the wider alternative left.

Conclusion

When the Homosexual Action Hamburg decided to campaign in the 1978 state elections—in a departure from the gay movement's previous antipathy to the parliamentary sphere—they did not back a candidate independently but stood as part of the *Bunte Liste* ("rainbow list," a precursor to the Greens), alongside environmental, feminist, and migrant-rights groups.[92] According to members, this "unity of action" was necessary, because "alongside the struggle against anti-gay prejudice" gays have other interests, which "arise first and foremost from our roles as worker, employee, pupil, student, tenant, and so on."[93] Similarly, activists in Munich explained that "it is only through the social emancipation of all groups that the social-sexual emancipation of homosexuals is possible."[94] These were not merely earnest phrases but ones indicative of the fact that oppression was understood—and experienced—as multidirectional and interrelated, as was liberation from that oppression. Certainly, concerns over autonomy remained, as seen in the *Tuntenstreit*, with the "male feminists" arguing that personal emancipation was a precondition for collective liberation. Alliances proved hard to build; a case in point was the failure of those same male feminists to win support from the women's movement. Yet this fraught wrangling does not mean that the 1970s gay movement can be conceptualized as a "single-issue" struggle, or one limited to the aim of winning social inclusion for gay men alone. Gerd-Rainer Horn is right to take seriously the "spirit of 1968," which he describes as "a ceaseless effort to construct a different and more egalitarian social order."[95] Though its place in the alternative left was at times somewhat precarious, the West German gay movement was very much part of this effort, part of this historical moment.

Craig Griffiths is a Senior Lecturer in Modern History at Manchester Metropolitan University and is a co-founder and co-convenor of the Seminar Series in the History of Sexuality at the Institute of Historical Research, London. His book, *The Ambivalence of Gay Liberation: Male Homosexual Politics in 1970s West Germany*, was published with Oxford University Press in 2021. His current research investigates the history of human rights through a queer historical lens.

Notes

* For their feedback and advice, I am grateful to the volume's editors, Stephen Milder, Belinda Davis, and Friederike Brühöfener; to Charlotte Faucher; and to the anonymous peer reviewers.
1. Dieter Rucht, "Linksalternatives Milieu und Neue Soziale Bewegungen in der Bundesrepublik: Selbstverständnis und gesellschaftlicher Kontext," in *Linksalternative Milieus und Neue Soziale Bewegungen in den 1970er Jahren*, ed. Cordia Baumann, Sebastian Gehrig, and Nicolas Büchse (Heidelberg: Universitätsverlag, 2011), 35. Unless otherwise stated, all translations are my own.
2. Andreas Pareik, "Kampf um eine Identität: Entwicklung, Probleme, Perspektiven der neuen Homosexuellen-Emanzipationsbewegung am Beispiel der Homosexuelle Aktion Westberlin" (Diploma dissertation, Berlin, 1977).
3. By using this term, I seek to bridge the gap between narrower organizational histories of the "New Left" or "radical left" and the literature on the amorphous networks and spaces that post-1968 protest groups gave rise to, often historicized under the category "milieu." See Sven Reichardt and Detlef Siegfried, eds., *Das alternative Milieu: Antiburgerlicher Lebensstil und linke Politik in der Bundesrepublik Deutschland und Europa 1968–1983* (Göttingen: Wallstein, 2010); Sven Reichardt, *Authentizität und Gemeinschaft: Linksalternatives Leben in den siebziger und frühen achtziger Jahren* (Berlin: Suhrkamp, 2014); and Cordia Baumann, Sebastian Gehrig, and Nicolas Büchse, eds., *Linksalternative Milieus und Neue Soziale Bewegungen in den 1970er Jahren* (Heidelberg: Universitätsverlag Winter, 2011).
4. See further Benno Gammerl, *anders fühlen: Schwules und lesbisches Leben in der Bundesrepublik—eine Emotionsgeschichte* (Munich: Carl Hanser, 2021), 35–140.
5. On the Gay Liberation Fronts in the United States (from 1969) and in London (from 1970), see Emily Hobson, *Lavender and Red: Liberation and Solidarity in the*

Gay and Lesbian Left (Oakland: University of California Press, 2016), and Lucy Robinson, *Gay Men and the Left in Post-war Britain* (Manchester: Manchester University Press, 2007). On France, see Dan Callwood, "Re-evaluating the French Gay Liberation Moment 1968–1983" (PhD thesis, University of London, 2017).

6. Aribert Reimann, "Zwischen Machismo und Coolness: Männlichkeit und Emotion in der westdeutschen 'Kulturrevolution' der 1960er- und 1970er Jahren," in *Die Präsenz der Gefühle: Männlichkeit und Emotion in der Moderne*, ed. Manuel Borutta and Nina Verheyen (Bielefeld: Transcript, 2010), 243.
7. As Marc Stein notes, the riots are often understood, incorrectly, as the first "first act of lesbian and gay resistance *ever*." See his *City of Sisterly and Brotherly Loves: Lesbian and Gay Philadelphia, 1945–1972* (Chicago: University of Chicago Press, 2000), 289.
8. The first such event in Germany took place in Bremen, Stuttgart, Cologne, and West Berlin on 30 June 1979, to mark the tenth anniversary of the Stonewall riots. "Zehn Jahre Stonewall Day," *Emanzipation* 5 (1979): 28–31.
9. Paragraph 175 dates back to the unification of Germany in 1871 but was radicalized by the Nazis in 1935 in order to more easily secure convictions. The 1969 liberalization decriminalized most forms of male homosexuality, setting the age of consent of twenty-one, while a further reform in 1973 reduced this to eighteen. Female homosexuality had never been criminalized. Paragraph 175 was repealed entirely in 1994.
10. I explain the emergence of the commercial gay press and the unfolding of gay liberation in more detail in *The Ambivalence of Gay Liberation: Male Homosexual Politics in 1970s West Germany* (Oxford: Oxford University Press, 2021).
11. According to an annual list kept updated by the Action Group Homosexuality in Bonn. *Addressen zur Schwulenemanzipation* (May 1980), Schwules Museum Berlin archives [hereafter, SMB archive].
12. The case for a link between 1968 and gay liberation is less clear in East Germany, both in terms of the political salience of "1968" and the very possibility of building a social movement. However, according to Josie McLellan, the events of the late 1960s were formative in the development of the gay and lesbian activists who would go on to found the first gay liberation group in Eastern Europe in 1973, the Homosexual Interest Group Berlin. McLellan, "Glad to Be Gay behind the Wall: Gay and Lesbian Activism in 1970s East Germany," *History Workshop Journal* 74 (2012): 107.
13. Kristina Schulz, "Feminist Echoes of 1968: Women's Movements in Europe and the United States," in *A Revolution of Perception? Consequences and Echoes of 1968*, ed. Ingrid Gilcher-Holtey (New York: Berghahn Books, 2014), 141.
14. Herbert Marcuse, *One-Dimensional Man: Studies in the Ideology of Advanced Industrial Society* (New York: Beacon Press, 2002), 260.
15. *du&ich* 5 (1977): 29.
16. HAW "vorläufige Grundsatzerklärung" (November 1971), printed as appendix to *HAW Info* 1 (1972).
17. Peter Schult, "Für eine sexuelle Revolution! Wider die linken Spießer," *Autonomie* 5 (1977): 92.
18. See further Erik Jensen, "The Pink Triangle and Political Consciousness: Gays, Lesbians, and the Memory of Nazi Persecution," *Journal of the History of Sexuality* 11

(2002). Sébastien Tremblay, "'Ich konnte ihren Schmerz körperlich spüren': Die Historisierung der NS–Verfolgung und die Wiederaneignung des Rosa Winkels in der westdeutschen Schwulenbewegung der 1970er Jahre," *Invertito* 21 (2019): 179–202. See also Jake Newsome, *Pink Triangle Legacies: Coming out in the Shadow of the Holocaust* (Ithaca, NY: Cornell University Press, forthcoming).
19. Cited in Dagmar Herzog, *Sex after Fascism: Memory and Morality in Twentieth-Century Germany* (Princeton, NJ: Princeton University Press, 2005), 155, from whom I have adapted this translation.
20. French and Italian activists certainly attended; other nationalities may have too. The HAW sent an English-language letter to British gay activists inviting "Sisters, Friends and Comrades" to the event. Letter dated 25 April 1973, Hall-Carpenter Archives, LSE, Ephemera/222/14.2.
21. Gabriele Dennert, Christiane Leidinger, and Franziska Rauchut, eds., *In Bewegung bleiben: 100 Jahre Politik, Kultur und Geschichte von Lesben* (Berlin: Querverlag, 2007), 47.
22. HAW, "Pfingstaktion '73: Die Unterdrückung der Homosexualität ist nur ein Spezialfall der allgemeinen Sexualunterdrückung" (1973), SMB archive.
23. See *HAW Info* 12 (1973), 16–19. Personal accounts include Andreas, "Meine persönliche HAW-Geschichte," in *Schwule sich emanzipieren lernen: Materialien zur Ausstellung*, ed. Peter Hedenström (Berlin: Rosa Winkel Verlag, 1976), 38–45; and Hans Hermann, "Ausgießung des heiteren Geistes," *him* 9 (1973), 6–7.
24. "Marsch der Lidschatten," *BILD*, 12 June 1973.
25. *HAW Info* 12 (1973), 16–19.
26. Ibid., 17. While this is not explicitly stated in the minutes, it seems that the Italian and French activists were from the fuori! (Fronte Unitario Omosessuale Rivoluzionario Italiano) and FHAR (Front Homosexuel d'Action Révolutionnaire) groups respectively.
27. This section on the *Tuntenstreit* is an adapted and abridged version of *The Ambivalence of Gay Liberation: Male Homosexual Politics in 1970s West Germany*, 166–76. Reproduced by permission of Oxford University Press.
28. Carsten Balzer, "The Beauty and the Beast: Reflections about Socio-historical and Subcultural Context of Drag Queens and 'Tunten' in Berlin," *Journal of Homosexuality* 46 (2004): 60.
29. On Britain, see Jeffrey Weeks, *Coming Out: Homosexual Politics in Britain from the Nineteenth Century to the Present* (New York: Quartet Books, 1990), 202–3. On the United States, see Betty Luther Hillman, "'The Most Profoundly Revolutionary Act a Homosexual Can Engage In': Drag and the Politics of Gender Presentation in the San Francisco Gay Liberation Movement, 1964–1972," *Journal of the History of Sexuality* 20 (2011): 153–81. On France, see Callwood, "Re-evaluating the French Gay Liberation Moment," and Julian Jackson, *Living in Arcadia: Homosexuality, Politics and Morality in France from the Liberation to AIDS* (Chicago: University of Chicago Press, 2009), 188–89.
30. *HAW Info* 12 (1973), 17.
31. Balzer, "Beauty and the Beast," 60.
32. HAW "vorläufige Grundsatzerklärung" (November 1971).

33. Martin Dannecker and Reimut Reiche, *Der gewöhnliche Homosexuelle: Eine soziologische Untersuchung über männliche Homosexuelle in der Bundesrepublik* (Frankfurt a.M.: Fischer Verlag, 1974), 345–76.
34. Ibid., 351 and 356. The data was based on surveys given to 789 homosexuals in 1971.
35. HAW Feministengruppe, "Feministenpapier" (October 1973), SMB archive.
36. Andreas, "Meine persönliche HAW-Geschichte," 40.
37. Ibid., 40.
38. "Feministenpapier," 20.
39. Helmut Ahrens et al., "Die Homosexualität in uns," in *Tuntenstreit: Theoriediskussion der Homosexuellen Aktion Westberlin* (Berlin: Rosa Winkel Verlag, 1975), 29, emphasis in the original. Originally published in *Kursbuch* 37 (1974): 84–112.
40. Edith und ihre Lehrerinnen, "Falsche Unmittelbarkeit? Gedanken zur 'Feministenfrage' von der Pädogogengruppe," *HAW Info* 13 (1974), 25.
41. Ibid., 26.
42. See further Robert Beachy, *Gay Berlin: Birthplace of a Modern Identity* (New York: Knopf, 2014), esp. 85–119.
43. See further Clayton Whisnant, *Male Homosexuality in West Germany: Between Persecution and Freedom 1945–1969* (New York: Palgrave, 2012), esp. 64–111, and Burkhardt Riechers, "Freundschaft und Anständigkeit. Leitbilder im Selbstversttändnis männlicher Homosexueller in der frühen Bundesrepublik," *Invertito: Jahrbuch für die Geschichte der Homosexualitäten* 1 (1999).
44. "Falsche Unmittelbarkeit?" 28.
45. "SDS schreibt an BILD," undated, printed in Astrid Czubayko, *Die Sprache von Studenten- und Alternativbewegung* (Aachen: Shaker, 1997), appendix 24.
46. Oskar Negt and Alexander Kluge, *Öffentlichkeit und Erfahrung: Zur Organisationsanalyse von bürgerlicher und proletarischer Öffentlichkeit* (Frankfurt a.M.: Suhrkamp, 1974 [1972]), 162–63.
47. *HAW Info* 12 (1973), 18 and 19.
48. "Doppelmitgliedschaft" (October 1972), printed as appendix to Pareik, "Kampf um eine Identität," 289–91.
49. Thorsten Graf and Mimi Steglitz [both pseudonyms], "Homosexuellenunterdrückung in der bürgerlichen Gesellschaft," in *Tuntenstreit: Theoriediskussion der Homosexuellen Aktion Westberlin* (Berlin: Rosa Winkel Verlag, 1975), 42. Originally published in *Probleme des Klassenkampfs: Zeitschrift für politische Ökonomie und sozialistische Politik*, 16 (1974): 17–50.
50. Graf and Steglitz, "Homosexuellenunterdrückung," 65 and 66.
51. Helmer, "Briefe an meine freunde, die Feministen!" *HAW Info* 13 (1974), 22–23.
52. Around twenty further members would leave the HAW in the aftermath of the *Tuntenstreit*. See further the introductory editorial note in HAW, *Tuntenstreit* [unpaginated section]. Manfred Herzer used the pseudonym Mimi Steglitz in the piece for *Problems of Class Struggle*.
53. "Es lebe der Feminismus!" *HAW Info* 16 (1974), 32.
54. Thorsten Graf [pseudonym] and Manfred Herzer, "Zur neueren Diskussion über die Homosexualität," *Das Argument: Zeitschrift für Philosophie und Sozialwissenschaften* 93 (1975): 871.

55. Ibid., 871 and 865.
56. Reimut Reiche, *Sexualität und Klassenkampf: Zur Abwehr repressiver Entsublimierung* (Frankfurt a.M.: Neue Kritik, 1968), 17.
57. Jennifer Evans, "Decriminalization, Seduction, and 'Unnatural Desire' in East Germany," *Feminist Studies* 36 (2010): 558.
58. See further Gerd Koenen, *Das rote Jahrzehnt: Unsere kleine deutsche Kulturrevolution, 1967–1977* (Cologne: Kiepenheuer & Witsch, 2001), and Andreas Kühn, *Stalins Enkel, Maos Söhne: Die Lebenswelt der K-Gruppen in der Bundesrepublik der 70er Jahre* (Frankfurt a.M.: Campus, 2005).
59. "Dokumentation: Schriftwechsel zwischen Kommunistischer Bund Westdeutschland und Homosexuelle Aktion Bremen" (March 1974), 3 and 11, SMB archive.
60. See further Joachim Häberlen, "Feeling Like a Child: Dreams and Practices of Sexuality in the West German Alternative Left during the Long 1970s," *Journal of the History of Sexuality* 25 (2016): 219–45.
61. For a fuller discussion, see Griffiths, *Ambivalence of Gay Liberation*, 107–11. Gerd Koenen points out that while older members of the illegal KPD took on most of the leadership roles in the newly constituted DKP, its ranks were filled by much younger activists influenced by the student movement and other parts of the alternative left. *Das rote Jahrzhnt*, 268.
62. "Feministenpapier," 13.
63. Ibid., 19.
64. Nikos Papadogiannis uses the term "dual militancy" in reference to female Communist Party members who also agitated in feminist groups outside of the party. Papadogiannis, *Militant around the Clock? Left-Wing Youth Politics, Leisure, and Sexuality in Post-dictatorship Greece, 1974–1981* (New York: Berghahn Books, 2015), 17.
65. Dennert et al., *In Bewegung bleiben*, 38.
66. Ahrens et al., "Die Homosexualität in uns," 29. The male feminists, of course, rejected this analysis and argued that only (unpoliticized) *Tunten* were guilty of this charge.
67. Cited in Ursula Linhoff, *Weibliche Homosexualität: Zwischen Anpassung und Emanzipation* (Cologne: Kiepenheuer & Witsch, 1976), 129.
68. Golda von Ostheim, "Machen Kleider Leute? Gedanken zum Schwulenfeminismus," *Emanzipation* 5 (1977): 24–25.
69. According to Monica Pater, there even existed a unity between the "Women's/Lesbian movement." Pater, "'Gegen geile Männerpresse—für lesbische Liebe': Der Andersen/Ihns-Prozess als Ausgangspunkt für das Coming-out von Lesben," *Invertito: Jahrbuch der Homosexualitäten* 8 (2006): 144.
70. Magdalena Beljan, *Rosa Zeiten? Eine Geschichte der Subjektivierung männlicher Homosexualität in den 1970er und 1980er Jahren der BRD* (Bielefeld: Transcript, 2014), 19.
71. Victoria Hesford, *Feeling Women's Liberation* (Durham, NC: Duke University Press, 2013), 260.
72. Nancy Fraser, "Rethinking the Public Sphere: A Contribution to the Critique of Actually Existing Democracy," in *Habermas and the Public Sphere*, ed. Craig Calhoun (Cambridge: MIT Press, 1992), 125.
73. See further Michael Warner, *Publics and Counterpublics* (New York: Zone Books, 2002).
74. Cf. the chapter by Bernhard Gotto in this volume.

75. *Schauplatz Gerichtstrasse—Schwulengruppe Bielefeld* (WDR, 30 January 1979), copy in the SMB archive. Roland Lange, "Brühwarm: Der erfüllte Traum von der Selbstverwirklichung," *Emanzipation* 5 (1976): 12–14.
76. On the legacy of the Situationist International in the alternative left more broadly, see Joachim Häberlen, *The Emotional Politics of the Alternative Left: West Germany, 1968–1984* (Cambridge: Cambridge University Press, 2018), 65.
77. "Wir sind schwul," *Stern* 41 (1978); "Wir haben abgetrieben!" *Stern* 24 (1971). Gay activists, especially in the Homosexual Action Hamburg, were centrally involved in recruiting participants for the *Stern* feature. See further "Schwule im Stern: Helden und Mäuschen," *Emanzipation* 3 (1978): 21–22.
78. Fraser, "Rethinking the Public Sphere," 123; Herzog, *Sex after Fascism*, 226.
79. *AHA Info Intern* (December 1978), 6.
80. Ödipus Kollektiv, ed., *Brühwarm: Ein schwuler Jahrmarkt* (1976), SMB archive.
81. See for example Hanno, "Schwule Gruppendynamik: Am Beispiel der Initiativgruppe Homosexualität Tübingen," *Emanzipation* 1 (1976): 2. On consciousness-raising groups in the women's movement, see Bernhard Gotto's contribution to this volume.
82. "Homosexuelle helfen Homosexuellen," *Emanzipation* 6 (1976): 13–16.
83. In 1977, gay cafes called *Anderes Ufer* opened in both Frankfurt and West Berlin. "Anderes Ufer: Ein Kaffeehaus in Berlin," *him* 7 (1977) 18–19; "An's andere Ufer gerettet," *Pflasterstrand* 15 (1977), 30–31.
84. "Die Homosexuelle Aktionsgruppe Nürnberg," *ID* 83 (1975), 8; "Von der Roten Zelle Schwul zum Schwulencafe," *Pflasterstrand* 14 (1978), 35–38; *Blatt* 145 (1979), 14–16 and 27–28; *INFO-BUG* 62 (1975), 6–7; "Rosa Winkel: Historisches Zeichen der Schwulenunterdrückung," *Carlo Sponti* 14/15 (1975), 9.
85. AStA (*Technische Hochschule*, Aachen) to Maczkiewitz-Nigge, 5 December 1973, SMB archive, NARGS box one, folder "Dokumentation Aachener Info-Tisch-Fall."
86. Similarly, Benno Gammerl has shown how, in the recollections of lesbian and gay activists, sexual identity was often closely associated with other political belongings, for example to the peace or environmental movements or the left-alternative milieu. Gammerl, *anders fühlen*, 183.
87. *Schwuchtel* 1 (1975), 1.
88. Ibid., 17.
89. "Wir sind schwul," 108.
90. Michael Schwartz, "'Warum machen Sie sich für die Homos stark?' Homosexualität und Medienöffentlichkeit in der westdeutschen Reformzeit der 1960er und 1970er Jahre," *Jahrbuch Sexualitäten 2016*, ed. Mari Borowski et al. (Göttingen: Wallstein, 2016), 69.
91. *Arbeiterkampf: Kampf der Schwulenunterdrückung!* (n.d.) and AG Schwule im KB, *Schwule Rechte jetzt!* (1979), both SMB archive.
92. HAH, "Ab jetzt gibt's unser Programm: Ein Schwuler kandidiert sich zur Bürgerschaftswahl," SMB archive, folder Hamburg–Schwulenbewegung–HAH.
93. HAH, *Schwulen-info* 1 (April 1978), n.p.
94. Cited in Gustl Angstmann, "Dokumentarische Information der Schwulenbewegung in München 1971–1975, HAG, HAM und Teestube," 2, SMB archive, folder München–Schwulenbewegung–HAG/HAM.

95. Gerd-Rainer Horn, *The Spirit of '68: Rebellion in Western Europe and North America, 1956–1976* (Oxford: Oxford University Press, 2007), 2.

Select Bibliography

Gammerl, Benno. *anders fühlen: Schwules und lesbisches Leben in der Bundesrepublik—eine Emotionsgeschichte*. Munich: Carl Hanser, 2021.
Häberlen, Joachim. *The Emotional Politics of the Alternative Left: West Germany, 1968–1984*. Cambridge: Cambridge University Press, 2018.
Hilman, Betty Luther. "'The most profoundly revolutionary act a homosexual can engage in': Drag and the Politics of Gender Presentation in the San Francisco Gay Liberation Movement, 1964–1972." *Journal of the History of Sexuality* 20 (2011): 153–81.
Homosexuelle Aktion Westberlin. *Tuntenstreit: Theoriediskussion der Homosexuellen Aktion Westberlin*. Berlin: Rosa Winkel, 1975.
Reichardt, Sven and Detlef Siegfried, eds. *Das alternative Milieu: Antiburgerlicher Lebensstil und linke Politik in der Bundesrepublik Deutschland und Europa 1968–1983*. Göttingen: Wallstein, 2010.
Warner, Michael. *Publics and Counterpublics*. New York: Zone Books, 2002.

Chapter 11

Radical Protest or Shadow Diplomacy?

The Decolonization of Zimbabwe and West German Maoism, 1960–80

David Spreen

In January 1977, a few months before hostilities between the Red Army Faction (RAF) and the West German state culminated in the "German Autumn," an employee of the German consulate in Durban, South Africa, encountered an article in the *Daily News*. The paper claimed that a Portuguese ship had just left Durban with unexpected cargo from Hamburg, Germany: three armored "combat vehicles" (albeit without arms), apparently a gift of the Communist League of West Germany (KBW) to "terrorist leader" Robert Mugabe, then based in Maputo, Mozambique. Not to be blindsided, the consulate reached out to a high-ranking official of the South African security police for information. They learned the following: the sender of the freight was indeed the KBW, but the vehicles were not, as claimed by the *Daily News*, of German make. Instead, they had been shipped from Sweden to Hamburg, where they were transferred to the Portuguese ship. Large posters that depicted "a black man and a black woman of the liberation movement" decorated the side of the vehicles. A KBW solidarity address to the Zimbabwe African National Union (ZANU) was printed on another poster.[1]

The event caused an uproar in South Africa, and the German consulate reported the story to the West German Foreign Office, which directed it to the interior minister. Because it seemed unlikely to both the South African security forces and the German consulate that the KBW had the means to purchase and ship military equipment across the globe, the Foreign Office asked the Interior Ministry to comment on the likelihood that the vehicles were actually bought by East Germany or the Soviet Union.[2] Both the Federal Criminal Police and the West German intelligence service, the Federal Office for the Protection of the Constitution (Bundesamt für Verfassungsschutz), were aware of KBW publications stating that the organization had collected money to support ZANU's armed liberation struggle.[3] In fact, the KBW had already shipped several Land Rovers to ZANU in 1975 and was in the process of raising money for guns for ZANU's armed wing—the Zimbabwe African National Liberation Army (ZANLA).[4]

It was unlikely, however, that the money came from the East Germans. Ideologically, the KBW—and other West German Maoists—were born of a Left that looked to China as an alternative to the Moscow-centric communist world. While material support during the Cold War did cross ideological lines, the East German Ministry for State Security (or Stasi) was well aware that support for Mugabe was in part motivated by the KBW's hostility to Moscow and East Berlin. In somewhat characteristic hyperbole, a 1978 ministry report exaggerated the KBW's motivation in raising money for Mugabe into the organization's chief ideological tendency: to mobilize the "Third World" against the Soviet Union and, by implication, the German Democratic Republic (GDR).[5] This report came after years of Stasi concern over the purported antisocialist activities of West German Maoists—sometimes exaggerated to the level of a conspiracy theory, in which Maoist parties themselves were imagined as an arm of the West German state.[6]

This chapter considers the relationship between West German Maoists and African decolonial movements as a dimension of West German activism after '68 that is neither easily assimilated into the formalistic determinations of New Social Movement theory nor consistent with the single-issue politics usually attributed to the extraparliamentary politics of the 1970s: the case of global Maoism.[7] With their rigid organizational structures, reputation for Marxist-Leninist dogmatism, and overt distaste for de-Stalinization, Maoist parties in the Federal Republic of Germany (FRG) defy many clichés about the activism of the 1970s.[8] Ostensibly neither "bottom-up" nor "undogmatic," Maoist parties have been portrayed as exceptions to the creative explosion of the "Global Sixties" and the pragmatic, issue-oriented, politics of the 1970s.[9] But Maoists were a substantial part of the 1970s West German Left, with an estimated eighty to one hundred thousand people coming through these parties or one of their numerous mass organizations throughout the decade.[10] More importantly, Maoists figured prominently in many of the 1970s campaigns that are now associated with the new social movements: the mobilizations against the "abortion paragraph" (§218) of West Germany's criminal code and the occupations of nuclear power plant construction sites. Maoists used both national and transnational networks to connect separate movements and citizens initiatives into what they hoped would be a global revolutionary movement sparked and made meaningful by decolonization and the global Cold War.

By foregrounding the collaboration between the KBW and Zimbabwean decolonial actors, this chapter argues that decolonization caused a decisive—and still often overlooked—transformation of the postwar Left in West Germany.[11] Similar to other facets of West German culture in the 1960s and 1970s, the Left took on an increasingly global perspective. But, as I have argued elsewhere, "global" did not mean boundless. Access to what some have described as a community of "global Maoism" differed between and within countries and was heavily mediated by a set of select transnational brokers.[12] Few West German Maoists were privileged enough to travel to Southern Africa or work with Zimbabweans at the KBW's printing press. More than anything, the Zimbabwe campaign depended on Zimbabwean brokers in Europe; they were the ones who took ownership of revolutionary politics in the European metropole. Students from Southern Africa traveling across Europe built networks of solidarity, and the Zimbabweans generally set the tone of the Maoist campaign. The KBW brought these causes into seemingly unrelated environmental or reproductive rights campaigns. In this light, what might have appeared to some West German activists as Marxist-Leninist dogmatism was—at least in part—also a shift of political and moral authority from the Global North to the Global South. If KBW activists were inflexible with West German activists in meetings and at protest sites, they also supported ZANU's demand that Zimbabweans be "their own liberators" while raising money and providing logistical support, technical skills training, and—eventually—an industrial printing facility and communications system to ZANU headquarters in Mozambique.[13]

Maoists' complete and utter failure to appeal to West Germany's working class has often been taken as a cause for ridicule; but this chapter suggests that their appeal and consequent numerical strength in the 1970s can nonetheless be explained: the KBW's collaboration with those who, by 1980, had become state actors in an independent Zimbabwe emerged from the decolonial contexts that undergirded much of 1960s radicalism and threw Maoists headfirst into the global Cold War. Maoist solidarity involved a bottom-up form of diplomacy, similar to what Christian Helm calls "people-to-people diplomacy" in his chapter on Nicaragua solidarity work in this volume. Maoists presented themselves abroad as representatives of an alternative "socialist" West Germany to such an extent that they could appear as "diplomatic competition" to the German state. Of course, most West German Maoists were not directly involved and worked on other campaigns: the attempts to mobilize West German workers inside factories and soldiers within the army, the campaign against West Germany's restrictive abortion law, or opposition to nuclear energy. Nonetheless, the Zimbabwe campaign alongside other solidarity campaigns (for Chile, for Iranians in Europe, for Albania) infused Maoists' work with significance that went far beyond revolutionary fantasy.

Due to the nature of available sources, literature on New Left solidarity continues to disproportionately focus on the agency of West German activists. But as Christian Helm has also demonstrated, solidarity was not a one-way street: In the case of the KBW's Zimbabwe campaign, the relationship itself was the result of ZANU's European networking activities, and Zimbabweans were able to assert both their specific material needs and their critique of the KBW's dogmatic adherence to Chinese foreign policy.[14] Moreover, the assertiveness of students and actors from the Global South toward the West German Left did not begin with 1970s Maoism. Indeed, the story of Maoism as a global, decolonial, and postcolonial Left was the culmination of a longer history of African decolonization and German attention to it running from the Algerian War to the breakup of Portugal's African empire.

Navigating a Changing World: African Decolonization on Campus

Although Germany surrendered its colonies in the aftermath of World War I, decolonization was part of daily reality in the two Germanies in the late 1950s and early 1960s. African decolonization became a diplomatic and ideological battleground for German-German competition, and both states evoked powerful memories of Germany's own colonial legacies. As a number of historians have demonstrated, East German commitments to national liberation in the 1960s cannot be divorced from the GDR's attempts to secure international recognition and to circumvent West Germany's Hallstein doctrine, by which the FRG attempted to forestall other countries from diplomatically recognizing the existence of a second German state.[15] Conversely, West German interest in Africa was at least partially motivated by a fear of communism gaining ground in the newly decolonizing world and a desire to develop and preserve trading relationships with African states. In an interview with *Der Spiegel*, Bundestag president Eugen Gerstenmaier was asked whether decolonization meant that there was a danger that Africa might "fall back into hereditary anarchy." His response: "I believe the worst thing that could happen in Africa would be the replacement of colonial domination with the dictatorship of communism."[16]

Gerstenmaier served as the first president of the West German Africa Society (Afrika-Gesellschaft), set up in 1956 with the support of the Foreign

Office. While the central significance of German colonialism for an understanding of modern German history is a relatively recent insight within the historiography,[17] the legacies of German colonialism were ubiquitous in the context of African decolonization: the Africa Society, for example, felt that contemporary young Germans lacked the kinds of professional opportunities in Africa they had had before 1914, and thus, the society embarked on a campaign to host "Africa Weeks" around the country in the early 1960s.[18]

In October 1960, the Africa Society organized the first German Africa Week. It consisted of fifty events, which took place across twenty-eight cities and included lectures as well as various art and cultural exhibits. Some 171 guests from several African countries took part. The event was met with immediate criticism. In West Germany, the older Africa Club (Afrika Verein) mounted attacks from both the Right and the Left. The Africa Club worried that Africa Week might alienate white Africans and hurt trade relations, but its members also likened the speaking tours and cultural events to a modern *Völkerschau*—a practice that began in the nineteenth century and only ended in the 1950s whereby German zoos exhibited so-called "natural peoples" to gawking audiences.[19] Naturally, East German officials were quick to condemn the West German events as nothing more than a thinly veiled form of neocolonialism. But of course, their own "Africa efforts," as genuine as they may have been, also had to contend with racist sentiments from within the East German population and bureaucracy.[20]

These critiques notwithstanding, at the local level, Africa Weeks provided an opening for West German engagement with its colonial legacies. Only a month after the first official Africa Week, the University of Freiburg—located near the French and Swiss borders in Germany's southwest—held its own version. In a newsletter distributed by the executive committee of the student government, the officer for information on Africa and Asia poignantly explained the need for more attention to the continent in a way that almost prophetically described the later trajectory of the student movement:

> Political education is mostly limited to topics that concern Germany or perhaps Europe. But the world-political developments of today force us to see in new dimensions. The question is no longer: What does this mean for Germany? But what does this mean for the world?[21]

The article went on to argue that the present was a period of global transformation and that these transformations were most prominent in Africa, Asia, and South America. Concretely, national economies were in the process of being transformed into global economies. The article optimistically called for students to learn about non-European cultures, study African languages, and start seeing Africans as equal partners.

None of this is to say that the article (and others beyond it) was free of condescension. Much of the later part of the text was dedicated to the need to educate West German experts who could take part in development efforts in Africa. The article also maintained that partnership with Africans required West Germans to avoid not only underestimating them but also to avoid overestimating them. The overall tone left little doubt about the nature and direction of the "partnership" that compelled students to learn about "African culture" so that they could take on the role of experts in developing countries. This attitude did not go entirely unchallenged, however. In their issue on Africa Week, the *Freiburger Studentenzeitung* praised the occurrence because "solidarity events matching Africa Week in effort and diligence had been a rare occasion before" and the turnout was encouraging: three hundred students had shown up. Nonetheless, the article also remarked that African culture had probably been received more as an interesting curiosity, making an end to talk of "primitives" and "illiterates" unlikely in the near future. Condemning claims of "Africa having no history," which the Africa Week was unlikely to have adequately contradicted, the author still remained hopeful that the event was the beginning and not the end of new interest in the African continent.[22]

The nascent New Left developed its own interest in Africa early on: starting in the 1950s, the Algerian Revolution put Africa on the map for a few left-wing journalists. In 1958, Klaus Rainer Röhl's *konkret* first published articles by Algerians directly involved with the Front de Libération Nationale (FLN).[23] Critical voices from France, particularly Jean-Paul Sartre, were published as well. At the same time, university landscapes were changing dramatically. The number of students from Africa and Asia at West German universities grew by a factor of sixty from 1951 to 1963.[24] Similarly, the number of students from Africa, Asia, and Latin America studying at universities in the United States grew sharply in the 1960s and 1970s.[25] Although fewer in terms of absolute numbers, forty-four thousand people from the Global South studied in East Germany. In the early 1960s, most came from West Africa, although the GDR's priorities shifted with the geopolitics of the Cold War in the Global South.[26] In December 1959, the University of Freiburg's student newspaper dedicated a whole issue to the emergence of African countries on the world stage. Fifteen years later, Freiburg would become an important base of operations for the KBW.[27]

Throughout the 1950s, the Freiburg student paper concerned itself with politics only to the extent that they directly affected student life, with the notable exception of regular articles about the "all-German question." But even here, the conditions for students in East Germany were the central concern. In December 1959, however, the paper tried something new: "to explore the problems of our foreign colleagues and let them contribute themselves."[28] The stated impetus was the ongoing Algerian War of Independence. The opening article complained that in the daily newspapers, politics were still understood exclusively in terms of the conflict between East and West: "But too easily—and sometimes happily—do we overlook that for years the peripheral regions of civilization have developed their own political life, which impacts upon the inner structures of our alliances and ultimately changes them."[29] Setting aside, for a moment, the language describing Algeria as "the edge of civilization," students raised the issue of a new political force in the world that would have a profound influence on the trajectories of the Cold War. In explaining the purpose of the issue, the *Freiburger Studentenzeitung* wondered if anybody had ever stopped to think about where the nearly twenty thousand foreign students would go when their German colleagues went home for Christmas.[30]

Soon, more serious concerns took center stage. The early 1960s were crucial years for the global Cold War as well, including the speedy breakdown of Sino-Soviet relations.[31] More importantly, they witnessed two events with major relevance for African and Asian students in West Germany. Following the death of Patrice Lumumba and a shutdown of Tehran University, students took to the streets in what Quinn Slobodian has designated "the first major intervention of African and Asian students and their first appearance in West German streets."[32]

War of Liberation Abroad: Zimbabwean Activists in Europe

Not only did students from Asia and Africa come to study at universities, but both German states also provided them with training grants to come to Europe and learn a variety of trades. In the case of West Germany and Zimbabwe, this was part of a complex double strategy. On the one hand, West German policy toward Southern Rhodesia after the unilateral declaration of independence by Ian Smith's white minority regime favored neutrality over anticolonial commitment. Despite officially supporting Black self-government in Southern Africa, the West German government also committed to noninterference in the Zimbabwean War of Independence. Furthermore, as several UN Security Council resolutions first condemned and then imposed sanctions on the Smith regime, West Germany—an observer, but not full member of the UN until 1973—did not ratify sanctions against

Rhodesia.[33] On the other hand, West Germany did provide funding for Zimbabwean war refugees to come to Germany via Mozambique, Zambia, and Botswana. When Robert Mugabe embarked on his first official visit to the Federal Republic in 1982, the government was optimistic: since independence, the relationship between West Germany and Zimbabwe had developed in a positive direction. West Germany's recognition of the new state and support for the reconstruction efforts after the War of Independence had supposedly endeared it to the Black majority government. More importantly, Mugabe's government supposedly remembered the generosity of West German stipends to Zimbabweans during the war.[34] In 1979, records from the Federal Ministry for Economic Cooperation and Development's "Southern Africa" program showed that 273 trainees from Southern Africa were currently in West Germany—the vast majority of them coming from "Rhodesia" via third countries.[35]

The story of Maoist solidarity with Zimbabwean activists did not begin in the minds of West German activists but with the organizing of Zimbabwean students in Europe. Before coming to London to study at the Institute of Transport, Rex Chiwara had been a shunter for Zambian Railways. He took over ZANU's London office as its representative to Western Europe in 1972.[36] As was the case for the West German Maoist parties and their predecessors in the student movement, ZANU built on (and sometimes inherited) the accomplishment of prior Zimbabwean student organizations.[37] The London office was originally founded by the Southern Rhodesian African National Congress. The office was passed on first to the National Democratic Party, and then later the Zimbabwe African People's Union (ZAPU). In 1963, the leader of the London office sided with ZANU against ZAPU, and thus transformed it into ZANU's London office.[38] The office became one of the hubs for organizing Zimbabwean nationalists in the United Kingdom—but not the only one: the Chinese embassy in London received ZANU representatives for social occasions, much like its representation in East Berlin received West German Maoists.[39] ZANU's China orientation also created natural collaborators among other liberation movements. ZANU shared its office with the South African Pan African Congress—another partner party of the KBW—as well as the National Union for the Total Independence of Angola.[40] The milieu of Zimbabwean nationalist activists also included ZAPU cadres and members of the Zimbabwe Student Union. After Ian Smith signed the Unilateral Declaration of Independence in 1965, Black Zimbabwean women and men—some of whom had fought as guerrillas or were trained to fight—came to Britain, often as students.[41] They worked with solidarity activists who organized speaking opportunities and helped with fundraising. This did not mean, however, that their efforts remained limited to the far Left. Some found a platform on the BBC and worked with Labour Party members of parliament. Already at the center of solidarity activity in Western Europe, Chiwara visited the KBW in 1974.

To celebrate the anniversaries of Guinea-Bissau's declaration of independence and the one-year anniversary of the commencement of Mozambique's War of Independence—on 24 and 25 September 1974 respectively—several European solidarity networks had decided at an April 1974 meeting in Oxford to host a solidarity week in their respective countries. During these events, Rex Chiwara met with KBW cadres in Mannheim on 24 September to solicit donations for several Land Rovers. The vehicles were crucial for the military campaign waged by ZANU's armed wing, ZANLA, in Southern Rhodesia. In October, the KBW's newspaper published a statement by ZANU chairman Herbert Chitepo, in which he wove together a narrative of the history of colonialism and resistance in Southern Rhodesia, alongside a letter to the KBW by Rex Chiwara referencing the 24 September meeting and urging the organization to raise money for at least two vehicles. Next to Chiwara's letter was also an urgent call from KBW chairman Joscha Schmierer to answer Chiwara's appeal.[42] Approximately one month later, the Committee for Southern Africa published its first special issue on Zimbabwe, including Chiwara's letter.[43] Thus began the relationship between ZANU and the KBW.

While the KBW was in charge of organization and logistics in West Germany, the Zimbabweans nonetheless repeatedly asserted their authority over the terms of the campaign. During the following six years, the KBW coordinated a number of fundraising and information campaigns, printed the *Zimbabwe News*, and shipped the newspaper to ZANU offices in Maputo, and met with ZANU representatives in England and West Germany. Donation campaigns ranged from collecting medical equipment and clothing to raising money for vehicles, and supporting the purchase of weapons for a "fully motorized company of the Zimbabwe National Liberation Army."[44] The success of these campaigns stemmed in part from the rigorous organization of regular fundraising events across the country and multiple speaking tours with representatives of ZANU, including its founder, Ndabaningi Sithole, and later president Robert Mugabe. Yet, in meetings with the KBW leadership, ZANU leaders repeatedly cautioned the KBW not to elevate Chinese doctrine over the interests of African peoples struggling for liberation. At a long discussion between the KBW's chairman and founding ZANU member Herbert Ushewokunze, the latter warned that China based its foreign policy too narrowly on the rejection of Soviet policy and ran the risk of undermining revolution in African states. Although the KBW continued to support Chinese foreign policy, there is every indication that they heeded the Zimbabwean advice to stay in their lane. But Ushewokunze had further-reaching critiques of the solidarity campaign: The production of the *Zimbabwe News* in Frankfurt am Main meant that too much of the money raised for armed struggle was now being spent on the newspaper. He urged a solution that would respect the "West German working class"—after all, the German donors believed they had given money to support a military campaign.[45] As a result, ZANU and the KBW together built a printing facility in Maputo, which was moved to Harare after independence in 1980.

"Guns for the Youth of Zimbabwe": The KBW's Campaign to Support ZANU

The relationship between the KBW, ZANU, and the West German government became tense in 1977–78. In 1977, the KBW started a new campaign to "equip a fully motorized company of ZANLA," but it faced legal challenges in multiple West German states—the most successful of which ended in the seizure of a KBW bank account containing over 100,000 Deutschmark (DM) by the regional government in Tübingen. After the seizure, donations continued to trickle into the account for about a month, such that the total amount held by the government amounted to DM 120,359.45. While both the KBW and ZANU battled the seizure in court, the KBW continued its collection. The result was that the confiscated funds only amounted to approximately 10 percent of the total money raised. By November 1978, nearly DM 800,000 had been transferred to ZANU, and an additional couple of hundred thousand DM were spent on shipping costs for material donations, telex communications, and the reproduction of ZANU materials. In other words, in 1978 alone, the KBW raised in excess of DM 1 million to support Robert Mugabe's forces.[46]

The West German state originally based its seizure of the account on article 26, paragraph 1 of the constitution, which, it argued, rendered all actions that endangered or disturbed a state of peace unconstitutional.[47] The KBW's lawyers argued, by contrast, that article 26 meant that foreign policy was bound by international law. Moreover, since 1970, Germany was bound, despite its blanket abstentions on this matter, by several UN resolutions that legitimized "armed struggle" when it served the purpose of establishing national self-determination and liberation from colonial and foreign domination.[48]

The most remarkable argument made by the state, however, was that support for ZANU in the civil war conflicted with the foreign policy of the Federal Republic, thereby elevating the KBW to a competing diplomatic body. In parallel suits in other federal states, the Foreign Office at first refused to comment on the matter but then argued that the KBW's fundraising campaigns interfered with the federal government's ambition to find peaceful resolutions to conflicts in Southern Africa. Accordingly, outside support for armed conflict endangered the Federal Republic's foreign policy objectives, which included an end to racist discrimination and the eventual independence of Zimbabwe. The fundraising campaign had to be prohibited because of this conflict.[49]

Unsurprisingly, the KBW disagreed with this interpretation, not because it denied that its position was at odds with the official West German position on the conflict in Zimbabwe but rather because the conflict itself was irrelevant. According to the KBW's lawyers, laws pertaining to the foreign policy of the federal government regulated which state offices had the right to represent the Federal Republic abroad (and here, the Foreign Office had an exclusive right), but these laws did not apply to nonstate actors. Furthermore, the KBW's lawyers argued that according to international law, there could not be any relationship between the Federal Republic and the internationally unrecognized Rhodesian state, which thus meant that there could not be any outside interference in that relationship.[50]

What does it mean that the state essentially treated the KBW campaign as an alternative foreign policy? It is tempting to dismiss the state's legal argument as merely strategic: after all, the state's attorneys mobilized a whole range of arguments to keep the campaign money frozen, and ultimately, the KBW failed to achieve a suspension of the injunction.[51] A parallel legal challenge by ZANU—which avoided the political challenges inherent to the KBW's line of argumentation by simply claiming that the money was raised before the campaign had been prohibited, and thus the government was now in possession of funds that were already the property of ZANU—failed as well.[52] Nonetheless, in some ways, the West Germans got to have it both ways.

Perhaps inadvertently, the seizure of the campaign assets—supported by the federal Foreign Ministry—made a spectacle of the state's commitment to cracking down on armed struggle. From a foreign policy perspective, this was certainly an important signal—both because of West Germany's own struggle with political violence in the 1970s, which led the FRG to seek an international antiterror consensus,[53] and the country's ongoing desire to not alienate economic partners in South Africa.[54] Simultaneously, the DM 100,000 seized represented only a fraction of the millions that the KBW raised for ZANU. Despite the ongoing legal battle, in fact, the fundraising campaign and collaboration with the Zimbabwe African National Union continued without inhibition. On the contrary, considering the construction of printing facilities in Maputo, it is fair to say the campaign picked up steam.

The KBW was able to mobilize seemingly disparate movements to support ZANU both politically and financially, not least due to a characteristic that proved an annoyance for much of the non-Maoist Left in West Germany: the KBW's propensity to infiltrate solidarity groups, *Bürgerinitiativen* (citizens initiatives), and neighborhood committees in an attempt to bring them closer to the party line. Here, the party's organizational structure meant that KBW members' presence in many different local and regional initiatives allowed them to carry their campaigns into seemingly unrelated contexts. In 1978, for example, the KBW's paper proudly reported that the Citizens Initiative against Nuclear Power Plants Hildesheim, the Coordinating Committee of the Working Group Against Nuclear Power Göttingen, the Citizens Initiative "No Nuclear Power Plant in the Bay of Eckernförde," and the Working Group Against Nuclear Power Salzgitter had all donated to the campaign to support ZANLA. Moreover, several of them passed resolutions in support of ZANLA.[55]

A press clipping held by the Federal Ministry for Education and Science described a similar action: students at the University of Cologne had initiated a boycott of their cafeteria in response to excessive prices. The student government set up an emergency booth selling soup to offset the deficit caused by the boycott. Unfortunately for them, the KBW-affiliated student organization Communist University Group (KHG) set up its own booth selling sandwiches and drinks. The article, published in the local *Kölner Stadtanzeiger* and titled "Geld Floss in den Urwald" (Money flowed into the jungle), alleged that the KHG raised around DM 10,000, while the student government operated at a loss of DM 16,000. Worse than that, the money was no longer available to benefit the students but had disappeared into the "jungle of Rhodesia."[56] Now, the student government sought legal action against the KHG, which proved difficult because it was unclear who was responsible for the group. A KHG brochure criticizing a variety of Africa-related seminars and classes at the university had a different version of the story: according to the brochure, a general assembly of the student body had approved a proposal by the KHG and other student groups involved in the boycott to send the proceeds from the sale of the sandwiches to ZANU.[57] Whichever version is true, the KHG certainly made no secret of its ongoing campaign for the recognition of ZANU by the federal government and its support for the armed liberation of Zimbabwe.

What did the campaign mean to activists from Zimbabwe and the KBW? With respect to the funds, the case was not decided until 1980, when the West German government sought to establish official relations with the newly independent nation of Zimbabwe, and the funds were released.[58] By that time, Maoism's influence on the West German Left was in serious decline. Still, the KBW was the only West German organization (other than the official government delegation) invited to the official events marking Zimbabwean independence.[59] When Mugabe visited West Germany in 1982, he insisted on meeting with a selection of solidarity activists that had helped ZANU before independence; to the anger of West German officials, this group included a KBW delegation.[60] Although officials thought the KBW delegation's inclusion might undermine the goals of the state visit, they decided against an attempt to persuade Mugabe to cancel the meeting because such a step was unlikely to succeed and might upset Mugabe.[61] A memo preparing the chancellor for the visit pointed out that Mugabe would not miss any opportunity to mention that while the KBW had brought him to West Germany already in 1976, neither the government nor the major parties would meet with him at that time.[62] Even the irritated officials planning Mugabe's visit recognized that Mugabe was showing gratitude to those that had helped him when nobody else would, and that this period was now over.[63] Indeed, ZANU's relationship with the KBW had caused the Zimbabweans problems before. On several occasions before independence, the Ministry of the Interior had denied ZANU representatives entry visas due to their close relationship with the KBW.[64] When ZANU sought to establish an office in Bonn, the internal Foreign Office memos mentioned ZANU's militancy and connection to the KBW as reasons to deny the request.[65] In a complaint to the West German government, ZANU explained that when they sought to establish relationships in Western Europe, the KBW was the only organization willing to help. Now that ZANU had a realistic expectation of governing in the near future, their relationship with the KBW would become increasingly unimportant.[66] In turn, the KBW (despite its insignificant working-class membership) was allowed to stand in for West German working-class radicalism abroad—a circumstance perhaps best encapsulated by an article in the *Zimbabwe News* about the West German government impounding funds "collected from German workers."[67]

Conclusion

Working within numerous campaigns, initiatives, and solidarity committees, West German Maoists had the infrastructure and reach to mobilize people from all different political backgrounds and engage them in a wide variety of campaigns in support of the Zimbabwe African National Union and thus for the decolonization of Southern Africa. But rather than arbitrarily bringing together different "single issues," the KBW understood its activities as a return to revolutionary politics in the context of a global revolutionary movement. Indeed, the story of West German Maoism's interactions with African decolonization built on a much longer history of people from the Global South asserting themselves within the West German postwar Left.

Yet the KBW's relationship with movements in the Global South also demands a reevaluation of the bifurcation of the post-1960s Left in West Germany into a dogmatic and an undogmatic wing. If Maoists appeared ideologically inflexible in encounters at antinuclear protests or in solidarity committee meetings, the KBW nonetheless yielded leadership to Zimbabwean activists who had approached them in the first place. This may well be because, measured by their ambition to be the revolutionary party of the West German working class, parties like the KBW were a complete failure. Some legitimacy, though, alongside their real contributions to seemingly liberal causes like reproductive choice and environmental protection, came from the decolonial context of the postwar Left and their subsequent entanglement in the diplomacies of the global Cold War—a situation both enabled by the West German state's repressive measures and validated by its later attempt to redefine Maoist diplomacy as West German generosity.

David Spreen is Assistant Professor of history at Harvard University where he is also resident faculty at the Minda de Gunzburg Center for European Studies and a faculty affiliate at the Weatherhead Center for International Affairs. Before coming to Harvard, he was a Postdoc at the Berlin Program for Advanced German and European Studies at the Freie Universität Berlin. He received his Ph.D. with his dissertation "Dear Comrade Mugabe: Decolonization and Radical Protest in Divided Germany, 1960-1980" from the University of Michigan in 2019.

Notes

* The author would like to thank Quinn Slobodian for suggesting the term "shadow diplomacy" at a conference many years ago. Many thanks also to Dzingai Mutumbuka and Anton Mlynczak for taking the time to speak with me; Timothy Scarnecchia, Friederike Bruehoefener, Belinda Davis, Stephen Milder for providing valuable feedback; and Julia Sittmann for editing the manuscript. Johanna Folland has read countless iterations of this work, and the project this chapter is drawn from was deeply impacted by her own scholarship and thinking about the Cold War. Funding for the research leading to this chapter has been provided by the Berlin Program for Advanced German and European Studies at the Freie Universität Berlin, the Central European History Society, as well as the Department of History and the Rackham School of Graduate Studies at the University of Michigan. Conclusions and mistakes are mine.

1. Bundesarchiv (hereafter BArch), B 106/124172, Deutsches Konsulat in Durban to Auswärtiges Amt, 25 January 1977.
2. BArch, B 106/124172, Auswärtiges Amt to Bundesministerium des Innern, 17 February 1977.
3. BArch, B 106/124172, Bundeskriminalamt to Bundesministerium des Innern, 17 March 1977; BArch, B 106/124172, Bundesamt für Verfassungsschutz to Bundesminister des Innern, 18 March 1977.
4. See "Kleider für die ZANU," *Kommunistische Volkszeitung*, 23 January 1975, 13; Archiv Außerparlamentarische Opposition und Soziale Bewegungen (APO-Archiv hereafter), APO-KBW 023 "Aufstellung: ZANU—Sammlungen," 14 July 1978.
5. BArch, MfS, HA II, Nr. 28979, "Operativ-Information B/346/11/78 über die materielle Unterstützung des bewaffneten Kampfes der 'Patriotischen Front' von Zimbabwe durch den 'Kommunistischen Bund Westdeutschlands' (KBW)," 2 November 1978, 3.
6. BArch, MfS, ZKG, Nr. 648, "Einschätzung der Jüngsten Aktivitäten der Maoistischen Kräfte und die sich daraus für das MfS ergebenden spezifischen Gegenmaßnahmen," 3 June 1975, 82. On the Stasi's theory of "political ideological diversion," which often combined China, the United States, West Germany, and various opposition movements and cultural groups (including the Esperanto Society) into one monolithic enemy, see Andreas Glaeser, *Political Epistemics: The Secret Police, the Opposition, and the End of East German Socialism* (Chicago: University of Chicago Press, 2011). It is, however, true that in the early 1960s, West German intelligence sought to briefly exploit the Sino-Soviet split to divide the East German Socialist Unity Party (SED). See Mascha Jacoby, "Frei Haus: Wie der Verfassungsschutz Anfang der Sechzigerjahre den Maoismus verbreitete," in *Ein kleines rotes Buch: Die "Mao-Bibel" und die Bücher-Revolution der Sechzigerjahre*, ed. Anke Jaspers, Claudia Michalski, and Morten Paul (Berlin: Matthes & Seitz, 2018), 117–30. This, however, did not mean that the West German state displayed any strategic "leniency" toward the Maoist organizations of the 1970s. See David Spreen, "Dear Comrade Mugabe: Decolonization and Radical Protest in Divided Germany, 1960–1980" (PhD diss., University of Michigan, 2019), 76–139.
7. On global Maoism, see Julia Lovell, *Maoism: A Global History* (London: Bodley Head, 2019); Alexander C. Cook, *Mao's Little Red Book: A Global History* (Cambridge: Cambridge University Press, 2014).
8. Some former participants have since taken the "authoritarian" character of Maoist cadre parties to mean that the Left of the 1960s prefigured the authoritarianism of the 1970s. See Götz Aly, *Unser Kampf: 1968—ein irritierter Blick zurück* (Frankfurt a.M.: Fischer, 2008); Gerd Koenen, *Das rote Jahrzehnt: Unsere kleine deutsche Kulturrevolution, 1967–1977* (Cologne: Kiepenheuer & Witsch, 2001). But even some scholarly literature—if it considered Maoists at all—has reproduced the idea of Maoism as a mere exception to the creative possibilities of the 1960s and 1970s Left. See, for example, Timothy Scott Brown, *West Germany and the Global Sixties: The Antiauthoritarian Revolt, 1962–1978* (Cambridge: Cambridge University Press, 2013).
9. To the extent that Maoism features as part of the Global Sixties, authors usually focus on the student movement's loose appropriations of Mao imagery and pro-

Chinese iconography. See, for example, Sebastian Gehrig, "(Re-)Configuring Mao: Trajectories of a Culturo-Political Trend in West Germany," *Transcultural Studies* 2, no. 2 (2011): 189–231. Quinn Slobodian's more recent typography of "Maoisms" is an exception to this trend. See Quinn Slobodian, "The Meanings of Western Maoism," in *The Routledge Handbook of the Global Sixties: Between Protest and Nation-Building*, ed. Chen Jian et al. (Abingdon: Routledge, 2018), 67–78.
10. See Koenen, *Das rote Jahrzehnt*.
11. Rita Chin has called for a much more thorough consideration of the effects of postwar waves of decolonization on the European New Lefts. See Rita Chin, "European New Lefts, Global Connections, and the Problem of Difference," in *A New Insurgency: The Port Huron Statement and its Times*, ed. Howard Brick and Gregory Parker (Ann Arbor, MI: Maize Books, 2015), 354–67. Quinn Slobodian's study of foreign students in the early 1960s is a start, but for Slobodian, the impact of foreign students subsides in the aftermath of the shooting of Benno Ohnesorg. See Quinn Slobodian, *Foreign Front: Third World Politics in Sixties West Germany* (Durham, NC: Duke University Press, 2012). For an argument about the role of people from the Global South on the French "New Radical Left," see Christoph Kalter, *The Discovery of the Third World: Decolonization and the Rise of the New Left in France, c.1950–1976* (Cambridge: Cambridge University Press, 2019).
12. See David Spreen, "Signal Strength Excellent in West Germany: Radio Tirana, European Maoist Internationalism and its Disintegration in the Global Seventies," *European Review of History: Revue européenne d'histoire* (forthcoming). For an argument about transnational intermediaries, see also Andrew Tompkins, "Grassroots Transnationalism(s): Franco-German Opposition to Nuclear Energy in the 1970s," *Contemporary European History* 25, no. 1 (2016): 117–42. For the argument that Maoism was a transnational community co-constructed by Maoists around the world, see Robeson Taj Frazier, *The East Is Black: Cold War China in the Black Radical Imagination* (Durham, NC: Duke University Press, 2015).
13. In retrospect, the KBW may have inadvertently contributed to a narrative in which ZANU-PF claimed ownership over Zimbabwean independence with far-reaching political implications. This claim to ownership has been enabled by a historiography that focuses narrowly on ZANU leaders and the guerrilla war. The classic example of this is David Martin and Phyllis Johnson, *The Struggle for Zimbabwe: The Chimurenga War* (London: Faber and Faber, 1981). More recently, historians have sought to destabilize this narrative by showing the ways in which ZANU depended on international connections and by illuminating contributions to independence beyond the battlefield. See David Moore, "ZANU-PF & the Ghosts of Foreign Funding," *Review of African Political Economy* 32, no. 103 (2005): 156–62; Gerald Chikozho Mazarire, "ZANU's External Networks 1963–1979: An Appraisal," *Journal of Southern African Studies* 43, no. 1 (2017): 83–106; JoAnn McGregor, "Locating Exile: Decolonization, Anti-imperial Spaces and Zimbabwean Students in Britain, 1965–1980," *Journal of Historical Geography* 57 (2017): 62–75. That the KBW in some small way enabled ZANU's official narrative should not distract from the fact that, in the 1970s, enthusiasm for Mugabe greatly transcended the far Left.
14. For the broader turn toward "solidarity" in the postwar period, see also the contributions to Frank Bösch, Caroline Moine, and Stefanie Senger, eds., *Internationale*

Solidarität: Globales Engagement in der Bundesrepublik und der DDR (Göttingen: Wallstein, 2018).
15. Ned Richardson-Little, *The Human Rights Dictatorship: Socialism, Global Solidarity and Revolution in East Germany* (Cambridge: Cambridge University Press, 2020); Jason Verber, "The Conundrum of Colonialism in Postwar Germany" (PhD diss., University of Iowa, 2010). On the Hallstein Doctrine, see Werner Kilian, *Die Hallstein-Doktrin: Der diplomatische Krieg zwischen der BRD und der DDR 1955–1973: Aus den Akten der beiden deutschen Aussenministerien* (Berlin: Duncker & Humblot, 2001).
16. "Karitas für Afrika," *Der Spiegel*, 26 October 1960.
17. The crucial work here is Susanne Zantop, *Colonial Fantasies: Conquest, Family, and Nation in Precolonial Germany, 1770–1870* (Durham, NC: Duke University Press, 1997). Zantop argues that colonial fantasies long preceded actual colonial projects and had long-lasting consequences. Since then, literature on German colonialism and its importance in German history abounds. For a few notable examples, see Sara Friedrichsmeyer, Sara Lennox, and Susanne Zantop, eds., *The Imperialist Imagination: German Colonialism and Its Legacy* (Ann Arbor: University of Michigan Press, 1998); Eric Ames, Marcia Klotz, and Lora Wildenthal, eds., *Germany's Colonial Pasts* (Lincoln: University of Nebraska Press, 2005); Bradley Naranch and Geoff Eley, eds., *German Colonialism in a Global Age* (Durham, NC: Duke University Press, 2014); Lora Wildenthal, *German Women for Empire, 1884–1945* (Durham, NC: Duke University Press, 2001); Sebastian Conrad, *German Colonialism: A Short History* (Cambridge: Cambridge University Press, 2012); Sebastian Conrad, *Globalisation and the Nation in Imperial Germany* (Cambridge: Cambridge University Press, 2010); Andrew Zimmerman, *Alabama in Africa: Booker T. Washington, the German Empire, and the Globalization of the New South* (Princeton, NJ: Princeton University Press, 2010); George Steinmetz, *The Devil's Handwriting: Precoloniality and the German Colonial State in Qingdao, Samoa, and Southwest Africa* (Chicago: University of Chicago Press, 2007).
18. Verber, "Conundrum of Colonialism," 63.
19. Ibid., 63–64. On the *Völkerschauen* and their European colonial contexts, see, among others, Eric Ames, *Carl Hagenbeck's Empire of Entertainments* (Seattle: University of Washington Press, 2009).
20. See the contributions in Quinn Slobodian, ed., *Comrades of Color: East Germany in the Cold War World* (New York: Berghahn Books, 2015). See also Young-Sun Hong, *Cold War Germany, the Third World, and the Global Humanitarian Regime* (Cambridge: Cambridge University Press, 2015).
21. Archiv Soziale Bewegungen Freiburg (hereafter ASB), 5.1.1.II, Zeitschriften, Informationen für Dozenten und Studenten der ALU Freiburg, 1960–1969, Dagobert Soergel, "Zur Afrika-Woche: Die Universität und die Entwicklungsländer," *Informationen für Dozenten und Studenten der Albert-Ludwigs Universität Freiburg im Breisgau*, no. 1, Special Issue on the Africa Week, 28 November to 3 December 1960.
22. H. M. Schmid, "Ihr lieben Weißen aus Freiburg . . . ," *Freiburger Studentenzeitung*, 6 January 1961.

23. Dorothee Weitbrecht, *Aufbruch in die Dritte Welt: Der Internationalismus der Studentenbewegung von 1968 in der Bundesrepublik Deutschland* (Göttingen: V&R Unipress, 2012).
24. Slobodian, *Foreign Front*, 17.
25. Odd Arne Westad, *The Global Cold War: Third World Interventions and the Making of Our Times* (Cambridge: Cambridge University Press, 2005), 37.
26. Compare Young-Sun Hong, *Cold War Germany*, 201. On African students in the GDR specifically, see Sara Pugach, "African Students and the Politics of Race and Gender in the German Democratic Republic," in *Comrades of Color: East Germany in the Cold War World*, ed. Quinn Slobodian (New York: Berghahn Books, 2015). For Iraqi students, see Julia Sittmann, "Illusions of Care: Iraqi Students between the Ba'thist State and the Stasi in Socialist East Germany, 1958–89," *Cold War History* 18, no. 2 (April 3, 2018): 187–202.
27. Landesarchiv Baden-Württemberg, Hauptstaatsarchiv Stuttgart (hereafter HStaSt), EA 2/302 Bü 63, Landeskriminalamt Baden-Württemberg und die Landespolizeidirektion Baden-Württemberg, "Arbeitspapier über Aktivitäten kommunistisch-maoistischer Gruppen im Raum Freiburg und Möglichkeiten staatlicher Gegenmaßnahmen," 3.
28. Hermann Bitzer, "Der Schlaf der Gerechten," *Freiburger Studentenzeitung*, December 1959, 1.
29. Ibid.
30. "Liebe FSZ Leser!" *Freiburger Studentenzeitung*, December 1959, 2.
31. Sergey Radchenko, *Two Suns in the Heavens: The Sino-Soviet Struggle for Supremacy, 1962–1967* (Washington, DC: Woodrow Wilson Center, 2009).
32. Slobodian, *Foreign Front*, 19.
33. Joseph Mtisi, Munyaradzi Nyakudya, and Teresa Barnes, "Social and Economic Developments During the UDI Period," in *Becoming Zimbabwe: A History from the Pre-colonial Period to 2008*, ed. Brian Raftopoulos and A. S. Mlambo (Harare: Weaver Press, 2009).
34. BArch, B/136/17439, "Länderaufzeichnung—Republik Simbabwe," in *Gesprächsmappe für den Besuch des Regierungschefs von Simbabwe*, 24–25 May 1982, 5.
35. APO-Archiv, APO-KBW 028, "BMZ-Programm Südliches Africa."
36. Mazarire, "ZANU's External Networks 1963–1979," 94–95.
37. Dan Hodgkinson, "Nationalists with No Nation: Oral History, ZANU and the Meanings of Rhodesian Student Activism in Zimbabwe," *Africa* 89, no. 5 (2019): S40; Dan Hodgkinson, "Subversive Communities and the 'Rhodesian Sixties': An Exploration of Transnational Protests, 1965–1973," in *The Routledge Handbook of the Global Sixties: Between Protest and Nation-Building*, ed. Chen Jian et al. (Abingdon: Routledge, 2018), 39–52.
38. Mazarire, "ZANU's External Networks 1963–1979," 93.
39. McGregor, "Locating Exile," 67–70.
40. Ibid., 69.
41. Ibid., 64.
42. "Bericht des Genossen Herbert Chitepo, dem Vorsitzenden des Zentralkommittees der Afrikanischen Nationalunion von Zimbabwe (ZANU), über den Befreiungskamp des Volkes von Zimbabwe"; Joscha Schmierer, "Es lebe der Befreiungskampf

des Volkes von Zimbabwe gegen das rhodesische Siedlerregime"; Rex Chiwara, "Aufruf zur Unterstützung," *Kommunistische Volkszeitung*, 16 October 1974, 16.
43. Rex Chiwara, "Aufruf zur Unterstützung," *Afrika Zeitung*, November 1974.
44. ZANU would later deny that money had been used to purchase weapons or that they were in the habit of paying for weapons at all. Politisches Archiv des Auswärtigen Amts (hereafter PA-AA) B 34-ZA/116812, "Betr: Verhältnis zu den Befreiungsbewegungen; hier: Vorsprache der ZANU-Funktionäre Shamuyarira (Mugabe)," 9 November 1978, 2.
45. APO-Archiv, APO-KBW 024, "Protokoll des Treffens der Delegationen der ZANU und des KBW am 10. und 11.6. in London," 4–6.
46. APO-Archiv APO-KBW 028, KBW ZK Sekretariat to KBW ZK Org. und Statistik "Betrifft: Abrechnung ZANU-Sammlung, Ausrüstung einer vollmotorisierten Kompanie der ZANLA," 3 November 1978. On average US$1 bought DM 2.01 in 1978. Adjusting for inflation, the KBW's fundraising efforts would amount to approximately US$2 million today.
47. APO-Archiv, APO-KBW 024, Landesanwaltschaft beim Verwaltungsgericht Sigmaringen to Verwaltungsgericht Sigmaringen, 10 April 1978, 2.
48. APO-Archiv, APO-KBW 024, Eberhardt Kempf, H.-Jürgen Borowsky, Birgit Laubach to Verwaltungsgericht Sigmaringen "In der Verwaltungsstreitsache Kommunistischer Bund Westdeutschland gegen das Land Baden-Württemberg," 15 April 1978, 3–4.
49. APO-Archiv, APO-KBW 024, Landesanwaltschaft beim Verwaltungsgericht Sigmaringen to Verwaltungsgericht Sigmaringen, 10 April 1978, 4.
50. APO-Archiv, APO-KBW 024, Eberhardt Kempf, H.-Jürgen Borowsky, Birgit Laubach to Verwaltungsgericht Sigmaringen "In der Verwaltungsstreitsache Kommunistischer Bund Westdeutschland gegen das Land Baden-Württemberg," 15 April 1978, 1–2.
51. APO-Archiv, APO-KBW 024, Verwaltungsgerichtshof Baden-Württemberg "Beschluß in der Verwaltungssache des Kommunistischen Bundes Westdeutschland vertreten durch das Zentrale Komitee, dasselbe durch den Sekretär Gerhard Schmierer gegen das Land Baden-Württemberg," 6 June 1978, 1–2.
52. APO-Archiv, APO-KBW 024, Eberhard Kempf, H.-Jürgen Borowsky, Birgit Laubach to Verwaltungsgericht Sigmaringen "In der Verwaltungsstreitsache Dr. E. Zvogo gegen das Land Baden Württemberg," 15 April 1978, 1–2.
53. For West Germany's efforts to achieve unified definition of "terrorism" across the United Nations, see Bernhard Blumenau, "The Other Battleground of the Cold War: The UN and the Struggle against International Terrorism in the 1970s," *Journal of Cold War Studies* 16, no. 1 (2014): 61–84. On political violence in West Germany, see Karrin Hanshew, *Terror and Democracy in West Germany* (Cambridge: Cambridge University Press, 2014); Jeremy Peter Varon, *Bringing the War Home: The Weather Underground, the Red Army Faction, and Revolutionary Violence in the Sixties and Seventies* (Berkeley: University of California Press, 2004); Patricia Melzer, *Death in the Shape of a Young Girl: Women's Political Violence in the Red Army Faction* (New York: New York University Press, 2015). For a critique of the literature on left-wing militancy that focuses narrowly on West German actors, see Quinn Slobodian, "The Borders of the Rechtsstaat in the Arab Autumn: Depor-

tation and Law in West Germany, 1972/73," *German History* 31, no. 2 (2013): 204–24.
54. For West Germany's "pragmatic" foreign policy approach to its relationship with Apartheid South Africa, see Sebastian Gehrig, "Reaching Out to the Third World: East Germany's Anti-Apartheid and Socialist Human Rights Campaign," *German History* 36, no. 4 (2018): 574–97. For a critique of Gehrig's reproduction of a rather ideology-ridden dichotomy between ideology and pragmatic foreign policy, see Johanna Folland, "Globalizing Socialist Health: Africa, East Germany, and the AIDS Crisis" (PhD diss., University of Michigan, 2019), 79.
55. "Bürgerinitiative für die Unterstützung der ZANU," *Kommunistische Volkszeitung*, 3 April 1978. For the reverse argument, that the strict organization of the *K-Gruppen* in combination with its wide networks aided the transnational antinuclear movement, see Robert Gildea and Andrew Tompkins, "The Transnational in the Local: The Larzac Plateau as a Site of Transnational Activism Since 1970," *Journal of Contemporary History* 50, no. 3 (2015): 581–605.
56. BArch, B/138/53093, "Geld Floss in den Urwald," *Kölner Stadtanzeiger*, 22 April 1977.
57. "WS 76/77 Köln: 10,000 DM Überschuß aus dem E-Raum Boykott von der Uni-VV an die ZANU gesandt," in Kommunistische Hochschulgruppe (KHG) Köln / Rhein-Sieg, *Die Pläne für die Ausbeutung und Unterdrückung der Völker Afrikas werden an der Hochschule ausgebrütet. Die Studentenbewegung unterstützt die Befreiungskämpfe der Völker Afrikas. Untersuchung über die imperialistische Afrikaforschung an den Kölner und Bonner Hochschulen*, 1978. Retrieved 27 July 2021 from www.mao-projekt.de/BRD/NRW/KOE/Koeln_Rhein-Sieg_VDS_1978_Voelker_Afrikas.shtml.
58. APO-Archiv, APO-KBW 028, Auswärtiges Amt to Vertretung des Landes Baden-Württemberg beim Bund, 11 March 1980; APO-Archiv, APO-KBW 028, "Zahlungsauftrag, Eberhardt Kempf to ZANU-PF Department of Finance."
59. APO-Archiv, APO-KBW 028, "Zimbabwe Independence Celebrations 1980: Provisional Directory of Official Delegations."
60. BArch, B/136/17439, "Besuch von PM Mugabe; hier: Privates Treffen Mugabes mit Vertretern u.a. des Kommunistischen Bund Westdeutschlands (KBW)," 24 May 1982.
61. BArch, B/136/17439, "Besuch des simbabwischen Regierungschefs PM Mugabe in Bonn vom 24.05.1982 bis 26.05.1982; hier: Treffen von PM Mugabe mit 'Solidaritätsgruppen' am 25.05.1982 im Rahmen des privaten Besuchsprogramms," 21 May 1982.
62. BArch, B/136/17439, "Besuch von Premierminister Mugabe in Bonn; hier: Gesprächsunterlagen für den Bundeskanzler," 3.
63. BArch, B/136/17439, "Besuch des simbabwischen Regierungschefs PM Mugabe in Bonn vom 24.05.1982 bis 26.05.1982; hier: Treffen von PM Mugabe mit 'Solidaritätsgruppen' am 25.05.1982 im Rahmen des privaten Besuchsprogramms," 21 May 1982.
64. PA-AA B 34-ZA/116812, "Betr: Kontakte zu rhodesischen Befreiungsbewegungen; hier: Absicht der ZANU (Mugabe), in Bonn ein ständiges Büro einzurichten," 25 August 1978, 3.

65. PA-AA B 34-ZA/116812, "Betr: Kontakte zu rhodesischen Befreiungsbewegungen; hier: Absicht der ZANU (Mugabe), in Bonn ein ständiges Büro einzurichten," 11 August 1978, 3.
66. PA-AA B 34-ZA/116812, "Betr: Verhältnis zu den Befreiungsbewegungen; hier: Vorsprache der ZANU-Funktionäre Shamuyarira (Mugabe)," 9 November 1978, 2.
67. "West German Government Seizes ZANU Funds," *Zimbabwe News* 10, no. 1 (1978), 34.

Select Bibliography

Blumenau, Bernhard. "The Other Battleground of the Cold War: The UN and the Struggle against International Terrorism in the 1970s." *Journal of Cold War Studies* 16, no. 1 (2014): 61–84.

Brown, Timothy Scott. *West Germany and the Global Sixties: The Antiauthoritarian Revolt, 1962–1978*. Cambridge: Cambridge University Press, 2013.

Friedrichsmeyer, Sara, Sara Lennox, and Susanne Zantop, eds. *The Imperialist Imagination: German Colonialism and its Legacy*. Ann Arbor: University of Michigan Press, 1998.

Hong, Young-Sun. *Cold War Germany, the Third World, and the Global Humanitarian Regime*. Cambridge: Cambridge University Press, 2017.

Kalter, Christoph. *The Discovery of the Third World: Decolonization and the Rise of the New Left in France, c.1950–1976*. Cambridge: Cambridge University Press, 2019.

Lovell, Julia. *Maoism: A Global History*. London: Bodley Head, 2019.

Mazarire, Gerald Chikozho. "ZANU's External Networks 1963–1979: An Appraisal." *Journal of Southern African Studies* 43, no. 1 (2017): 83–106.

McGregor, JoAnn. "Locating Exile: Decolonization, Anti-Imperial Spaces and Zimbabwean Students in Britain, 1965–1980." *Journal of Historical Geography* 57 (2017): 62–75.

Slobodian, Quinn. *Foreign Front: Third World Politics in Sixties West Germany*. Durham, NC: Duke University Press, 2012.

Weitbrecht, Dorothee. *Aufbruch in die Dritte Welt: Der Internationalismus der Studentenbewegung von 1968 in der Bundesrepublik Deutschland*. Göttingen: V&R Unipress, 2012.

Chapter 12

Supporting a Revolution

West German Nicaragua Solidarity and Its Transnational Connections with the Nicaraguan Sandinistas

Christian Helm

"Dear friend, our organization has come to know about you and your vocation for justice."[1] In early 1978, several West German organizations and groups with a track record of activism or interest in liberation struggles in the so-called Third World received a letter from Nicaragua. Its author, the Foreign Commission of the Sandinista National Liberation Front (Frente Sandinista de Liberación Nacional, FSLN), addressed the letter's recipients as potential supporters of their fight against the authoritarian dictatorship of the Somoza family. Attached to the letter was a brochure with more information on the Sandinistas' cause and the repressive situation in Nicaragua. The addressees were asked to spread the information to local media and were promised more newsletters with continuous updates on the struggle.

The Sandinistas were lucky. The information contained in their newsletters soon began to appear in West German leftist periodicals with national outreach. In the course of the following months, Nicaragua became a regular topic. By July 1979, when the guerillas managed to overthrow the Somozas, leftist circles and the general public in West Germany were well aware of the situation in the Central American country. Nicaragua had become the focal point of a solidarity movement that included the whole spectrum of West Germany's contemporary Left and had even reached into liberal circles and Christian church groups. By the mid-1980s, around three hundred local solidarity groups engaged in activism to support the Sandinista revolution. Similar support movements spread in the Americas and around the globe; the West German movement was among the liveliest in Western Europe.

As the above-cited letter from the FSLN's Foreign Commission indicates, Nicaraguan actors were involved in the solidarity movement's development from the very beginning. This state of affairs defies the descriptions of the movement found in most chronicles written by former activists, who tend to neglect the agency of their Nicaraguan counterparts. During the 1970s and 1980s, and in the context of divided Germany, West German activists may have neglected mentioning Nicaraguans' role in order to avoid conservative criticism that their actions were "remotely controlled" by a liberation movement with links to the communist sphere. Continued neglect in later testimonials, however, suggests that many West German activists neither recognized Nicaraguan agency at the time nor came to realize its existence in retrospect.[2] Drawing from three case studies, one from the movement's formative phase and two from its height in the mid-1980s, I will present further evidence of decisive collaboration from within Nicaragua. In so doing, I will also argue that West German Nicaragua solidarity was hardly a movement that fit within a local or national container. Instead, it had significant transnational aspects not only in its overall focus and program but also in terms of organization and actions. The case studies further illustrate that activists consistently sought to influence state politics. While many of them came from the alternative scene and were keen to preserve their autonomy from traditional politics, the latter still remained a major addressee of their claims. By the mid-1980s, however, not only had Nicaragua solidarity achieved parliamentary representation but its members had also actively engaged in people-to-people diplomacy and thus defied official diplomacy as a realm of the government.

Looking at the Nicaragua solidarity movement in West Germany and beyond adds nuance to existing theoretical assumptions about social movements after '68 and reveals how activists developed a variety of connections with transnational partners, politics, and other contemporary social movements. Social scientists, such as Keck and Sikkink in their study *Activists beyond Borders* or Bob in his monograph *The Marketing of Rebellions*, have shown that activism in solidarity with groups in the Global South is often influenced by the latter.[3] In order to raise awareness for their cause, Southern activists need to establish communication channels with potential supporters abroad and frame their message in a way that resonates with target audiences. Once the transnational communication network is established, a continuous flow of information is key to maintain attention and make support persistent. As Thomas Olesen has argued, communication—in both ways, back and forth—acts as a kind of "glue" between the geographically distant partners.[4] This is also true for the present case, where the absence of any major historical connections between West Germany and Nicaragua before 1978/79 contrasts with widespread support for the Sandinistas during the 1980s. To get their message across, the Sandinistas' communication profited from intercultural knowledge about potential supporters and their local context as well as from an effective representation of their cause as a common one for both parties involved. In his contemporary poem "Wo liegt Nicaragua?" the West German poet Erich Fried portrays the country as a global symbol of imperialist and capitalist oppression.[5]

Their very quest for "solidarity" put the Sandinistas and their cause in a long tradition of leftist internationalism.[6] West German actors did the same by denominating their support network a "solidarity movement."[7] Acting on a common ground of ideological and moral principles helped to stabilize the transnational ties.[8] While acknowledging the ideological roots of the term "solidarity movement" and its use by contemporary activists, I will henceforth adhere to it for pragmatic and analytic reasons. Social scientists also use the term to denote a specific category of social movements that engage in support activities for distant others, such as liberation struggles in the Global South. According to Dieter Rucht, this measure of altruism is what differentiates them from other social movements.[9] A growing body of research on Nicaragua solidarity from a transnational perspective has highlighted the manifold links and personal contacts between Nicaraguans and their solidary counterparts, thus defying the definitional notion of "Distant Issue Movements."[10] The following sections, which address campaigns against West German aid to Somoza and against foreign intervention in Sandinista Nicaragua, further illustrate this point.

Stopping Funds for the Dictatorship

Under the heading "Development aid for Somoza," one of the movements' earliest brochures presented astoundingly detailed information on how the Somoza family used its power within the state apparatus and national economy to appropriate aid funds.[11] Several members of the Somoza clan were introduced. The brochure explained how their respective key positions in public institutions or state enterprises enabled them to plunder public funds and redirect foreign development aid into their own pockets. However, the brochure represented more than just a collection of disclosures. First, it was the result of successful communication from within Nicaragua to the Sandinistas' transnational supporters in West Germany. Second, it provided the latter with substantiated arguments for lobbying the West German public and government to end financial support of the Somoza regime.

Concerning the first point, West German activists could rely on Sandinista communication from Nicaragua in print and in person. One of their best-known representatives at that stage was famous poet and liberation theologian Ernesto Cardenal, who had secretly joined the FSLN.[12] His poems and especially the published description of his small Christian commune on Solentiname Islands in Lake Nicaragua had earned him a growing fan base within left-leaning Christian groups.[13] From the mid-1970s onward, he traveled regularly throughout West Germany to read from his books or to attend the annual national gatherings of the Catholic and Protestant churches as a guest.[14] Since West Germany experienced an explosion of left-wing terrorism in autumn 1977, pleading the case of a leftist guerrilla movement was a difficult task. Thanks to his personal background, however, Cardenal managed to reach out to church groups, intellectuals, and left-wing liberals. His lobbying efforts were complemented by the work of a number of Nicaraguan students, exiles, and immigrants. Upon hearing about an upsurge of Sandinista guerrilla attacks and the ensuing massive repression from the Somoza regime in late 1977, they decided to take action and found the first solidarity groups. These decentralized efforts in cities like Tübingen, Göttingen, Wuppertal, or West Berlin were soon unified and expanded on a national level. Enrique Schmidt Cuadra, who had studied in Cologne and later returned to West Germany as a political exile after having been imprisoned and tortured in Nicaragua, became one of their main representatives.[15] Like Cardenal, he had experienced the repressive dictatorship firsthand and thus emanated a special authenticity in his public call for solidarity. Also like Cardenal, Schmidt Cuadra and his fellow Nicaraguan activists had direct contacts to Nicaragua to supply West Germans with recent, "authentic" information.

Together, they embarked on speaking tours all over West Germany, drawing on networks of Latino exiles, leftist radicals, and, so-called Third World groups. Schmidt Cuadra and Cardenal's German editor initiated the Information Office Nicaragua (Informationsbüro Nicaragua, IBN) in Wuppertal. It soon became the central hub of West German Nicaragua solidarity.[16] Together with a growing number of local solidarity groups, the IBN committed to disseminating information, to lobbying the public and politicians, and to collecting funds for the (armed) opposition in Nicaragua.

As the preceding paragraphs illustrate, Nicaraguan agency played a major role in the establishment of transnational communication channels. The constant flow of Sandinista brochures, periodicals, pamphlets, and communiqués was distributed by a network of Nicaraguans. By mid-1978, IBN's new bulletin *Nicaragua Nachrichten* (Nicaragua News), but also other existing and renowned periodicals in the alternative scene (*Lateinamerika Nach-*

richten, ila-info, blätter des iz3w), republished news from Nicaragua with relatively short delays of just a few days or weeks.

Such direct communication channels, which avoided the filters of international news agencies, were an enormous advantage and provided news about Nicaragua with a special aura of authenticity. Thanks to this network, the Sandinistas were able to comment rapidly on new incidents in Nicaragua, to portray themselves as the spearhead of national resistance, and to share their political program. A German translation of their thirty-point social-revolutionary program was published in late summer 1978. On account of strong public demand, four consecutive editions were printed within one year.[17] Thanks to their transnational communication network, Sandinistas had soon managed to familiarize supporters in West Germany with their program and their vision for Nicaragua's political future.

Getting information across was certainly one important goal of the transnational communication network. Providing transnational solidarity groups with concrete tasks was another. In its publications, the FSLN's Foreign Commission voiced a clear vision of solidarity and how their transnational supporters should act. The adjectives "effective" and "concrete" were regularly used in their quest for solidarity. By "effective" the Sandinistas referred to unification of forces and efforts. In order to gain strength, the FSLN and their representatives repeatedly called for the broadest alliance possible within a leftist spectrum and beyond. Every political and social force willing to support their struggle against the dictatorship should be welcome within the solidarity movement.[18] Well informed about their supporters abroad, they criticized factionalization and the existence of different solidarity groups in cities divided by leftist ideological competition.[19] Schmidt Cuadra, familiar with the contemporary West German context, was aware of the ideological quarrels that had debilitated Chile solidarity only a few years earlier. Together with his fellow Nicaraguans, he stressed the necessity of joining forces "without defending party interests."[20] By "concrete," the Sandinistas meant that solidarity must transcend the theoretical level of addresses and statements. "We want this solidarity to be put into practice," a Sandinista communiqué requested.[21] According to Tomás Borge, one of the FSLN's best-known leading figures, solidarity was neither muttered commentary nor to be mistaken for commiseration. For him, it was a specific activity pursued within one's trade union, at one's university, or in one's workplace.[22]

To spread examples of best practices, early FSLN periodicals had a special rubric called "International Solidarity," within which actions by solidarity groups in various American or European countries were described.[23] This practice illustrates how information between the Sandinista Foreign Commission and transnational solidarity groups circulated in both directions. The former was informed about support activities abroad and in turn highlighted them in its publications, thus inviting imitation. To a similar end, the FSLN and its representatives used every publication as well as the regional and national meetings of support groups or public solidarity events to provide a list of five concrete tasks.[24] These included: the permanent denouncement of corruption and repression in Somoza Nicaragua; moral and material support for the Sandinista guerrillas and their civil representation—often framed in more general terms as "national resistance" against the dictatorship; lobbying of the respective local government to end diplomatic, military, and economic cooperation with the Somoza regime; support for the formation of a new, democratic government in Nicaragua; and last but not least, the denouncement of any kind of foreign intervention in the Nicaraguan conflict—especially US financial, diplomatic and military support for the Somoza regime, which had long been a close US ally in Central America.

All five points were well suited to the possibilities and needs of transnational support groups. They remained concrete and feasible, they could easily be translated into actions, and thus they instilled solidarity activities with a sense of purpose. They centered on public lobbying efforts, and the continuous flow of information from within Nicaragua provided solidarity activists with the facts and background they needed to organize an up-to-date lobbying campaign. As the efforts to end West German development aid for Somoza Nicaragua demonstrate, the latter proved crucial.

The brochure mentioned at the beginning of this section contained more than an article on the Somoza family's corrupt regime and its deviation of aid funds. It also included a plea to take action by addressing the West German government about its financial support for a dictatorship. Confronted with growing numbers of protest letters, the Ministry of Foreign Relations and the Ministry for Economic Cooperation and Development responded that ending any financial cooperation with Nicaraguan partners would only cement the present state of power—a perspective that IBN saw as plainly naïve.[25] By referring to detailed knowledge about the Somoza regime obtained from within Nicaragua and confirmed by development workers on a recent mission to this country, the IBN claimed expert status and countered "that every Deutsche Mark from West German taxpayers helps to cement Somoza's power."[26]

Raising the issue of development aid funds and financial cooperation also provided solidarity activists with a plausible connection between Nicaragua and West Germany. "We cannot act like Nicaragua had nothing to do with us," read the title of one flyer.[27] It went on to explain that West German taxpayers' money was ending up in the pockets of a dictator and helping him to repress, prosecute and torture the local opposition. Schmidt Cuadra and his fellow activists often referred to the fact that West Germany was Somoza Nicaragua's third most important trade partner.[28] Last but not least, all the information about West German engagement in Nicaragua also served a dual purpose for many leftist radicals since it represented a welcome base to criticize the moral double standards of the contemporary government coalition of social democrats and liberals.[29]

At the height of repression in September 1978, activists received information that the federal government had greenlighted the disbursement of a US$10 million credit. Even if ministry officials argued that the disbursement was part of a larger development project and had nothing to do with the present state of repression, the solidarity groups reverted to massive public protest. The concerns activists voiced in individual letters, on a television talk show, and at the annual meeting of West German Catholics prompted the ministry to stop the disbursement.[30] The moratorium was then closely monitored by the solidarity movement during the following months until July 1979, when the Sandinistas took power.

While the campaign to end development aid was successful, the Sandinista and West German activists' efforts to lobby for the severance of official diplomatic relations with Somoza Nicaragua did not yield success before the dictatorship was overthrown in July 1979. During the following years, the federal government remained a central target of the solidarity movement's lobbying activities. However, the latter's stance toward official politics in West Germany was fraught with complexity. On the one hand, the activists sought to retain autonomy by remaining distant from official politics. On the other hand, however, they actually managed to have a representative in parliament.

Scandal in West Germany's Parliament

"Mr. Kohl! Support for the USA in Nicaragua means complicity concerning the death of Albrecht Pflaum!" read the message in bold white letters on a bedsheet-size banner facing the members of West Germany's parliament during chancellor Helmut Kohl's State of the Nation address.[31] After only a few seconds, the banner was removed by parliamentary service personnel; such protests were strictly prohibited by the West German parliament's procedural rules. Thus, press photographers had eagerly documented the scandalous action. Petra Kelly, a leading member of the Green Party, later explained in an official speech why she and a colleague had unrolled the banner.[32] She accused Kohl and his government coalition of conservatives and liberals of a moral double standard. While criticizing the communist block for Human Rights violations, the West German government nonetheless supported abominable anticommunist military regimes as well as the brutal reality of US warfare in Central America. Kelly's banner drew attention to the death of the West German citizen Albrecht Pflaum, a state-funded development worker on a long-term mission to Nicaragua. Pflaum had been killed in an ambush by counterrevolutionary rebels who were supported by the administration of US president Ronald Reagan. According to Kelly, Kohl's siding with Reagan, the claim that Sandinista Nicaragua represented a communist threat to US national security, and the ensuing military engagement in Central America had ultimately resulted in the death of a German citizen. "It is your silence and actions regarding Central America that has made the Federal Government complicit in the murder of one of its own development aid workers,"[33] Kelly said amid angry outcries from the benches of the conservative party.

The Green Party had just entered the West German parliament for the first time after the general election, which had been held only a few weeks earlier. While the party's name hinted that the ecological movement was its main basis, the party itself was largely conceived as the political arm of several contemporary social movements, including the women's movement, the antinuclear movement, the peace movement, and, last but not least, the so-called "Third World Movement" and its various solidarity groups.[34] In the weeks leading up to the election, the party had reached out to institutions of solidarity activism for Nicaragua, El Salvador, and Guatemala.[35] The idea was to have them suggest independent candidates for the party's electoral list and thus enable solidarity activism to represent and pursue its issues at the center of West Germany's parliament.

The response from within the solidarity movement was ambivalent. Unlike in other European countries, where Nicaragua solidarity was strongly connected to leftist political parties, the West German movement had emphasized political autonomy since its very beginning.[36] The reasons for this particularity were recent experience and the special political context of West Germany. The disruptive ideological quarrels within the Chilean solidarity movement a few years earlier, which had occurred after radical leftist factions had tried to monopolize solidarity with Chile, have already been mentioned.[37] Other contemporary examples of organized solidarity activism, such as solidarity movements with Cuba or Vietnam, were controlled by the country's small communist party and ultimately by East Germany. These movements were just as abhorrent for the vast majority of West Germany's Nicaragua activists.[38] In contrast to these other movements, Nicaragua activists considered themselves a radical and independent opposition even to the Social Democrats. What is more, the concept of decentralized, grassroots democracy adopted by West Germany's Nicaragua solidarity movement also contradicted any close party affiliation.

This critical stance toward party politics also permeated a January 1983 newsletter published by the IBN, which discussed the issue of cooperation with the Green Party.[39] While welcoming the opportunity presented by the Greens' plan to organize open electoral lists, the IBN emphasized the Nicaragua solidarity movement's autonomy and reiterated that candidates on the Greens' electoral lists were not required to join the party. It noted the significance of the chance to provide knowledge and experience that would influence the party's future programs, but nonetheless preferred the informal framework of local working groups for cooperation with Green Party institutions, which allowed the solidarity groups to maintain their autonomy. And, while stressing the opportunities for public relations, media, and information work that would come with parliamentary representation, the IBN remained firm that "party politics, electoral races, and parliamentary work are not the lever for political change."[40] In large part, the IBN's conclusions echoed contemporary attitudes among West Germany's leftist alternative scene.[41] And yet, despite the IBN's many reservations, the newsletter ended with an introduction of persons with a track record of leftist and solidarity activism who would run as independent candidates for the Green Party.[42] One of them was Gabriele ("Gabi") Gottwald. A few weeks later, a Green Party convention voted to make her the eighth candidate on its electoral list.[43]

On 6 March 1983, Gottwald, indeed entered the West German Bundestag as part of the Green Party's parliamentary group. It was she who unrolled the banner together with Kelly during chancellor Kohl's speech in parliament. In May 1983, the annual federal meeting of Nicaragua solidarity groups addressed her as "Our Woman in Parliament."[44] The protocol of this meeting formulated two main tasks for Gottwald and the Green Party as the movement's official parliamentary arm. Gottwald and the Greens should provide access to infrastructure and information on official political proceedings that had been hard to obtain before, and they should act as a pressure group for Nicaragua solidarity in parliament.[45]

Although she was not a party member, Gottwald became the spokesperson for Central American affairs in the Green parliamentary group and made extensive use of the opportunities open to parliamentary representatives for political and public lobbying in support of Sandinista Nicaragua. Not only did her office keep close contact with the Nicaraguan Embassy in West Germany but it was also well connected with the solidarity movement.[46] Her official telephone line could be used for expensive calls to Nicaragua. Transcripts of her information requests to the government, copies of her official letters to chancellor Kohl, and minutes from parliamentary debates on Central America were published in solidarity journals, thus documenting Gottwald's interventions.[47] Her office even compiled reports of its parliamentary work or Gottwald's official visits to Nicaragua and sent them to solidarity movement representatives.[48]

While these activities had little political impact insofar as they did not change the critical attitude and policy of the governing conservative-liberal majority toward Sandinista Nicaragua, they were relevant in keeping the country in public discussions and providing an alternative view on it in parliament. In line with the solidarity movement's implicit strategy, Gottwald—as well as other Green and Social Democrat representatives friendly to the cause—made use of their position to provide Sandinista voices from Nicaragua with a public platform. To this end, they capitalized on the official prestige of the parliament to host meetings and press events with Nicaraguan officials.[49]

In emergency situations like the one that occurred in November 1984, when the low intensity warfare waged by US forces edged toward open war and military intervention seemed imminent, Green parliamentarians quickly joined forces with the solidarity movement. The Greens' parliamentary group created an emergency task force that coordinated parliamentary and public lobbying efforts calling for the Kohl administration to exert pressure on its ally and demand an end to US military aggression in Nicaragua.[50]

Although the movement's acceptance of Gottwald as an independent candidate and the ensuing parliamentary-level activities convinced a majority of activists that a closer cooperation with the Green Party was principally possible, neither the party nor Gottwald's office became a new epicenter of the movement.[51] Gottwald admitted that expectations concerning her parliamentary work as well as her personal availability for solidarity events could hardly be met.[52] Also, the decentralized nature of West German Nicaragua solidarity complicated communications between her office and the movement. The agency for campaigns and major events thus always remained with local solidarity groups and the IBN in Wuppertal.

In the long run, this proved to be beneficial. At the end of March 1985, Gottwald rotated out of parliament according to the Green Party principle's and made way for another Green representative. While solidarity work remained a topic of the parliamentary group, Gottwald's successor as spokesperson for Central America did not have the same genuine connection to the movement. The parliamentary connection lost momentum.

Working from inside the parliament had only been one inroad to the realm of official politics in order to influence the bilateral relations between Nicaragua and West Germany, however. Since 1981, Nicaraguans and West

German solidarity activists had also been working on a strategy to establish a transnational people-to-people diplomacy.

Campaigning against US Intervention

"You, too, are defense fighters of the Nicaraguan Revolution . . . 18 months after the Sandinista victory, we value the significance of international solidarity more than ever."[53] The words of Tomás Borge, one of the most prominent Sandinistas and minister of the interior, were well received by about three hundred activists from forty-two mostly Western countries. They had gathered in Managua in April 1981 to participate in the first official meeting of international solidarity representatives convened by the FSLN.[54] Facing mounting pressure from recently inaugurated US president Ronald Reagan, who openly advocated regime change in Nicaragua, Borge and other high-ranking Sandinistas who spoke at the meeting referred to transnational solidarity activism as a defense mechanism for the revolution.[55] Just as before July 1979, public information work and political lobbying was to exert and maintain pressure on Western governments, especially the US and its close allies like West Germany, in order to delegitimize and prevent a military intervention in Nicaragua.

The meeting in Managua marked a turning point in the relationship between the Sandinistas and their transnational support network. After the euphoria of summer 1979 and the internationally celebrated literacy campaign of the following year, solidarity activism in West Germany and elsewhere had been slowly subsiding. On the activist side, disappointment about the Sandinistas' actual policy gained ground. For some, it did not meet their expectations of a radical revolution. For many others, increasing examples of the FSLN's authoritarian grip on power collided with their vision of a new kind of humanistic and nondictatorial revolution. The beginning of a civil war between pro-revolutionary Sandinistas and an armed opposition group, known as the "Contra," also complicated the picture. While solidarity activists had little sympathy for the Contra, which counted on financial and material aid from the US government, the violently escalating conflict between the Sandinista-controlled government and the Indigenous peoples of Nicaragua's Atlantic coast, who sought autonomy, had a dampening effect on solidarity activism.[56]

On the Sandinista side, the transnational support network had, in the meantime, become less important. As the dominating party in Nicaragua's new provisional government, the FSLN now enjoyed direct diplomatic contacts with Western governments, and the country was initially offered a great deal of development aid in order to keep Nicaragua from becoming part of the socialist bloc. One example of these new priorities, which left a deep impression with movement leaders, was the absence of an official Sandinista representative during the regular meeting of West European solidarity groups in early 1980.[57] At the same time, the formerly continuous stream of Sandinista news from Nicaragua dwindled or was replaced by heavy-handed propaganda material. "The flow of information has been interrupted, the FSLN has other issues and there are partners who are more important and donors who are more potent,"[58] summarized one activist in late 1980.

Not until the beginning of US president Reagan's term and the simultaneously slowing financial and diplomatic support from other Western governments did the transnational relationship between activists and the FSLN improve again. The Managua meeting demonstrated the Sandinistas' renewed interest in their transnational support network. At the same time, indignation about Reagan's military and financial efforts to effect regime change in Nicaragua resonated with West German leftists on account of their critical attitudes toward the United States and especially US "imperialism."[59]

Now, the speaking tours and lobbying efforts of Sandinista representatives in West Germany were complemented by West German visitors to Nicaragua who had experienced the warlike situation firsthand. One activist, who had been to Nicaragua with his church group in 1982, reported: "The threat is real. There is a war going on in Nicaragua, which cannot be overlooked. This is a daily reality for the local population. There are deaths every day."[60]

After July 1979, Nicaragua had been virtually flooded by international supporters who wanted to witness the revolutionary changes personally. With some reservations, the Sandinistas had accepted this kind of revolutionary, political tourism.[61] At the meeting in Managua, Borge ended his speech with an invitation for solidarity activists—called "internationalists" by the FSLN according to leftist traditions—to come to Nicaragua.[62] During following meetings at a West European level, the idea of "working brigades," which combined working in a social project with a political program and touristic excursions, gained ground.[63] But it was in fall 1983 that the idea of working brigades really gained momentum.

At that time, increasing military hostilities on the part of the United States provoked fears of an upcoming military intervention and a violent end of the Sandinista revolution. Following up on an idea brought forward by US Christian organizations, which sought to send US citizens into border regions of Nicaragua in order to prevent an intervention and to pray for peace ("Witness for Peace"), the Sandinistas launched a campaign to invite international solidarity brigades.[64] At first, leading Sandinistas had turned down such offers, as they feared that foreign citizens getting harmed in hostilities might not only provoke a negative backlash but also serve the US and other Western governments as the very pretext for a military intervention. The US intervention that overturned the leftist government in Grenada in late October 1983 and international solidarity's support for the idea ultimately led the Sandinistas to change their minds, however.

Neither the name nor the concept of international brigades was new. The name made reference to the volunteers within the republican army during the Spanish Civil War, and the combination of political tourism and volunteer work in the harvest of cash crops had been practiced for a long time in other countries ruled by leftist regimes, like Cuba.[65] What was new in Nicaragua, however, was that not only did the brigadiers volunteer in the coffee harvest but they also functioned as human shields. In their official call, the FSLN was very clear about the warlike situation in Nicaragua's borderlands, and the IBN, the coordinating office in West Germany, stressed this point, too.[66] In order to avoid diplomatic strain, the Sandinistas had every future brigadier sign a declaration in which he or she renounced litigation against Nicaragua for any possible incident.[67]

The resonance was nonetheless impressive. The IBN in Wuppertal received around one thousand applications from interested West Germans. On 20 December 1983, the first brigade of 162 West German brigadiers boarded a plane for Nicaragua, where they joined hundreds of other volunteers from all over the Western world. They were welcomed by official acts with leading politicians. A special Sandinista organization for transnational solidarity was in charge of attending to the brigadiers, choosing a coffee finca at which volunteers would work, and organizing the additional political and touristic program.[68]

Since the feared US intervention did not materialize, the FSLN officially declared the campaign to be finished in March 1984. Due to the campaign's wide resonance, however, a national meeting of the West German solidarity movement decided to continue the program. As the harvesting period came to an end, the Sandinistas and their West German counterparts agreed on several new projects mostly aimed at building homes for resettled farming families in regions affected by the civil war between FSLN and the armed opposition. A new slogan of the West German campaign was, "We reconstruct what Contras destroyed."[69] Until summer 1986, several hundred volunteers participated in these efforts, and at the same time they aimed to serve as human shields for the local population. When two major Contra attacks demonstrated that brigade volunteers could no longer be regarded as functional shields, the Sandinistas gave in to pressure from the West German government and consequently withdrew the brigades from dangerous areas in 1986.[70]

However, these brigades were far from the only emissaries of West German solidarity. In addition to the aforementioned brigades, the Sandinistas offered similar arrangements for local solidarity groups, who had been raising funds for a social project in Nicaragua and wanted to pay a visit. From 1983 onward, members of solidarity committees in leftist parties, trade unions, boy scout groups, church chapters, artist groups, high schools, and universities were regular short-term visitors. Their stays typically lasted up to six weeks and combined volunteer work in "their" project with a touristic and political program. Meetings with representatives of government agencies and FSLN organizations alternated with trips to political events, visits to institutional symbols of social reforms like cooperatives or newly built facilities for education and healthcare, and, last but not least, trips to the beach and other touristic highlights.[71]

Both, visitors and Sandinistas were all well aware that the main output of these solidarity brigades was not the financial and economic contribution for a certain project. The solidarity brigades were rather seen as a catalyst for a transnational people-to-people diplomacy aimed at defending the revolutionary transformation in Nicaragua. Strategy and concept papers of both Sandinista officials and West German organizers stressed the visits as an opportunity to strengthen bilateral relationships and enhance the subjective experience of solidarity.

On the one hand, the very presence of the brigadiers allowed Nicaraguans to experience international support for the Sandinista revolution personally. The Sandinista daily newspaper *Barricada* covered the official solidarity campaign in 1983/84 with titles like "Internationalists: Solidarity and Admiration—Nicaragua Is Hope for People All Over the World." Reports on later visiting groups were published on a regular basis.[72] At the local level, a Sandinista official voiced his hopes that the brigades might serve as a source of motivation for Nicaraguans themselves.[73] Similarly, the West German coordination office stressed the importance of sending solidarity brigadiers even to areas affected by Contra attacks as a sign that solidarity groups and Sandinistas had not given up on them.[74]

On the other hand, these experiences—even the experience of living with Nicaraguan locals for several weeks—were intended to have an impact on West German activists too. In a poll among former brigadiers in 1985, a vast majority agreed that their visit had furthered their commitment to the cause.[75] The establishment of personal and emotional bonds between activists and locals was surely one reason for it, even though language barriers complicated the interaction. Thanks to personal encounters and their description in travel reports, Nicaraguans ceased to be an abstract mass of people affected by war and the ensuing precarious living conditions. "Now I know that this can happen to people I know and who have become friends,"⁷⁶ a Christian activist stated upon her return. For many other West Germans too, meeting Nicaraguans who had lost family members and loved ones in the armed conflict made its consequences tangible.

The war situation was not the only thing that made a deep impression on the West German activists, however. The experience of rural poverty and the corresponding revolutionary efforts to improve living conditions by providing financial and material support for the farmers as well as programs for education and healthcare also left their mark. Brigadiers assumed that they had "learned what it meant to live in a liberated country of the Third World" and that they had seen what revolutionary change meant for locals and their lives.⁷⁷

These personal experiences provided visitors with so-called "authentic" experience, which was highlighted as one of the best prerequisites for public lobbying work back home in West Germany. Also, this kind of subjective firsthand information was positively distinguished from reports by West German media that were discarded on account of perceived anti-Sandinista bias. The FSLN regarded solidarity brigades as the "best propaganda tool for the development of the Popular Sandinista Revolution."⁷⁸ A group of West German radicals agreed, stating that the brigade work brought "More motivation, more illustration, more and more recent detailed facts, e.g., what it means to be in danger by imperialist aggression."⁷⁹

Upon their return, many visitors engaged in public relations work focused on condemning military hostility against Nicaragua and defending the Sandinistas' political project. They organized talks and published articles, which due to their motivation and the circumstances of their stay, were often partial.⁸⁰ However, this is not to imply that activists avoided any criticism or were not aware of problems under the Sandinista rule. One brigadier frankly conceded in 1986 that his idea of collecting clear information had been naïve and that the situation in Nicaragua was too complex for an unambiguous assessment.⁸¹ He and his fellow activists usually addressed problematic issues within the framework of so-called "critical solidarity," which meant "being solidary with the [FSLN]'s principle aims considering always the conditions and explanations shaping their actions, but not approving of them automatically."⁸²

Moreover, by collecting funds for construction and infrastructure projects in Nicaragua, the solidarity movement and its brigades claimed to replace the official development aid that was curbed or withdrawn by the West German government due to criticism of the Sandinista regime. In terms of a people-to-people diplomacy, they aimed at representing another better and solidary West Germany to the Nicaraguan people and at differentiating themselves from the official policies of their government back home.

However, this message was hard to convey to Nicaraguan locals who often regarded their solidary counterparts as official emissaries of their home country.[83] In an interview, a thirty-six-year-old Nicaraguan schoolteacher admitted she was confused by the activists' self-representation. On the one hand, they were claiming to be in opposition to their government; on the other hand, they were applying for and receiving official funds to support projects in Nicaragua. "What I do not understand is, how can they be in opposition to their government and still receive funding from it?"[84] This doubt was understandable for someone unfamiliar with the German federal system. While the federal government blocked most of its official development aid, activists could still apply for funds from leftist governed federal states (*Bundesländer*) or city councils. Initiatives for town twinning between West German and Nicaraguan cities were one example of this. Not only were town-twinning initiatives seen as an instrument to further people-to-people diplomacy but they were also considered an opportunity to institutionalize solidarity and get access to public funding.

The Sandinistas had furthered the idea of town twinning early on. In spring 1982, a government official from the secretary for municipal affairs asked the West German Social Democrats for their support in establishing such municipal partnerships.[85] In the following years, local leftist party chapters, as well as independent solidarity groups, used their contacts to Nicaragua to realize this idea.[86] In 1988, the Federal Republic counted over forty such initiatives, some of which had already received official recognition from their respective town councils. Statistically, the number of initiatives was second only to the United States, and there were far more town twinning projects in West Germany than anywhere else in Western Europe.[87]

Town twinning or partnerships between schools also provided for more mutual exchange and travel in both directions. Although in much smaller in numbers, Nicaraguans soon started to visit their West German counterparts too. For the Sandinistas, this part of a people-to-people diplomacy fit their larger outline of an intensive public and cultural diplomacy.[88] Since the early speaking tours of Ernesto Cardenal (who went on to serve as Nicaragua's minister for cultural affairs from 1979 until 1988) or Enrique Schmidt Cuadra (who served as minister for post and telecommunication until he died in an ambush in 1984), the stream of Sandinista officials touring Western Europe and visiting its solidarity groups for public informational events had never really decreased. Every year, the IBN in Wuppertal organized at least one tour. Sometimes, officials were joined by Nicaraguan folk music bands, which also toured West Germany on a regular basis. Financially supported by the Sandinista government, these music tours offered a chance to get to know the country from a different angle and provided local solidarity groups with an opportunity to enhance their public lobbying activities. Speakers and musicians visited not only West Germany's large cities but also smaller towns in the countryside.

Conclusion

In the late 1970s and especially after the Sandinista guerrillas had taken power in 1979, Nicaragua became a focus point of radical and left-leaning circles in West Germany. Despite all of their actions, the solidarity movement still seems to have failed its main aims, namely to stop the military aggression against Sandinista Nicaragua, to enable the FSLN to pursue its agenda of political and social transformation in peace, and, ultimately, to stay in power. While much could be said about the authoritarian turn of the Sandinista regime and the context of the global Cold War, these three points remained far beyond the capabilities of solidarity groups, even on a worldwide basis.[89] Indeed, the West German movement seemed to have failed to change even the minds of West German politicians and shift the government's approach to Nicaragua. Or did it?

In 1978, the solidarity groups successfully challenged West German loans to the Somoza dictatorship. In 1983/84, West German activists protested US intervention in Central America by bringing the issue into the West German parliament and, last but not least, by traveling to Nicaraguan borderlands in order to serve as human shields. Such actions shed light on how the movement interfered with West German foreign politics and worked on establishing an alternative people-to-people diplomacy. With a continuous stream of information from within Nicaragua to support their lobbying, activist groups maintained an important position for the Central American country within West German politics for more than a decade. In the end, even the reigning conservative and liberal parties had to react. From the mid-1980s onward, they organized their own Nicaragua events—events that aimed at discrediting the FSLN and promoting support for local conservative opposition parties.[90] Furthermore, solidarity activists were also able to raise millions of German marks over the years to directly support the FSLN and its policies of social reform, especially after the FSLN had been largely cut off from official development aid.[91]

Aside from these particular achievements, the true success of contemporary West German Nicaragua Solidarity might lie elsewhere. The territorial spread of solidarity activism for Sandinista Nicaragua from large university cities to rural areas and from Southern Bavaria to the North Sea is a striking feature, which sets this movement apart from other examples. A second one is its persistence throughout the 1980s, which in some cases even continued after the FSLN lost the 1990 general election. The movement's territorial spread and its endurance was based, first of all, on the establishment of a transnational communications network that allowed information and people to circulate between the two countries. The Sandinistas were not solely recipients of solidarity but were actively engaged in the establishment of transnational connections. The framework of people-to-people diplomacy provided for personal encounters, for the establishment of individual connections, and furthered a mutual understanding of the situation in Sandinista Nicaragua. In some cases this even resulted in the institutionalization of bilateral relationships in the form of official town twinnings, some of which still exist to this day.

Again, all of these activities illustrate the collaboration between West German actors and their Nicaraguan counterparts. In terms of its focus and actions, then, West German Nicaragua solidarity was hardly a social movement that fit within a local or national container.

Christian Helm's PhD research focused on the transnational communications network between West Germany's Nicaragua solidarity movement and the Frente Sandinista de Liberación Nacional (1977–90). Other topics covered in his publications include the phenomenon of revolutionary tourism, the role of images in solidarity networks, and the transnational practices of their formation.

Notes

1. Archive Informationszentrum 3. Welt (iz3w), Freiburg, folder "Nicaragua ZB 1978 I," FSLN Comisión Exterior, Sub-Comisión de Información to Estimado Amigo, no date. The translation of this quote and the following ones are mine.
2. Cf. Klaus Hess and Barbara Lucas, "Die bundesdeutsche Solidaritätsbewegung," in *Die Revolution ist ein Buch und ein freier Mensch: Die politischen Plakate des befreiten Nicaragua 1979–1990 und der internationalen Solidaritätsbewegung*, ed. Otker Bujard and Ulrich Wirper (Cologne: PapyRossa Verlag, 2007), 306–17; Erika Harzer and Willi Volks, eds., *Aufbruch nach Nicaragua: Deutsch-deutsche Solidarität im Systemwettstreit* (Berlin: Christoph Links Verlag, 2008); Werner Balsen and Karl Rössel, *Hoch die internationale Solidarität: Zur Geschichte der 3.-Welt-Bewegung in der Bundesrepublik* (Cologne: Kölner Volksblatt Verlag, 1986); and an exception to this rule is Rosemarie Karges, *Solidarität oder Entwicklungshilfe? Nachholende Entwicklung eines Lernprozesses am Beispiel der bundesdeutschen Solidaritätsbewegung mit Nicaragua* (Münster: Waxmann, 1995).
3. Margaret Keck and Kathryn Sikkink, *Activists beyond Borders: Advocacy Networks in International Politics* (Ithaca, NY: Cornell University Press, 1998). Clifford Bob, *The Marketing of Rebellions* (Cambridge: Cambridge University Press, 2005).

4. Thomas Olesen, *International Zapatismo: The Construction of Solidarity in the Age of Globalization* (New York: Zed Books, 2005), 53.
5. Erich Fried, *Gesammelte Werke*, vol. 3 (Berlin: Wagenbach Verlag, 1993), 529–31.
6. Cf. Departamento de Propaganda y Educación Política del FSLN, ed., *El programa histórico del FSLN* (Managua, 1984 [1969]); Tomás Borge, "Combatientes de la Solidaridad y Defensa de la Revolución," in *La Dirección Nacional en el Primer Encuentro Internacional de Solidaridad con Nicaragua "El Salvador Vencerá,"* ed. Departamento de Propaganda y Educación Política del FSLN (Managua, 1981), 89–105.
7. For activists' self-positioning in leftist internationalism as a means to provide their quest with additional legitimacy, cf. Helm, *Botschafter der Revolution*, 8–9. For the mutual relationship between the emergence of the radical new left and their idea of a "Third World" in the case of France in the long 1960s, cf. Christoph Kalter, *Die Entdeckung der Dritten Welt: Dekolonisierung und neue radikale Linke in Frankreich* (Frankfurt a.M.: Campus, 2011).
8. Sally Scholz, *Political Solidarity* (University Park: Penn State University Press, 2008), 6.
9. Dieter Rucht, "Distant Issue Movements in Germany: Empirical Description and Theoretical Reflections," in *Globalization and Social Movements: Culture, Power, and the Transnational Public Sphere*, ed. John Guidry, Michael Kennedy, and Mayer Zald (Ann Arbor: University of Michigan Press, 2000), 78f.
10. Cf. the result of my own PhD research, Christian Helm, *Botschafter der Revolution: Das transnationale Kommunikationsnetzwerk zwischen der FSLN und der bundesdeutschen Nicaragua-Solidarität 1977–1990* (Berlin: DeGruyter, 2018); Ágreda Portero, José Manuel, and Christian Helm, "Solidaridad con la Revolución Sandinista: Comparativa de redes transnacionales; Los casos de la República Federal de Alemania y España," *Naveg@merica* 17 (2016), http://revistas.um.es/navegamerica/article/view/271921; Friederike Apelt, "Between Solidarity and Emancipation? Female Solidarity and Nicaraguan Revolutionary Feminism," in *Making Sense of the Americas: How Protest Related to America in the 1980s and Beyond*, ed. Jan Hansen, Christian Helm, and Frank Reichherzer (Frankfurt a.M.: Campus, 2015), 175–96; Benjamin Huhn, *Internationalismus und Protest: Solidarität mit Lateinamerika in der Bonner Republik der 1970er/1980er Jahre* (Mannheim: Röhrig Universitätsverlag, 2018); for Nicaragua solidarity in East Germany, see Stefanie Senger, "Getrennte Solidarität? West- und ostdeutsches Engagement für Nicaragua Sandinista in den 1980er Jahren," in *Internationale Solidarität: Globales Engagement in der Bundesrepublik und der DDR*, ed. Frank Bösch, Caroline Moine, and Stefanie Senger (Göttingen: Wallstein Verlag, 2018), 64–92; for Nicaragua solidarity in Western Europe and the United States, see Kim Christiaens "States Going Transnational" Transnational State Civilian Networks and Socialist Cuba and Sandinista Nicaragua Solidarity Movements in Belgium (1960s–1980s)," *Revue Belge de Philologie et d'Histoire* 89 (2011): 1277–305; Kim Christiaens, "Between Diplomacy and Solidarity: Western European Support Networks for Sandinista Nicaragua," in *European Review of History* 4 (2014): 617–34; Eline van Ommen, "La Revolución Sandinista en los Países Bajos: Los comités de solidaridad holandeses y Nicaragua (1977–1990)," *Naveg@merica* 17 (2016), http://revistas.um.es/navegamerica/article/view/271861; Héctor Perla, "Heirs of Sandino: The Nicaraguan Revolution and the U.S.-Nicaraguan Solidarity Movement," in *Latin American Perspectives* 6 (2009): 80–100.

11. Peggy Lorenz, "Entwicklungshilfe für Somoza," in *Endet das Schweigen*, ed. Informationsbüro Nicaragua (Wuppertal: IBN April 1978), 29.
12. Ernesto Cardenal, *Die Jahre in Solentiname* (Wuppertal: Peter Hammer Verlag, 2002), 251, 257.
13. Ernesto Cardenal, *Das Evangelium der Bauern von Solentiname*, 2 vols. (Wuppertal: Peter Hammer Verlag, 1976/1978).
14. Helm, *Botschafter der Revolution*, 41f., 98–101; for the memories of Cardenal's German editor, see Hermann Schulz, "'Endet das Schweigen': Von den Anfängen der Nicaragua-Solidarität," *Lateinamerika Nachrichten* 301/2 (1999): 32.
15. Hermann Schulz, "Enrique Schmidt Cuadra und der Beginn der Solidaritätsarbeit für Nicaragua," in *Enrique Presente: Enrique Schmidt Cuadra; Ein Nicaraguaner zwischen Köln und Managua*, ed. Hans Hübner et al. (Cologne: Schmidt von Schwind Verlag, 2004), 25f.
16. "Büro Nicaragua in Wuppertal nimmt Arbeit auf," *ila-info* 14 (1978), 15; "Nicaragua: Informationsbüro in der BRD eröffnet," *blätter des iz3w* 67 (1978), 13f.
17. *Für was kämpfen die Sandinisten? Programm der Sandinistischen Front*, ed. AELA München (Munich, 1978); see also IISH, ASK, Dose 51, Informationsbüro Nicaragua, Materiallisten, here vol. 1 (1980).
18. Forschungs- und Dokumentationszentrum Chile Lateinamerika (FDCL), Berlin, Folder "Nicaragua–P–Solidarität 1980–86," Encuentro de Comités de Nicaragua de Europa, Driebergen 30 March –1 April 1979.
19. IISH, ASK, Dose 50, FSLN a comités de solidaridad y demás organizaciones, April 1979.
20. Ibid.
21. FDCL, Folder "LA Nicaragua, Dokumente I," Pronunciamiento del Frente Proletario al pueblo de Nicaragua y el mundo, 3 October 1978.
22. FDCL, Folder "LA Nicaragua, Presse I," AK Mittelamerika, Kann man Nicaragua den Rücken zukehren? Fall 1977.
23. E.g., "Alemania. Los Comités de Solidaridad redoblan su lucha," *Lucha Sandinista* April (1978), 19.
24. For an early example, cf. iz3w, Folder "Nicaragua ZB 1978 I," Manifiesto del FSLN a todas las fuerzas democráticas, progresistas, patrióticas y anti-imperialistas del mundo, January 1977 [=1978, C.H.].
25. IBN: BMZ uneinsichtig, *Nicaragua Nachrichten* 2 (1978), 4.
26. Ibid., 5.
27. IISH, IBN, Folder "Komitee Arbeit," IBN, Nicaragua im Generalstreik, January 1978.
28. Cf. IBN, ed., *Nicaragua—ein Volk in Familienbesitz* (Reinbek: Rowohlt Verlag, 1979), 81; IISH, IBN, Folder "Rundbriefe Komitees," Lateinamerika-Komitee München: Rede von Enrique Schmidt, München 7 November 1978.
29. Letter cited in: "Nach den Septemberkämpfen," *Lateinamerika Nachrichten* 64 (1978), 13.
30. IBN, "Bonner Kreditpraxis und Somoza," *Nicaragua Nachrichten* 6 (1978), 8.
31. Protokoll der Plenarsitzung des Deutschen Bundestages, 4 May 1983, 71, http://dipbt.bundestag.de/doc/btp/10/10004.pdf.
32. Ibid., 130.

33. Ibid.
34. Cf. Silke Mende, *"Nicht rechts, nicht links, sondern vorn": Eine Geschichte der Gründungsgrünen* (Munich: DeGruyter Oldenbourg, 2011).
35. IISH, IBN, Folder "Grüne—Bundesarbeitsgemeinschaft Internationalismus," IBN an alle Nicaragua-/Mittelamerikakomitees, Wuppertal 1 July 1983.
36. Cf. IISH, IBN, Folder "Rundbriefe Komitees," IBN: Grundsatzpapier für die Nicaragua-Solidaritätsbewegung in der BRD, October 1980.
37. On West German Chile solidarity cf. Huhn, *Internationalismus und Protest*; Georg Dufner, "West Germany: Professions of Political Faith, the Solidarity Movement and New Left Imaginaries," in *European Solidarity with Chile 1970s–1980s*, ed. Kim Christiaens (Frankfurt a.M.: Peter Lang, 2014), 163–86.
38. Cf. Helm, *Botschafter der Revolution*, 166–67.
39. IISH, IBN, Folder "Grüne—Bundesarbeitsgemeinschaft Internationalismus," IBN an alle Nicaragua-/Mittelamerikakomitees, Wuppertal 1 July 1983.
40. Ibid., Annex "Zusammenarbeit mit den Grünen."
41. Cf. Sven Reichardt, *Authentizität und Gemeinschaft: Linksalternatives Leben in den siebziger und frühen achtziger Jahren* (Frankfurt a.M.: Suhrkamp Verlag, 2014).
42. IISH, IBN, Folder "Grüne—Bundesarbeitsgemeinschaft Internationalismus," IBN an alle Nicaragua-/Mittelamerikakomitees, Wuppertal 1 July 1983, Annex CV Gabriele Gottwald.
43. "Dritte Welt-Fachfrau in den Bundestag?," *ila-info* 63 (1983), 26f.
44. IBN Archive, Wuppertal, Folder "Intern, Brigadenprotokolle 1982/83," Bernd, Protokoll der AG Zusammenarbeit mit den Grünen, Nicaragua-Bundestrefffen, May 1983.
45. Ibid.
46. Frank Bösch, *Zeitenwende 1979: Als die Welt von heute begann* (Munich: C. H. Beck, 2019), 128.
47. E.g., "Bundesregierung mitschuldig," *ila-info* 66 (1983), 5; "Kleine Anfrage der Fraktion der Grünen an die Bundesregierung betreffs 'Kämpfe in Mittelamerika,'" *IBN Rundbrief* 5 September 1983, 2–5; "Drogenhändler, Geheimpolizisten, Politische Gefangene," *Mittelamerika Magazin* 36 (1984), 18f.
48. IISH, IBN, Folder "Grünen Fraktion im Bundestag," Gaby Gottwald, MdB, Bericht über meinen Aufenthalt in Nicaragua im Juli und August 1983; also in this folder: Gottwald, MdB, Tätigkeitsbericht, December 1983; IISH, IBN, Folder "Grünen Fraktion im Bundestag," Gottwald, Entwurf für einen Artikel in der Frankfurter Rundschau, 14 March 1984.
49. Cf., e.g., Archiv Grünes Gedächtnis (AGD), Berlin, 2B 5860, Dokumente zum Besuch Tomás Borges 1983; Die Grünen im Bundestag, ed., *Krisenherd Mittelamerika: Mit Auszügen aus dem Zentralamerika-Hearing der Grünen im Bundestag, 17.–18.3.1984* (Bonn, 1984).
50. AGD, 2B 5838, Jochen Hippler, Präsentation Krisenstab Mittelamerika, November 1984, AGN, 2B 5838, Jochen Hippler, Abschlussbericht Krisenstab, 30 January 1985.
51. IBN Archive, Folder "Intern, Brigadenprotokolle 1982/83," Bernd, Protokoll der AG Zusammenarbeit mit den Grünen, Nicaragua-Bundestreffen, May 1983.
52. IISH, IBN, Folder "Grünen Fraktion im Bundestag," Gottwald, Tätigkeitsbericht, December 1983.

53. Borge, "Combatientes de la Solidaridad," 99.
54. Ruedi Balmer, "Erstes Treffen der Solidaritätsgruppen in Managua," *Nicaragua Aktuell* 10 (1981), 28–30.
55. Cf. Thomas Walker and Christine Wade, *Nicaragua: Living in the Shadow of the Eagle*, 5th ed. (Boulder, CO: Westview Press, 2011), 47; Robert Kagan, *A Twilight Struggle: American Power and Nicaragua, 1977–1990* (New York: The Free Press, 1996).
56. Helm, *Botschafter der Revolution*, 243f.; Ruben Quaas, *Fair Trade: Eine globallokale Geschichte am Beispiel des Kaffees* (Cologne: Böhlau Verlag, 2015), 214f. From a contemporary activist perspective: Niña Boschmann and Willibald Fredersdorff, "Nicaragua Solidarität: Zwischen Wunsch und Wirklichkeit," *blätter des iz3w* 101 (1982), 43–46.
57. FDCL, Folder "Nicaragua Nachrichten, Infostelle Nicaragua," Lutz Kliche, Kurzer Bericht über das Treffen der europäischen Nicaragua-Solidaritätskomitees, Vienna 13–15 June 1980.
58. Hubertus, "Ein Brief aus Nicaragua," *Nicaragua Aktuell* 8 (1981), 7.
59. Reinhild Kreis, "'Eine Welt, ein Kampf, ein Feind'? Amerikakritik in den Protesten der 1980er Jahre," in *All We Ever Wanted . . .' Eine Kulturgeschichte europäischer Protestbewegungen der 1980er Jahre*, ed. Hanno Balz and Jan-Henrik Friedrichs (Berlin: Karl Dietz Verlag, 2012), 136–55; Philipp Gassert, "Mit Amerika gegen Amerika: Antiamerikanismus in Westdeutschland," in *Die USA und Deutschland im Zeitalter des Kalten Krieges 1945–1990: Ein Handbuch*, vol. 2, ed. Detlef Junker et al. (Stuttgart and Munich: Deutsche Verlags-Anstalt, 2001), 750–60.
60. Nicaragua-Gruppe der Luthergemeinde Offenbach, *Die Kinder sind die Zukunft unseres Landes: Bericht aus Nicaragua* (Offenbach: Private Publishing Venture, 1982), 22.
61. For a closer analysis of political tourism to Nicaragua, see my article "'The Sons of Marx Greet the Sons of Sandino': West German Solidarity Visitors to Nicaragua Sandinista," *Journal of Iberian and Latin American Research* 2 (2014): 153–70.
62. Borge, "Combatientes de la Solidaridad," 105.
63. IISH, IBN, Folder "Europäische Koordination 1979–81," Dokumente des 6. Europäischen Treffens der Nicaragua-Solidarität, Genf 6–8 November 1981, Protocolo del trabajo de la comisión III: Relaciones Comités-FSLN.
64. Perla, "Heirs of Sandino," 88f.; Edward Griffin-Nolan, *Witness for Peace: A Story of Resistance* (Louisville, KY: Westminster John Knox Press, 1991), 23–42.
65. For Cuba, cf. Christiaens, "States Going Transnational," 1286–89 and 1296.
66. Archiv IBN, Folder "Brigaden II Kommunikation," FSLN, Proyecto de Brigadas, 4f; Archiv IBN, Folder "Brigaden 1984/85," CNSP, Normativa para las Brigadas, 3; and in the same Folder, IBN, Informations- und Fragebogen für den Einsatz in Nicaragua, circa 1983/84.
67. Archiv IBN, Folder "Brigaden II Kommunikation," Telex, Jorge Granera/DRI an IBN, Managua 16 November 1983.
68. FSLN had its own Department for International Relations (DRI) to connect with transnational supporters abroad. Its subinstitution Comité Nicaragüense de Solidaridad con los Pueblos (CNSP) was responsible for the solidarity brigades.

69. Cf. the official call "Brigaden für das befreite Nicaragua: Unterstützung des Befreiungskampfes in El Salvador," *blätter des iz3w* 117 (1984), 6; "Wir bauen auf, was die Contra zerstört," *Mittelamerika Magazin* 50 (1985), 13–18.
70. In May 1986, Contra troops kidnapped an entire West German brigade and held them as prisoners for several weeks. Two months later, a German internationalist died with five colleagues when his car convoy was attacked near Matagalpa in Northern Nicaragua. For a contemporary assessment, cf. Ralf Leonhard, "Sperrzonen für alle Aufbauhelfer," *die tageszeitung*, 13 August 1986, 1, 6.
71. Among many other examples, e.g., Dengler Susi et al., *Solidarität ist die Zärtlichkeit der Völker: Berichte aus Nicaragua*, ed. Bundesvorstand der Jungsozialisten (Bonn: Bundesvorstand der Jungsozialisten, 1983).
72. Internacionalistas: Solidaridad y admiración—Nicaragua es una esperanza para todos los pueblos, *Barricada*, 4 January 1984.
73. Archiv IBN, Folder "Brigaden II Kommunikation," FSLN, Proyecto de Brigadas; Hess, Klaus, "Nicaragua—Arbeitsbrigaden," *blätter des iz3w*, 117 (1984), 4.
74. Archiv IBN, Folder "Brigaden 1984/85," IBN an zukünftige Brigadisten, Wuppertal April 1984.
75. Klaus Hess, "Auswertung der Arbeitsbrigadenkampagne," *IBN Rundbrief* 5 (1986), 15–23.
76. Barbara Wolf, "Unter Palmen und Gewehren: Blitzlichter einer vierwöchigen Nicaraguareise," *bundesforum: Zeitschrift der katholischen Landjugendbewegung Deutschlands* 3 (1985): 5.
77. "Postkarten aus Nicaragua für den Wiederaufbau von 'Oro Verde,'" in *IBN Rundbrief*, 5 September 1984, 19.
78. Archive IBN, Folder "Brigaden II Kommunikation," FSLN, Proyecto de Brigadas, 2.
79. Letter of a brigade in Pantasma, March 1985, cited in Hess, "Auswertung der Arbeisbrigadenkampagne," 19.
80. Hess, "Auswertung der Arbeitsbrigadenkampagne," 16.
81. Johannes Riehm, *Leben mit dem unerklärten Krieg: Berichte von einem Aufenthalt in Ocotal/Nicaragua im Sommer 1986* (Wiesbaden: Private Publishing Venture, 1986), 5; Hess, "Auswertung der Arbeitsbrigadenkampagne," 17.
82. Hess and Lucas, "Die bundesdeutsche Solidaritätsbewegung," 313.
83. Karges, *Solidarität oder Entwicklungshilfe*, 277–83.
84. Cit. in Karges, *Solidarität oder Entwicklungshilfe*, 281.
85. Archiv der Sozialen Demokratie, Bonn, SPD-Parteivorstand, Referat Jungsozialisten, 7628, Sonia García an Roland Röscheisen, Managua 12.5.1982.
86. Klaus Hess, "Städtepartnerschaften zwischen deutschen und nicaraguanischen Städten," in *Die Revolution ist ein Buch und ein freier Mensch: Die politischen Plakate des befreiten Nicaragua 1979–1990 und der internationalen Solidaritätsbewegung*, ed. Otker Bujard and Ulrich Wirper (Cologne: PapyRossa Verlag, 2007), 318–21.
87. Ronald van der Hijden et al., eds., *European Conference on City-Linking with Nicaragua: An Example of North-South Cooperation and Dialogue; Report* (Amsterdam: Private Publishing Venture, 1988), 49.
88. Cf. Helm, *Botschafter der Revolution*, 148–64.

89. David Close, Salvador Martí i Puig, and Shelley McConnell, eds., *The Sandinistas and Nicaragua since 1979* (Boulder, CO: Lynne Rienner Publishers, 2012); Lynn Horton, *Peasants in Arms: War and Peace in Nicaragua (1979–1994)* (Athens: Ohio University Press, 1998); John Coatsworth, "The Cold War in Central America, 1975–1991," in *The Cambridge History of the Cold War*, vol. 3: *Endings*, ed., Melvyn Leffler and Odd Arne Westad (Cambridge: Cambridge University Press, 2010), 201–21.
90. Cf. Bösch, *Zeitenwende 1979*, 133–36.
91. Cf. Frank Bösch, "Internationale Solidarität im geteilten Deutschland: Konzepte und Praktiken," in *Internationale Solidarität: Globales Engagement in der Bundesrepublik und der DDR*, ed. Frank Bösch, Caroline Moine, and Stefanie Senger (Göttingen: Wallstein Verlag, 2018), 30–32.

Select Bibliography

Ágreda Portero, José Manuel, and Christian Helm. "Solidaridad con la Revolución Sandinista: Comparativa de redes transnacionales; Los casos de la República Federal de Alemania y España," *Naveg@merica* 17 (2016), http://revistas.um.es/navegamerica/article/view/271921.

Bösch, Frank. "Internationale Solidarität im geteilten Deutschland: Konzepte und Praktiken." In *Internationale Solidarität: Globales Engagement in der Bundesrepublik und der DDR*, eds., Frank Bösch, Caroline Moine, and Stefanie Senger, 7–34. Göttingen: Wallstein Verlag, 2018.

Christiaens, Kim. "States Going Transnational: Transnational State Civilian Networks and Socialist Cuba and Sandinista Nicaragua Solidarity Movements in Belgium (1960s–1980s)." *Revue Belge de Philologie et d'Histoire* 89 (2011): 1277–305.

Close, David, Salvador Martí i Puig, and Shelley McConnell, eds. *The Sandinistas and Nicaragua since 1979*. Boulder, CO: Lynne Rienner Publishers, 2012.

Helm, Christian. "'The Sons of Marx Greet the Sons of Sandino': West German Solidarity Visitors to Nicaragua Sandinista." *Journal of Iberian and Latin American Research* 2 (2014): 153–70.

———. *Botschafter der Revolution: Das transnationale Kommunikationsnetzwerk zwischen der FSLN und der bundesdeutschen Nicaragua-Solidarität 1977–1990*. Berlin: DeGruyter, 2018.

Huhn, Benjamin. *Internationalismus und Protest: Solidarität mit Lateinamerika in der Bonner Republik der 1970er/1980er Jahre*. Mannheim: Röhrig Universitätsverlag, 2018.

Perla, Héctor. "Heirs of Sandino: The Nicaraguan Revolution and the U.S.-Nicaraguan Solidarity Movement." *Latin American Perspectives* 6 (2009): 80–100.

Walker, Thomas, and Christine Wade. *Nicaragua: Living in the Shadow of the Eagle*. 5th ed. Boulder, CO: Westview Press, 2011.

Chapter 13

East German Environmental Activism and the West

Connections, Common Ground, and Difference across the Iron Curtain

Julia E. Ault

In 1986, West German journalist Peter Wensierski wrote of his experiences reporting on East German pollution and societal responses to it. Addressing a West German audience, he declared that since Chernobyl it had become ever more apparent that "environmental problems are transboundary in character and can only be solved in mutual cooperation."[1] This statement was one that many West Germans likely shared in light of growing environmental consciousness in the Federal Republic of Germany (West Germany, FRG) since at least the 1960s. Wensierski, then, pivoted to explaining environmental challenges next door in the communist dictatorship, East Germany (German Democratic Republic, GDR). For a West German readership that was environmentally aware but not necessarily familiar with the GDR, he illuminated environmental devastation, a repressive system that restricted access to important data, and a small but active protest movement. Wensierski's work is but one example of transnational environmental connections after '68.

In the GDR, new sources of frustration—or new approaches to existing problems—brought about activism akin to Western social movements in the years after '68. Without large-scale student protests or a Prague Spring–type movement in '68, however, the expression of concerns about human rights, peace, the environment, and other "socio-ethical" issues took on different forms.[2] The Protestant Church, as the only sizable semi-independent institution in the GDR, emerged as a key site for discussion of such concerns and as a refuge for groups that sought to tackle such issues.

Over time, church-based groups increasingly used socio-ethical topics to critique and undermine the GDR's ruling Socialist Unity Party (SED). The secret police (Stasi) understood these groups as a threat. Thus, the Stasi infiltrated the groups, spied on individual activists, and shut down meetings. As a result, opportunities for collective action were significantly more restricted than in the FRG. Still, church-based groups discussed themes and took political orientations similar to those found in Western social movements.

When West German activists, politicians, and scholars looked eastward, they quickly found these parallels and responded to them in a variety of ways. They aided groups in the GDR and informed the West German public about conditions behind the Iron Curtain through radio, newspaper, and television reporting. Through visits, letters, and other means of communication, West Germans established connections with East Germans that grew into transnational networks. At the same time, East German dissidents eagerly sought to connect their activism with the related transformations in Western countries, which lent their work legitimacy and allowed them to speak of an emerging civil society in the GDR.[3] During and after the "Peaceful Revolution" of 1989, former East German activists drew on these contacts and parallels to situate themselves in a unified and democratic Germany.

The case of environmental activism elucidates the asymmetrical entanglements between East and West Germans and social movements in their respective states.[4] The conservation movement, as a predecessor to modern environmentalism, dated back to Wilhelmine Germany where it had enjoyed widespread support.[5] Environmental concern continued to exist in a variety of forms in both Germanys during the postwar division. In the 1970s and 1980s, that activism underwent an "ecologization" in East and West, a development that revealed that environmental activism was not an isolated phenomenon but a shared one.[6] Whether in response to water or air pollution, acid rain, or nuclear power, grassroots initiatives were emblematic of the movement in both states.[7] Given that West Germans had more freedom to travel, Western activists, politicians, and observers played a larger role in similar, more restricted initiatives in the GDR than did East Germans in the FRG.

While opportunities, chronologies, and legacies of social movements differed between the East German dictatorship and the West German democracy, the environment provided a window into "the other side" and created a sense of mutual responsibility. In the 1960s and 1970s, independent environmental groups within the East German Protestant Church were part of a trend toward more environmental awareness that was developing all around the globe, including in the FRG. By the 1980s, East Germans leaned on West Germans for data and practical aid that were difficult to obtain in the GDR. At the same time, West Germans learned about both environmental problems and political challenges under communism. Activists established networks across the German-German border, sharing information and resources and occasionally organizing joint protests. As the GDR collapsed, the environment became one source of frustration in the mass demonstrations of 1989 and helped shape analyses of East German social movements after the fact. This chapter argues that a look at green activism in East and West reveals shared sensibilities about the environment, its protection, and its importance to sustaining human life in Cold War Germany. Though interactions between East and West Germans did not occur without misunderstandings, engagement in environmental affairs illuminates growing connections across the Iron Curtain that are often overlooked in divided environmental histories of the two Germanys.

The Origins of Environmental Activism in the GDR

Independent environmental activism first found a foothold within the Protestant Church in the late 1960s and early 1970s. By the late 1960s, growing international attention to ecology fed into fears about pollution—and its impact on humans—in the GDR. In this context, the Protestant Church became invested in environmental questions and supported parish-based environmental groups. As in the FRG, environmentalism gained significance among certain segments of East German society in the 1970s and 1980s. With increased contact between the two Germanys in this period, the East German environmental movement grew not as a copycat of the more popular Western movement but in relationship with it. East German activists reacted to domestic conditions and global debates, but they strategically employed West German and international influences to bolster their critiques of environmental degradation and to challenge the SED.

Because the social and political landscape was markedly different in the GDR than in the FRG, the possibilities for activism were also quite distinct. Assembling or organizing events without the explicit permission of the SED or the state was virtually impossible. Any sort of association was either funneled into officially sanctioned party or state organizations or banned outright. Indeed, even church-based activities were closely monitored. Both the Protestant and Catholic Churches were suspect in the eyes of the state and regularly antagonized throughout the first half of the GDR's existence.[8] Beyond the churches, police quickly disbanded unsanctioned gatherings, while the Stasi kept close tabs on East Germans. In fact, over the course of the GDR's existence, the Stasi grew, doubling in size between 1968 and

1982 alone.⁹ By 1989, the Stasi employed over 91,000 full-time officers, meaning that in a country of roughly 17 million people, there was roughly one officer for every 180 East German citizens. Additionally, the Stasi paid some 173,000 unofficial informants to tattle on family, friends, coworkers, and neighbors.[10] Activism was thus far more limited behind the Iron Curtain. Fewer people joined activist groups, meetings were less public, and the stakes were higher.

The Protestant Church became involved in ecological questions in the 1960s, in large part thanks to transnational connections. It soon developed into a refuge for environmental activists.[11] The Church's participation in the World Council of Churches (WCC) spurred a reflection on Christianity's relationship with the natural world at a moment when many countries around the world were grappling with the challenges of consumption, pollution, and population growth.[12] The Church's "Committee on Church and Society," which interfaced with the WCC, assembled experts to consider the place of the environment in the GDR.[13] A collection of clergy, technical experts who were active in the Church, and others, this committee explored the impact of environmental pollution at home while also contemplating how to speak to international Christian audiences. This work included Provost Dr. Heino Falcke's presentation about the "environment under socialism" at the WCC's 1979 conference on "Faith, Science, and the Future" in Boston.[14]

At the same time, the environmental problems that East German Christians identified were intrinsically local. Air and water pollution levels were incredibly high, especially in industrial areas such as the Chemical Triangle, a name given to the area surrounding Halle and Bitterfeld. Open-pit coal mining scarred the landscape, lowered local water tables, and destabilized the ground. What is more, East German coal was of low quality and laced with sulfur, producing sulfur dioxide when burned. Such conditions led to acid rain killing the forests (and damaging buildings), high rates of chronic bronchitis, and unsafe drinking water.[15] Yet environmental data was nearly impossible to obtain. After 1982, the state classified it as "secret," meaning that East Germans could not access statistics that confirmed the devastation they observed all around them. As citizens' initiatives took off across the FRG, the environment also became a subject of intense debate in East German church circles.[16]

In 1978, the Church further solidified its support for environmental activism when it reached a détente with the SED and committed itself to being the "Church in Socialism." In recognizing the SED as the ruling party of the GDR, the Church garnered relative freedom for itself and was able to champion politicized causes, such as peace, human rights, gay rights, and women's rights.[17] Women for Peace and the Initiative for Peace and Human

Rights were prominent in the GDR, and both were deeply connected to Europe-wide activist networks.[18] In this climate, environmentalism found fertile ground. Parish-based groups sprang up across the GDR with the Church's backing, revealing that the environment attracted attention in the Church both from the top down and the bottom up.[19]

By the early 1980s, a number of church-based environmental groups regularly met and held events across the GDR. Groups emerged in numerous towns and cities, not only in major industrial centers. Schwerin, Rostock, Berlin, Magdeburg, Leipzig, Halle, Dresden, and other smaller towns all boasted environmental groups. In 1988, the Ecclesiastical Research Center in Wittenberg tallied at least fifty-eight active groups across the GDR, while specific events could attract hundreds of participants, an impressive feat in light of constant Stasi surveillance.[20] These groups navigated the confines of the East German dictatorship to learn about and act on behalf of the environment. They typically stated a number of objectives in their fliers and internal writings, such as improving their own understanding of ecological interconnection, learning about local pollution, and protesting against environmental destruction. Participants related anecdotes, planted trees, hosted environmental church services, and organized bicycle demonstrations.

Environmental activism expanded dramatically after Chernobyl in 1986. After learning about the disaster from Western media, East Germans voiced growing frustration with the regime. New groups popped up and began to discuss the dangers of nuclear power and to learn about their potential exposure to radiation from the disaster in Ukraine. These groups included, most famously, the Environmental Library at the Zion Church in East Berlin.[21] The new groups met on the parish level as well as at more central church-hosted events. The "Eco-Seminars" at the Environmental Library, for example, drew participants from all over the GDR as well as international observers from the FRG and Eastern Europe.[22] East Germans who attended returned to their local groups to disseminate what they had learned, which created a more connected network of activists.

Practically, East Germans relied on their Western counterparts for environmental data as well as ideas about how to protest. Numerous groups in the GDR stated their desire for West German data and environmental materials. A group in Greifswald, for example, requested magazines and journals from the FRG that contained relevant content.[23] Given that environmental data was classified as secret in the GDR in 1982, hard numbers were important for verifying personal observations. In fact, activists from across Eastern Europe reached out to West Germans for environmental information.[24] In 1984, for example, a Hungarian wrote to the West German Green member of parliament Erika Hickel to ask for a copy of Fritjof Capra's *Green Politics*, which was not available in Hungary. The swelling green movement along with the convenience of German-language articles, not to mention personal ties, made the FRG an important point of contact and comparison for East Germans. Moreover, West German examples provided East Germans with concrete alternatives to failing SED policies.

East German environmental activism evolved in the Protestant Church in response to both local conditions and international trends. Though their meetings were smaller than the mass demonstrations that became increasingly common in the FRG, East German activists worked on a grassroots level within the Church, which was also invested in environmental questions. While parish-based groups relied on the Church and used a Christian rhetoric to critique the SED, they also drew inspiration from a range of sources, some of which were West German. The movement in the GDR did not therefore simply "copy" or "catch up" with West German social movements; it developed in relationship with them. East German activists strategically applied certain aspects of West German and global trends to their own situation while relying on outside information to bolster their own protests.

West German Engagement with East German Environmentalism

The surge in environmental activism in the FRG coincided with an easing of tensions between the two Germanys, most notably through the signing of the Basic Treaty in late 1972. The improved relations between the FRG and the GDR enabled increased contact and travel between the two states. In particular, it became easier for West Germans to travel eastward, which led to stronger networks between activists across the Iron Curtain. Journalists, as well as activists and politicians, made connections with environmental activists in the GDR, learning about the movement there and sharing information with others back in the FRG. Additionally, after the West German Green Party entered parliament in 1983, that party's official visits to the GDR opened up another avenue of communication between East and West German activists. By the late 1980s, West German media reports about environmental conditions in the GDR were commonplace, appearing in newspapers and magazines and on television and the radio. The improved networking also led to some joint protests, especially regarding waste disposal, in the GDR's final years. Through these types of interactions, a sense of common concern about the conditions in the GDR emerged for some activists.

West German activists and journalists visited the GDR and supported the independent movement in various ways, such as reporting on it back home. These actions garnered the Stasi's attention and inspired it to interfere in interactions between West and East German activists. Peter Wensierski was a prominent example of this phenomenon. He was a West Berlin–based journalist who became the youngest Western travel correspondent active in the GDR thanks to his position at the Protestant News Service (Evangelischer Pressedienst). Beginning in 1979, he reported on East German environmental issues, connecting them to the green movement in the FRG and bringing them into the Western eye. His engagement with pollution in the GDR earned him a specific mention in the SED's 1982 decision to classify all environmental data, making it virtually impossible to collect information about pollution.[25] Wensierski nevertheless published numerous books and articles on pollution in the GDR based on personal observations and conversations with the people he encountered in East Germany.[26] His 1985 exposé in *Der Spiegel* highlighted the seriousness of acid rain pollution and "forest death" (*Waldsterben*), as well as the lack of funds for improving conditions, which stood "in contrast to the situation in the Federal Republic."[27] Wensierski was banned from entering the GDR that same year.

The parish-based nature of independent activism in the GDR reminded the West German greens of their own grassroots structure and locally based initiatives. Wensierski employed familiar language and examples that helped draw in West German audiences. The green movement's successes and entrance into electoral politics in the late 1970s and early 1980s served as a point of comparison (and contrast) for his West German readership.[28] Wensierski teased out the local orientation of environmental protest, connecting parish-based organization to the grassroots democratic character of the green movement in the FRG.[29] This emphasis on local initiatives complemented the nonhierarchical and grassroots, or *basisdemokratisch*, approach so popular to environmental activism in the FRG. Direct participation in politics, such as through citizens' initiatives (*Bürgerinitiative*) that responded to local polluters, were a quintessential element of the West German green movement in the 1970s.[30] Over time, East German groups embraced the term *basisdemokratisch* to explain their intentions too, despite not living in a democratic system.[31] Their goal, at least in part, was to connect their efforts to successful methods in the West.

Wensierski and others, such as West German Green Party politician Dr. Wilhelm Knabe, personified the transnational component of the environmental movement. They traveled back and forth across the Iron Curtain bringing information and ideas with them, entangling developments in the two countries. Wensierski referred to church-based environmentalists as "the

Greens (East)," further highlighting the similarities between East and West.³²
The comparison between environmental movements in the FRG and the
GDR not only familiarized West Germans with changes in the GDR but
also lent credibility to East German activists. The work of Wensierski and
others brought East German environmental groups to West Germans' attention, which led to international recognition and status for the East German
groups.

The West German Green Party politician Wilhelm Knabe played an important part in this work. Knabe had long fostered contacts in the GDR,
which he and his family had fled in 1959. These contacts strengthened connections between Eastern and Western greens and raised the profile of these
small East German groups.³³ In 1983, Knabe was part of an official Green
Party delegation that visited the GDR to take part in meetings with officials
as well as church-based environmental activists.³⁴ Knabe made numerous
further trips to the GDR in his position as a Green Party politician, aiding church-based groups as many became increasingly oppositional toward
the SED. He consistently smuggled in banned materials for East German
groups. His contacts tended to be in Berlin, and from there, the materials
he brought could be distributed across the GDR through church networks.
Most famously, using his diplomatic status as a member of parliament,
Knabe smuggled in a printing press for the Environmental Library at the
Zion Church in Berlin-Mitte.³⁵ The Environmental Library's publication,
Umweltblätter, went from print runs of two hundred to two thousand between 1986 and 1989—thanks in part to the new machine—making it one
of the most circulated underground, or samizdat, publications in the GDR.³⁶
Issues of *Umweltblätter* made their way from Berlin to Leipzig, Dresden, and
other East German towns and cities, shaping the debate around the environment, pollution, and the SED dictatorship. Over the next three years, the
Environmental Library and its publications became increasingly critical of
the regime, in part thanks to Western data that revealed the extent of East
German pollution.

In the early 1980s, Wilhelm Knabe's son, Hubertus, became increasingly
interested, and personally involved, in church-based "socio-ethical" groups in
the GDR. He too spent time with activists, and in his popular and academic
writing he explicitly compared the rise of environmental groups, as well as
other East German activist groups, to the West German social movements
of the 1970s.³⁷ He compared the discussions of modernization and highly
industrialized societies in Western Europe to those under state socialism in
Eastern Europe, specifically the GDR, which were often considered preconditions for the West German social movements of the 1970s.³⁸ The younger
Knabe noted affinities between peace, environmental, and other groups in

the Church—referring to them as "alternative political orientations"—and similar movements in the FRG. He emphasized the groups' grassroots structure, the "postmaterial" orientation of their interests, and their attractiveness for young, well-educated participants.[39] Knabe considered these various groups to comprise an "overarching counterculture," though he created typologies of the topics and aims instead of treating groups' objectives holistically as part of a broader picture of human life.[40]

The younger Knabe not only published on East German activism but also gave interviews on West German radio, familiarizing audiences in the FRG with the situation in the GDR. His explanations of the "socio-ethical" groups helped West Germans to understand similarities, but he also emphasized important differences. Knabe explained that the party and state attempted to co-opt potential social movements, and the lack of civil society under socialism made it difficult to counteract the regime's monopoly on power. The SED's meddling in the peace movement and the 1980 creation of the "Society for Nature and Environment" in the party's Cultural League were but two of the most prominent examples.[41] Still, in a 1983 radio interview with *Bayerischer Rundfunk*, Knabe explained that a thousand Christians attended church events in Dresden to discuss the "crisis of the environment."[42] Given the limitations on independent movements in the GDR, this number was not insignificant, and interest continued to grow in subsequent years. The Knabes and Wensierski helped raise awareness about East German pollution in the FRG as well as in the GDR.

One of the most famous instances of East and West German collaboration on the environment was the creation of the documentary *Bitteres aus Bitterfeld* in 1988. The thirty-minute film exposed the devastating environmental conditions in and around the town of Bitterfeld in the Chemical Triangle. East German activists filmed the documentary and smuggled it into the FRG where Wensierski then handled the editing and airing of the documentary on West German television.[43] This piece highlighted the GDR's pollution problem for West Germans who learned about pollution that flowed from the Mulde River into the Elbe and across the border to impact them.[44] East Germans who secretly watched West German programming learned about conditions at home. In the months that followed, environmental groups in the Church set up screenings and discussions of the documentary as well as other smuggled content, such as videos on forest death in the Ore Mountains along the East German–Czechoslovak border and industrial animal production.[45] Such connections raised awareness about pollution and created a common sense of concern in the two Germanys.

Cooperation between East and West German environmental activists remained relatively limited, though, and the challenges of working in a dictatorship remained quite clear. In a letter to a Greenpeace chapter in Hamburg, two church-based environmentalists in Leipzig enlightened the West Germans as to the practical realities of life in a dictatorship. They explained that if Greenpeace sent a letter with the logo on it, the authorities would immediately open it; there was no right to privacy.[46] They further described the difficulties of raising awareness when it was illegal to publicly display bulletins or photos of sludgy rivers or dying forests; nor could they freely publish materials to inform citizens about the devastation.[47] These complications inhibited their ability to effect change, and the potential consequences of joining a social movement, such as being spied on or even imprisoned, kept people away. The authors illustrated disparities in a social movement's opportunities under a dictatorship even as they sought information and materials from the other side.

The proximity of West Berlin, an island surrounded by the GDR, offered East Germans the means to critique the SED's handling of pollution. In Berlin, East Germans invoked West Berlin's "smog alarm" in petitions to the authorities. The alarm consisted of television and radio warnings regarding the air quality in the city.[48] In their letters, East Berliners asked why West Berliners were notified of high sulfur dioxide and carbon monoxide levels but they were not. As one petition noted, "We know that the pollution levels are just as high if not higher" on the GDR side of the border.[49] The *Umweltblätter* also reported that, "from the window of the Environmental Library, we can see the buildings of the West Berlin district of Wedding," and concluded that pollution levels had to be nearly identical, even if East German media did not report on them. The authors encouraged East Berliners to listen to West Berlin television and radio for air quality updates.[50] The divided city proved problematic for the SED, which tried to hide environmental data, given that not only pollution but also television and radio signals defied the political boundary.

Beyond relying on West German information, East and West Germans jointly protested the issue of waste disposal. In the 1980s, the GDR accepted waste from the FRG in return for hard currency. The SED, being strapped for cash, adopted a number of strategies to bring in Western money, one of which was to dispose of West German trash.[51] The FRG approved of this arrangement, because paying the GDR to take it was cheaper than disposing of it at home.[52] A side effect of strict environmental regulation in the FRG was costlier waste disposal; as a consequence, waste was exported instead. Thus, in the GDR's final years, East and West Berlin environmental groups worked together to protest East German dumps that took West German waste and, of course, did not follow the same level of environmental care that the West German companies would have been obligated to implement at home.

To protest a new incinerator at one dump, the West Berlin–based Robin Wood and the Environmental Library held a joint demonstration in the GDR on 1 November 1988.[53] Robin Wood activists attempted to block West Berlin trash trucks from crossing the border into the GDR near Lichtenrade and then join East Berliners demonstrating at the landfill in Schöneiche. Organizational confusion, however, accidentally led to the Stasi being tipped off ahead of time. A press conference about the upcoming protest in West Berlin made the Stasi aware of the groups' protest, and so it was broken up before anyone could reach the site. As one participant later wrote in the *Umweltblätter*, "By 11:30, there wasn't an unguarded bush" in Schöneiche county anymore, and police rounded up the demonstrators.[54] Protests such as these underscored the common concerns that East and West German activists shared as well as the challenges in undertaking joint projects.

Most West German activists focused on domestic issues or looked westward for transnational cooperation. A few, however, also looked to the GDR and Eastern Europe.[55] Those activists, politicians, and journalists made West Germans aware of environmental conditions behind the Iron Curtain, and they supported the severely restricted independent movement in the GDR. In the communist dictatorship's final years, collaboration and interactions across the German-German border helped to expand the movement and demonstrated a sense of common purpose. While the East German movement remained small—there were no mass environmental protests in the GDR, and fewer people were involved in environmental activism than in the FRG—fears about East German pollution existed in the GDR and the FRG.

1989 and Understanding East German Environmentalism After the Fact

In the years after 1989–90, East and West Germans alike sought to understand the East German environmental movement of the 1980s and its significance. For both it was useful to compare environmental activism—and by extension the citizens' movements of 1989—in the GDR to West German social movements after '68. First, they were connected by the sharing of information and joint protests. Second, similarities in the East and West German movements, such as their emphases on human rights and the environment, helped to make sense of the groundswell of protest in the fall of 1989. Third, for East German activists, association with West German social movements provided a sense of importance to their work after the fact. Comparisons between the FRG's social movements after '68 legitimized East

German activism and helped explain the "peaceful revolution" both in the moment and in the years that followed.

In the fall of 1989, as the GDR collapsed, many sources of frustration brought East Germans into the streets to demonstrate against the SED. Communist parties in other countries, such as Poland and Hungary, had already ended their monopoly on power, putting pressure on the SED to do likewise. Beginning in September, new "citizens' movements" began demanding reform in the GDR. Some of those involved in environmental groups were also founding members of the citizens' movements. Nearly every citizens' movement incorporated ecological planks into its platform, suggesting how central the environment was to East Germans' demands for transparency and reform. In November, some activists founded an East German Green Party that gave the environment primacy over virtually all other frustrations with the regime.[56] The overlap between environmental activists and the leaders of the 1989 citizens' movements connected church-based groups to the mass demonstrations.

While not the driving force behind the protests, environmental issues were part of Leipzig's Monday Demonstrations and continued to play a role throughout unification. The connection between environmental activism and citizens' movements in 1989 defies simple explanations. The environment alone did not bring tens of thousands of people into the streets, but it fed into a larger disillusionment with the SED that mobilized East Germans. As unification progressed, earlier activism, the lived experience of pollution, and German-German cooperation of the 1980s helped to make environmental cleanup a relatively noncontroversial topic; the need to ameliorate East German pollution was self-evident. West German chancellor Helmut Kohl made that clear when he included the environment as an important part of his unification strategy. His Ten Point Plan, which he introduced in late November 1989, referenced environmental protection and cooperation in three of its ten points.[57] A greening of both East and West German society—and the interactions between them—created a common interest in cleanup.[58]

A unified Germany presented new challenges to the formerly East German environmental groups and tested their resilience. In particular, the revelations of Stasi unofficial informants (*inoffizielle Mitarbeiter*, IM) further challenged cooperation among former oppositional and environmental figures. Henry Schramm, for example, had been an important figure in Halle's environmental scene and even became a party speaker for the East German Green Party before it merged with the West German one in December 1990. Later, it was revealed that he had been an IM since 1983 and actively disrupted environmental protests, reported on fellow activists, and even sought to lure them back to the movement when they drifted away.⁵⁹ With the opening of Stasi files in the 1990s, former dissidents learned who had previously betrayed them, a set of revelations that created deep rifts and undermined any remaining sense of solidarity. Along with a new socioeconomic order that was profoundly disorienting, distrust and feuds among members of the East German groups hindered environmental action after 1989.

Confronting this past and securing the opposition's legacy—not further environmentalism—became the top priority for a subset of the former dissidents. In many ways, pollution became less of an issue as the newly unified German parliament committed to spending hundreds of millions of marks on environmental cleanup in the former GDR.⁶⁰ In the early 1990s, many former members of the Berlin-based Environmental Library, a prominent environmental and oppositional group from the 1980s, began to preserve the memory of their work. A core of the activists turned the library into an archive and information center about the injustices of the SED dictatorship.⁶¹ The Robert Havemann Society, named after the prominent East German dissident and chemist, produced exhibits and publicized documents relating to 1980s dissident groups and their role in the 1989 revolution. The Havemann Society's publications emphasized the connection between church-based groups, citizens' movements, and the collapse of the GDR. Thus, the content of the dissidents' engagement changed significantly from opposing the regime in the 1980s to documenting their activism in the 1990s.

Numerous activists also turned to penning personal accounts of dissidence in the GDR and describing their leading roles in the peaceful revolution. Some were closely connected to the Robert Havemann Society, while others pushed against its narrative, revealing how the distrust and rifts that were created in the 1980s carried forward. Prominent memoirs include Carlo Jordan's *Arche Nova: Opposition in der DDR, Das "Grün-ökologische Netzwerk Arche," 1988–90*, Wolfgang Rüddenklau's *Störenfried: DDR-Opposition, 1986–1989*, and Michael Beleites's *Untergrund: Ein Konflikt mit der Stasi in der Uran-Provinz.*⁶² All three works recount personal involvement and run-ins with the Stasi, which they supplement with documents from their respective environmental groups. These authors and others prioritized cementing their personal contributions over untangling the conflation of groups, citizens' movements, and mass protests in 1989.

With East German academics and universities generally discredited after unification, Western scholars took on the task of explaining 1989.⁶³ The question of dissidence and opposition in the GDR continued to dominate the scholarly debate. Hubertus Knabe published his book on environmental conflicts in the GDR and Hungary in 1993, which now incorporated communism's rapid demise and argued that pollution played a significant role in that process.[64] Other social scientists used the West German model to track East German groups as they transitioned to a liberal democratic order. Many of these scholars had first written about social movements in the FRG or Western Europe and only turned to studying the GDR after 1990. As a result, they sometimes came to unflattering conclusions that did not take the challenges of protest under a dictatorship into account. Three prominent scholars claimed in the 1990s, for example, that "East groups" after 1990 were less resistant to the "pressure to conform in the direction of institutionalization" than the "New Social Movements of the West." The scholars argued that East German groups were less robust and less able to withstand pressure.[65] The Western social movements remained the gold standard for successful protest and resistance to state pressure, though they arose in a different sociopolitical context than the East German groups.

Over time, scholars—especially those who had contacts in the GDR prior to 1989—developed more nuanced approaches to East German activism as well as its relationship to Western social movements. Sociologist Detlef Pollack, who began his book *Politischer Protest* with a vignette about visiting friends in Leipzig in June 1989, and others referred to "political alternative" or "socio-ethical" movements."[66] They used the terms to define the similarities and illustrate differences between the systems, teasing out the relationship between East German movements, the Church, and the state. Another sociologist, Karl-Werner Brand emphasized differing opportunities for mobilization and evolution, arguing that the church-based groups in the GDR only expanded into a larger movement in the context of East German collapse (instead of being a latent social movement or the cause of its demise).[67] In doing so, scholars clarified why these groups appeared when they did in the history of the GDR and offered contingency in their relationship to 1989. With more distance (and greater access to sources), scholars provided more insight to the continuities and ruptures in (East) German history while avoiding value-laden assessments about "catching up" with the West.

As a participant in the activism of the 1980s and a scholar, Hubertus Knabe became personally invested in studying the role of the Stasi in the GDR. He completed his doctorate in political science at the Free University of Berlin in 1991 and shortly thereafter began to work for the Federal Commissioner for the Stasi Records. Later, he became the scientific director of the Berlin-Hohenschönhausen Memorial and penned numerous publications on repression in the dictatorship.[68] In 2019, he left that position under a range of accusations. His vice director had allegedly sexually harassed female employees, and the memorial had accepted funds from an association with ties to the far-right Alternative for Germany (AfD).[69] Throughout his career, Knabe had maintained close ties with dissidents who experienced imprisonment in the GDR but drifted away from social movement research.

In the 1990s, former activists and scholars alike sought to make sense of East German environmental activism through the lens of social movements and the peaceful revolution. The relationship between these three phenomena (environmental activism, social movements, and the peaceful revolution) was more complicated than often portrayed in the years immediately following unification. Conflating their origins and motivations was at times intentional as activists sought to legitimize their dissidence in the 1980s and West German scholars sought comparisons that were familiar. East German activism, West German social movements, and the mass demonstrations of 1989 were absolutely related to one another, but the complexity of their impulses, interactions, and networks became clearer with temporal distance.

Conclusion

The environmental activism that developed in the East German Protestant Church in the 1980s was both the product and subject of transnational exchanges of knowledge. Consumption, population growth, and their impact on the environment became sources of concern within the Church as early as the late 1960s and early 1970s. Connections to international organizations raised environmental awareness within the Church and laid the groundwork for grassroots environmental activism at the parish level. That activism evolved in response to local environmental conditions and pushed against the SED's attempts to hide damning data about the extent of the devastation. The motivations for environmental activism—as limited as it was in the dictatorship—were varied.

East Germans active in the church-based or independent (sponsored by neither the party nor the state) movement gained knowledge and credibility through contacts with the West. West German social movements, and later the West German Green Party, became sources of inspiration as well as of practical support. East Germans strategically used contacts with the West to critique the SED dictatorship. And while instances of joint protests were limited, they nevertheless complicate divided narratives of environmental activism in the two Germanys. The differences between the political systems were real, but both sides cultivated transnational networks and illuminated common values. Some of the connections suggest older, pre–Cold War traditions of nature conservation in a German context, while others speak to an environmental zeitgeist in the 1970s and 1980s.

Finally, the relationship between East German activism and 1989 defies simplicity while also highlighting the centrality of environmentalism across political systems. Protest against pollution alone did not bring down communism, but frustration over living conditions, public health, and environmental degradation did contribute to dissatisfaction with the SED. Groups such as the Environmental Library in East Berlin used West German values, information, and contacts to fuel that discontent. As the East German dictatorship collapsed, the state of the environment became increasingly intertwined with other motivations for protest, such as the lack of a right to travel and inadequate material standards of living. The "big social movement" moment in the GDR, namely the mass demonstrations of 1989, brought down the regime, but it drew on transnational interactions and networks that had been built over the previous two decades. This perspective also helps to explain the general popularity of environmental cleanup in the former GDR in the 1990s. Environmentalism in the two Germanys—and across the 1989 divide—is more connected than often acknowledged.

Julia E. Ault is an Associate Professor of History at the University of Utah. Her book, *Saving Nature under Socialism: Transnational Environmentalism in East Germany, 1968-1990* was published with Cambridge University Press in 2021. Her research interests include the environment, transnational networks, social movements, socialism, and the Cold War.

Notes

1. Peter Wensierski, *Von oben nach unten wächst gar nichts: Umweltzerstörung und Protest in der DDR* (Frankfurt a.M.: Fischer Taschenbuch Verlag, 1986), 1.
2. Anna von der Goltz has complicated this narrative in her article "Making sense of East Germany's 1968: Multiple Trajectories and Contrasting Memories," *Memory Studies* 6, no. 1 (2013): 53–69.
3. Scholars and dissidents alike connect dissidents in Eastern Europe to the "rebirth of civil society." See Barbara Falk, *Dilemmas of Dissidence in East-Central Europe: Citizen Intellectuals and Philosopher Kings* (Budapest: Central European University Press, 2003), 2–3, or Jürgen Kocka, *Civil Society and Dictatorship in Modern German History* (Hanover, NH: Brandeis University Press, 2010), 41–42.
4. Christoph Kleßmann, "Introduction," in *The Divided Past: Rewriting Post-war German History*, ed. Christoph Kleßmann (New York: Berg Publishers, 2001), 2–3. While using environmental activism as a case study, I readily acknowledge it evolved in conjunction with related movements, such as peace and human rights.
5. John Alexander Williams, *Turning to Nature in Germany: Hiking, Nudism, and Conservation, 1900–1940* (Stanford, CA: Stanford University Press, 2007).
6. Jens Ivo Engels, *Naturpolitik in der Bundesrepublik: Ideenwelt und politische Verhal-*

tensstile in Naturschutz und Umweltbewegung, 1950–1980 (Paderborn: Ferdinand Schöningh, 2006), 294.
7. Environmental histories of postwar Germany tend to focus on either the FRG or the GDR. For the FRG, examples include Engels, *Naturpolitik in der Bundesrepublik*; Stephen Milder, *Greening Democracy: The Anti-nuclear Movement and Political Environmentalism in West Germany and Beyond, 1968–1983* (New York: Cambridge University Press, 2017); Frank Uekötter, *The Greenest Nation? A New History of German Environmentalism* (Cambridge, MA: MIT Press, 2014). For the GDR, histories include Tobias Huff, *Natur und Industrie im Sozialismus: Eine Umweltgeschichte der DDR* (Göttingen: Vandenhoeck & Ruprecht, 2015); Christian Möller, *Umwelt und Herrschaft in der DDR: Politik, Protest und die Grenzen der Partizipation in der Diktatur* (Göttingen: Vanderhoeck & Ruprecht, 2020). A few works move beyond this dichotomy, notably Astrid M. Eckert, *West Germany and the Iron Curtain: Environment, Economy, and Culture in the Borderlands* (New York: Oxford University Press, 2019).
8. Mary Fulbrook, *Anatomy of a Dictatorship: Inside the GDR, 1949–1989* (New York: Oxford University Press, 1995), 87–125.
9. Gary Bruce, *The Firm: The Inside Story of the GDR* (New York: Oxford University Press, 2010), 41.
10. Ibid., 10–11.
11. From this point on I will refer to the Protestant Church as the "Church" in order to be more concise.
12. Donella H. Meadows et al., "Forward," in *The Limits to Growth: A Report for the Club of Rome's Project on the Predicament of Mankind* (New York: Universe Books, 1972), 9.
13. Evangelisches Zentralarchiv (EZA) 101 633, "Protokoll über die 8. Sitzung des Ausschusses Kirche und Gesellschaft am 4./5. Februar 1972 in Berlin, Auguststrasse 80."
14. Bundesarchiv (BArch) DO 4/801, "Vorschläge zur Gliederung 'Umweltschutz und Kirchen,'" 30 December 1983.
15. Archiv Bürgerbewegung Leipzig (ABL), Kirchliches Forschungsheim Wittenberg, "Die Erde ist zu Retten," 1985, 1; Tobias Huff, *Natur und Industrie im Sozialismus: Eine Umweltgeschichte der DDR (Göttingen: Vandenhoeck & Ruprecht, 2015)*, 226–29; BArch DK 5/2145, "Bericht über Ergebnisse des Umweltschutzes in der Deutschen Demokratischen Republik, 1981."
16. The SED was also invested in environmental protection in the GDR and created the Ministry for Environmental Protection and Water Management in 1972. For more party and state efforts, see Huff, *Natur und Industrie im Sozialismus*; Möller, *Umwelt und Herrschaft in der DDR*; Julia E. Ault, *Saving Nature under Socialism: Transnational Environmentalism in East Germany, 1968–1990* (Cambridge: Cambridge University Press, 2021).
17. Fulbrook, *Anatomy of a Dictatorship*, 107–9.
18. Fulbrook, *Anatomy of a Dictatorship*, 212; Ned Richardson-Little, *The Human Rights Dictatorship: Socialism, Global Security, and Revolution in East Germany* (New York: Cambridge University Press, 2020), 192–96.
19. Julia E. Ault, "Defending God's Creation? The Environment in State, Church and Society in the German Democratic Republic, 1975–1989," *German History* 37, no. 2 (2019), 205–26.

20. RHG Ki 18/02, "Die Karteibroschüre der kirchlichen Umweltgruppen in der DDR: Stand vom November 1988."
21. Wolfgang Rüddenklau, ed., *Störenfried: DDR-Opposition 1986–1989, mit Texten aus den "Umweltblättern"* (Berlin: BasisDruck, 1992), 69.
22. Robert Havemann Gesellschaft (RHG) SWV 02/01, "Drittes Berliner Ökologieseminar," undated. BArch, MfS, BV Bln AG XXII 275, "Erste Erkenntnisse zum sogenannten 3. 'Berliner Ökologieseminar' vom 28.11.1986 bis zum 30.11.1986 in der Evangelischen Kirchgemeinde Zion." The Ecology Working Group (a subset of the Friedrichsfelde Peace Circle) started the seminars a few years earlier, but starting in 1986 the Environmental Library hosted them.
23. RHG Ki 18/02, "Die Karteibroschüre der kirchlichen Umweltgruppen in der DDR: Stand vom November 1988."
24. Archiv Grünes Gedächtnis (AGG) B II 3 1176, Letter from Imre Hronszky, 10 November 1984.
25. BArch DK 5/1982, "Bericht über Probleme des Geheimnisschutzes bei Informationen zum Umweltschutz," 5 October 1982.
26. Peter Wensierski and Wolfgang Büsche, *Beton ist Beton—Zivilisationskritik aus der DDR* (Hattingen: Scandica, 1981); Wensierski, *Von oben nach unten wächst gar nichts*.
27. Peter Wensierski, "'Wir haben Angst um unsere Kinder': Report über die Umweltverschmutzung in der DDR (I)," *Der Spiegel* 28 (1985), 65–66.
28. Stephen Milder, "Between Grassroots Protest and Green Politics: The Democratic Potential of 1970s Antinuclear Activism," *German Politics and Society* (Winter 2015): 25.
29. RHG HK 1, "'Erste Hilfe für die Umwelt': Ökologisches Engagement in den evangelischen Kirchen der DDR," Bayrischer Rundfunk, 26 September 1983.
30. Roland Roth and Dieter Rucht, eds., *Neue soziale Bewegungen in der Bundesrepublik Detuschland* (Frankfurt: Campus Verlag, 1987), 20.
31. RHG RG S 01 03, Initiative Leben—Leipzig, January 1989.
32. Wensierski, "'Wir haben Angst um unsere Kinder,'" 65.
33. "Forstmann, Umweltaktivist, Mitbegründer der Grünen und der Heinrich-Böll-Stiftung: Wir erinnern an Wilhelm Knabe," https://www.boell.de/de/2016/02/24/eine-haelfte-des-lebens-fuer-andere-einsetzen, accessed 2 March 2022. Hubertus was born shortly after they arrived in the West, but he also developed an interest in the GDR, including having a partner who applied for and was granted permission to emigrate.
34. AGG A 56, "Besuch von den Grünen," *Der Sonntag: Gemeindeblatt der Evangelisch-Lutheranisch Landeskirche Sachsens*, 18 November 1983, Personalbestand: Wilhelm Knabe.
35. "Schmuggel für die Umweltbibliothek," Bundesbeauftragter für Stasiunterlagen der ehemaligen DDR, retrieved 22 June 2021 from https://fallofthewall25.com/mauer geschichten/schmuggel-fuer-die-umwelt-bibliothek.
36. "Environmental Pamphlets [*Umweltblätter*] (1987)," retrieved 22 June 2021 from https://germanhistorydocs.ghi-dc.org/sub_image.cfm?image_id=2836. The press was later confiscated by the Stasi.
37. AGG A 56, Correspondence between Wilhelm Knabe and Erich Honecker, 10 October 1984.

38. Hubertus Knabe, "Neue Soziale Bewegungen im Sozialismus: Zur Genesis alternativer politischer Orientierungen in der DDR," *Kölner Zeitschrift für Soziologie und Sozialpsychologie*, 40 (1988): 551–53.
39. Ibid., 556, 562. Karl-Werner Brand, "'Neue Soziale Bewegungen' auch in der DDR? Zur Erklärungskraft eines Konzepts" in *Zwischen Verweigerung und Opposition: Politischer Protest in der DDR, 1970–1990*, ed. Detlef Pollack and Dieter Rink (Frankfurt a.M.: Campus, 1997), 235–51.
40. Ibid., 558.
41. Knabe, "Neue Soziale Bewegungen im Sozialismus," 565.
42. RHG HK 01, "Erste Hilfe für die Umwelt: Ökologisches Engagement in den evangelischen Kirchen der DDR," Bayerischer Rundfunk, 26 September 1983.
43. AGG POL 509-3, "Teil II. Die Grünen aus dem Blickwinkel der Bürgerbewegungen der DDR," undated.
44. BArch DO 4/1022, Correspondence between Hans Reichelt and Willi Stoph, 6 October 1988. "Müll: Grube ohne Grenze," *Der Spiegel*, 18 July 1983, 48–49.
45. BArch, MfS, BV Bln Abt. XX/3780, "5. Ökologie Seminar, 1988—Abschlußbericht." BArch, MfS, BV Bln AKG 632, "Den '1. Berliner Umwelttag' am 3. und 4. Juni 1989 in der Bekenntniskirche in Berlin-Treptow," 7 June 1989.
46. ABL 22.14, Letter to Wolfgang Lohbeck, Hamburg (Greenpeace member), 18 December 1984. Ault, *Saving Nature under Socialism*, 137.
47. Ibid.
48. BArch DK 5/1982, "Bericht über Probleme des Geheimnisschutzes bei Informationen zum Umweltschutz," 25 October 1982.
49. RHG RG B 08, Der Friedens- und Umweltkreis der Pfarr- und Glaubenskirche Lichtenberg, "Eingabe: Betr. Zeite besonders hoher Schadstoffkonzentrationen in der Berliner Luft?" 11 January 1985.
50. "Stellungnahme der Umwelt-Bibliothek zum Smog in Westberlin," *Umweltblätter*, February 1987.
51. Astrid Mignon Kirchhof, "'For a Decent Quality of Life': Environmental Groups in East and West Berlin," *Journal of Urban History* 41, no. 4 (April 2015): 625–46.
52. "Müll: Grube ohne Grenze," *Der Spiegel*, 18 July 1983, 29.
53. RHG RG/B 19/09, "Robin Wood und Umwelt-Bibliothek gegen Giftmüllexport." Ault, *Saving Nature under Socialism*, 193-194.
54. Ibid.
55. Andrew S. Tompkins, *Better Active than Radioactive! Anti-nuclear Protest in 1970s France and West Germany* (New York: Oxford University Press, 2016).
56. Carlo Jordan, "Greenway—das osteuropäische Grüne Netzwerk (1985–1990)," in *Beiträge zur Zeitgeschichte: 30 Jahre Grüne in West und Ost* (Berlin: Archiv Grünes Gedächtnis, 2010), 43.
57. "Helmut Kohl's Ten-Point Plan for German Unity (November 28, 1989)," retrieved 28 June 2021 from https://germanhistorydocs.ghi-dc.org/sub_document.cfm?document_id=223.
58. How that cleanup happened and what caused the simultaneous rise in unemployment in the former GDR is a different issue.
59. Merrill E. Jones, "Origins of the East German Environmental Movement," *German Studies Review* 16, no. 2 (May 1993), 257. Ault, *Saving Nature under Socialism*, 235.

60. Sebastian Knauer, "Ein Fluß geht baden," *Der Spiegel* 30/1990, 23 July 1990, 45.
61. "Robert Havemann," retrieved 7 September 2016 from http://www.havemann-gesellschaft.de/index.php?id=46.
62. Micheal Beleites, *Untergrund: Ein Konflikt mit der Stasi in der Uranprovinz* (Berlin: BasisDruck, 1991); Carlo Jordan and Hans Michael Kloth, eds., *Arche Nova: Opposition in der DDR, "Das Grün-ökologische Netzwerk Arche," 1988–1990* (Berlin: BasisDruck, 1995); Rüddenklau, *Störenfried*.
63. Konrad H. Jarausch, *The Rush to German Unity* (New York: Oxford University Press, 1994), 204.
64. Hubertus Knabe, *Umweltkonflikte im Sozialismus: Möglichkeiten und Grenzen gesellschaftlicher Problemartikulation in sozialistischen Systemen; Eine vergleichende Analyse der Umweltdiskussion in der DDR und Ungarn* (Cologne: Verlag Wissenschaft und Politik, 1993), 26–27.
65. Barbara Blattert, Dieter Rink, Dieter Rucht, "Von den Oppositionsgruppen der DDR zu den neuen sozialen Bewegungen in Ostdeutschland?" *Politische Vierteljahresschrift* 36, no. 3 (1995): 420.
66. Detlef Pollack, *Politischer Protest: Politisch alternative Gruppen in der DDR* (Opladen: Springer Fachmedien Wiesbaden, 2000). Nathan Stoltzfus, "Public Space and the Dynamics of Environmental Action: Green Protest in the German Democratic Republic," *Archiv für Sozialgeschichte* 43 (2003): 385–403. Gareth Dale, *Popular Protest in East Germany, 1945–1989* (New York: Routledge, 2005).
67. Brand, "Neue Soziale Bewegungen' auch in der DDR?" 236.
68. Hubertus Knabe, "Vita," retrieved 28 June 2021 https://hubertus-knabe.de/biographie/. For example, Hubertus Knabe, *Die Täter sind unter uns: Über das Schönreden der SED-Diktatur* (Berlin: PropylSen Verlag, 2007). The title alludes to the 1946 rubble film, *Die Mörder sind unter uns*, which was supposed to force viewers to consider German atrocities during World War II.
69. "Hubertus Knabe muss Stasi-Gedenkstätte verlassen," *Der Spiegel*, 26 September 2018, retrieved 11 September 2019 from https://www.spiegel.de/kultur/gesellschaft/hubertus-knabe-direktor-der-stasi-gedenkstaette-berlin-hohenschoenhausen-muss-gehen-a-1230033.html.

Select Bibliography

Eckert, Astrid M. *West Germany and the Iron Curtain: Environment, Economy, and Culture in the Borderlands*. New York: Oxford University Press, 2019.

Huff, Tobias. *Natur und Industrie im Sozialismus: Eine Umweltgeschichte der DDR*. Göttingen: Vandenhoeck & Ruprecht, 2015.

Kleßmann, Christoph, ed. *The Divided Past: Rewriting Post-war German History*. New York: Berghahn Books, 2001.

Knabe, Hubertus. "Neue Soziale Bewegungen im Sozialismus: Zur Genesis alternativer politischer Orientierungen in der DDR," *Kölner Zeitschrift für Soziologie und Sozialpsychologie* 40 (1988): 551–69.

Pollack, Detlef. *Politischer Protest: Politisch alternative Gruppen in der DDR*. Opladen: Springer Fachmedien Wiesbaden, 2000.

Chapter 14

Activists Divided?

Continental Imaginations in West Germany's 1968 and Beyond

Anna von der Goltz

The May 1968 edition of *FU Spiegel*, a popular West Berlin student newspaper, gave powerful expression to the idea that the activists of the late 1960s crossed borders with ease. The cover image showed a group of flag-waving protesters leaping across a map of Europe in leftward motion. Various stars marked recent flashpoints of protest, from Milan to Oslo and from Madrid to London. Although the revolts of the late 1960s took place on a continent divided into different political systems—capitalist liberal democracies in the west and north, the communist bloc in the east, and capitalist right-wing dictatorships in the south—the image depicted a united continent without national frontiers. Most strikingly, less than seven years after the East German communist regime had built a border wall around the Western part of the city in which the paper was published, it showed a Europe that was not bifurcated by the political cartography of the Cold War. There was no "Iron Curtain" and no Berlin Wall. Warsaw and Prague were simply featured alongside Paris, Brussels, and Copenhagen as sites of recent demonstrations. A caption underneath read "International Student Revolt."[1] This image perfectly captured the idea that the student movement of 1968 was not just a West German phenomenon but a transnational and Pan-European one.

Recently, scholars have indeed often emphasized the Europeanism of the years around 1968. That this was a truly international moment that linked young people across the continent and beyond has become a hallmark of a literature that regards Europe as a key site of the "global 1960s."[2] Even the "Iron Curtain" has come to be understood as more of "a semi-permeable membrane," a porous barrier that allowed a sustained exchange of ideas, people, and goods.³ Given such linkages across the blocs, some scholars have explicitly portrayed the so-called '68ers as vanguards of European integration, a generation that anticipated the growing together of the divided continent that occurred after 1989—a unity the cover of *FU Spiegel* had already hinted at two decades earlier.⁴

The two Germanys, with their geographical proximity, shared history and language, and extensive kinship ties, have been identified as particularly rich cases in which to study trans-bloc solidarities and transfers in the global 1960s. Scholars have examined, for instance, how New Left thought, anti-imperialist critiques, antiauthoritarianism, and the counterculture manifested themselves in two closely connected locations with contrasting ideological settings.⁵ As a contributor to this literature, I have cautioned elsewhere against the temptation to view 1968 through the prism of 1989/90—to read backward from unification to narrate the history of activism in divided Germany as a uniform one.⁶ This chapter revisits these questions to suggest a number of different ways in which we might rethink the meaning that the Cold War East held for activists in West Germany—first, by offering a more nuanced assessment of how activists of the Left viewed the communist bloc and Europe over time and, secondly, by redirecting our historical gaze to take in the spectrum of political diversity characterizing the West German student experience of 1968.⁷

The first part of the chapter examines why, at least around 1968, East-West encounters among leftists were often as noteworthy for the incomprehension that accompanied them as for any sense of political connection they engendered—in spite of strongly imagined solidarities. As we will see, the *FU Spiegel*'s cover image was at most aspirational. Significant obstacles hampered the emergence of a shared political culture and language that could easily transcend the Cold War divide, and communist Eastern Europe—including East Germany—did not, in fact, feature prominently on the mental maps of most West German New Leftists.⁸ Their political imaginations were usually more global than continental.⁹ A sustained interest in the struggles of those in the communist bloc only arose after 1968, with the rise of Charter 77 and the Solidarity movement in the late 1970s and 1980s.

However, this does not mean that, around 1968, West German activists generally disregarded the communist East and German division. As the second part of this chapter shows, these were, in fact, key issues for some activists in this period—students of the center-right. They populated the Association of Christian Democratic Students (Ring Christlich-Demokratischer Studenten, RCDS) as well as a number of new center-right umbrella groups that were founded at West German universities from 1967 onward. These activists participated in 1968 in manifold ways and left their mark on (West)

German political culture in the years after, particularly during Helmut Kohl's chancellorship in the 1980s. Like their peers on the Left, these student activists were critical of many aspects of the "post-45 settlement" and saw a need for increased participation by ordinary citizens to revive West German democracy, but most nevertheless chose to effect change through established political channels—by running for office or joining political bureaucracies in the state capitals or at the federal level.[10]

Comparing and contrasting the New Left's and center-right's political imaginations and the very different ways in which German and European division featured within them, this chapter aims to rethink the intricacies of activist internationalism in the wake of 1968. In doing so, it helps to break out of the confines of the existing literatures on 1968 and the New Social Movements, which strongly privilege activism of the Left. Writing center-right activists back into the history of 1968 and its afterlives reminds us that student activism in these years was a broader, more versatile, and, ultimately, more consequential phenomenon than the traditionally narrower focus on left-wing radicals allows. It also demonstrates that the Left around 1968 and the social movement activists of the 1970s and 1980s did not operate in a vacuum but in an environment that was structured by the center-right in significant ways.

A Porous Border

The "Iron Curtain" was indeed porous in divided Germany, and critiques of the "repressive system" operative in both capitalist and state socialist settings percolated across the divide.[11] In the late 1960s, New Left activists on both sides of the divide imagined themselves as part of the same worldwide struggle against authority, imperialism, technocratic domination, and political hypocrisy.

Easterners obtained information about the Western student movement in a number of different ways. For one, it was covered regularly in the Eastern press. Although skeptical that students, rather than workers, were behind most of the West German demonstrations, Eastern newspapers welcomed them as evidence of a latent longing for socialism in the Federal Republic—at least prior to the Warsaw Pact's intervention in Czechoslovakia, which hardened the regime's stance toward youth protest. Moreover, the majority of East Germans could receive Western television stations and radio channels, which regularly covered student protests. By 1971, 85 percent of GDR citizens owned a television, and viewing Western programs was extremely common.[12]

The two halves of Berlin were an especially important zone of exchange. Visits by Westerners to the Eastern half of the city were severely restricted between the Wall's construction in 1961 and 1972, when the Four Power Agreement took effect. However, the close ties between Western and Eastern inhabitants of the city that had characterized the entire postwar period were not severed completely by the Wall, thanks to various travel permit agreements that provisioned for visits on a limited scale and enabled the exchange of ideas via texts, books, records, and other goods that visitors often brought with them.[13] As a result, activists from both halves of the city corresponded and met in person. There was even a commune in East Berlin, the Kommune I Ost, that was modeled, at least in part, on its Western predecessor Kommune 1, an offshoot of the SDS and the first West German political commune set up to break out of the constraints of the bourgeois nuclear family.[14] Some of the founders of Kommune 1 visited East Berlin on several occasions where they were hosted by the East Berlin dissident circle that clustered around the scientist Robert Havemann, the singer Wolf Biermann, and the sculptor Ingeborg Hunzinger. Under the ever-watchful eye of at least one Stasi informant, the activists discussed the divergent possibilities for meaningful political change in East and West.[15]

Some East and West German activists were also bound by longstanding family or friendship ties—an important factor in a divided country that had seen a massive exodus from East to West before 1961. Jürgen Holtfreter, for one, a graphic designer for the radical left-wing paper *Agit 883*, was originally from East Germany and had left the GDR in the late 1950s. He had first got involved in the leftist scene as an art student in Stuttgart where he helped to design a famous SDS poster that showed Marx, Engels, and Lenin next to the slogan "Everybody talks about the weather. We don't."[16] Holtfreter's brothers had stayed in the East, and, once he had settled in West Berlin, he became the single point of contact for a number of different East German oppositional groups that sought support from the West. Holtfreter regularly ferried books, brochures, and newspapers in his children's diapers. As he recalled in an interview:

> Those were the days of the Extra-Parliamentary Opposition in West Berlin and it was exactly their [the Easterners'] thing. . . . The atmosphere from West Berlin at the time reached East Berlin every day, via the media, TV and radio and so on. They were keen to lay their hands on it all, anything one could smuggle over. And that's what I did for a long, long time. I was their smuggler in chief.[17]

Goods and information did not just flow seamlessly between the two Germanys. Some West German leftists also showed a keen interest in reform socialist movements in other Eastern Bloc countries. At the time, the most notable among these was, of course, the Prague Spring, the experiment to create "socialism with a human face" in Czechoslovakia. Sibylle Plogstedt, a West German SDS activist who would later help found the feminist magazine *Courage*, spent the summer of 1968 in Prague conducting research on the Czechoslovak economy. There she met young Czech reformers from Charles University who fascinated her. As she recalled in her memoir: "I had never witnessed this kind of resistance. I didn't want to miss a single moment. . . . No comparison to what happened in West Berlin in 1968."[18] Plogstedt returned to Prague in the fall of 1968 and joined the Revolutionary Youth, a newly formed dissident group around activist Petr Uhl with whom she began a relationship. They practiced trans-bloc "socialism in one bed," as she put it.[19]

Lost in Translation

Such evidence of a porous "Iron Curtain," reciprocal interest, and intimate ties notwithstanding, encounters between Eastern and Western activists of the Left were actually often quite fraught in the late 1960s. Envisioning how change could be brought about in two fundamentally different political systems was not easy.[20] The Westerners typically emphasized the need to build a mass following via publicly visible protests and performative rule-breaking—protest repertoires that were much more difficult and dangerous to employ in socialist dictatorships that circumscribed expressions of nonconformity far more extensively than Western liberal democracies.[21] Oblivious, as some Western activists no doubt were, to the level of fear that marked daily life in the East, they could perceive Easterners as insufficiently radical, timid, or even boring.[22] Eastern dissidents' reform-mindedness, in particular, could make them awkward partners for a Western Left that dreamt of revolution.

Conversely, many Easterners thought that activists in the West were self-centered and dismissive of Easterners' longing for more democracy and affected a revolutionary superiority toward them.[23] Some Easterners who fled to the Federal Republic found it particularly difficult to speak about communist repression. "Many [on the Left] didn't like it. . . . Those [Easterners] who spoke openly of their . . . prison experiences were automatically put in the right-wing corner," recalled Steffi Recknagel, who had been involved in GDR oppositional groups and imprisoned for her beliefs before she arrived in West Berlin in the 1970s.[24] Fearing, as they did, that critiquing state socialism would undermine communist ideals in general and divert attention from the anti-capitalist cause, New Left activists in the West indeed struggled to find ways to openly address the repressiveness of Eastern Europe's socialist regimes.

Ideas also got lost in translation.[25] Eastern activists who met West German SDS icon Rudi Dutschke often recalled that his Marxist-inspired jargon had put them off. Dutschke had come of age in East Germany before fleeing west in 1961. He frequently visited the socialist bloc in the late 1960s, making him more attuned than most Westerners to the conditions to the east of the "Iron Curtain." Nevertheless, his Marxist vocabulary echoed the Eastern regimes' official rhetoric and, as such, did not seem persuasive to many of his Eastern interlocutors who had developed serious doubts about Marxism's emancipatory potential.[26] Such observations were neither limited to Dutschke nor to the German context. Polish activist Aleksander Smolar, who ended up in Paris as a result of the Polish anti-Zionist campaign, recalled similar barriers to East-West communication.

> The West, churned up by 1968, fascinated me; but I also felt lonely and alien. The people I met in Bologna and Paris were often near to me in age, sensitivity, and literary taste, but at the same time terribly distant. This began at the level of language. . . . The Western prisoners of semantics . . . were describing the world in the same language as Brezhnev and Gomulka. That was enough to block conversation, not to mention agreement.[27]

This should give us some pause when trying to conceive of 1968 as a moment that anticipated German or European unity, particularly among leftists. The former West German SDS chair K. D. Wolff put it bluntly when interviewed in 2008: "We did not feel all-German. I still don't feel all-German."[28]

Such recollections have no doubt been bolstered by post-unification debates about the proverbial "Wall in the head." However, it is worth noting that contemporary student publications—particularly those on the center-right—already picked up on this incomprehension between Eastern and Western activists. The popular West Berlin student paper *Colloquium*, for one, a publication with a strong antitotalitarian bent and centrist politics, repeatedly carried reports about trans-bloc communication problems on the Left.[29] In April 1967, the paper ran an article in German translation that had originally been published in the Prague-based student paper *Student*. The piece discussed the tensions that had surfaced during a recent meeting between West German SDS activists and members of the official Czechoslovak youth organization. The Westerners' fervent anti-capitalism and lack of knowledge about the actual political conditions in the Eastern Bloc had given them an utterly utopian idea of socialism, the authors argued. The Easterners had tried to explain that a socialist revolution in the West would not solve the world's problems, least of all those of the "Third World." The Westerners, in turn, had denounced the Easterners as "bureaucrats"—a favorite *Situationist* insult—the article reported.[30]

At the height of the Prague Spring, another *Colloquium* piece openly mocked Western leftists' global imagination.

> In Poland and Czechoslovakia, a number of liberal reforms are needed that "troublemakers" in Western democracies already benefit from. One consequence is that some groups on our side deem evolution boring and instead prefer to tell the Latin Americans and Vietnamese—from a safe distance—to have their heads kicked in. The students in the socialist countries understand much better how to sensibly combine protest and working within the system. The liberalization there, incidentally, is primarily driven by forces of a type that over here are condemned as managers, slaves to practical constraints, positivists, and one-track specialists.[31]

The piece ended by admonishing members of the Western "would-be-revolutionary elite" to turn their gaze back to their own continent. They should stop wasting their time trying to grow "Castro beards" and "change their travel plans for a cheaper ticket to Prague," the paper suggested.

About a decade later, in the late 1970s and 1980s, new oppositional movements in Eastern Europe, such as the Czechoslovak Charter 77 and Poland's Solidarity, found novel ways of mobilizing against the communist dictatorships that centered on open and peaceful defiance and human rights. At a time when the Cold War confrontation between the superpowers became more heated, Western leftists, who had begun to rethink their own revolutionary politics after 1968, began to enthusiastically embrace the cause of Eastern dissidents, leading to a deeper and more sustained engagement that lasted until 1989 and beyond.[32] As a result of this rapprochement, some New Left activists grew critical of the movement's previous blind spots. One of them was Christian Semler, who had been a leading figure in the West Berlin SDS in the 1960s, a Maoist activist in the 1970s, and who had dedicated himself to the cause of Eastern dissidents in the 1980s. With hindsight, he lamented that, in 1968, the GDR had been "terra incognita" for activists in the West, a place one had tried to avoid except for obligatory family visits.[33] His old acquaintance Dutschke had begun to rethink the Western Left's mental maps even earlier. In one of the last interviews he gave before his death in 1979, he recalled that, a decade prior, few Westerners had understood why the Easterners' fight had targeted communist systems. For him and his peers in the West, capitalist liberal democracy had been the chief culprit, he explained.

> I remember that within the core of the SDS, the majority thought alike as to the question of Eastern Europe. Nobody even discussed it. It was considered secondary, so we just didn't bring it up. . . . But no understanding whatsoever of the situation and what the real stakes were in [Czechoslovakia]. This is the main reason why the left in Western Europe did not understand the dynamics of social and political emancipation in Eastern Europe. Because of this, communication and cooperation became impossible.[34]

The post-'68 West German Left, he concluded, had to recognize that a meaningful political transformation in Western Europe would only occur if it went hand in hand with political and social emancipation in the East.

In a recent interview with the political scientist and public intellectual Claus Leggewie, the Franco-German former student leader Daniel Cohn-Bendit extended these self-reflections to include New Left conceptions of Europe as a political category. Although he has often been held up as the archetypical European in the literature on 1968, he cautioned: "Europe was not an issue, not at all. . . . We enjoyed the mobility, traveled back and forth . . . yes. But 'Europe' was not on our minds much, not as a grand idea and not as the basis for political institutions either."[35]

Continentalists

In fact, "Europe" was a far more salient theme for student activists of the center-right. In 1968, the Association of Christian Democratic Students called directly on the Christian Democrats to make a united Europe their chief political goal. In doing so, the organization was following in the footsteps of the Christian Democratic parties of the late 1940s, which had been a major driving force behind the early project of European integration.[36]

Center-right students relied primarily on formal channels of international exchange to liaise with student activists from other Western European democracies. The RCDS was a founding member of the International Union of Christian Democrat and Conservative Students (ICCS), which had been set up in 1961 and which organized regular meetings between like-minded students from across Western Europe.[37] At one such meeting held in 1970, the participants identified the belief in a "permanent reform of society . . . by evolutionary means" as their binding conviction, and they called on European politicians to help young reformers defeat the left-wing revolutionaries by "making parties and institutions more transparent, strengthening democracy within parties, communicating more with their citizens, and increasing the incentive to become politically active."[38]

Above all, it was their similar experiences of being put onto the defensive by a resurgent Left that strengthened the bonds between West German Christian Democratic students and their peers across the continent.[39] The fact that left-wing protest around 1968 was itself strongly transnational shrunk the political distance between different national student groups that opposed it. "Europe has to be seen as a unit in this regard as well. That is why the RCDS is trying to activate a European International of Students. All students that seek a free, democratic, and parliamentary Europe can collaborate," RCDS delegates to the association's annual federal convention agreed in 1969.[40] They envisaged this new body as a counterweight to the Prague-based, pro-Communist International Student Union after the dissolution of its main Western competitor, the International Student Conference (ISC), in February 1969 had left a political vacuum on the right.[41] Although the new organization never quite got off the ground, the "fight against the extreme Left . . . [remained] an absolute link" between European Conservative and Christian Democratic student groups well into the 1970s, as Friedbert Pflüger, a young Christian Democrat who served as deputy chairman of their renamed international association, the European Democrat Students (EDS), recalled.[42]

Although this cooperation primarily involved students from the Western European democracies, center-right activists always kept a close eye on political developments in the Eastern Bloc. Their habitual anticommunism and belief in evolutionary change meant that they regarded Eastern dissidence as closely compatible with their own politics—despite the fact that, prior to 1989, many Eastern dissidents sought to improve, rather than abolish, communist systems.[43] Protests against communist regimes in the Eastern Bloc were central to how West German center-right activists made sense of their own politicization. In oral history interviews and written autobiographies, former student activists often invoked events that symbolized communist repression to narrate the story of their politicization and to connect their own activism with German history.[44] Peter Radunski, for one, a leading activist in West Berlin's RCDS, who became the CDU's chief campaign strategist during Kohl's tenure as party leader, noted his presence during several iconic Cold War protests in his published autobiography. He recalled that, on 17 June 1953, as a teenager, he had cycled to the Brandenburg Gate to get a glimpse of the tanks on the Eastern side of the border, where workers' demonstrations against a 10 percent rise in work norms had turned into a broader antiregime revolt. His first political demonstration, he noted, was a protest of about two thousand high school students marching against the crushing of the anti-Soviet Hungarian Uprising in 1956.[45] The early political experiences he included in his autobiography thus conveyed a staunch anticommunist mindset.

East Germany's 17 June 1953 and the Hungarian Uprising were frequent reference points, but the construction of the Berlin Wall was a particularly important staging post in many accounts—one that activists invoked regularly to signal the centrality of German division to their politics. The events of 13 August 1961 led to "never-ending personal and political deliberations," according to Radunski. "The changed situation touched me emotionally, much like the other students who now came to Berlin more than ever."[46] As the frontline city of Cold War Europe, divided Berlin indeed exerted a particular fascination on students of the center-right. While West German students with left-wing political leanings flocked to the island city for other reasons—notably its cosmopolitan reputation and the prospect of avoiding conscription—it was the barbed-wire symbolism of the walled city that caught the imagination of the center-right, representing, as it did, the inhumanity of socialism in practice. For a young activist of the center-right, the city was the perfect place to demonstrate anticommunist commitment. Their intense focus on the Berlin Wall and Germany's Cold War division represented a marked contrast to activists of the Left, whose main points of political reference often lay outside Germany's—and Europe's—borders. "We had a different socialization into these topics [of student politics in the 1960s]. Our socialization was the Wall," Radunski asserted.[47]

Radunski's student peer Horst Teltschik, who in the 1980s would become Kohl's chief foreign policy advisor—and effectively the Federal Republic's "clandestine foreign minister"— equally stressed the important ways in which Berlin's division had shaped his views as a student activist.[48] He had arrived in West Berlin in the fall of 1962, merely one year after the Wall had gone up, and he claimed that, throughout his time there, he had found it impossible to ignore what was going on to the east of the barrier; the repression that ordinary East Germans suffered had simply been ever-present to him, Teltschik recalled. As a West German living in the city, Teltschik could visit its Eastern half even before the Quadripartite Agreement on Berlin came into effect in 1972, and he did so frequently, meeting various people that an East German friend put him in touch with. "I experienced firsthand how much GDR citizens suffered," he explained. Even their youngest children already knew what was permissible to say in the company of strangers, Teltschik remembered. "This showed the whole brutality and inhumanity of the system. I'm saying this because of course it shaped my conflict with the Left."[49]

Teltschik recalled that, viewed from the vantage point of West Berlin, the radical Left's revolutionary internationalism seemed particularly misplaced to him because there had appeared to be far more pressing problems closer to home. He charged the '68 Left with having been willfully ignorant about conditions in the Eastern Bloc while cultivating a naïve and deeply flawed revolutionary internationalism—a trope that, as we saw above, had already circulated in center-right publications at the time.

> I never understood it. Including Dutschke, who came from the GDR. . . . The Wall had just been built. Against the backdrop of the Wall, barbed wire, the Wall dead, the Soviet intervention against the Prague Spring in '68—that it wasn't an issue! Vietnam was a huge issue. . . . Overnight the U.S. was suddenly the devil. Just Vietnam, Vietnam, Vietnam! . . . The Wall, human rights abuses in East Berlin, in Moscow. That's who my enemies are, actually.[50]

Teltschik's recollections highlight the extent to which center-right students' political imagination continued to be structured by the mental cartography of the Cold War. He was adamant, however, that the RCDS had not simply remained stuck in the rigid anticommunist mindset of the 1950s. Indeed, in the 1960s, not only did Christian Democratic students speak out against the "irrational anticommunism" of the previous decade, but they also supported the legalization of the West German Communist Party, which had been banned in 1956.[51] Moreover, even before the Social-Liberal coalition under Willy Brandt began to pursue its *Neue Ostpolitik* of rapprochement with the Soviets and Eastern Bloc in 1969, the RCDS had begun to favor closer ties with the GDR, advocating German-German contacts on all levels.[52] In 1968, the West Berlin RCDS chapter debated the desirability of recognizing the Oder-Neisse Line, thereby calling into question the long-standing official policy of seeking a restoration of the German borders of 1937.[53] The RCDS's basic program of 1969 similarly called for recognizing Poland's western border and for the total revocation of the Hallstein Doctrine.[54] In doing so, the student activists edged closer to the stance of the Social Democrats at the time, who had held the Foreign Ministry during the Grand Coalition years and begun to lay the ground for Brandt's later initiatives. Most established Christian Democratic politicians, on the other hand, opposed accommodation with the GDR—a position that would initially only harden once the SPD began to implement its new course after 1969.[55]

Their more relaxed and pragmatic attitude toward state socialist regimes was also reflected in the considerable interest that center-right students displayed in reform communist movements to the east of the "Iron Curtain," particularly in the Prague Spring. They paid close attention to the liberalization of the Czechoslovak economy that began in the mid-1960s and interpreted the reformist cause adopted by Communist Party leader Alexander Dubček in 1968 as a cautious first step toward Western-style democracy. Some young Christian Democrats even openly revered Dubček—so much so that Chancellor Kurt Georg Kiesinger expressed consternation about the phenomenon in internal discussions with CDU leadership.[56] All this led to a somewhat bizarre spectacle during the World Festival of Youth and Students in Sofia, organized by the Communist-controlled International Student Union in the summer of 1968: West German Christian Democratic students, who brandished their anticommunist credentials at home, now applauded the official Czechoslovak delegation when they came in carrying pictures of the Communist Party leader. Members of the antiauthoritarian wing of the West German SDS, on the other hand, displayed their preference for alternative revolutionary socialist models from the "Third World" when they shouted "Castro-Mao-Guevara" instead.[57] Such were the intricacies of student internationalism in sixties Cold War Germany.

The Soviet military intervention of 21 August 1968 ultimately saved center-right activists from having to think more deeply about the—at best complicated—relationship between Dubček's attempt to build "socialism with a human face" and capitalist liberal democracy. The brutal clampdown on the Czechoslovak experiment made August 1968 a symbol of communist repression, akin to 1953 and 1956. Rather than exemplifying the promises of a more humane form of socialism, as it had once done, "Prague '68" became a cudgel to wield against the socialist Left. "Can socialism be a political solution for a generation that wants freedom, if socialism has historically always been the political enemy of free development? We will ask all those who propagate socialism in Germany for their measures to safeguard freedom, because we want to hold on to the civil liberties that the citizens of Czechoslovakia lost before they were even won fully," Teltschik wrote in guidelines for student speakers on how to attack the extraparliamentary opposition for its lackluster response to the Soviet intervention.[58] Over the next ten years and more, Christian Democratic students would frequently commemorate the Soviet intervention to highlight communism's repressive nature and what they regarded as proof of the antithetical relationship between socialism and democracy.[59]

Anticommunist Human Rights

The 1970s witnessed major transformations of West German activism on the Left. As Jan Eckel has demonstrated, the rise of human rights discourse and activism—a key feature of 1970s social movement activism in Europe, as indeed globally—represented a major departure for a post-utopian Left that sought to preserve its idealism while focusing on achieving meaningful change on a smaller scale.[60] By contrast, embracing the cause of human rights required no major pivot for West German center-right activists—if any turn at all.[61] The politics of major human rights organizations like Amnesty International (AI), which is often associated with the post-1968 Left, were in many ways closely aligned with center-right self-conceptions.[62] The antipolitical image AI projected sat very comfortably with activists who had long railed against "ideology" and the Left's revolutionary aspirations. Working to "make the world a slightly less wicked place"—AI's motto—was also very much in line with the center-right's gradualist impulses. As early as 1973—several years before AI achieved truly global stature—the leading Christian Democratic student magazine declared its "solidarity" with Amnesty's "prisoners of the month," a Somali, a Greek, and a Soviet citizen, and asked its readers to write letters on their behalf to their respective country's head of government.[63] Christian Democratic student publications also regularly called for donations to the human rights group.

Talking about human rights in the years after 1968 allowed center-right activists to continue to push many themes that Christian Democrats had long since championed, not least the inviolability and dignity of the "human person" against the totalitarian collective, a concept that was derived from Catholic social teaching. Moreover, anticommunism could easily be reframed as a human rights issue.[64] Christian Democratic student magazines, for instance, described the German-German border as the "most inhumane border in the world" and championed a politics of empathy with East German escapees and individual dissidents.[65] These included the prominent East German reform socialists Rudolf Bahro and Robert Havemann, who faced repressive measures ranging from imprisonment to house arrest, and the Protestant pastor Oskar Brüsewitz, whose self-immolation in protest against the oppression of religion in the GDR in August 1976 had shocked the world.[66] Christian Democratic students also ran individualized campaigns in support of Soviet dissidents such as Boris Evdokimov, a historian and publicist who had been committed to a psychiatric asylum in the USSR for his political views, and Vladimir Maksimov, a dissident writer who had been stripped of his Soviet citizenship in 1973 and, living in Parisian exile, who published a dissident magazine evocatively named *Continent*.[67]

As Lora Wildenthal has shown, appeals to human rights had already been made constantly in postwar West Germany, but generally on behalf of other Germans, notably those living in the GDR, the expellees, bombing victims, and POWs held captive in the Soviet Union.[68] Younger center-right activists built on these traditions when stepping up their human rights work in the years after 1968. Europe, German division, and the communist regimes in the Eastern half of the continent always remained central reference points. At the same time, they began to carefully project ideological equidistance by condemning human rights violations in communist states alongside those in right-wing dictatorships, such as Pinochet's Chile.[69] In doing so, they were able to reinvigorate the longstanding center-right critique of communist regimes in the now universally popular political vocabulary of international human rights. This gave the postwar European conservative and Christian Democratic version of anticommunist human rights a more self-consciously global and overtly apolitical form.

Conclusion

As this chapter has shown, activists had very different mental maps in the years after 1968. For all the people-to-people ties and imagined solidarities between activists in East and West Germany, political communication across the blocs could be quite difficult, especially in the late 1960s when revolution was the stated goal of many on the West German Left. Western leftists expanded their political vision globally in this period and increasingly looked to "Third World" liberation movements for inspiration, convinced that the Federal Republic was a major cog in the worldwide machinery of imperialist oppression. In looking south rather than east, they consciously reworked the mental political cartography of the Cold War—so much so that the "Iron Curtain" did not feature at all on the May 1968 cover of *FU Spiegel* discussed at the beginning of this piece. European division did not move toward the center of their vision until the Cold War threatened to get hot again at the dawn of the 1980s.

By contrast, center-right students did not feel the need to redraw their mental maps in the years after 1968 to nearly the same extent, even as they picked up new causes and repertoires such as campaigning for global human rights. They never questioned the Cold War framework in fundamental ways and continued to find their political inspiration much closer to home. While they may not have been ardent cold warriors in the vein of the 1950s—as their more pragmatic approach to the GDR and interest in movements of socialist reform in the Eastern Bloc signified—anticommunist conviction always animated much of their activism. As a result, they opposed any movement that couched its goals in communist rhetoric, be it domestic student groups or the North Vietnamese, and their human rights activism continued to include a prominent anticommunist angle. To them, the walled-in city of

West Berlin remained a powerful symbol of defiance in the face of communist repression, and Germany's and Europe's division continued to structure much of their thinking.

The center-right's evident Europeanism, in particular, has major repercussions for how we understand the legacies of sixties student internationalism. Historians have frequently portrayed the left-wing '68ers as forerunners of European unity, who anticipated the growing together of a divided continent that happened after 1989. While many left-wing '68ers indeed turned into emphatic Europeans over time, "Europe" had been at most a secondary political category for them around 1968. Their political imagination was far more global than continental. Student activists of the center-right, on the other hand, made German and European division a central aspect of their campaigning in the years around 1968 and thereafter. While the radical Left sought to overcome Europe's division more indirectly, via a socialist revolution that would transform the West alongside the East, center-right activists focused their critique on the repressive nature of the regimes in the Eastern Bloc.

All of this matters because, for better or worse, the center-right's version of internationalism was the one that won out in the long run. If we strip this statement of the normative baggage and political point scoring that all too often accompany assessments of 1968 and its legacies, it is difficult not to come to this conclusion. European politics certainly developed in ways that center-right activists welcomed. In 1989, dissident-directed reform movements, people power, symptoms of socialist collapse, and a reformer in the Kremlin coalesced to bring about the demise of Europe's state socialist regimes while leaving Western political systems largely unchanged.[70] This was an outcome that the center-right celebrated—in contrast to a West German Left for whom 1989 and its aftermath was a moment of considerable disappointment.[71]

What is more, in Germany, this transformation occurred under Christian Democratic auspices, and former student activists of the 1960s and 1970s played key roles in shaping the course of unification and helping to craft the post–Cold War order in Europe. Horst Teltschik, who had railed against the Left's revolutionary internationalism around 1968 and who reported that his experience as a student in West Berlin had profoundly influenced him, shaped Kohl's foreign and German policy more than any other figure. In the 1980s, he helped to orchestrate a closer West German relationship to the United States, advocated for the continuation of engagement with the GDR, and was intimately involved in the negotiations surrounding German unification.[72] When historians seek to understand the links between 1968 and 1989—and indeed the internationalist imagination of West German activists in the years after 1968—the center-right deserves to be a much bigger part of the story. Studying their mental maps helps to explain why the world looks the way that it does today—and much less like the way the revolutionary Left envisaged it in the late 1960s and beyond.

Anna von der Goltz is associate professor of German and European history at Georgetown University. She has published widely on activism in both German states in the years around 1968. Her most recent book is *The Other '68ers: Student Protest and Christian Democracy in West Germany* (Oxford University Press, 2021).

Notes

1. "Internationale Studentenrevolte," *FU Spiegel* 64 (May 1968), cover.
2. Martin Klimke and Joachim Scharloth, eds, *1968 in Europe: A History of Protest and Activism, 1956–1977* (Basingstoke: Palgrave Macmillan, 2008); Richard Ivan Jobs, "The Grand Tour of Daniel Cohn-Bendit and the Europeanism of 1968," in *May 68: Rethinking France's Last Revolution*, ed. Julian Jackson, James S. Williams, and Anna-Louise Milne (Basingstoke: Palgrave Macmillan, 2011), 231–44; Robert Gildea, James Mark, and Anette Warring, eds, *Europe's 1968: Voices of Revolt* (Oxford: Oxford University Press, 2013); Timothy Scott Brown, *Sixties Europe* (Cambridge: Cambridge University Press, 2020).
3. Michael David Fox, "The Iron Curtain as Semi-Permeable Membrane: The Origins and Demise of the Stalinist Superiority Complex," in *Cold War Crossings: International Travel and Exchange across the Soviet Bloc, 1940s–1960s*, ed. Patryk Babiracki and Kenyon Zimmer (College Station, TX: Texas A&M University Press, 2014), 14–39.
4. Richard Ivan Jobs, *Backpack Ambassadors: How Youth Travel Integrated Europe* (Chicago: University of Chicago Press, 2017), 98.
5. Timothy Scott Brown, "'1968' East and West: Divided Germany as a Case Study in Transnational History," *American Historical Review* 114, no. 1 (2009): 69–96; Roland Roth and Dieter Rucht, eds, *Die sozialen Bewegungen in Deutschland seit 1945: Ein Handbuch* (Frankfurt a.M.: Campus, 2008), 30; Axel Schildt, Detlef Siegfried, and Karl Christian Lammers, eds., *Dynamische Zeiten: Die 60er Jahre in den beiden deutschen Gesellschaften* (Hamburg: Hans Christian, 2000).
6. Anna von der Goltz, "Attraction and Aversion in Germany's '1968': Encountering the Western Revolt in East Berlin," *Journal of Contemporary History* 50, no. 3 (2015): 536–59; Anna von der Goltz, "Making Sense of East Germany's 1968: Multiple Trajectories and Contrasting Memories," *Memory Studies* 6, no. 1 (2013): 53–69; see also Tobias Hochscherf, Christoph Laucht, and Andrew Plowman, eds., *Divided, but Not Disconnected: German Experiences of the Cold War* (New York: Berghahn Books, 2010); Christoph Klessmann, "Das Jahr 1968 in westlicher und östlicher Perspektive," *Historische Literatur* 1, no. 1 (2003): 39–45.

7. This chapter reuses material from several previous articles and my most recent book to tease out the role that German and European division played in the political imagination of West German student activists across the political spectrum. Some of the material is taken from Anna von der Goltz, "Attraction and Aversion"; James Mark and Anna von der Goltz, "Encounters," in Gildea, Mark, and Warring, *Europe's 1968*, 131–64; Anna von der Goltz "'Other '68ers' in West Berlin: Christian Democratic Students and the Cold War City," *Central European History* 50, no. 1 (2017): 86–112; and Anna von der Goltz, *The Other '68ers: Student Protest and Christian Democracy in West Germany* (Oxford: Oxford University Press, 2021).
8. Christian Semler, "1968 im Westen—was ging uns die DDR an?" *Aus Politik und Zeitgeschichte*, B 45 (2003), 3–5.
9. Robert Gildea and James Mark, "Conclusion: Europe's 1968," in, Gildea, Mark, and Warring, *Europe's 1968*, 326.
10. On the history and politics of these groups, see von der Goltz, *The Other '68ers*. On the "post-45 settlement," see Geoff Eley's contribution as well as the introduction to this volume.
11. Brown, *Sixties Europe*, 24–25.
12. Patrick Major, *Behind the Berlin Wall: East Germany and the Frontiers of Power* (Oxford: Oxford University Press, 2010), 193; Frank Bösch and Christoph Classen, "Bridge over Troubled Water? Mass Media in Divided Germany," in *A History Shared and Divided: East and West Germany since the 1970s*, ed. Frank Bösch (New York: Berghahn Books, 2018), 551–602.
13. Michael Lemke, *Vor der Mauer: Berlin in der Ost-West-Konkurrenz 1948 bis 1961* (Cologne: Böhlau, 2011).
14. Timothy Scott Brown, "A Tale of Two Communes: The Private and the Political in Divided Berlin, 1967–1973," in *Between Prague Spring and French May 1968: Opposition and Revolt in Europe, 1960–1980*, eds. Martin Klimke, Jacco Pekelder, and Joachim Scharloth (New York: Berghahn Books, 2011), 132–40; von der Goltz, "Attraction and Aversion."
15. See the Stasi report about the meeting held on 27 January 1968 marked MfS, no. 276/68, in Robert Havemann Gesellschaft (RHG), file RH 280, 8.
16. Gabriele Renz, "Das Plakat der Bewegung," *Frankfurter Rundschau*, 14 May 2008, retrieved 9 December 2020 from https://www.fr.de/politik/plakat-bewegung-11592120.html.
17. Jürgen Holtfreter, interview with author, Berlin, 25 June 2010.
18. Sibylle Plogsted, *Im Netz der Gedichte: Gefangen in Prag nach 1968* (Berlin: Ch. Links, 2001), 15.
19. Plogstedt, *Im Netz der Gedichte*, 26; Mark and von der Goltz, "Encounters," 134.
20. Paulina Bren, "1968 in East and West: Visions of Political Change and Student Protest from across the Iron Curtain," in *Transnational Moments of Change: Europe 1945, 1968, 1989*, ed. Gerd-Rainer Horn and Padraic Kenney (Lanham, MD: Rowman and Littlefield, 2004), 119–36. See also Julia Ault's contribution to this volume.
21. See further Brown, *Sixties Europe*, 23–29.
22. K. D. Wolff, interview with author, Berlin, 28 May 2008.

23. Bettina Wegner, interview with author, Berlin, 2 May 2010; Mark and von der Goltz, "Encounters," 331.
24. Steffi Recknagel, interview with author, 5 January 2010; von der Goltz, "Attraction and Aversion," 153.
25. Bren, "1968 in East and West"; Mark and von der Goltz, "Encounters"; Nick Rutter, "Look Left, Drive Right: Internationalisms at the 1968 World Youth Festival," in *The Socialist Sixties*, ed. Anne Gorsuch and Diane Koenker (Bloomington: Indiana University Press, 2013), 193–212; Brown, *Sixties Europe*, 23–29.
26. Florian Havemann, *Havemann: Eine Behauptung* (Frankfurt a.M.: Suhrkamp, 2007), 882; Mark and von der Goltz, "Encounters," 151; Bren, "1968 in East and West."
27. Aleksander Smolar, "Years of '68," *Transit* 35 (2008), retrieved 7 December 2020 from https://www.eurozine.com/years-of-68/?pdf.
28. K. D. Wolff, interview with author, Berlin, 28 May 2008.
29. James F. Tent, *The Free University of Berlin: A Political History* (Bloomington: Indiana University Press, 1988), 78–79.
30. "Verständigungsschwierigkeiten," *Colloquium*, no. 4 (April 1967), 10–11; see also "Der Student lebt nicht von Marx allein: Die soziale Situation der jugoslawischen und ungarischen Studenten," *Colloquium*, no. 8 (August 1968), 9; and *Actio: Eine deutsche Studentenzeitschrift*, 4, nos. 2/3 (1968). On "bureaucracy" as a synonym for Soviet-style socialism in *Situationist* parlance, see Brown, *Sixties Europe*, 7.
31. "Prag liegt näher," *Colloqium*, no. 4 (April 1968), 2–3.
32. Mark and von der Goltz, "Encounters," 335.
33. Semler, "1968 im Westen."
34. Rudi Dutschke, interview with Jacques Rupnik, first published in English in *European Journal of International Affairs*, no. 6 (1989), reprinted in *Eurozine* (16 May 2008), available at https://www.eurozine.com/the-misunderstanding-of-1968/?pdf.
35. Daniel Cohn-Bendit and Claus Leggewie, "1968: Power to the Imagination," *New York Review of Books*, 10 May 2018, 6; on Cohn-Bendit as the archetypical European, see Jobs, "Grand Tour."
36. Dieter Ibielski and Wolfgang Kirsch, "Geschichte: Der RCDS als vordenkende Gruppe in der Politik," in *RCDS-entschieden demokratisch: Geschichte, Programm und Politik*, ed. Wolfgang Kirsch, RCDS-Schriftenreihe no. 8 (n.d. [1971]), 43. On the Catholic and Christian Democratic origins of European integration, see Wolfram Kaiser, *Christian Democracy and the Origins of European Union* (Cambridge: Cambridge University Press, 2007); Richard Vinen, *Bourgeois Politics in France 1945–1951* (Cambridge: Cambridge University Press, 1995), 152; and Martina Steber, *Die Hüter der Begriffe: Politische Sprachen des Konservativen in Großbritannien und der Bundesrepublik Deutschland 1945–1980* (Berlin: De Gruyter, 2017).
37. It was renamed European Union of Christian Democrat and Conservative Students (ECCS) in 1970, and renamed European Democrat Students (EDS) in 1975. For an organizational overview: Holger Thuss and Bence Bauer, *Students on the Right Way: European Democrat Students 1961–2011* (Brussels: European Democrat Students, 2012).
38. ACDP, 4/6/43/1, *Aktuell*, 24 April 1970.

39. Archiv für Christlich-Demokratische Politik (ACDP), 4/6/13/2, "What is ECCS?" *Taurus* 1, no. 1 (1974).
40. ACDP, 4/6/10, "Europäische Allianz der gemäßigten Studenten," Beschlüsse der 19. Ordentlichen Delegierten-Versammlung des RCDS, 11.–15. März 1969 in Soest-Westfalen, 42.
41. Philip G. Altbach, "The International Student Movement," *Journal of Contemporary History*, 5, no. 1 (1970): 156–74.
42. Friedbert Pflüger, interview with author, Berlin, 13 June 2013.
43. Annemarie Dittmann, "'Sag mir wo Du stehst . . .' Der Oktober-Klub in Ost-Berlin," *Colloquium*, no. 8 (August 1968), 14–15.
44. von der Goltz, *The Other '68ers*, chap. 2.
45. Peter Radunski, *Aus der politischen Kulisse: Mein Beruf zur Politik* (Berlin: B&S Siebenhaar, 2014), 26–27.
46. Radunski, *Hinter der Kulisse*, 37.
47. Peter Radunski, interview with author, Berlin, 26 October 2009.
48. Andreas Wirsching, *Abschied vom Provisorium: Geschichte der Bundesrepublik Deutschland 1982–1990*, vol. 6 (Munich: DVA, 2006), 182.
49. Horst Teltschik, Interview with author, Munich, 3 June 2013.
50. Ibid.
51. Hoover Institution Archives (HIA), BFW, box 84, "RCDS-SDS," in *Akut: Nachrichtenblatt der Bonner Studentenschaft* 40 (May/June 1968); ACDP, 4/6/8, "Nachtrag zu den Beschlüssen der 17. ord. Delegiertenversammlung vom 16.–20. März 1967 in Heidelberg."
52. ACDP, 4/6/1/2, Wulf Schönbohm, "Innerdeutsche Politik im Wandel"; *Jürgen-Bernd Runge Private Papers*, file Politischer Beirat, Martin Kempe, "Protokoll des Außenpolitischen Arbeitskreises des Bundesverbandes des RCDS, 19.–21. Januar 1968"; Ibielski and Kirsch, "Geschichte: Der RCDS als vordenkende Gruppe in der Politik," 41–42.
53. ACDP, 4-6-1-2, Wulf Schönbohm, "Innerdeutsche Politik im Wandel"; Runge Papers, file "Politischer Beirat," Martin Kempe, "Protokoll des Außenpolitischen Arbeitskreises des Bundesverbandes des RCDS, 19.–21. Januar 1968."
54. "Grundsatzprogramm des RCDS: 39 Thesen zur Reform und zu den Zukunftsaufgaben deutscher Politik," in Kirsch *RCDS-entschieden demokratisch*, 53–54.
55. Clay Clemens, *Reluctant Realists: The CDU/CSU and West German Ostpolitik* (Durham, NC: Duke University Press, 1989); Julia von Dannenberg, *The Foundations of Ostpolitik: The Making of the Moscow Treaty between West Germany and the USSR* (Oxford: Oxford University Press, 2008), 101.
56. Kiesinger's remarks in a meeting of the CDU's federal board on 21 June 1968. *Kiesinger: "Wir leben in einer veränderten Welt" (1965–1969), Die Protokolle des CDU-Bundesvorstandes*, vol. 5, ed. Günter Buchstab (Düsseldorf: Droste, 2005), 969–70; also *Jürgen Bernd Runge Private Papers*, file "Politischer Beirat," Frank Breitsprecher, "Liberalisierungstendenzen in der tschechischen Wirtschaft"; Detlef Stronk, "Die Notwendigkeit einer konkreten Humanisierung," in Kirsch, *RCDS-entschieden demokratisch*, 17.
57. Quinn Slobodian, *Foreign Front: Third World Politics in Sixties West Germany* (Durham, NC: Duke University Press, 2012), 195.

58. ACDP, 4/6/42/2, Horst Teltschik, "Die Argumentation der Außerparlamentarischen Opposition (APO) zur Entwicklung in der CSSR," Rednerdienst, no. 4 (November 1968).
59. See ACDP, 4/6/44/3, RCDS Pressemitteilung, no. 41, 22 August 1969; "Vor 10 Jahren: Prager Frühling," *Der Grüne Punkt: Hochschulzeitung des RCDS Berlin* (Sommersemester 1978), 2.
60. Jan Eckel, *The Ambivalence of Good: Human Rights in International Politics since the 1940s* (Oxford: Oxford University Press, 2019).
61. Stefan-Ludwig Hoffmann, "Introduction," in *Human Rights in the Twentieth Century*, ed. Stefan-Ludwig Hoffmann (Cambridge: Cambridge University Press, 2011), 20; Jan Eckel and Samuel Moyn, eds., *The Breakthrough: Human Rights in the 1970s* (Philadelphia: University of Pennsylvania Press, 2014).
62. Tom Buchanan, "'The Truth Will Set You Free': The Making of Amnesty International," *Journal of Contemporary History* 37, no. 4 (2002): 575–97; Jan Eckel, "The International League for the Rights of Man, Amnesty International, and the Changing Fate of Human Rights Activism from the 1940s through the 1970s," *Humanity* 4, no. 2 (2013): 183–214.
63. "Die Arbeit von Menschenrechtsorganisationen unterstützen," *Demokratische Blätter* 13 (April/May 1977), 13; "Die Gefangenen des Monats," *Demokratische Blätter* 1 (1973), 4.
64. Samuel Moyn, *Christian Human Rights* (Philadelphia, PA: University of Pennsylvania Press, 2015); Marco Duranti, *The Conservative Human Rights Revolution: European Identity, Transnational Politics, and the Origins of the European Convention* (Oxford: Oxford University Press, 2017); Udi Greenberg, "Militant Democracy and Human Rights," *New German Critique* 42, no. 3 (2015): 169–95.
65. "Die unmenschlichste Grenze der Welt," *Demokratische Blätter* 18 (January 1978), 12–16.
66. Ibid.
67. ACDP, 4/6/45/1, Beschlüsse der 27. O. BDV, Bonn, 5–7 March 1976; HIA, Folkmar Koenigs Collection, Box 3, RCDS leaflet "Freiheit für Boris Ewdokimov."
68. Lora Wildenthal, *The Language of Human Rights in West Germany* (Philadelphia: University of Pennsylvania Press, 2013), 9.
69. See further von der Goltz, *The Other '68ers*, chap. 4.
70. For an analysis of the economic, social, and political effects of unification on West Germany—what he terms "cotransformation"—see Philipp Ther, *Europe Since 1989* (Princeton, NJ: Princeton University Press, 2016), 259–87.
71. Konrad Sziedat, *Erwartungen im Umbruch: Die westdeutsche Linke und das Ende des "real existierenden Sozialismus"* (Munich: De Gruyter, 2019).
72. Wirsching, *Abschied vom Provisorium*, 182, 512, 659. See also Horst Teltschik, *329 Tage: Innenansichten der Einigung* (Berlin: Siedler, 1991); Christian Hacke, *Weltmacht wider Willen: Die Außenpolitik der Bundesrepublik Deutschland* (Frankfurt a.M. and Berlin: Ullstein, 1993), 441; Mary Sarotte, *1989: The Struggle to Create Post–Cold War Europe* (Princeton, NJ: Princeton University Press, 2009), 159. For a more detailed discussion of Teltschik's trajectory, see von der Goltz, *The Other '68ers*, chap. 6.

Select Bibliography

Bren, Paulina. "1968 in East and West: Visions of Political Change and Student Protest from across the Iron Curtain." In *Transnational Moments of Change: Europe 1945, 1968, 1989*, edited by Gerd-Rainer Horn and Padraic Kenney, 119–36. Lanham, MD: Rowman and Littlefield, 2004.

Brown, Timothy Scott. *Sixties Europe*. Cambridge: Cambridge University Press, 2020.

Eckel, Jan. *The Ambivalence of Good: Human Rights in International Politics since the 1940s*. Oxford: Oxford University Press, 2019.

Gildea, Robert, James Mark, and Anette Warring, eds, *Europe's 1968: Voices of Revolt*. Oxford: Oxford University Press, 2013.

von der Goltz, Anna. *The Other '68ers: Student Protest and Christian Democracy in West Germany*. Oxford: Oxford University Press, 2021.

Conclusion

Democracy in the Streets, Social Change in the Countryside: Grassroots Struggles, Solidarity Work, and Political Power after '68

Stephen Milder

In November 1975, the future Green Party cofounder Petra Kelly wrote a statement with the provocative title, "What is to be Done??? Some possibilities for Action for the West European Socialists."* With her characteristic overuse of capital letters and punctuation marks, Kelly's two-page manifesto promoted "GRASSROOTS RESISTANCE!!!!!" She called on the West European Socialists (WES), a new group comprising left-wing dissidents from the West German and Danish Social Democratic Parties, to learn from rural antinuclear activists and other participants in the "movements for the protection of life." Though her statement shared its title with Lenin's famous 1901 pamphlet, Kelly presented a decidedly different pathway to power than the Bolshevik leader had. Instead of attributing to the West European Socialists the role of vanguard party, she called on the group's members to study and build upon the work of local antinuclear activists through "action research, contact with various grassroots groups, [and] 'spectacular actions.'" If the WES deployed the models that had been put to use by grassroots movements, Kelly explained, it could help create a "Peace Power Europe."¹

In drawing on local organizing and aiming at the transformation of Europe, Kelly eschewed national politics. Many 1970s social activists, from urban activists to feminists, from peace activists to participants in solidarity movements, shared that outlook. And yet, the ways in which activists' grassroots work, their transnational visions, and their seeming neglect of national politics fostered broad social change and opened new pathways to political power have been left out of most accounts of activism in the 1970s and 1980s. Instead, scholars have interpreted the neglect of "high politics" as a limitation of activism after '68.[2] Todd Gitlin, for example, criticized the US Left for "battling for the English Department" while the Right "won the White House."[3] Tony Judt framed his own criticism of post-'68 activism in Europe within a juxtaposition of narrowly conceived "single-issue" movements that emphasized "identity politics" with social democratic parties based on the broad constituencies of "class or occupation."[4] In short, the emergence of grassroots initiatives and of movements ostensibly focused on particular people or "single issues" has widely been considered essential to the breakdown of the classical labor movement and the mass social democratic and communist parties that had defined the Left over the previous century.[5]

In the West German case, such arguments have served in part to focus scholarly attention on the Green Party (Die Grünen), which with its founding in 1980 supposedly led the way out of the divided 1970s by reuniting the Left's errant factions into a single, nationally organized political party.[6] Joschka Fischer, a "street-fighting anarchist" in the early 1970s who joined the Greens in 1982 and became Germany's foreign minister and vice chancellor in 1998, has been made to embody the Left's return to relevance—not to mention political power—through the Greens.[7] Yet, as Joachim Jachnow argued in his forceful 2013 critique, the Green Party was not the sum of the goals and ideals of 1970s activists. On the contrary, Jachnow proposed that the Greens represented "the blockage of earlier emancipatory struggles."[8] For him, in other words, the fragmented movements of the 1970s offered something that the united Greens did not—or at least that they no longer offered as a professionalized parliamentary party.

The "emancipatory potential" of activism after '68 has been explored throughout this volume. The cases studied here demonstrate that potential and show its rootedness in bottom-up approaches to politics and the ability to connect oneself, one's own experiences, and one's particular concerns with broader, sometimes distant struggles. One group of contributions to this collection considers how activism that grew from the bottom up, cleaving to an approach that Petra Kelly described as "start[ing] where you are," connected basic, individual concerns with far-reaching political debates and thus augured toward the transformation of society. Thus, experimental living arrangements became the basis for participants' rethinking of what represents social change and how to enact it, while tenants' campaigns and student rent strikes comprised part of a multifaceted struggle for the right to the city.[9] Participation in such experiments and protest actions was a means of self-empowerment, as evidenced by apprentice workers' efforts to deploy self-organization when union leadership failed to properly represent them, let alone work to redress their concerns.[10]

Another group of contributions to this anthology addresses a different form of empowerment, revealing how activists made common cause with others near and far, and thus "learn[ed] to live in solidarity." These cooperations were rarely straightforward, and they were not always based on equal partnership, but they did enable activists to connect themselves with broader causes, big ideas, and even global struggles. Solidarity movements, through which West Germans empowered themselves to circumvent the Foreign Office and conduct "people-to-people diplomacy" in support of liberation struggles in Nicaragua or southern Africa, were only the most outwardly obvious examples of such cooperative work.[11] Feminists learned, through emotional work, to transcend their differences in the name of a shared political project, while gay liberation activists described their own struggle as "inseparable from the structural injustice of the capitalist system and hence intimately connected with other forms of social and racial exclusion."[12] Attempts to cooperate across the iron curtain provide particularly strong evidence of the difficulty of working in solidarity with others in different situations, but also of cooperation's sometimes unanticipated benefits.[13]

This conclusion reflects on how the striving toward self-empowerment and the openness to others that characterized the movements studied in this volume were premised on activists' firsthand experiences of mainstream politics' limitations as well as on their belief that acting in solidarity enabled grassroots struggles to resonate across wide spaces. To this end, it returns to Petra Kelly's manifesto for the WES and the grassroots antinuclear protests that prompted her to write it. Drawing on this example—and referencing other cases explored in this anthology—the essay argues that in linking together grassroots struggles through solidarity work, activists worked toward new forms of inclusion and thus enabled themselves to wield real political power and contribute to social transformation in the years after '68.

Grassroots Struggles

Analyzing the social movements that helped transform West German society in the years after '68 requires getting out from under interpretations that begin with the "fragmentation" of the 1960s student movement.[14] On the basis of comparisons with their purportedly unitary predecessor, scholars were long preoccupied with classifying the movements and groupings of the 1970s, sorting them into categories like dogmatic communist "K-Groups," reformist groups in the orbit of the Social Democratic Party of Germany

(SPD), terrorist organizations, and New Social Movements, all apart from those who were deemed to have withdrawn from "politics" altogether.[15] Even within each category, efforts to identify individual organizations and sort out various single-issue movements have offered taxonomists endless work, the outcome of which has been presented as further evidence of rancorous division and endless infighting among the groups under study.[16] In contrast to the powerful parties of the postwar social democratic Left, then, the movements of the years after '68 are framed as splinter groups alien to the mass of society and proudly distant from the levers of political power. Yet, the vast majority of the movements and groupings that might be said to have collectively comprised the post-'68 Left were neither as distinct from one another nor as ideologically inflexible as they are made out to be.

A closer look at the West European Socialists, to whom Petra Kelly sent her November 1975 proposal for action, makes the pitfalls of overclassification readily apparent, revealing the salience of an approach to activism after '68 that focuses on ideas about inclusion and collectivity. Indeed, the WES could, at first glance, be said to epitomize the Left's supposed fragmentation after the demise of the Socialist German Student League (Sozialistische Deutsche Studentenbund, SDS) in 1970. Led by Richard Bünemann, a member of Schleswig-Holstein's state parliament who was purged from the SPD in February 1975 on account of "insufficient separation from Communists," the WES was a short-lived attempt to create a socialist party to the Left of the SPD.[17] The perception that the WES was self-absorbed and distant from political power was most obviously supported by its allergy to questions about participation in parliamentary elections. Invited by Bünemann to join the group, the former student movement leader Rudi Dutschke made the mistake of proposing that the "party question" had to be "open for debate" at a November 1975 gathering in West Berlin. The audience was taken aback by Dutschke's forthright interest in forming a new party and his mention of the upcoming Bundestag election: "They whispered, laughed, and doubted Rudi's mental health."[18] That the very idea of competing with the parties of the political establishment in a parliamentary election could be equated with mental illness (and in essence attributed to the lingering effects of Dutschke's 1968 shooting) suggested a deep antipathy toward political power as traditionally conceived in a liberal democracy. The WES's estrangement from parliamentary politics was made even more clear at a February 1976 meeting when Peter Brückner, one of the group's primary organizers, explained rather flippantly that he had no interest in forming a political party and was "here in order to organize [him]self."[19]

Despite this disregard for parliamentary politics and emphasis on organizing, there can be little doubt that members of the WES thought a great deal about power and inclusion—or that the group brought activists together in new ways. As a collaboration between Danes and Germans, the organization was premised on the idea that political parties should not conform to national political boundaries. Its name and international membership directory implied that people from all over the European Communities comprised a common polity that transcended the national states of Western Europe. Kelly pushed the group to make more of this transnationalism. She argued that the WES could work above and beneath the national level at once, since she saw organizing at the grassroots level and advocating transborder districts in the upcoming direct election to the European Parliament as a means of building up her desired Peace Power Europe. Though she did not focus on traditional centers of political power, Kelly's concerns certainly went beyond individuals and single issues, aiming toward the formation of what might anachronistically be termed geopolitical "soft power."[20]

As she explained in her action proposal, Kelly's ideas drew heavily on "experiences related to the resistance in the area around Wyhl (the Kaiserstuhl region, etc.)."[21] Her reference was to the struggle of local citizens' initiatives against the construction of the proposed Wyhl nuclear power plant. At first glance that struggle suited the antinuclear movement's image as a narrowly conceived, single-issue, New Social Movement focused on a particular "quality of life issue."[22] The struggle at Wyhl seemed primarily to pit local farmers and vintners, who feared for their crops, against the state government, which promoted the reactor alongside the quasi-public Badenwerk utilities company. Other activists' initial reactions to the fight over the Wyhl reactor seem to provide evidence of the sort of infighting and fragmentation that scholars have emphasized in their treatments of the 1970s. One K-Group from the nearby university town of Freiburg, for example, denounced the struggle at Wyhl as a battle of bourgeois "doctors and big vintners" interested only in protecting their own property.[23] From further afield, anti-reactor protests like the one at Wyhl were easily cast as remote and provincial.[24] Perhaps most damningly, the struggle at Wyhl appeared aloof from important questions of energy economy that were essential in political power centers and—after the oil shock—central to efforts to restore economic growth that might benefit the working class.[25] Superficially, at least, Kelly's celebration of the grassroots struggle at Wyhl as a potent model for action could easily be countered with the argument that such rural activism was a provincial sideshow that completely overlooked the core issues of material politics.

But a clash between rural reactor opponents and police at the Wyhl reactor construction site in February 1975 convinced even proponents of class struggle of anti-reactor activists' militancy, thus attracting them to the cause. After police used water cannons to attack middle-aged activists who were occupying the construction site and then arrested nearly fifty of them, a dozen distinct activist groups, ranging from K-Groups to squatters and from peace activists to environmentalists, organized a spontaneous solidarity demonstration thirty kilometers away in the city of Freiburg.[26] What had been discounted as a limited, single-issue movement was now cast as an impetus for action by Freiburg activists from a whole host of organizations, which seemed to have very little in common with one another.

Kelly, who was then an employee of the European Communities' Economic and Social Committee, made her first visit to Wyhl several weeks later. At an Easter Monday demonstration of more than ten thousand people, she took the stage and proclaimed that advocates of progressive change in Brussels had been "waiting for Wyhl!"[27] An advertisement for that same demonstration, which was used by West Germany's Federal Association of Citizens' Initiatives for Environmental Protection (Bundesverband Bürgerinitiativen Umweltschutz, BBU) to attract activists from across the FRG and beyond, declared that "whatever happens in Wyhl will affect all future developments. . . . Our struggle is your struggle."[28] Furthermore, in the wake of mass protests that continued throughout Spring 1975, the Baden-Württemberg chapter of the Communist League of West Germany (Kommunistische Bund Westdeutschlands, KBW) described the struggle against the Wyhl reactor as the immediate precursor to the coming "solidary coalition of the millions of oppressed or exploited in our country."[29] For Kelly, for the BBU, and eventually also for the KBW, the finite and specific Wyhl struggle served as a model for a bigger, all-encompassing struggle to come.

Solidarity Work

Despite the excitement, the local organizers of the Wyhl protests remained uninterested in leading the exploited masses in a revolution. What they wanted was control over their own lives and the future of their region. Thus, their vision of power, illustrated in a new version of the German patriotic anthem "The Watch on the Rhine," written by a local singer-songwriter and set to the tune of an Appalachian strike song, emphasized personal and regional empowerment vis-à-vis political power centers.[30] But they did not assert themselves by launching a new party or taking steps that might lead to regime change in the state capital of Stuttgart, let alone the federal capital in Bonn; they did so by protesting in the woods outside the village of Wyhl where the state government had decided to build a nuclear reactor. And despite the remoteness and rootedness of their struggle, it served as a model for numerous other site-specific protests in the years after '68.

These actions, which included attempted occupations of other nuclear reactor construction sites, blockades of military bases where NATO missiles were to be stationed, and the protests against the Frankfurt Airport's new west runway, were frequently linked by their protagonists to the struggle at Wyhl, evidencing a connective tissue that held together grassroots protests across the Federal Republic and far beyond.[31] These individual struggles were also moments of connection and solidarity building, since they served, as Tim Warneke has put it, as "opportunities to bring the various currents of society" together regardless of differences. Warneke argues that such convergent protests were the "focal points of a broad cultural struggle between the alternative movement and the establishment."[32] But we should not allow the idea of an "alternative movement" to suggest that such protests were limited only to self-described opponents of the established order, as is exemplified by the important role of the "doctors and big vintners" in the Wyhl protests. Nor should we adopt a narrow definition of "cultural struggle," since protests against nuclear energy, airport expansion, and nuclear weapons challenged the underpinnings of the West German economy and the military strategy of the NATO alliance.[33]

The broad coalitions that developed in support of the anti-reactor movement and contemporaries' countervailing interpretations of the Wyhl protest's meaning provide evidence that we ought to understand this particular, closely focused campaign as a seminal part of multiple, broad struggles. Doing so effectively requires understanding solidarity work. Andrei Markovits has given solidarity pride of place in his accounts of the changes to politics brought about by activists after '68. He describes activists' successful efforts to "[bring] those who were previously excluded into the realm of the legitimate and acceptable" as the basis of a new "politics of compassion."[34] Thinking in this framework, Markovits considers empathy essential to the coalitions that developed in support of "emancipatory movements" like the women's movement or the gay rights movement, since others who were not themselves women or gay could understand and share the feelings of repression that members of these groups faced.[35] Markovits's emphasis on empathy underscores the importance of seeking to understand one another and building common ground that were so essential to social movements after '68. But his approach also hints at the ways in which even well-meaning solidarity could be misguided or overly dependent on one's own (mis)understanding of another's struggle.[36]

Indeed, the ways in which activists projected their own purposes and interests onto the Wyhl struggle suggests that empathy alone does not tell the entire story of solidarity after '68. Thus, Theodor Ebert, a West Berlin–based academically credentialed expert on social movements, whom anti-reactor activists called upon for help in the struggle at Wyhl, was initially reluctant to join the fight. His hesitance, he explained, was based in the fact that he was "not personally certain" that local people's "existence was in fact threatened" by the proposed reactor.[37] Despite his breathtaking lack of empathy, Ebert came to Wyhl to support the anti-reactor movement as soon as he heard about the mass protests taking place there in spring 1975. He was excited by the goings-on at Wyhl because he claimed to have discovered "the most significant explicitly nonviolent protest campaign since the founding of the Federal Republic."[38] This excitement, and the idea that the grassroots protests at Wyhl could reshape politics well beyond rural Baden, motivated many others like Ebert to engage themselves in distant Wyhl.

In other words, empathy with the affected population of the villages near the proposed Wyhl reactor may well have motivated some activists to join the anti-reactor struggle. Empathy was certainly an important motivation after the brutal February 1975 police crackdown on middle-aged rural protesters, for example. But pushing forward one's own vision of protest or the particular ideas and interests of specific groups or individuals played an important part in the formation of a large coalition at Wyhl too. Though they were ostensibly fighting for the interests of the farmers who lived near the reactor site, participants in the broad anti-reactor coalition were also focused on themselves. Self-interest can doubtless lead to the narcissism of minor differences, a phenomenon that has frequently been emphasized in critical looks at the politics of the years after '68.[39] But self-interest need not obliterate empathy completely; it can also be a basis for diverse coalitions, as it was at Wyhl. Indeed, precisely such an ability to use self-interest as an important element of coalition building was evident in gay activists' insistence that the struggle for gay liberation was part of the broader struggle against the capitalist order, or the ways that Maoists understood solidarity with liberation movements in Southern Africa as an opportunity to join "what they hoped would be a global revolutionary movement."[40] Solidarity work, then, was a means of finding common ground, of realizing that even—or perhaps especially—people with diverse backgrounds, outlooks, and needs could make common cause, and that doing so was the key to empowering themselves and realizing the change they aspired to effect.

Political Power

So how should we evaluate the impact of protests that so blatantly rejected traditional political frameworks and seemed so distant from political power but managed to bring together broad coalitions? Histories of the Federal

Republic frequently turn this question on its head, taking a teleological approach that presents the movements of the 1970s as the most important predecessors of the new Green Party, which entered its first state parliament in 1979 and won seats in the federal parliament in 1983.[41] The Greens effected significant changes to the FRG's parliaments by their very presence and eventually held power in a number of German states as well as at the federal level.[42] From the time of the Greens' formation, however, many grassroots activists approached the new party with deep reservations. Much like Nicaraguan solidarity activists, who consented to engage with the Green Party only on the basis of their own continued independence, antinuclear activists considered the Greens at odds with their approach, arguing that they could build broad coalitions from the grassroots up precisely because they eschewed partisanship.[43]

Beginning with activists' hesitancy to join the Greens, let alone celebrate their emergence, then, another analysis of the impact of activism after '68 might begin far from parliamentary work and emphasize the ways individuals and communities changed on account of their involvement. The vintner Annemarie Sacherer, for example, began to think of herself as an environmentalist, adopted organic farming techniques, and decided to run for local office only after participating in the anti-reactor protests at Wyhl.[44] Such poignant personal transformations seem to lack a claim to political power beyond the local level, but, as Geoff Eley points out, individual stories of transformation were "replicated many, many times" among post-'68 activists. What is more, Eley continues, on the basis of a "shared collective sensibility," such individual stories of engagement functioned collectively, bringing former activists into positions of administrative and political power, but also opening up new perspectives and alternative possibilities to the people with whom they came into contact—constituting, in other words, a collective story of what Rudi Dutschke famously referred to as "the long march through the institutions."[45]

The research presented in this volume provides the basis for a deeper reconsideration of the nature and the meaning of personal transformations and public engagement in the years after '68. The cases studied here link the local, the national, and the transnational by focusing on the opportunities to wield power apparent in the protests of broad coalitions at single pressure points. At first glance, rural struggles over particular construction projects that outside activists joined out of their own self-interest hold no candle to the unified imagery of the "male muscular Left."[46] And yet, such struggles effected salient political and social change. For one thing, they led to reforms and new directions in policymaking in various fields, ranging from particular, moderate advances in gay rights to the legal framework for the promotion of renewable energy sources that has underpinned Germany's celebrated energy transition (*Energiewende*).[47] More meaningfully still, they broadened the circle of actors expected to participate in the practice of popular sovereignty in the FRG and expanded the varieties of democratic praxis deemed acceptable within the framework of parliamentary democracy, cementing an important role for popular politics alongside the formal work of governance. Inclusion—even in a society increasingly aware of its internal diversity, which was reflected by the movements themselves—was the seminal achievement and key to the political power of activism after '68.

Though they comprised particular groups and individuals with a variety of interests, then, the solidary coalitions of the 1970s and 1980s must nonetheless be regarded as more than loose networks of individual actors. They should be seen instead as a means of realizing individual inclusion and popular political participation in a polity that could be remarkably hostile to perceived newcomers and unconventional ideas and, indeed, to meaningful politics from below altogether. Sven Reichardt, in his comprehensive analysis of the 1970s in West Germany, shows how self and community were linked together with a poignant quote by none other than Petra Kelly, who called for "a loving, nonviolent world in which human relationships are based on tenderness, kindness, equal rights, solidarity, and freedom."[48] Since Kelly sought to bind kind and tender relationships with equal rights, solidarity, and freedom, her political approach has far more to do with the traditional politics of the Left than her emotive language sometimes leads critics to assume.[49] It is in this relationship that both the emancipatory potential and the aspiration to political power embedded in activism after '68 become most clear and resonate most profoundly in the present. Some of the first significant protests against the Trump administration, for example, developed out of concerns for immigrants and travelers from seven majority Muslim nations, not the (implicitly white, male) universal citizen, and yet activism at airports against Trump's "Muslim Ban" mobilized people from all across society. On the basis of individual examples, not only have activists in the #MeToo movement focused attention on the extent and the pervasiveness of sexual violence directed against women but they have also transformed political cultures and changed who holds political power and how that power is wielded. Given the increasing diversity of the FRG, effective activism in Germany too requires warm human relationships that can transgress difference and promote inclusion. But such warm relationships need not prevent various groups from retaining their identities and seeing their interests reflected in particular actions or protest campaigns. Thus, the inclusive, kaleidoscopic imagery invoked by activists after '68 is a valuable political tool in the present. It certainly suggests a far more promising strategy for practicing collective politics than does denouncing particularisms and exalting an imagined universal subject.

Stephen Milder is lecturer on modern history at the University of the German Armed Forces in Munich. He is the author of *Greening Democracy: The Anti-Nuclear Movement and Political Environmentalism in West Germany and Beyond, 1968-1983*.

Notes

* Work on this chapter was conducted with support from the German Research Foundation (Deutsche Forschungsgemeinschaft, DFG), project no. 423371999.
1. Petra Kelly, "WAS TUN??? Einige Aktionsmöglichkeiten für die Westeuropäischen Sozialisten!" (November 1975), Petra Kelly Archiv (PKA) 534,2.
2. Even Michael Foley, who has written a celebratory history of 1970s and 1980s activism in the United States, admits that national politics became a "spectator sport" during this "forgotten heyday" of grassroots activism. Foley, *Front Porch Politics: The Forgotten Heyday of American Activism in the 1970s and 1980s* (New York: Hill and Wang, 2013).
3. Todd Gitlin, *The Twilight of Common Dreams* (New York: Metropolitan, 1995), 126ff., esp. 151–59.
4. Tony Judt, *Postwar: A History of Europe since 1945* (New York: Penguin, 2005), 486.
5. Daniel Rodger's description of the period since the 1970s as an "age of fracture" is well-suited to these interpretations and also suggests that they extended far beyond the political Left. Daniel Rodgers, *Age of Fracture* (Cambridge, MA: Harvard University Press, 2011).
6. See, for example, Andrei Markovits and Philip Gorski, *The German Left: Red, Green, and Beyond* (Oxford: Oxford University Press, 1993).
7. The quote is taken from Paul Hockenos's book *Joschka Fischer and the Making of the Berlin Republic: An Alternative History of Postwar Germany* (Oxford: Oxford University Press, 2008), 4, which presents perhaps the most emphatic version of this argument. But scholars like Edgar Wolfrum have made the same point in their histories of postwar Germany. See Wolfrum, *Die geglückte Demokratie: Geschichte der Bundesrepublik Deutschland von ihren Anfängen bis zur Gegenwart* (Stuttgart: Klett-Cotta, 2006), 479.
8. Joachim Jachnow, "What's Become of the German Greens?" *New Left Review* 81 (May–June 2013): 95–117.
9. See Freia Anders's and Belinda Davis's contributions to this volume.
10. See David Templin's contribution to this volume.
11. See Christian Helm and David Spreen's contributions to this volume.
12. See Bernhard Gotto and Craig Griffiths's contributions to this volume.
13. See Julia Ault and Anna von der Goltz's contributions to this volume.
14. Geoff Eley, *Forging Democracy: The History of the Left in Europe, 1850–2000* (Oxford: Oxford University Press, 2002), 418.

15. See, for example, Wolfrum, *Die Geglückte Demoratie*, 267–68
16. Several studies emphasize the differences and even the penchant for infighting among groups within these categories. Gerd Koenen has written on the various K-Groups in *Das Rote Jahrzehnt: Unsere kleine deutsche Kulturrevolution, 1967–1977* (Cologne: Kiepenheuer und Witsch, 2001), esp. 183–206. For a contrasting perspective, see David Spreen's contribution to this volume. In *Die Soziale Bewegungen in Deutschland seit 1945: Ein Handbuch* (Frankfurt a.M.: Campus, 2008), Dieter Rucht and Roland Roth have painstakingly differentiated the various new social movements of the 1970s from one another.
17. "Bünemann, geh nicht voran!" *Die Zeit*, 5 December 1975.
18. Gretchen Dutschke-Klotz, *Wir hatten ein barbarisches, schönes Leben: Rudi Dutschke: Eine Biographie* (Cologne: Kiepenheuer & Witsch, 1996), 362. And "APO: Gefühl des Gewinns," *Der Spiegel*, 15 December 1975.
19. Peter Brückner in Frankfurter Rundschau, quoted in Dutschke-Klotz, *Wir hatten*, 363.
20. On soft power, see Joseph Nye, *Soft Power: The Means to Success in World Politics* (New York: Public Affairs, 2004).
21. Kelly, "WAS TUN???"
22. On the antinuclear movement as a new social movement motivated by postmaterial values, see Karl-Werner Brand, Detlef Büsser, and Dieter Rucht, *Aufbruch in eine andere Gesellschaft: Neue Soziale Bewegungen in der Bundesrepublik* (Frankfurt a.M.: Campus, 1983).
23. "500 Kaiserstühler Bauern demonstrieren gegen Kernkraftwerk," *Klassenkampf: Extra Blatt*, 19 September 1972. Archiv Soziale Bewegungen Freiburg (ASB), "Wyhl die Anfänge," 3581.
24. Even sympathetic observers of the protest, like the sociologist Dieter Rucht, noted that in contrast to protests against particular nuclear reactors, which were primarily local affairs, protests against nuclear fuel storage or reprocessing facilities had the potential to stop the entire nuclear program. Dieter Rucht, *Von Wyhl nach Gorleben: Bürger gegen Atomprogramm und nukleare Entsorgung* (Munich: Beck, 1980), 210–11.
25. Jan-Werner Müller has explained the Left's initial difficulty in relating to environmental protests with the quip that "it was clearly much more difficult for thinkers and political parties of an ultimately Marxist inspiration to break with a belief in the beneficial nature of industrial production." Müller, *Contesting Democracy: Political Ideas in Twentieth Century Europe* (New Haven, CT: Yale University Press, 2011), 211.
26. Aktion Dritte Welt, AK-Frieden, Bewohner der besetzten Häuser Belfortstr. 34–36, Evangelische Studentengemeinden, Fachschaftsräte Soziologie-Physik-Jura, Gruppe Internationale Marxisten, Gewaltfreie Aktion, Kommunistischer Bund West Deutschland, Kommunistische Hochschulgruppe, Kommunistischer Studentenverband, Arbeitskreis Umweltschutz an der Universität Freiburg, Deutsche Kommunistische Partei, "Das KKW wird nicht gebaut!" (20 February 1975). ASB, "Wyhl die Anfänge," 3450.
27. Petra Kelly, Untitled Speech [Wyhl, 31 March 1975]. PKA 3166.
28. Bundesverband Bürgerinitiativen Umweltschutz, "Oster-Treffen aller Atomkraftgegner in Wyhl." PKA 3168.

29. KPD Regional Komitee Baden-Württemberg, "Kein KKW in Wyhl," 23 February 1975. ASB, "Wyhl die Anfänge," 3599.
30. On this new version of the song, the lyrics to which were written by the Freiburg singer-songwriter Walter Mossmann, see, Mossman and Peter Schleunig, eds., *Alte und neue politische Lieder: Enstehung und Gebrauch, Texte und Noten* (Reinbek: Rowohlt, 1978). See also Stephen Milder, *Greening Democracy: The Anti-Nuclear Movement and Political Environmentalism in West Germany and Beyond, 1968–1983* (Cambridge: Cambridge University Press, 2017), 51–52.
31. On grassroots antimilitarization protests and their wide ramifications, see Adam Seipp's contribution to this volume.
32. Tim Warneke, "Aktionsformen und Politikverständnisse der Friedensbewegung: Radikales Humanismus und die Pathosformel des Menschlichen," in Sven Reichardt and Detlef Siegfried, eds., *Das Alternative Milieu: Antibürgerlicher Lebensstil und linke Politik in der Bundesrepublik Deutschland und Europa, 1968–1983* (Göttingen: Wallstein Verlag, 2010), 461.
33. On the ways in which antinuclear protests affected the German energy economy, see, for example, Dolores Augustine, *Taking on Technocracy: Nuclear Power in Germany, 1945 to the Present* (New York: Berghahn Books, 2018); and Carol Hager, "Germany's Green Energy Revolution: Challenging the Theory and Practice of Institutional Change," *German Politics and Society* 33, no. 3 (Autumn 2015): 1–27. On the influence of peace protests on NATO strategy, see Adam Seipp's contribution to this volume, and Susan Colbourn, *Euromissiles: A Transatlantic History* (Ithaca, NY: Cornell University Press, 2022).
34. Andrei Markovits, "From Red to Green: A Transfer of Power on Germany's Left," *American Institute for Contemporary German Studies*, 28 July 2021, retrieved 18 August 2021 from https://www.aicgs.org/2021/07/from-red-to-green/.
35. Markovits presents this definition of empathy and highlights its importance for the politics of compassion in his account of dog rescue, where he differentiates empathy and compassion following the logic that dog rescuers cannot truly understand the emotions of the dogs they rescue, but humans can understand—and thus empathize with—the plight of other humans, even if those humans have different experiences or identities. Andrei Markovits and Katherine N. Crosby, "Introduction," in *From Property to Family: American Dog Rescue and the Discourse of Compassion* (Ann Arbor: University of Michigan Press, 2014), 9–10.
36. On misunderstandings of others' struggles, see Julia Ault's contribution to this volume.
37. Theodor Ebert to Heinz Siefritz, 3 September 1974. Archiv der Badisch-Elsässische Bürgerinitiativen (ABEBI) Haag Lore 8HL6.
38. Theodor Ebert, "Als Berliner in Wyhl: Friedensforschung und Konfliktberatung vor Ort," *Gewaltfreie Aktion* 23, 24, 25 (1975).
39. See, for example, Christopher Lasch, *The Culture of Narcissism* (New York: Norton, 1979).
40. On the gay liberation movement, see Craig Griffiths's contribution to this volume. The quote is from David Spreen's contribution to this volume.
41. See, for example, Marovits and Gorski, *German Left*; and: Silke Mende, *"Nicht rechts, nicht links, sondern vorn": Eine Geschichte der Gründungsgrünen* (Munich: Oldenbourg Wissenschaftsverlag, 2011).

42. On the Greens' achievements, see, for example, Andrei Markovits and Joseph Klaver, "Thirty Years of Bundestag Presence: A Tally of the Greens' Impact on the Federal Republic of Germany's Political Life and Public Culture," *AICGS German-American Issues* 14 (2012).
43. I expand on this argument in Milder, *Greening Democracy*.
44. Annemarie Sacherer, "Zehn Jahre danach," in *Wyhl: Der Widerstand geht weiter; Das Bürgerprotest gegen das Kernkraftwerk von 1976 bis zum Mannheimer Prozeß*, ed. Christoph Büchele, Irmgard Schneider, and Bernd Nössler (Freiburg: Dreisam-Verlag, 1982), 38.
45. See Geoff Eley's contribution to this volume. Dutschke began to use the slogan "long march through the institutions" in 1967. The phrase has been taken up by many others, and interpreted in various ways, but Dutschke describes it as "the path of permanent revolutionaries" who move through various institutions, offering "direct support" to wage-dependent workers and helping them to "call late-capitalist society into question." Rudi Dutschke, "Vorwort" in Stefan Reisner, ed., *Briefe an Rudi D. mit einem Vorwort von Rudi Dutschke* (Berlin: Voltaire Verlag, 1968), vii-viii.
46. Eley, *Forging Democracy*, 490.
47. On the links between antinuclear protest and the German energy transition, see, for example, Hager, "Germany's Green Energy Revolution"; and Arne Jungjohann and Craig Morris, *Energy Democracy: Germany's Energiewende to Renewables* (New York: Palgrave MacMillan, 2016).
48. Kelly to Ingeborg Hübner (1978). Quoted in Sven Reichardt, *Authentizität und Gemeinschaft: Linksalternatives Leben in den siebziger und frühen achtziger Jahren* (Berlin: Suhrkamp, 2014), 887, and in Saskia Richter, *Die Aktivistin: Das Leben der Petra Kelly* (Munich: Deutsche Verlags-Anstalt, 2010), 116.
49. On Kelly's use of emotive language, see Friederike Brühöfener's contribution to this volume.

Select Bibliography

Eley, Geoff. *Forging Democracy: The History of the Left in Europe, 1850–2000*. Oxford: Oxford University Press, 2002.

Hockenos, Paul. *Joschka Fischer and the Making of the Berlin Republic*. Oxford: Oxford University Press, 2008.

Jachnow, Joachim. "What's Become of the German Greens?" *New Left Review* 81 (May–June 2013): 95–117.

Markovits, Andrei, and Philip Gorski. *The German Left: Red, Green, and Beyond*. Oxford: Oxford University Press, 1993.

Reichardt, Sven. *Authentizität und Gemeinschaft: Linksalternatives Leben in den siebziger und frühen achtziger Jahren*. Berlin: Suhrkamp, 2014.

Richter, Saskia. *Die Aktivistin: Das Leben der Petra Kelly*. Munich: Deutsche Verlags-Anstalt, 2010.

Rucht, Dieter, and Roland Roth. *Die Soziale Bewegungen in Deutschland seit 1945: Ein Handbuch*. Frankfurt a.M.: Campus, 2008.

Index

abortion, 51, 74, 205
  "abortion paragraph" (§218), 13, 95, 182–183, 239–241
  fight for the abolition of, 13, 74, 93–95, 229
activism, 2–6, 12–13, 25–36, 46–47, 90–91, 135, 175, 239, 259–260. *See also* protest
  center-right activism, 305, 311–312, 315
  environmental activism (*see* environmentalism)
  feminist activism (*see* women's movement)
  gay activism (*see* gay movement)
  grassroots or basisdemokratisch, 3–7, 10, 29, 50–53, 118, 121–123,135, 197, 203–205, 284, 288–291, 297, 324–332 (*see also* democracy)
  peace activism (*see* peace movement)
  post-'68, 226, 304, 324–325, 333
  solidarity activism (*see* solidarity)
Adorno, Theodor, 31–34, 37, 78
Aktionsherbst, 84, working group, 133–134, 138, 145–146
Ali, Tariq, 24
Alternative for Germany (Alternative für Deutschland), 14, 59, 297
anticapitalism, 12, 122–123, 179, 197, 220–221, 223, 227, 308–309
anticommunism, 147, 265–266, 309, 311–316
antiauthoritarianism, 75–76, 114, 118–119, 156, 195–196, 199, 201–202, 218, 226, 304. *See also* Sponti
anti-/Alterglobalization Movement, 79–82
American Civil Rights Movement. *See* United States of America

Amnesty International, 315
apprentices' movement, 11, 194, 198–200, 207–209, 325–326
Arendt, Hannah, 77
Association of Christian Democratic Students (Ring Christlich-Demokratischer Studenten, RCDS). *See* students

Basic Law, *Grundgesetz* (West Germany), 8, 46–49, 53, 56–57
Berlin, 36, 71, 77, 93, 99, 100, 117–120, 154, 162, 165, 166, 196–198, 203, 229, 287–289
  Berlin Wall, 303, 306–313
Berndt, Heide, 116
Biess, Frank, 88, 181
Bloch, Ernst, 24
borderlands, 23–24, 271, 275
Borge, Tomás, 263, 269–270
Bundeswehr, 138, 173, 176–177, 181–185
Brandt, Willy, 6, 49, 52,176, 313
  and the "Decree on Radicals," 52, 158
  Neue Ostpolitik, 313
Bretton Woods System, 4–5, 28

capitalism, 29, 37, 90, 179
  capitalist restructuring, 28–31, 35–37
Cardenal, Ernesto, 262
Chernobyl, 179, 283, 287
Christian Democratic Union (CDU), 48, 51–52, 58, 147. *See also* Students and Student Groups
Christian Social Union (Christliche Soziale Union, CSU), 48, 51, 52, 58

citizenship, 5–6
 activist citizenship, 29
 democratic, 24, 55
 grassroots, 29, 36
 political, 8 46, 51–54, 58
 social, 25, 29
citizens' initiatives (*Bürgerinitiativen*), 2, 13, 46–47, 52–58, 115, 139–140, 193, 197, 202, 208, 240, 249, 286, 289, 328–329
 Federal Association of Citizens' Initiatives for Environmental Protection (Bundesverband Bürgerinitiativen Umweltschutz, BBU), 142, 329
civil disobedience, 56–57, 196, 228
Cohn-Bendit, Daniel, 24, 75–77, 166, 195, 310
consciousness, 74, 77, 91, 221–222, 284
 consciousness industry, 70–71, 74
 consciousness raising, 91, 229
Cold War. *See under* war
communication, 12, 79, 154–155, 156, 284, 288, 308
 communication centers, 205, 229, 247
 communication network, 260–263
communism, 28, 54, 197, 241, 226, 285, 303–304. *See also* Maoism
 collapse of, 30–31, 298 (*see also* nineteen eighty-nine*)*
 Communist League (Kommunistischer Bund, KB), 197, 230
 Communist League of West Germany (KBW), 13, 226, 238–241, 246–251, 329
 Communist University Group (Kommunistische Hochschulgruppe KHG), 249
 Communist Youth Federation (Kommunistischer Jugendverband, KJV), 204
 eurocommunism, 26, 37, 40
 German Communist Party (DKP), 1, 121, 123, 198–199, 204, 226, 230
 K-Gruppen, 119, 124, 226, 326, 329

 League of Communists of Yugoslavia, 195
 Socialist Unity Party of Germany (SED) (*see under* socialism)
churches, christian, 47, 177, 259, 262, 270, 272, 283–284
 East German Protestant Church and environmentalism, 285–297 (*see also* environmentalism)
Christopher Street Day, CSD. *See under* gay movement
Czechoslovakia, 28, 137, 305, 307–314
 Charter, 77 304, 309
 Prague Spring, 113, 283, 307– 314

Debray, Régis, 70
decolonization, 240–242
 Africa Weeks, 242
 Africa Club (Afrika Verein), 242
 West German Africa Society (Afrika-Gesellschaft), 241–242
De Gaulle, Charles, 28, 72–73
 Gaullism
democracy, 5–8, 23–25, 27, 46–47, 52–59, 69, 311–314
 council democracy, 8, 51
 direct, 51, 195
 grassroots, 50–53, 202, 266–267
 liberal, 9, 53, 303, 307, 310, 327
 militant democracy, 6, 51
 parliamentary democracy, 6–7, 14, 27, 53, 333
 participatory democracy, 6–8, 27, 33, 53, 58–59, 196
 representative, 51, 53, 202
Do-It-Yourself (DIY), 36, 193
Dubček, Alexander, 314
Dutschke, Rudi, 70–71, 76–77, 123, 166, 184, 196, 308–309, 313, 327, 332, 337n45

ecological movement. *See* environmentalism
emotions, 11, 50, 54–55, 58, 174–176, 178–18. *See also* feelings
 expressions of, 50, 58, 90, 180–181

and the women's movement, 88–101,
and Wohngemeinschaften, 155,
162–163
environmental destruction, 5, 140–142,
283–287, 291–292
environmentalism, 13, 140–142, 176,
283–298, 329
BURN—Citizens' Action for
Environmental Protection
Rhine-Neckar / Bu*rgeraktion
Umweltschutz Rhein-Neckar, 140
environmental destruction, 5, 10, 283
(*see also* pollution)
new environmental movement, 113,
135, 140–142, 174, 285, 289–290,
293
Federal Association of Citizens'
Initiatives for Environmental
Protection (Bundesverband
Bürgerinitiativen Umweltschutz,
BBU), 329
"forest death" (*Waldsterben*), 292, 289,
291 (*see also* pollution)
Enzensberger, Hans Magnus, 69–75
expression, 7, 50–52, 58, 73–74, 157,
203–204, 283, 303, 307
of emotions (*see* emotions)
freedom of, 8, 49, 58, 73
political, 6–7, 46, 51–52, 156, 186
extraparliamentary opposition
(Außerparlamentarische Oppositons
APO), 27–28, 37, 69–71, 118–119,
154, 166, 180, 184, 239, 314

Federal Scout Association (Bund
Deutscher Pfadfinder, BDP),
204–205
feelings, 54, 88–92, 96–101, 179–181.
See also emotions
Feminism, 27, 34, 38–39, 88–99, 162,
176, 180, 183, 219, 223–229. *See
also* women's movement
Feminist, 9, 74, 89–92, 95, 97–98, 100
Feminist activism, 89, 93, 176,
182–185, 223, 227
Feminist Consciousness, 91–93, 97–98

Ferguson, Niall, 5
Ferree, Myra Marx, 89
Fischer, Joschka, 161, 169, 325
Flaubert, Gustav, 72,
Foucault, Michel, 67, 78–79
And the Information on Prisons
Group (Groupe d'information sur
les prisons), 78–79
Frankfurt Provos. *See* urban movements
Frankfurt School, 116–117, 220
Freyhold, Michaela von, 175–176
Fulda Gap, 10, 133, 144–145. *See also*
United States of America

gay movement, 12, 218–231
Christopher Street Day, CSD, 219
General Homosexual Committee
(Allgemeine Homsexuelle, AHA),
225
Homosexual Action West Berlin
(Homosexual Action West Berlin,
HAW), 217, 220–225, 226, 230
Lesbian Action Centre (LAZ), 221
Stonewall, 219
gender, 11, 23–24, 88, 90, 159–160,
161, 169, 174–175, 202, 218,
222–225, 227
generations, 24–26, 35, 37–41, 93–95,
113–114, 159, 182, 199, 304
German Trade Union Confederation
(Deutscher Gewerkschaftsbund,
DGB), 119, 122, 199
German Peace Union (Deutsche Friedens
Union, DFU). *See under* peace
movement
Germany
Federal Republic of Germany (FRG)/
West Germany, 1–2, 6, 8, 27, 47–
54, 134–135, 138, 140, 143–145,
173, 176, 194, 239, 241, 247–248,
274, 316, 331
German Democratic Republic
(GDR)/East Germany, 13,
137–138, 143, 239, 243, 283–297,
309
Gottwald, Gabriele ("Gabi"), 267–268

grassroots activism. *See* activism
grassroots democracy. *See* democracy
grassroots politics. *See* politics
Green Party (East Germany), 294
Green Party (West Germany), 113, 138–146, 177, 179, 182–183, 266, 267–268, 288–290, 325, 332
Greenpeace, 292
Group 47 (Gruppe 47), 68–71

Habermas, Jürgen, 50, 117
Häberlen, Joachim, 89, 100, 179
Hartung, Klaus, 156–157, 164, 169
Hitler, Adolf, 47–48, 57
Hobsbawm, Eric, 4–5, 37
Horkheimer, Max, 33, 37
human rights, 54, 256–266, 284, 286, 293, 309, 314–316

IG Metall (Industrial Union of Metalworkers), 114
intellectual, change of, 67
    archetypical, universal intellectual, 68–75
    feminist intellectual, 74
    Marxist intellectual, 74, 79
    new type of intellectual, 70–74, 78–79
Iron Curtain, 13, 284 286, 293, 308
    connections across, 12, 13, 285, 288–289, 326
    as "porous," 303–307
Institute for Peace Policy (Institut für Friedenspolitik), 143
International Union of Christian Democrat and Conservative Students (ICCS). *See* students

Jarausch, Konrad, 5

Kelly, Petra, 10, 143, 175, 179–180, 184, 265–267, 324–329, 233
Klein, Naomi, 67, 79–82
Knabe, Hubertus, 290–291, 295–297
Knabe, Wilhelm, 289–290
Kohl, Helmut, 177, 182, 265–268, 294, 305

Kommune 1 and 2. *See Wohngemeinschaft*
Krahl, Hans-Jürgen, 32–33, 38, 219
Krohn, Wolfgang, 193

Langhans, Rainer, 156, 164
Lefebvre, Henri, 10, 113, 195
Lenz, Ilse, 89
Lüth, Erich, 49

Maoism, 73, 78–79, 121
    global, 239–241
    Maoist Communist League of West Germany (Kommunistischer Bund Westdeutschlands, KBW), 13, 226, 238–241, 245–251, 329
    Maoist solidarity with Zimbabwe, 245–250 (*see also* solidarity)
    West German, 239–241, 245, 250–251, 309
Marcuse, Herbert, 24, 31–35, 39, 116, 220
marxism, 118–119, 308
    marxist radicals, fear of, 52
    Marxist-Leninists, 196–199, 204, 225–226
    Trotskyist International Marxist Group (Gruppe Internationale Marxisten, GIM), 199
McCaughin, Kathy, 2
Meinhof, Ulrike, 119–120
Melucci, Alberto, 174–175
Miliband, Ralph, 24, 37
Mitscherlich, Alexander, 115–117
Mossmann, Walter, 1–3
Mugabe, Robert, 238–239, 245–246, 247, 250

NATO (North Atlantic Treaty Organization), 10, 133, 135–148, 177–178, 182, 330. *See also* United States Military)
New Left, 4, 68, 69, 70–71, 74–77, 90, 116, 174, 180, 181, 184, 194–196, 198, 204, 218–220, 241, 243, 304–305, 307–310
neoliberalism, 29, 36, 112–114, 209

new social movements (NSM), 2–10,
13, 29, 34–37, 46–58, 74–76,
80, 111–114, 135, 154, 174–175,
193–194, 196, 203, 208, 217–218,
239–240, 260–261, 266, 283–284,
290–292, 293, 296–298, 305, 215,
327–328, 330. *See also* sixty-eight
in contrast to the "old" social
movements, 3–4, 29–30, 193–194,
198, 200, 204
as "single-issue" movements, 5–6, 120,
218–219, 227–228, 239, 325–329
politics, 27–31, 35–38, 41
theory of, 112, 239
Nicaragua, 259– 275
international brigades, 271–273
Sandinista National Liberation Front
(Frente Sandinista de Liberación
Nacional, FSLN), 13, 259,
262–264, 269–273, 275–276
Sandinista guerilla, 262, 264, 275
Sandinista Revolution, 259, 269,
272–273
Somoza family and regime, 259,
261–262, 264–265, 275
the death of Albrecht Pflaum, 265–266
transnational communication network
(*see* transnational)
West German solidarity with, 13,
259–276 (*see also* Nicaragua)
nineteen eighty-nine (1989), 30–31, 38,
156, 284–285, 293–298, 304, 309,
311, 317
Peaceful Revolution, 284, 294–297
nineteen sixty-eight (1968). *See* Sixty-
Eight ('68)
nonviolence, 55–57

Objectivity, 50, 54, 58, 179
Oil Shock, 328

Paragraph, 175 (West Germany), 219,
232n9
Plogstedt, Sibylle, 97, 307
Powell, Colin, 142–143
Powell, Enoch, 27

Peace Movement, New, 6, 36, 134–136,
146, 174, 178, 184, 266, 291
German Peace Union (Deutsche
Friedens-Union, DFU), 184
Peace activism, 34–36, 135, 177–178
Frauenwiderstandscamp (women's
resistance camp), 178
Pletchford, Herb, 1–2
Politics, 12, 14, 15–16, 27–31, 34,
50–55, 135, 154–164, 168–169,
175, 177–179, 201–202, 208,
217–218, 239, 260, 265–268, 275,
289, 308–309, 311–312, 317,
324–326, 330–333
of everyday life, 153–168
Grassroots, 3, 12 (*see also* activism)
"high," 10, 12, 325
Identity Politics, 112, 162, 325
Parliamentary, 6, 10, 183, 328–239,
330
Participatory, 7, 14, 52
Party, 7, 168, 267–268
of the personal, 90, 153, 155–156, 218
Popular, 3–6, 10, 186, 333
Single-issue, 217, 227, 239
Sexual, 36, 218–220, 224
Pollution, 283–298. *See also*
environmental destruction
in Bitterfeld, Chemical Triangle East
Germany, 286, 291
"forest death" (*Waldsterben*), 286, 289,
291–292
Postwar, 3–8, 24–36, 134, 153–155,
186, 306, 315–316, 327
activism, 3–4, 8
culture and cultural changes, 23–26,
69
economic boom, 3, 8, 28, 30, 32, 36
settlements, 24–25, 29, 35–36
Prague Spring. *See* Czechoslovakia
Protest, 1–4, 8, 28, 46–49, 51–52,
54–59, 69–70, 74, 80, 89,
113–116, 120–127, 133, 137–142,
144–148, 176–178, 180, 185, 196,
198–200, 225–226, 228, 264–265,
275, 287–288, 292–298, 303, 305,

307, 311–312, 325–326, 333. *See also* activism
Antinuclear, 53–58, 176–179, 251, 325–326, 328–332
at Bonn's Hofgarten (1979), 1–4, 177–178
grassroots (*see* activism)
movements, 33–34, 77, 95, 113–116, 285 (*see also* new social movements)
pressure as protest, 50–56, 267–268, 269, 332
student protest (*see* students)
pupils' movement (Schülerbewegung), 196, 119, 224

Reagan, Ronald, 31, 177–178, 266, 269–270
Radunski, Peter, 311–312
Red Army Faction (RAF), 119, 137, 239
Red Cells
Redgrave, Vanessa, 24
Rent strikes. *See* urban movements
Revolt. *See* uprisings
Revolution, 1, 27–28, 30, 47, 70–72, 122, 206, 226, 240–241, 250–251, 307–309, 313, 329, 331
Algerian, 243
Counterrevolution, 97
French, 30
in Nicaragua (*see* Nicaragua)
nineteen eighteen (1918), 47, 51
Peaceful (1989) *see nineteen eighty-nine*
Portuguese, 28
Prague Spring (*see* Czechoslovakia)
Revolutionary action, 70–71, 122–123, 153, 155–158, 168–169, 195–196, 200–201
Revolutionary Subject, 74, 77, 220
revolutionary transformation, 13, 30, 54, 153, 155–158, 196, 205, 226
sexual, 164, 22
socialist, 203, 206, 218, 309, 317
Rucht, Dieter, 261, 317, 335f24

Sander, Helke, 24, 159–160, 178–179, 180, 182

Sapiro, Gisèle, 74, 79
Sartre, Jean-Paul, 24, 37, 68, 72–73, 75–76, 79, 243
Schmidt Cuadra, Enrique, 262–265, 274
Schmidt, Helmut, 176–177, 182
Schröder, Gerhard, 1
Schmidt-Harzbach, Ingrid, 26
Schwarzer, Alice, 97, 176–177
Self, 5–6, 10–12, 90–92, 97–101, 111–112, 157–165, 174, 181, 200, 202–203, 209, 333
self-awareness, 181, 202
self-defense, 54, 56
self-determination, 202, 247
self-empowerment, 92, 200, 325–326
self-expression, 53–54
self-help, 111, 114, 122, 196, 205, 229
self-organization, 10–12, 193–206, 208–209, 326
self-management, 11–12, 27, 28, 194–196, 201–202, 205–209
self-reflection, 70, 72, 75–76, 96, 98, 112, 155, 181, 310
Sixty-Eight ('68), 3, 27–28, 31, 39–41, 58, 67, 81–82, 153, 193–195, 219–220, 231, 303–305, 308, 310–311, 317
and nineteen forty-five, 35, 37
and nineteen eighty-nine, 30, 38, 112–114, 303–304
Global 1960s
"long 1968," 23–24, 42n2
'68-movement(s), 24, 68–70, 113, 166, 228 (*see also* new social movements)
May 1968 (France), 68, 71–72, 75, 77–78, 113, 1952
Post sixty-eight, 2–4, 6–7, 9–10, 37,58, 69, 78, 134, 153, 156, 158, 239, 293–294, 315–316, 325–327, 330–332
Sixty-Eighters, 5, 26, 36–38, 317
Smith, Ian, 244–245
Smolar, Aleksander, 308
Social Democracy, 26, 29, 324–325

Social Democratic Party of Germany (Sozialdemokratische Partei Deutschlands, SPD), 6, 47, 48, 115–116, 122, 177, 197, 218, 265, 268, 274, 326–327
Social Democratic University Union, 184
Socialism
  Socialist Youth of Germany (Sozialistische Jugend Deutschlands, SJD—Die Falken), 204
  Socialist Unity Party of West Berlin (SEW), 226, 230
  Socialist Unity Party of Germany (SED), 284–290, 293–294
  West European Socialists (WES), 324–328
Solidarity, 2–3, 12–14, 28, 31, 40, 91, 94–96, 142, 218, 222, 225, 226, 229, 239–241, 245–250, 266–269, 295, 304, 324–326, 329–331, 333
  Solidarność, 309
  Nicaragua solidarity movement (*see* Nicaragua)
Sölle, Dorothee, 175, 183–184
Southern Rhodesia, 244–246
Sovereignty, West German, 10, 135–136, 138–139, 143–144, 148
Spontis, 1, 114, 127, 166–167, 197–198, 204, 206, 226
Space, 10–12, 24, 27, 37–38, 67, 111–114, 116, 127, 154, 157, 162–163, 166, 203, 205–208, 218, 220, 228, 326
  Political space, 27, 41, 48, 134
Squatting. *See* urbanity
Steedman, Carolyn, 24
Stonewall. *See* gay movement
Students and Student Groups, 31–34, 39–41, 46–51, 68–71, 73, 78, 96, 99, 115–116, 119, 121, 124–127, 138, 162, 180, 193–195, 229, 240–245, 249, 262, 303–305, 308, 310–318, 326–327
  Association of Christian Democratic Students (Ring Christlich-Demokratischer Studenten, RCDS), 304, 310–315
  European Democrat Students (EDS), 311
  International Union of Christian Democrat and Conservative Students (ICCS), 310–311
Rent Strikes (*see* urban movements)
Student Movement, 2, 6, 27–28, 31–33, 69, 119, 195–196, 197, 218, 219–220, 226–227, 242–243, 304, 305
Socialist German Student Union (Sozialistischer Deutscher Studentenbund, SDS), 69, 71, 76, 115–118, 156, 164, 180, 182, 189, 196, 198, 218, 219, 222, 306–309, 314, 327
Union Students' Group (GSG, Hamburg), 199–200
Subjectivity, 31, 54, 89–90, 98, 179, 181, 185, 196, 201–203. *See also* Self

Teltschik, Horst, 312–314, 317
"The personal is political." *See* women's movements
Therborn, Göran, 30
Third World Movement, 266
Transnational movements, 2–3, 79–80, 134–135, 166, 260–264, 269–270
  Transnational communication, 239–240, 260, 262–263, 276
  Transnational People-To-People Diplomacy, 13, 240, 260, 269, 272–276, 326
Tuntenstreit. *See* gay movement

United States of America, 33–34, 77, 80, 120, 138, 177, 181–182, 194, 196, 219–220, 243, 264–271, 274, 317
  Civil Rights Movement, in United States, 34, 55, 196, 220
  US Women's Movement (*see* women's movement)

United States Military
  AirLand Battle doctrine, 137–138, 146
  NATO fall maneuvers, 10, 133, 137–139, 144–145 (*see also* Fulda Gap)
  Presence in Germany, 134–148
Uprising, 1953 in East Germany's, 311–312, 314
Uprising, 1956 in Hungary, 312, 314
Urbanity, 10, 30, 111–127, 197
  and Frankfurt Provos, 115–116
  Red Gallus group, 121–122
  Rent Strikes, 123, 124–126, 198
  Squatting, 10, 55, 124, 126, 153
  Urban Movements, 111–114, 119, 127

Vietnam War. *See* war
Violence, 26–27, 33, 38, 50, 54–58, 90, 100, 113–114, 117, 119, 157, 175, 181, 185, 248, 333
Vollmer, Antje, 148, 179, 182

Wainwright, Hilary, 24
War, 38, 138–148, 155, 173–175, 184–185,
  Algerian, 72, 241, 244
  Cold, 25, 79, 135, 144–148, 175, 178–179, 183, 239–240, 243–244, 251, 275, 285, 304–314, 316
  Contra, 268–273
  First World, 8, 47, 241
  Indochina, 28
  Nuclear, 180
  Second World, 8, 26, 72, 88, 148, 173, 183
  Spanish Civil, 271
  Third World, potential, 11, 144–148
  Vietnam, 34, 80, 185, 226
  Zimbabwean Independence, 244–246

Warsaw Pact, 10, 137, 177
West Germany. *See* Germany
Whitehouse, Mary, 27
Williams, Raymond, 24, 37, 40
Wohngemeinschaft (WG), 11, 153–169
  as family, 155
  Kommune 1, 156–157, 163–164, 306
  Kommune I Ost, 306
  Kommune 2, 155–157, 159, 168
  and the women's movements, 160–162
Wolff, K. D., 24, 121, 308
Women's movement, New, 9, 51, 161, 174, 180, 182–183, 201–202, 206, 219, 223, 227–229, 230–231, 266, 330. *See also* feminism
  Autonomous West German Women's Movement, 88–101
  Generational divides (*see* generations)
  "The personal is political," 90, 153
Wensierski, Peter, 283, 289–291
Working Group Westend (Arbeitsgruppe Westend, AGW), 121–122
Wyhl, protest surrounding the nuclear power plant, 328–331

Youth Center, 113, 120, 154, 205–206
Youth Center Movement, 201–207

Ziemann, Benjamin, 143
Zimbabwe, 240, 244, 246, 248, 249
  Zimbabwe African National Liberation Army (ZANLA), 239, 246, 247, 249
  Zimbabwe African National Union (ZANU), 13, 238–240, 245–250
  Zimbabwe African People's Union (ZAPU), 245
  Zimbabwean War of Independence. *See* War

www.ingramcontent.com/pod-product-compliance
Lightning Source LLC
Chambersburg PA
CBHW071147070526
44584CB00019B/2695